The European Culture Area

The European Culture Area

A Systematic Geography

ALEXANDER B. MURPHY,
TERRY G. JORDAN-BYCHKOV,
AND BELLA BYCHKOVA JORDAN

ROWMAN & LITTLEFIELD PUBLISHERS, INC.
Lanham • Boulder • New York • Toronto • Plymouth, UK

ROWMAN & LITTLEFIELD PUBLISHERS, INC.

Published in the United States of America
by Rowman & Littlefield Publishers, Inc.
A wholly owned subsidiary of The Rowman & Littlefield Publishing Group, Inc.
4501 Forbes Boulevard, Suite 200, Lanham, Maryland 20706
www.rowmanlittlefield.com

Estover Road, Plymouth PL6 7PY, United Kingdom

British Library Cataloguing in Publication Information Available

Library of Congress Cataloging-in-Publication Data

Printed in the United States of America

♾™ The paper used in this publication meets the minimum requirements of American National Standard for Information Sciences—Permanence of Paper for Printed Library Materials, ANSI/NISO Z39.48-1992.

Murphy, Alexander B., 1954-
The European culture area : a systematic geography / Alexander B. Murphy,
Terry G. Jordan-Bychkov, and Bella Bychkova Jordan.—5th ed.
    p. cm.
Rev. ed. of: The European culture area / Terry G. Jordan-Bychkov and
Bella Bychkova Jordan. 4th ed.
Includes bibliographical references and index.
ISBN-13: 978-0-7425-5671-3 (cloth : alk. paper)
ISBN-10: 0-7425-5671-9 (cloth : alk. paper)
ISBN-13: 978-0-7425-5672-0 (pbk. : alk. paper)
ISBN-10: 0-7425-5672-7 (pbk. : alk. paper)
    1. Europe—Geography. 2. Europe—Description and travel. I. Jordan-Bychkov, Terry G.,
1938- II. Bychkova Jordan, Bella. III. Jordan-Bychkov, Terry G., 1938- European culture area.
IV. Title. D907.J67 2009
914—dc22

2008024842

*Alec Murphy and Bella Bychkova Jordan
dedicate this book to Susan N. Gary
and the memory of Terry Jordan-Bychkov—
partners who made Europe, and so much more,
come alive for us.*

Contents

Preface

The fifth edition of *The European Culture Area* is the latest incarnation of a book begun in 1973 by Terry Jordan. Terry's original idea was to write a text on Europe reflecting geography's rich humanistic tradition—one that sought to situate economic, social, and political circumstances within the broader story of the region's evolving cultural-historical geography. Terry carried that tradition through four editions, but sadly succumbed to cancer before a fifth edition could be launched. He left the fifth edition in the hands of his fourth-edition co-author and a new lead author. We have undertaken an extensive revision for this edition, but we have endeavored to stay true to Terry's original vision. Hence, the book still views present patterns against the backdrop of changing geographical arrangements and ideas over time, and a substantial array of historical and contemporary maps remains at the core of the text.

Europe has undergone dramatic changes since the last edition of the book was published. The region has been swept up in economic and geopolitical shifts unfolding at the global scale, the European Union has almost doubled in size, and strides have been made toward addressing long-standing problems—even as new divisions and challenges have emerged. Capturing these developments required more than updating statistics and introducing more contemporary examples. We needed to rethink the balance among topics and the way they were presented.

The present edition reflects the results of that rethinking. Our fundamental goals were several. We sought to situate Europe more fully within the wider world—focusing attention on how the region's interactions with the rest of the globe have affected its development. We also aimed to problematize the idea of Europe itself—to consider how Europe has been understood geographically through time and how those understandings shape events and circumstances. Finally, we wanted to say more about political and social developments, for sweeping recent changes on these fronts are altering the nature and significance of Europe. Our goals for the book are reflected in entirely new chapters on social and ethnic geography and on the future of European integration; in a significant reworking of sections focused on political, economic, and cultural developments; and in a broad-ranging effort to put Europe and the wider world in dynamic tension with one another.

In tackling this edition, we were able to draw on extended past experiences in Europe, as well as our own research and writing on European themes. Our endeavor was also greatly aided by others. Alec Murphy owes a deep debt of gratitude to several University of Oregon graduate students who contributed to the project. Corey Johnson played a significant role in crafting the chapter on social and ethnic geography, Matthew Landers and Hunter Shobe provided invaluable research assistance during various stages of the project, and Marie Javdani offered helpful ideas for the updating of the language chapter. Matthew Derrick, a gifted geographer-cartographer, produced scores of new or revised maps and graphs for this edition of the book. Building on the attractive cartographic work of Dr. John Cotter from prior editions, Matt brought exceptional commitment, attention to detail, and skill to the project. The book would, quite simply, not have been completed without his dedication. A good number of Dr. Cotter's maps remain as well, and we are grateful to him for his past efforts.

Beyond the individuals who contributed directly to this book, Alec has benefited from being a part of a community of colleagues and students at the University of Oregon who have shared ideas about Europe over the past twenty years. Among colleagues, special acknowledgement goes to Ronald Wixman, whose insights encouraged new and important ways of thinking about Europe's geographical character, and to Everett Smith, who shared his perspectives on the European city during a team-taught seminar many years ago. General thanks also go to a number of former and present Oregon graduate students with European interests who have shared ideas and insights: David Keeling, George White, Amber Kemp, Dominique Salliard, Anne Hunderi-Eli, Nancy Leeper, Sara Press, Anthea Fallen-Bailey, Joanna Kepka, Robert Kerr, Roberto Serralles, Minna Pavulans, Adam Lake, and Megan Dixon. On a more personal level, Alec would like to acknowledge his partner, Susan Gary, and his sons, Richard and George, whose presence enriched joint explorations of Europe and who provided support and encouragement during the writing process.

The authors owe a special debt to the team at Rowman & Littlefield—most particularly Susan McEachern, whose belief in this project and gentle but persistent encouragement were essential to bringing it to fruition. Thanks also to Jessica Gribble, who was in charge of the art program, and to Alden Perkins, who oversaw production. Their efforts and professionalism are much appreciated.

A Note about Place Names

Decisions about how to render toponyms are complicated, and our general preference is to defer to indigenous forms. Since most readers of this book will be English speakers, however, we have decided to use the English forms of place names in cases where an English variant is in wide use (e.g., Naples instead of Napoli and Flanders instead of Vlaanderen). The danger in this approach is that it can lead to confusion. One American tourist bound for the wonders of Florence reportedly refused to get off the train at the station bearing the placard "Firenze," convinced that the conductor intended to cheat him! But the indigenous names of some places in Europe are not well known to most English speakers (Hrvatska, as opposed to Croatia), and most readers—including those of a variety of languages other than English—are more likely to identify with Vienna than Wien. Moreover, using the English term provides a convenient way of designating geographic features that extend across international and linguistic boundaries (e.g., the Danube, which is, at various places along its course, known as Donau, Duna, and Duanrea).

As for the names of independent countries, we have opted for commonly used anglicized short forms rather than formal country names (Germany instead of Federal Republic of Germany or Bundesrepublik Deutschland). The one case that might be less familiar to readers concerns the Czech Republic. Increasingly one hears the short form Czechia. Even though that name is not as widely known as other truncations (e.g., Slovakia for the Slovak Republic), we have decided to use Czechia for consistency and to reflect its growing use in the country itself.

Finally, when we capitalize the adjective in the compound terms Western Europe and Eastern Europe, we are referring to the two distinct parts of Europe that were a product of the geopolitical division that existed from the late 1940s through 1989. When the adjectives are not capitalized in these compounds, the intent is to refer to general parts of Europe without invoking Europe's post-World War II partitioning. Thus "western Europe" does not denote a precise territory with a particular geopolitical and temporal association, but the western portion of the European landmass.

CHAPTER 1

What Is Europe?

The title of this chapter raises a complicated question, for Europe represents, in the words of Norwegian geographer Leif Ahnström, "an elusive notion." Anyone who has followed the debate over the geographical limits of the European Union (EU) knows there is little consensus over what constitutes Europe. Yet the term has deep historical roots, and we use it all the time. One of the core concerns of the discipline of geography is to make sense of the ways the world is organized—both in our minds and on the ground. So any study of a world region should properly begin with consideration of why the area being studied is considered to be a region in the first place.

Europe as a Physical Entity

Most people would define Europe as a **continent**. You may recall from elementary school days reciting the names of the family of continents, in which Europe held a place of full membership. Support for the continental status of Europe appears in various dictionaries. For example, *Webster's New World Dictionary* defines Europe as a "continent between Asia and the Atlantic Ocean." In this view, we are led to believe that Europe constitutes a distinct physical entity because a continent is a sizable landmass standing more or less separate from other landmasses. North and South America, connected by the narrow Isthmus of Panama, form continents. Africa is linked to Asia only by the severed land bridge at Suez. Australia is fully separated from other landmasses by surrounding seas.

Europe, however, does not really satisfy the definition of a continent since it is not a separate landmass. To be sure, the Mediterranean Sea provides a separation from Africa in the south, while the Atlantic and Arctic Oceans well define Europe's western and northern limits. But, in the east, the notion of continentality founders. Only the beginning of a water separation appears in the southeastern fringe, where an arm of the sea reaches northward from the Mediterranean; through the Aegean, Dardanelles, and Bosporus to the Black Sea; and still beyond to the Sea of Azov. There, the division ends, for to the north stretches the vast East European Plain. Instead of a narrow

Figure 1.1.   World map drawn by the ancient Greek geographer Hecataeus about 500 B.C.E. He erroneously linked the Caspian Sea to the open ocean so that Europe and Asia joined only at the Caucasus isthmus. *Source:* adapted from Parker 1960.

isthmus similar to Panama or Suez, the map reveals a wedge of land broadening steadily to the east, welding Europe and Asia into one large continent called **Eurasia**. A glance at a map of the Eastern Hemisphere reveals Europe as simply one rather small appendage of Eurasia, merely a westward-reaching peninsula. At most, Europe forms only about one-fifth of the area of Eurasia.

The belief that Europe possesses the characteristics of a continent can be traced to the civilizations of the ancient Mediterranean, in particular, the Greeks and Romans (fig. 1.1). The Greco-Roman worldview, in turn, owed much to other, older cultures. One theory concerning the origin of the words *Europe* and *Asia* relates them to the Semitic Assyrian-Phoenician *ereb* (sunset) and *acu* (sunrise). Living along the eastern shores of the Mediterranean, the Assyrians were aware of two different cultural realms located in the direction of the sunrise and the sunset. Another theory has it that an

Figure 1.2. **World map of the Roman geographer Pomponius Mela,** drawn in 43 C.E. The Caspian Sea is still depicted as an arm of the ocean, but Russia has also been narrowed to form an isthmus. *Source:* adapted from Parker 1960.

ancient, mythological ruler of Sidon in Phoenicia had daughters named *Europa* and *Asia.* The legendary Europa married the Greek king of gods, Zeus, and accompanied him back to the Aegean, while her sister remained in the east.

Whatever the origins of the words may have been, the ancient Greeks, from their vantage point on the Aegean, perceived a world divided into three parts: one to the north and west (Europe), one to the south and west (Africa—then called Libya), and one to the east (Asia). Greece was always a nation of seafarers, and its sailors from the time of Ulysses and earlier had charted the marine separation between Europe and Africa. In addition, the classical Greeks knew of the division of Africa and Asia because the Phoenicians before them had circumnavigated the African continent. The Argonauts and other Greek explorers had probed into the Black Sea, founding trading colonies as far away as present-day Ukraine. Intrepid Greek merchants went beyond the Black Sea to the shores of the landlocked, saltwater Caspian Sea. Certain Greek scholars evaluating the information brought back by traders assumed that the saline Caspian was part of the ocean. They believed that the isthmus between the Black and Caspian Seas was the only land bridge connecting Europe and Asia (fig. 1.1). Little did they know that the Caspian was an inland sea without any opening to the ocean and that north of the Caspian stretched a huge expanse of land. The Romans carried on this view. Their maps whittled down the expansive Russian plains to a narrow land bridge (fig. 1.2). These ideas about divisions in the physical world were reinforced by the sense that widely different cultures occupied the territories to the north, south, and east.

From the Greeks and Romans, the three-continent concept passed to monastic scholars of the medieval period. Perpetuation of the classical view was guaranteed when

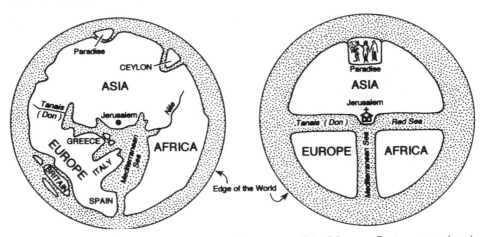

Figure 1.3.   Two versions of the medieval European "T in O" map. Europe remained, as in classical times, a separate continent. *Source:* adapted from Woodward 1985.

Christian religious significance was attached to it. Religious-inspired cartography produced the famous "T in O" map. The church simplified the map of the known world in such a way that the pattern of land and seas formed the letters "T" for *terrarum* (earth) and "O" for *orbis* (circle), suggesting that God had shaped the world in a sort of Latin shorthand. The Mediterranean Sea represented the lower bar of the "T." The top of the map was east rather than north. The Nile River (or Red Sea)–Aegean Sea–Black Sea–Don River line formed the horizontal bar of the "T."

Some medieval Christian scholars created water separations of Europe, Asia, and Africa by severing Suez and widening the Don to marine proportions. The letter "O" lay between the outer perimeter of the three continents and the presumed edge of the world (fig. 1.3). On many such ethnocentric Christian maps, the center of the world was the holy city of Jerusalem, while the lost Garden of Eden lay far out in the inaccessible reaches of Asia. We should not judge "T in O" maps by modern standards, because their purpose, as interpretative art, was to depict religious mysteries and offer a stylized stage for the Christian drama, rather than to picture the world accurately. In any case, medieval scholars perpetuated the pre-Christian notion of a clear distinction between Europe and Asia.

Even after the European **Age of Discovery** produced more precise understandings of the physical configuration of the earth's surface, the idea of Europe as a distinct continent persisted. Yet this view had to be sustained against the backdrop of increasingly accurate world maps showing that, instead of a relatively narrow land bridge separating the western and eastern portions of Eurasia, a 2,000-kilometer-wide wedge of land lay between the White Sea in the north of Russia and the Sea of Azov in the south. Yet discarding a 2,000-year-old belief is not easy. Hence, in the absence of an isthmus, geographers began looking for other environmental features that might mark Europe's eastern border. The Swedish geographer Philip J. von Strahlenberg lamented in 1738 that "every one who is conversant in Geography knows that there

Figure 1.4. The Ural Mountains, long regarded by many as the eastern border of Europe. The view here is in the far north, near the Arctic Ocean, on the eastern boundary of Russia's Komi Republic. The month is June, but snow still caps the northern Urals. Farther south, the Urals did not act as a major barrier to east-west movement (Photo by T.G.J.-B., 1997).

has, for a considerable time, been a disagreement among geographers about the certainty . . . of the boundaries between . . . Europe and Asia."

Attention soon fell upon the Urals, a low mountain range running in a north-south direction across the heart of Eurasia, as the best border. Many adopted this view (fig. 1.4). These mountains had never represented a significant barrier to west-east movement, but they served the purpose of suggesting a divide in the physical environment that was really historical in nature. (To this day, many publications treat the Urals as the divider between Europe and Asia.) Farther to the south, the more impressive snow-capped Caucasus Mountains, stretching between the Black and Caspian Seas, provided another link in the effort to bound Europe. But many different physical features have been proposed as markers of the border between Europe and Asia (fig. 1.5). The Don River formed one part of Strahlenberg's proposed border, and the Dnieper and Ural Rivers were accorded similar honor by certain scholars. The suggestion was also made that Europe should exclude all areas of interior, Arctic, and Indian Ocean drainage, leaving as European only those lands whose rivers drain to the Atlantic Ocean as well as the Baltic, Mediterranean, and Black Seas.

Still others proposed a climatic border, defining Europe as a temperate, well-watered land flanked by deserts, steppes, and frigid, subarctic wastes. The geographer Herbert Louis adopted this southern border, placing it at the limits of nonirrigated

Figure 1.5. Proposals for defining Europe physically. Mountain ranges, rivers, drainage basins, terrain patterning, and climatic traits have all been suggested. Borders: **1** = Eastern border of small discrete terrain regions, beyond which lie boundless plains; **2** = Western border of interior-Arctic-Indian Ocean drainage; **3** = Louis' borders, based on warmth and rainfall; **4** = Northern limit of the steppe grasslands; **5** = Northern limit of temperate climates; **6** = Europe narrowly defined, including lands accepted by all who seek to bound Europe on a physical environmental basis; **7** = Europe most broadly defined, including lands accepted by at least one scholar seeking a physical boundary; **8** = Southern border of Arctic tundra; and **9** = Most widely accepted border of Europe today. Europe, environmentally, thus becomes a temperate, well-watered land of variegated terrain. Louis oddly extended it far into southern Siberia, off our map. *Sources:* Hahn 1881, plate 3; Louis 1954, map following 80; Wolf 1982, 31; Parker 1953; Parker 1960.

farming. He further proposed that Europe reached only as far north and east as those lands having at least two months averaging 15° Celsius or warmer and a total of four months above 10°C, a limit judged critical for grain cultivation (fig. 1.5). Some scholars suggested excluding from Europe the steppe grasslands that intrude from Asia north of the Black Sea, regarding them as alien in appearance and utilization.

But of what value are these diverse suggestions for an environmentally determined Europe? Why, in fact, has the concept of Europe survived so long after continentality, in the conventional sense, has been disproven? Why do we teach courses in the geography of Europe instead of Eurasia? Why is there a European Specialty Group within the Association of American Geographers? Indeed, why do the Europeans themselves continue to believe that a separate and distinct Europe exists? Clearly, the answers do not lie in the contrived and discordant physical boundaries previously discussed. Instead, we must agree with the Russian geographer, E.M. Murzayev, who concluded that "any attempt to divide Europe from Asia on a systematic physical-geographical basis is doomed to fail."

Europe as a Human Entity

An alternative is to see Europe as a human, rather than environmental, entity. Following this approach, some have argued that Europe is a distinct **culture area**. A culture has been defined as a community of people who hold numerous features of belief, behavior, and overall way of life in common, including ideology, technology, social institutions, and material possessions. With this in mind, geographer W. H. Parker has argued that Europe represents "a cultural concept" and that "its eastern limits have been cultural and never long stable." Europeans, by this logic, belong to a cultural community rooted in a Judeo-Christian-Hellenic heritage.

This view of Europe has deep historical roots. As late as the 1200s, Europe continued to mean simply a continent, though by then some had adopted the view that Europeans were distinctive as the descendants of Japheth, one of the sons of the biblical Noah. Slowly, from 1300 to 1600, Europe came to mean "Christendom," says Denys Hay, "and the emotional content of the word Europe significantly increased." A European self-consciousness, centered in the church, emerged. By 1571, the pope revealingly referred to "Europeans, or those who are called Christians." Europe acquired a specific cultural meaning, and Europeans now had a distinctive worldview based in a vivid and flattering self-image.

Of course, parts of what we now consider to be Europe were not part of Christendom during the so-called European Middle Ages. Islam held sway in the Iberian Peninsula (until the late fifteenth century) and in the lands east of the Adriatic Sea, and Christianity had not fully taken root in parts of northern Scandinavia. Hence, Europe as Christendom was less a precise territorial construct than a geographically loose category based on a sense of cultural difference. That does not mean that Europe was seen in unified terms, however. At the broadest geographical scale, the official division of Europe between the Western and Eastern Churches in 1054 formalized a rift in the cultural practice that supposedly gave Europe its distinctiveness. For those living in the western parts of the "continent," it also fostered a sense of core and periphery in Europe that is still with us today. From their perspective, those oriented toward the Western Church were the true Europeans, whereas the Eastern Orthodoxy realm was one of transition.

Moving forward to the contemporary era, in 1991, another pope in Rome exhorted Europe to return "to its Christian roots." In that same year, the president of

Turkey, frustrated at the failure of his predominantly Muslim country to be accepted as a member of the EU, lamented that "some people maintain that the EU should be a Christian club." A few years later, a British periodical described "a Muslim crescent curling threateningly around the southern and eastern edges of Europe" (*Economist*, 6 August 1994). Finally, in 1999, Turkey's candidacy for EU membership was accepted, but it is currently on hold, and there is considerable doubt as to whether the application will ever be approved.

In the early 2000s, a vigorous debate developed over whether the preamble to a proposed constitution for the EU should include reference to the area's Christian heritage. Although not ultimately accepted, the debate revealed the degree to which there remains at least an historical sense of Europe being a Christian realm. And social fault lines still follow religious lines, affecting relations between Spaniards and Arabs, Greeks and Turks, Russians and Chechens, Serbs and Bosnian Muslims, and on and on. Even in the very heart of Europe and within the past century, the religious issue remained sufficiently potent to deny European residence, and even life itself, to Jews.

Christianity has not functioned as the sole historical marker of Europe as a human entity. With the Age of Discovery came an us-versus-them worldview that was rooted not just in economic and technological differences, but in racial differences. The idea took root of a world divided among three races—termed Caucasoid, Negroid, and Mongoloid—with explicit geographical connotations attached to each, respectively, European, African, and Asian. This view was reinforced and tied to the religious conception of Europe through the idea that the three sons of the biblical Noah—Ham, Shem, and Japheth—fathered, respectively, the African, Asian, and European races.

An additional cultural trait that has often been used to define Europe as a human entity is language. The great majority of Europeans speak one or another of the **Indo-European** tongues, an extended family of related languages that share common historical roots. Flanking the Indo-Europeans are speakers of other language families, such as Uralic, Altaic, Caucasic, Afro-Asiatic, or Euskera. Using language to define Europe is a more recent development, reflecting the rise of systematic inquiries into the relationships among languages that began in the nineteenth century. But the very term, *Indo-European*, reflects the close tie between a linguistic category and a geographical view of Europe as a region.

Despite the historical significance of the three previously described human characteristics—religion, race, and language—in conceptualizations of Europe as a human entity, they are no more helpful than physical characteristics in delimiting Europe geographically. As figure 1.6 suggests, there is no boundary in the east separating areas that do not have those three characteristics from areas where they are present. Of course, a map at this scale hides smaller areas within Europe, where, for example, Islam is the dominant religion.

Yet still, the idea of Europe as a distinctive entity persists, and, even though there is little agreement on its boundaries, a variety of widely referenced social and political indicators associated with the western portion of Eurasia tend to reinforce conceptions of European distinctiveness. Among the most common of these are:

Figure 1.6.   Europe defined on the basis of religion, language, and race. This formerly common approach to regionalization is fraught with problems because it is based on categories that are not well defined (especially race) and that do not necessarily reflect a sense of identity. Even these variables, however, show the problem of delimiting Europe based on the traditional Uralian boundary.

1. *A well-educated population.* More than 90% of the population is literate, and, in some places, it is illegal not to be. In Germany, for example, 99% of the population can read and write, and in Spain, the proportion is 97%. By contrast, as near as the southern shore of the Mediterranean, in Morocco, only a little over 60% of the people are literate.

2. *A healthy population.* The population enjoys a life expectancy far above average—well in excess of 70 years in many countries. Perhaps an even better measure of health is provided by the **infant mortality rate**, the number of children per thousand who do not survive to the age of one year. For much of what is conventionally viewed as Europe, the rate stands below 10, whereas, across the Aegean Sea, one encounters rates such as Turkey's 27.5.

3. *Low population growth rates.* The population is scarcely growing at present, and it is even declining in countries such as Germany and Ukraine. **Zero population growth** has essentially been achieved. By contrast, all countries in neighboring North Africa as well as in Africa and Asia at large experience more than 1.5% annual natural increase in the population.

4. *A wealthy population.* Standards of living are very high, as judged by standard socioeconomic indicators, with eight of the world's top ten countries in terms of per capital gross national product lie in what is conventionally thought of as Europe. In adjacent areas to the south and east, significant numbers of peoples achieve a bare subsistence.

5. *An urbanized population.* The vast majority of the population lives in cities and towns with populations of 10,000 or more and, in some countries, the proportion exceeds 80%. By way of comparison, only 28% of the people in India, 32% in China, 45% in Egypt, and 53% in Morocco are urbanites.

6. *An industrialized or post-industrial economy.* All sectors of industry, especially the services, are well-developed in what is conventionally defined as Europe, and they collectively employ the far greater part of the labor force. By contrast, agriculture remains the dominant form of economy in most regions lying to Europe's south and east.

7. *Freely elected governments.* Democracy is the dominant political form throughout what is conventionally termed as Europe. Competing ideologies are tolerated, and considerable deference is given to the rights of individuals. Forms of political governance are much more diverse in areas lying to the south and east.

These indicators are all foundations on which notions of Europe's geographical distinctiveness rest. They are a subset of a larger process of **othering**—that is, defining Europe in opposition to other areas—that has unfolded over the past several centuries (table 1.1). The ingredients at the heart of the othering process are reflected in statements by commentators such as David Gress, who refers to European culture as "a synthesis of democracy, capitalism, science, human rights, . . . individual autonomy, and the power of unfettered human reason." Such conceptualizations hark back to ancient Greece and Rome and then add layers rooted in the Renaissance, Enlightenment, modern science, and the rise of the modern state. They lie at the heart of that elusive concept known as Western Civilization.

There are two problems with defining Europe in these terms, however. One is that the criteria used to highlight European difference, for example, those listed previously, are highly selective, focusing primarily on matters widely viewed as positive. Inevitably, Europe's character and legacy is much more complex. Racism, the subjugation of distant peoples, and genocide are also part of the European story. A second problem is that the presence of things such as a healthy, urbanized population and high literacy rates in Europe cannot be understood by looking at Europe alone. These are the product in part of Europe's encounters with other parts of the world. Most obviously, Europe's colonial empires were integral to its rise to economic primacy, and recent immigrants have played a key role in sustaining the European economy in the contemporary era.

This second point raises a fundamental geographical issue. No region can be understood in isolation. The interconnections among places run deep, both in extent and in time. Even before the Age of Discovery, Europe's encounters with places to the east and south shaped its character. As those encounters intensified from the fifteenth century onward, Europe's character and destiny became increasingly intertwined with other parts of the world. Geographer James Blaut suggests that the rise of Europe was

Table 1.1.   European Self-Identity: A Checklist

Category	Europe/Self	Non-European/Alien
Physical Habitat	Marine	Continental
	Occident	Orient
	Temperate	Extreme
	Rimland	Heartland
	Northern	Southern
Religion	Christian	Non-Christian
	Roman Catholic	Orthodox Christian
	Secular	Believer
Race	Fair complexion	Dark complexion
Ideology/politics	Democratic	Authoritarian
	Uniting	Dividing
	Postnational	Nationalist
	Social democracy	Communism
	Peace/stability	War/turmoil
Culture	Civilization	Nature/barbarism
	Reason	Emotion
	Teacher	Pupil
	Progress	Stasis
	Cosmopolitan	Parochial
	Tolerance	Intolerance
	Wisdom	Immaturity
	Postmodern	Traditional/modern
Economy	Postindustrial	Industrial/agrarian
	Tertiary	Primary/secondary
	Core	Periphery
	Developed	Colonial

Source: Adapted, with modifications and addenda, from Painter 2000.

not due to the superiority of its culture, but it was instead due to the wealth that Europeans seized through conquest and colonialism.

We are then left with no clear sense of Europe as either a physical or a human entity. This does not mean that Europe has no meaning as a geographical construct. Indeed, the very fact that many people treat Europe as a distinct region gives it significance. But approaching the study of that region in a geographically informed fashion requires at least three things. First, it must be based on a recognition that no precise physical or functional boundaries circumscribe the region. Second, it must treat the region not solely as the product of internal arrangements and processes, but also in relation to other places, peoples, and forces. Finally, it must recognize that Europe is a constantly shifting, contested geographical idea.

Placing Europe

The complexities of defining Europe present a challenge for a book such as this. What geographical space should be the focus of analysis, even as we look outside as well as inside that space for the forces shaping Europe? There is no good answer to this question as any space one chooses will necessarily be arbitrary. Clearly, it makes more sense to look toward cultural rather than physical variables; however, the very notion of European distinctiveness is a cultural product. But considering the perceptions of Europeans about what constitutes Europe hardly provides clarity. Consider the following revealing, if sometimes bigoted, comments:

- "Africa begins at the Pyrenees." (Alexandre Dumas, French writer)
- "We were once, and will be again, Europeans." (Latvia's prime minister, 1991)
- "Russians: a European people or some mongrel Asian one?" (Steven Erlanger, 1995)
- "Can we become a part of Europe?" (anonymous Albanian, 1992)
- "Turkey—the Europe you don't know; the Asia you will discover." (Turkish National Tourist Bureau, 1995)
- "I want to say that Europe must give itself borders, that not all countries have a vocation to become members of Europe, beginning with Turkey, which has no place inside the European Union." (Nicolas Sarkozy, current French president, during presidential campaign, 2007).
- "With our mother country Croatia behind us, we will unite not with the barbaric hordes, but with Europe." (Kresimir Zubac, Bosnian Croat politician, 1996)
- "You're thinking of Europe as Germany and France. I don't. I think that's old Europe."(former US Secretary of Defense Donald Rumsfeld, 2003, in response to a reporter's question)

These remarks highlight the debate over what constitutes Europe. The status of Russia and its immediate neighbors is particularly contested. One member of the Ukrainian parliament recently distinguished the Europeanized Slavs in the western part of his country from the Russo-Slavs of the eastern region. Witold Orlowski, a Pole, noting that his country would soon create a barrier-border along its eastern frontier at the instigation of the EU, declared that "Europeans are drawing the borderline of Europe for the next fifty years and don't care about Ukraine, Belarus, and Russia."

Yet we should not forget that Mikhail Gorbachev, the former Russian leader, coined the term "our common European home." Historically, many geographers have drawn the border of Europe through Russia, claiming the western part of it, **Eurorussia**, for the European culture area (fig. 1.7). But seeking a sharp cultural border for Europe is futile, especially in the east. As long ago as the 1920s, geographers had "largely emancipated themselves from the hypnotic effect of terms like Europe and Asia," wrote the geographer Marion I. Newbigin, stressing instead the gradual transition from European to non-European.

The absence of sharp boundaries for the European culture area becomes even more apparent when efforts are made to map the types of previously mentioned human characteristics that are often invoked to distinguish Europe. A broad transitional zone emerges. From a core in central and northwestern Europe, where all the defining traits are found, the presence of these traits declines gradually to the peripheries, especially in the east and south (fig. 1.8). "But," you might protest, "how could Greece, the widely accepted birthplace of Europe, display fewer than half of the European

Figure 1.7. Proposed culture-based borders of Europe. Key: **1** = Western border of Russia; **2** = Eastern border of Europe proposed by the Russian geographer Murzayev, based upon internal administrative units; **3** = Border proposed by the German geographer Banse, 1912; **4** = Border proposed by the French geographer Thevet, 1575; **5** = Border of the "European space economy," according to geographer Andrew Dawson, 1993; and **6** = Borders of "sedentary agricultural Europe," proposed by the Frenchman Delaisi, 1929. The border shown as **7** is the one used when defining Europe for statistical purposes throughout this book. *Sources:* Parker 1960; Delaisi 1929, 24–25; Hahn 1881, plate 3; Murzayev 1964; Dawson 1993.

traits?" Such an observation nicely highlights the difficulties and controversies surrounding efforts to define Europe in these terms.

As we have already seen, the idea that some part of western Eurasia and adjacent areas might constitute a major region is traceable to the ancient world. But what actual territories are included has shifted greatly though time? About 1000 B.C.E., a small nucleus had formed around the shores of the eastern Mediterranean. The Greeks fought with peoples to the east to expand their infant culture. By the beginning of the Christian Era, Europe coincided with the territorial extent of the Roman Empire, a considerable expansion from the nucleus of 1000 B.C.E., even though the core still lay in the Mediterranean basin. The passage of still another millennium, to about 1000 C.E., brought dramatic areal changes. The Arabs, driven by the evangelical spirit of a new religion, Islam, had spread across all of North Africa, through the larger islands in the Mediterranean Sea, and into most of Iberia. The Arabs eventually reached into central western France, where they were turned back on the battlefield of Tours. Horsemen from the east, the Magyars, penetrated as far as southern Germany, where a major battle was

Figure 1.8. A measure of "European-ness," by province, based upon twelve traits that are sometimes (albeit controversially) associated with Europe. The resulting pattern reflects the way that some people, at least subconciously, view Europe. Key: **1** = Over 80% Christian or of Christian heritage; **2** = Over 80% Indo-European speakers; **3** = Over 90% Caucasian; **4** = Infant mortality rate below 12%; **5** = Per capita gross domestic product is at least 40% of the European Union average; **6** = Over 90% of people literate; **7** = 300 or more kilometers of highway per 100 square kilometers of territory; **8** = Less than 25% of workforce employed in agriculture; **9** = Over 50% of people live in towns and cities; **10** = Less than 0.5% annual natural population increase; **11** = Lies inside the European zone of continuous settlement (see fig. 3.1); and **12** = No substantial restrictions on democracy today.

fought on the Lechfeld in 955 C.E. After long years of raiding, these mounted warriors eventually abandoned all but a foothold in the grassland of Hungary, where their linguistic descendants still remain today. The first thousand years of the Christian Era were not, however, entirely years of retreat. The loss of North Africa to Christendom was paralleled by an expansion into Germanic and Slavic realms by Christian missionaries.

The territorial ebb and flow of Europe continued into the present millennium. Spaniards and Portuguese, gripped by a religious fervor reminiscent of the earlier Muslim expansion, drove the Arabic Moors from Iberia, a reconquest that was completed in 1492. But, in the southeast, the Muslim Turks overwhelmed the Greeks and pressed on beyond the Dardanelles–Bosporus to seize the center of eastern Christendom, Constantinople, which they renamed Istanbul. From there, the Turks spread northward to occupy most of the Balkan Peninsula. Repeatedly, an alliance of warriors gathered to turn the Turks back from the gates of Vienna (Wien) and also at Lepanto off the Greek coast. The Turkish tide gradually receded, leaving only Muslim relics in the Balkans and a small Turkish bridgehead on the northern shore of the Dardanelles and Bosporus around Istanbul. Even the most persistent efforts by Europeans failed to destroy this bridgehead.

The truly spectacular European expansion, however, has been accomplished over the past 400 to 500 years. Germanic-speaking peoples, in particular the English, created overseas Europes in Anglo-America, Australia, New Zealand, and South Africa, while Spaniards and Portuguese transplanted much that is European in large parts of Latin America. The overseas activities of the Iberians and northwestern Europeans coincided with a major Slavic expansion overland, accomplished by the Russians, who busily pushed Europe deep into the previously alien heartland of Eurasia and beyond to the Pacific shore.

In addition to the middle- and upper-latitude areas to which large European populations were transplanted bodily as well as by destroying or subjugating the native peoples, great tropical colonial empires were established by the Spaniards, Portuguese, British, French, Dutch, Belgians, and Germans. In the entire world, only China, Japan, Thailand, Iran, Arabia, and Turkey avoided falling under European imperial rule at some time between 1500 and 1950. Colonialism brought the imprint of Europe. Consequently, India has a railroad system founded by the British, Haitians speak a form of French, and Filipinos adhere to the Roman Catholic faith. Europeans carried their mode of life throughout the world, transplanting it to thinly occupied lands or grafting it onto societies too firmly rooted to be dislodged (fig. 1.9). The world has been Europeanized in numerous, fundamental ways. Even those few areas never ruled from Europe have felt its cultural impress. Japan accepted the Industrial Revolution, China adopted Marxist socialism, and Turkey replaced Arabic script with the Latin alphabet.

At the same time, other parts of the world also helped shape Europe. Influence flowed both ways, and the European way of life has been profoundly altered in the process. Indeed, prior to about 1500 C.E., Europe could best be regarded as peripheral to the great culture centers of the Eastern Hemisphere, receiving far more than it gave. Even Christianity, the traditional basis for much of Europe's distinctiveness, originated in the so-called Middle East and attained its first major foothold in what was long called Asia Minor, that is, modern-day Turkey. African Arabs taught Iberians some of the navigational secrets that permitted the Age of Discovery, and Muslims preserved and advanced much ancient Greco-Roman knowledge during Europe's lengthy Dark Age. Agriculture originally reached Europe from a western Asian hearth, and the later introduction of Native American crops, such as the potato, tomato, tobacco, and maize, greatly altered the European agrarian system.

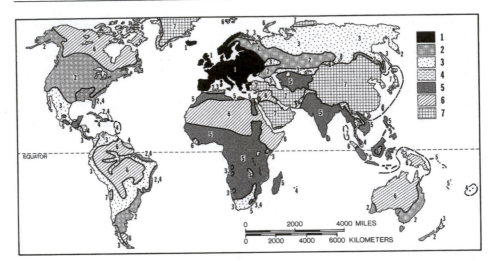

Figure 1.9.   The Europeanization of the world. Key: **1** = European hearth area, 1500 C.E.; **2** = Neo-European areas: population and culture almost wholly of European derivation; **3** = Mixed European and aboriginal areas, but culture strongly influenced or dominated by European practices; **4** = Plantation culture: small European-derived minority traditionally dominated a large non-European labor force; **5** = Exploitive or custodial occupation by Europeans in colonial era: minute numbers of Europeans implanted some durable customs and artifacts; **6** = Loose, ineffective, or brief European control and impact; and **7** = Areas never directly occupied or controlled by Europeans but indirect penetration of European influence often significant. *Source:* Modified from Zelinsky, W. 1966. *A Prologue to Population Geography*, Englewood Cliffs: Prentice Hall, 74–75.

Nor has European influence always found acceptance overseas. Recent events suggest a substantial, rising resistance to Europeanization. In Africa, Islam rather than Christianity is the fastest-growing religion, and generations of Christian missionaries failed to make significant inroads in India, China, or Japan. Finally, demographic stagnation means that Europeans form an ever-smaller part of the world population, a trend that may well further undermine their influence.

This Book's Approach

Given the complexities surrounding what constitutes Europe, no single approach to this geographical construct can be entirely satisfactory. Yet we cannot let this stop us from an effort to understand Europe. However much we might debate its geographical extent and meaning, Europe is a significant idea and place, regardless of how it is defined. With that in mind, this book starts from the premise that Europe's contested areal extent is one of its interesting geographical features. We proceed under the assumptions that (1) there is wide consensus that Europe at least encompasses the western portions of the area mapped in figure 1.6 and the consensus diminishes as one moves east and that (2) Europe is not a product simply of internal developments, but it has been constantly reinvented in relation to other places near and far.

This still leaves open the question of what territory will be the focus of attention in the book. In some places, a relatively sharp border seems simple to draw, as is true in the Arctic Sea, the Atlantic Ocean, and the Mediterranean Sea. Even in the Mediterranean, however, delineation is not as straightforward as it might initially seem. The different shores are widely viewed as belonging to contrasting cultural realms, but migrations have complicated the cultural picture. Moreover, the Mediterranean includes places such as the island of Cyprus, which is divided between Greek and Turkish sectors that some see as representative of different continental realms, but others do not.

As should already be clear from the discussion earlier in the chapter, beyond the Mediterranean, the picture becomes even more complicated. Not only are there no clear physical or cultural boundaries, in recent times, conflicts have raged over the cultural and political status of areas in and around Europe. For instance, in Bulgaria, expulsions of ethnic Turks flared anew in the late 1980s. In Azerbaijan, the Armenian Christian minority in Nagorno–Karabakh province rebelled. In Georgia, Abkhazi Muslims seceded amid civil war in 1993. In the Russian Caucasus, Islamic Chechnya continues a struggle for independence.

A convenient, albeit somewhat problematic, approach to the problem of boundary definition in the east can be found by looking to the EU in its recently expanded form (fig. 1.10). With the EU now encompassing areas that were once under Soviet domination in Eastern Europe, a functional order is coming into being that provides some basis for focusing attention on the lands that lie to the west of the eastern border of the EU. In recognition of this, this book's principal focus of attention in terms of discussion and analysis is those areas lying to the west of that border. In recognition of the artificiality of this pragmatic approach, however, our maps and statistical generalizations about Europe reflect a more expanded notion of the region, as represented by the solid line (#7) in figure 1.7. These, together with some commentary on developments in this geographically expanded conception of Europe, serve as important reminders of the inevitable messiness associated with the geographical concept of Europe.

In substantive terms, the goal of this book is to give the reader an appreciation not just of Europe's character as a place, but of the nature and significance of a geographical perspective on the region. Many people associate geography with memorizing lists of capital cities, mountains, and rivers. This conception often comes from elementary and secondary school classrooms where, at best, cursory attention is given to where things are located. Then they are only a background to discussions of social, historical, or environmental issues. Geography comes across as a dry, boring backdrop to questions of interest.

Yet it is no more accurate to see place-name memorization as the essence of geography than it would be to treat the memorization of dates as the essence of history. Place names provide a vocabulary that allows us to talk about the world, and they can sometimes reveal interesting things about past cultural influences on places. But geography's real interest and importance comes from the insights that can be gained from

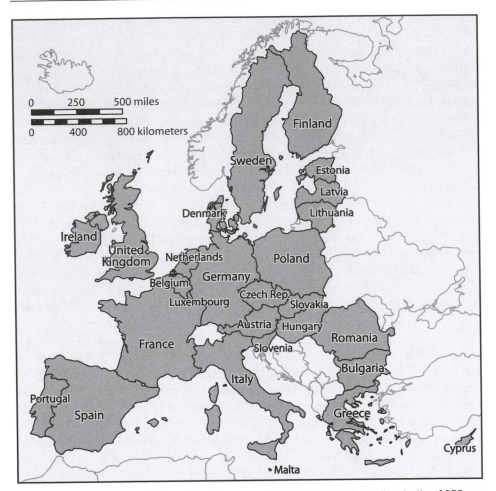

Figure 1.10.   Member states of the European Union. From its founding in the 1950s as an economic organization involving six countries, the European integration project has expanded to encompass 27 states and a range of issues beyond the strictly economic (migration, environmental change, infrastructure, foreign aid, etc.).

exploring not just where things are located, but why they are there and how particular geographical arrangements and patterns affect and influence the world around us. Geography is an integrative discipline concerned with the nature and significance of the patterns, places, and landscapes that make up the earth's surface. What can shifting vegetation patterns tell us about climate change? Why have migrants from North Africa ended up in some parts of Europe more than others? How does the changing character of the French-German political boundary along the upper Rhine affect peoples' sense of place and their approach to common problems? Questions such as these are at geography's core. They are the ones that make studying Europe from a geographical perspective such an interesting and important endeavor.

Against this backdrop, this book is focused not just on where things are, but why they are there and why that matters. Europe is a complex amalgam of physical, demographic, cultural, political, economic, and social arrangements and processes—each influencing the other. The goal of the book is to facilitate understanding of the region through investigation of the physical and sociocultural patterns that have shaped Europe's character and landscape through time. Toward that end, the book treats various aspects of Europe's geography like the layers of a cake. We begin with the physical setting, looking at the patterns and processes that help explain the physiographic, climatic, and vegetative complexes found in Europe. We then move to basic demographic issues, looking not just at underlying patterns and processes, but how they relate to the physical geographic issues presented earlier. We then add further layers to the cake, turning to language and religion, the evolution of the region's political pattern, and economic and social arrangements. By the end of the book, the reader should have at least an introductory understanding of many of the key geographical arrangements and processes that have shaped and continue to shape this fascinating part of the world.

The advantage of taking this approach is that it allows us to cut across many of the usual divisions found in studies of Europe. We will look not just at the physical environment, demographic dynamics, or political forces, but at how those are interrelated. Constructing our multilayered cake allows us to treat layers not just as isolated phenomena, but as interrelated parts of a whole. With the background provided in this book, a reader should be able to cut down through the layers of the European cake in different places and see some of the key geographical arrangements and processes at work.

The principal limitation of this approach is that it requires us to tackle a vast array of subject areas. To deal with them in a modest-length book, we necessarily have to operate at a fairly high level of generalization. Each of the topics discussed in this book has been addressed extensively by geographers and others. The bibliographies at the ends of chapters provide an entrée into deeper exploration of individual topics

Finally, it is worth noting that our fundamental approach to discussing and explaining Europe's geographical character is cultural-historical. Many geographical studies of world regions focus on the characteristics of contemporary spatial structures and arrangements with a particular emphasis on economic and demographic matters. We are interested in these as well, but emphasis is on how and why spatial structures and arrangements came to be, which means directing central attention to the ways in which cultural ideas and practices shaped their evolution. To put it another way, our book consistently explores how cultural-historical processes—many of which are deeply intertwined with economic and political processes—have given rise to the geographical patterns and landscapes that are at the heart of contemporary Europe. This is certainly not the only path that could be taken, but we believe it provides telling insights into why the patterns and processes discussed in this book have taken that form that they have.

Why Study Europe?

Before launching into the substance of the book, it is worth pausing for a moment to consider why Europe is a region worthy of study. The most obvious answer is that the western part of Eurasia, however defined geographically or viewed historically, is a place that, for better or for worse, has had an impact on the world that is greatly disproportionate to its size. As such, studying this region can provide important insights into developments of global import.

To appreciate the degree to which Europe has shaped the contemporary world, consider how many influential concepts and inventions of the last millennium trace their origins to this region (fig. 1.11). The concept of democracy came from classical Greece. It reappeared in medieval Iceland, the infant Switzerland, the Magna Carta of England, and Teutonic city-states of the Middle Ages before bursting forth over much of Europe in the late 1700s and 1800s. The European Age of Discovery, primarily the product of Italian and Iberian Europeans, allowed Europe to discover (from its perspective) and, in many cases, dominate much of the remainder of the world.

The printing press employing moveable type, a gift from the artisans of the German Rhine Valley, had a tremendous impact in most parts of the world, revolutionizing people's means of communication. The concept of the earth's sphericity, developed by the classical Greeks, was revived by Italians and Iberians in the Age of Discovery. The Polish astronomer Nicolaus Copernicus was the first to proclaim the heliocentric concept that the earth revolves about the sun. If Copernicus dealt a first great blow to human ego by removing the earth from the center of the universe, his fellow European, Charles Darwin, struck another in his theory of evolution by proposing that humans were animals with traceable biological ancestry. Gregor Mendel provided the basis for genetic science. Sigmund Freud, born a short distance from Mendel in Czechia, founded modern psychology, the scientific study of the mind.

Englishman Isaac Newton, in his laws of motion and gravity, established modern physics. The German-born Swiss resident, Albert Einstein, through his theory of relativity, greatly enhanced our understanding of the universe. Discovery of bacterial and viral causes of disease, the beginning of modern medicine, was the work of the German country doctor, Robert Koch and the Frenchman Louis Pasteur. Marie Sklodowska Curie, a native of Poland and citizen of France, pioneered the study of radioactivity, with her husband Pierre, ushering in the atomic and nuclear age. (The word *curie* became the unit of measurement for the property of radioactivity.) Russian Dmitry Mendeleyev developed the periodic table of chemical elements, working in St. Petersburg in the 1890s. Dutch and Italian inventors perfected the first microscope and telescope, allowing humans for the first time to inspect objects too small or too distant to be studied with the naked eye.

Perhaps Europe's most far-reaching impact resulted from the **Industrial Revolution**, the invention of diverse machines and harnessing of inanimate power that began in Great Britain in the 1700s. It led to countless crucially influential inventions, including the steam engine, railroad, internal combustion engine, automobile, expressway, radio, orbital satellites, manned space flight, and digital computer, to mention but a few (fig. 1.11). Prometheus was unbound, and it was Europeans who loosened his bonds. **Modernity** and the concept of progress, quintessentially European, sprang into being.

Figure 1.11.   Sources of selected European concepts and inventions. Key: **1** = Democracy (ancient Greece, French Revolution, Magna Carta); **2** = Age of Discovery (Genoa, Venice, Cádiz, Lisbon); **3** = Printing press (Gutenberg, at Mainz); **4** = Concept of the spherical earth (classical Greeks at Miletus, now in Turkey); **5** = Concept of heliocentric solar system (Copernicus in Frombark); **6** = Industrial Revolution (English Midlands); **7** = Steam engine (Watt in Glasgow); **8** = Railroad (northeast England); **9** = Internal-combustion engine (Lenoir in Paris, Otto and Daimler in Germany); **10** = Automobile (Daimler and Benz in Germany); **11** = Laws of motion and gravity, providing the basis of modern physics (Newton in England); **12** = Science of modern genetics (Mendel in Morava); **13** = Theory of evolution (Darwin in England); **14** = Theory of relativity (Einstein in Bern); **15** = Discovery of bacterial and viral causes of diseases (Koch in Ostpreussen and Pasteur in Paris); **16** = Radio (Marconi in Bologna); **17** = Modern study of the mind (Freud in Vienna); **18** = Socialism (Marx in Trier and London, Campanella in Italy); **19** = Productive capitalism (Holland and Flanders); **20** = Nationalism (Switzerland and France); **21** = Nation-state (Greece); **22** = Expressways (Germany); **23** = Orbital satellites and manned space flight (Russia); **24** = Microscope and telescope (Lippershey and Janssen in Holland; Galileo in Padua); **25** = Digital computer (Babbage in England); **26** = Early research on radioactivity (Curie in France); and **27** = Periodic table of the elements (Mendeleyev in St. Petersburg).

Other cornerstones of modernity were also laid in Europe, including capitalism, socialism, nationalism, and the modern state. Capitalism, distinguished by the application of capital to innovation in order to elevate levels of production, spread from an early nucleus in the 1500s in the Low Countries, and overtly commercial values soon permeated European civilization, leading to an economic boom that spread material prosperity through a larger segment of the population than ever before in world history. When linked to the Industrial Revolution, capitalism reshaped the world. Socialism arose in Europe as a movement to spread prosperity still more widely and to prevent the migration of great wealth back into the hands of the few. Rooted in Italian Tommaso Campanella's 1602 *City of the Sun,* socialism appeared as a fully developed ideology in the nineteenth-century works of Karl Marx, a German. In certain forms, socialism produced the enviable quality of life achieved in the Scandinavian welfare states, but it also underlay the economic and political deprivations of Russian Communism.

Nationalism, in which citizens transferred allegiance from the monarch to the state, began perhaps in medieval Switzerland and later appeared more forcefully in revolutionary France. Still later came another European innovation, the **nation-state** idea, in which nationality became conceptually linked to a common language and/or religion in a sovereign political territory. The nation-state idea was subsequently spread throughout the world.

Collectively, the impact of these diverse European concepts and inventions has been prodigious. Try to imagine a world never touched by them. As a result, some people jump to the Eurocentric conclusion that European culture is superior. Certainly, many Europeans have believed this to be true. Listen, for example, to the words of the great German writer, Thomas Mann. In his 1924 novel, *The Magic Mountain,* Mann described two opposed principles in conflict for possession of the world:

> force and justice, tyranny and freedom, superstition and knowledge, permanence and change. One may call the first Asiatic, the second European because Europe was a center of rebellion, the domain of intellectual . . . activity leading to change, while the Orient was characterized by quiescence and lack of change.

Similar, even stronger views found expression in the works of the famous Greek author, Nikos Kazantzakis, who grew up confronting an alien culture. Kazantzakis, in his book *Report to Greco,* compared his own culture to that of Asia Minor. He wrote that Greece "is the filter which . . . refines brute into man, eastern servitude into liberty, barbaric intoxication into sober rationality." Cultural impulses received from the East, that is, Asia, were refined and transubstantiated by the Greeks into more civilized forms. Kazantzakis said Greece's fated location on the borders of Asia produced "a mystic sense of mission and responsibility," a buffer against the "barbaric" and "bestial" East, that is, Turkey.

When confronted by **Eurocentricism** and cultural arrogance, we should remind ourselves that the region had no lock on innovation and that many European inventions came about because of Europe's encounters with other parts of the world. Moreover, some of the region's innovations proved malevolent and destructive. In some cases, they threatened the very existence of the human race. Europe gave us ethnic cleansing, genocide, fascism, religious inquisitions, imperialism, colonialism, and mechanized total warfare. In the words of geographer Yi-fu Tuan, Europeans, by discarding "the ageless fear of the greater power and potency of nature," assumed "an arrogance based on the presumed availability of almost unlimited power." Europe means progress, but where that progression ultimately will lead—to good or evil—remains unclear. Europeans developed a complex, sophisticated culture, but, in the final analysis, it could not prevent them from committing unspeakable atrocities in the German heart of Europe, nor does it allow them to control the powerful technology they unleashed.

Still, the importance of Europe remains uncontestable and profound. It is thus vital that we understand something about it. Moreover, many readers of this book will be in North America, a place that cannot be understood without reckoning with Europe's imprint. Recognition of that helps to explain the extraordinary flow of visitors each year who travel from North America to Europe. Many readers of this book will visit Europe at some point during their lives, if they have not done so already. The matters discussed here can, at a minimum, help enrich a traveler's experience in Europe. And they might even provide a foundation on which new transatlantic understandings and insights can be built. So let us turn our attention now to a geographical analysis of this small, but influential, corner of the world.

Sources and Suggested Readings

Ahnström, L. 1993. Europe: Culture Area, Geo-Ideological Construct or Illusion? *Norsk Geografisk Tidsskrift* 47 (2): 57–67.

Barzini, L.G. 1983. *The Europeans*. New York: Simon and Schuster.

Beeley, B.W. 1978. The Greek-Turkish Boundary: Conflict at the Interface. *Transactions of the Institute of British Geographers* 3 (3): 351–366.

Berdiaev, N. 1990. *Istoki i Smysl Russkogo Kommunizma*. Moskva: Nauka.

Berezin, M., and M. Schain. 2003. *Europe without Borders: Remapping Territory, Citizenship, and Identity in a Transnational Age*. Baltimore: Johns Hopkins University Press.

Blaut, J.M. 1993. *The Colonizer's Model of the World: Geographical Diffusionism and Eurocentric History*. New York: Guilford Press.

Cuisenier, J. 1979. *Europe as a Cultural Area*. The Hague: Mouton.

Dodgshon, R.A. 1992. The Role of Europe in the Early-Modern World-System: Parasitic or Generative? *Political Geography* 11 (4): 396–400.

Fells, J., and J. Niznik. 1992. What Is Europe? *International Journal of Sociology* 22 (1/2): 201–207.

Fischer, E. 1943. *The Passing of the European Age: A Study of the Transfer of Western Civilization and its Renewal in Other Continents*. Cambridge: Harvard University Press.

Gachechiladze, R.G. w. R.A.F. 1995. *The New Georgia: Space, Society, Politics, Eastern European Studies No. 3*. College Station: Texas A & M University Press.

Gress, D. 1998. *From Plato to Nato: The Idea of the West and its Opponents*. New York: Free Press.

Hahn, F.G. 1881. Zur Geschichte der Grenze Zwischen Europa und Asien. *Mitteilungen des Vereins für Erdkunde zu Leipzig*: 83–104.

Hasson, S. 1996. Frontier and Periphery as Symbolic Landscapes. *Ecumene* 3 (2): 146–166.

Hauner, M. 1990. *What Is Asia to Us? Russia's Asian Heartland Yesterday and Today*. Boston: Unwin Hyman.

Hay, D. 1968. *Europe: The Emergence of an Idea, Edinburgh University Publications; History, Philosophy and Economics, No. 7*. Edinburgh: Edinburgh U.P.

Hebbert, M., and J.C. Hansen, eds. 1990. *Unfamiliar Territory: The Reshaping of European Geography*. Aldershot: Avebury.

Jedlicki, J. 1999. *A Suburb of Europe: Nineteenth-Century Polish Approaches to Western Civilization*. Budapest: Central European University Press.

Jönsson, C., S. Tägil, and G. Törnqvist. 2000. *Organizing European Space*. London: SAGE Publications.

Kazantzakis, N. 1966. *Report to Greco*. New York: Bantam Books.

Kuus, M. 2004. Europe's Eastern Expansion and the Reinscription of Otherness in East-Central Europe. *Progress in Human Geography* 28 (4): 472–489.

Lewis, M.W., and K. Wigen. 1997. *The Myth of Continents: A Critique of Metageography*. Berkeley: University of California Press.

Louis, H. 1954. Über Den Geographischen Europabegriff. *Mitteilungen der Geographischen Gesellschaft in München* 39: 73–93.

Lyde, L.W. 1926. *The Continent of Europe*. London: Macmillan.

Meinig, D.W. 1969. "A Macrogeography of Western Imperialism." In *Settlement and Encounter*, eds. F. Gale and G.H. Lawton, 213–240. Melbourne: Oxford University Press.

Murphy, A.B. 2005. "Relocating Europe." In *Engaging Europe: Rethinking a Changing Continent*, eds., E. Gould and G. Sheridan, 81–101. Boulder: Rowman and Littlefield.

Murzazev, E.M. 1964. Where Should One Draw the Geographical Boundary between Europe and Asia? *Soviet Geography: Review and Translation* 5: 15–25.

Newbigin, M.I. 1924. *The Mediterranean Lands: An Introductory Study in Human and Historical Geography*. New York: A.A. Knopf.

Pagden, A., ed. 2002. *The Idea of Europe: From Antiquity to the European Union, Woodrow Wilson Center Series*. Washington, DC; Cambridge, UK: Woodrow Wilson Center Press; Cambridge University Press.

Painter, J. 2000. "Transnational Citizenship and Identity in Europe." In *9th Congress of the International Geographical Union*. Seoul.

Parker, W.H. 1953. Europe and the New Civilization. *Canadian Geographer* 3: 53–60.

———. 1960. Europe: How Far? *Geographical Journal* 126: 278–297.

Strahlenberg, P.J. v. 1738. *An Historico-Geographical Description of the North and Eastern Part of Europe and Asia*. London: J. Brotherton et al.

Tuan, Y-F. 1989. Cultural Pluralism and Technology. *Geographical Review* 79 (3): 269–279.

Whittlesey, D.S. 1949. *Environmental Foundations of European History*. New York: Appleton-Century-Crofts.

Wintle, M.J., ed. 1996. *Culture and Identity in Europe: Perceptions of Divergence and Unity in Past and Present, Perspectives on Europe. Contemporary Interdisciplinary Research*. Aldershot: Avebury.

Wolf, E.R. 1982. *Europe and the People without History*. Berkeley: University of California Press.

Woodward, D. 1985. Reality, Symbolism, Time, and Space in Medieval World Maps. *Annals of the Association of American Geographers* 75 (4): 510–521.

Zelinsky, W. 1966. *A Prologue to Population Geography, Prentice-Hall Foundations of Economic Geography Series*. Englewood Cliffs, NJ: Prentice-Hall.

CHAPTER 2

Habitat

Europe's human drama has been acted out on a small peninsula composed of many even smaller peninsulas attached to the western extremity of Eurasia. In this chapter, we consider Europe's physical geography. The goal is to provide insight into fundamental environmental features and forces that have shaped the region over time. Because Europeans have massively altered that environment, however, humans must be part of the picture. To the geographer, environment, people, and place are inextricably intertwined.

At the broadest level of generalization, several features of Europe's physical geography are of notable importance. First, Europe has a very long coastline in relation to its landmass. Only in the eastern part of Europe can one find land that lies more than 600 kilometers from a coast. The vast majority of Europeans live within less than 200 kilometers of a coast.

Also of great importance is Europe's position at the western edge of a large northern-hemisphere continent—abutting a large ocean. Moreover, Europe does not have a major north-south trending mountain range near its western edge. Instead, its higher mountains tend to be oriented in a west-east direction. As we will see, these characteristics have important implications for the region's climate, to say nothing of patterns of human movement.

A final notable aspect of Europe's physical geography is its northern location. Many Americans mistakenly think that Europe sits at more or less the same latitudes as does the United States. Actually, Europe is notably farther north. Rome lies on roughly the same latitude as New York City. If Brussels were in North America, it would lie along the southern shores of Hudson Bay. With these overarching features in mind, let us turn to four basic aspects of Europe's physical geography: its **geomorphology** and **hydrogeography**, its climate, its vegetation, and its soils.

Europe's Geomorphology and Hydrogeography

The European land is highly varied, ranging from high, rugged mountains to featureless flat plains (fig. 2.1). At first glance the physical patterns shown on a map of terrain regions may look dizzyingly complex, but they start making more sense if one

Figure 2.1.   Terrain regions. *Sources:* Raisz 2000; Embleton 1984.

considers the basic forces that have shaped the region over time. One of those forces is the movement of tectonic plates. As figure 2.2 shows, Europe lies near the western edge of the vast Eurasian plate, just north of the boundary between the Eurasian and the African plates. One of the dominant influences on Europe's landscape has been the movement of the Eurasian plate in relation to other plates. Between c. 280 and 240 million years ago, a huge supercontinent known as Pangaea was formed when prior amalgamations of tectonic plates crunched together. What came to be Europe lay at the heart of the supercontinent, and the enormous stresses and strains associated with its formation caused tremendous folding and faulting—particularly in the west and northwest part of what was to become Europe. This long-ago mountain-building period is called the **Hercynian period** in Europe. Geographers have identified three basic processes that contribute to landscape formation: uplift, erosion, and deposition.

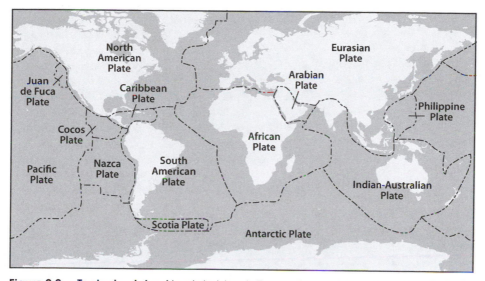

Figure 2.2.   Tectonic plates. No plate bisects Europe. Instead, the plate boundaries lie at Europe's southern and western edges. This explains why earthquakes and volcanic activity are common in the Mediterranean and in Iceland but not elsewhere.

Because many of the mountains formed during the Hercynian have been severely eroded through time, scientists used to think that the Hercynian was followed by a quiet period. We now know better. Beginning about 225 million years ago, Pangaea began to break up and folding and faulting continued, albeit it at a less intense level. Gradually, however, the higher Hercynian-era mountains were reduced in elevation by erosion—many taking on a more rounded, hilly look. Then between c. 100 and 60 million years ago, the African plate began pressing up against the Eurasian plate from the south, initiating an intensification of faulting and folding in the north. This period of tectonic activity, sometimes called the **Alpine period**, led to substantial mountain building in a west-east direction at a location somewhat inland from Europe's southern edge. These more recently uplifted mountains have had much less time to erode—and in some places they continue to grow. Europe's highest peaks are associated with these relatively recent uplifts.

Faulting and folding in conjunction with the movement of tectonic plates is not the only major influence on Europe's landscape. The other is erosion, and no source of erosion has been quite as dramatic as the advance and retreat of glaciers. Since at least the beginning of the Pleistocene era some 1.65 million years ago, the earth has been in an **ice age** characterized by multiple cold periods, called glacials, interrupted by periodic warmer periods known as interglacials. The Serbian astronomer Milutin Milankovitch came up with the most widely accepted explanation for these oscillations—attributing them to cyclical changes in (1) the shape of the earth's orbit, (2) the tilt of the earth on its axis, and (3) the earth's position in its orbit at equinox. Each of these cycles has a different periodicity, but they interact with one another to

Figure 2.3.   Glaciers in Europe during the height of the most recent glaciation. Far-northern Europe lay under thick layers of ice. All of Europe's climate zones were shifted significantly to the south.

produce irregular colder and warmer periods in keeping with what is known as the **Milankovitch cycle**.

The modern European landscape is a product in particular of the most recent glacials, during which enormous ice sheets built up in northern Europe, and glaciers colonized the taller mountains farther south (fig. 2.3). The ice sheets scraped off and ground up most surface materials in the north—depositing them at the feet of the glaciers as they retreated, or grinding them into fine particles that were distributed by wind throughout Europe's middle section. In the mountainous areas, glaciers carved craggy peaks and created U-shaped valleys as they wound their way down from the upper elevations. With a significant percentage of the earth's water in the form of ice on land, sea levels were much lower during glacial periods, and U-shaped valleys could extend into areas that are now below water. When the ice melted and sea levels rose, those U-shaped valleys below current sea-level filled with water, creating what are known today as fjords.

Europe entered the current interglacial period some 10–12 thousand years ago, although it experienced a return to somewhat colder temperatures between c. 1200 and 1850 in what is sometimes termed the Little Ice Age (a misleading term because the temperature shift was not nearly as great as that associated with major glacial advances). With the melting of the ice sheet, Europe's northern bedrock was exposed and the area of glacial deposits farther south could start supporting rich vegetation. The retreat of the glaciers exposed highly sculpted tall mountains, and caused considerable sculpting of some shorter mountains with Hercynian roots.

Armed with these insights, we can begin making sense of Europe's terrain—the pattern of mountains, hills, and plains shown in figure 2.1. We will then look at the region's hydrogeography and the ways in which humans have modified Europe's physiographic character.

MOUNTAINS

Europe's taller mountains lie largely in the southern half of the continent, and most ranges are oriented in a west-east direction. This concentration can be explained by the Alpine-era tectonic forces described above. Moving from west to east, the Bética Mountains parallel the south coast of Spain and consist of several ridges, including the Sierra Nevada. The Bética stretch from the Rock of Gibraltar to the vicinity of Valencia, where they disappear beneath the sea, only to reemerge to the east as the Balearic Islands. The Bética area, which includes peaks of more than 3,350 meters, served as the final stronghold of the Moors (Arabs originally from North Africa). The southernmost ridge of the Bética range fronts on the Mediterranean Sea, creating a rocky and picturesque coast.

Central Iberia is bisected by the Central Sierras, and along the north coast lie the Cantabrian Mountains (*Cordillera Cantabrica*), reaching 2,600 to 2,750 meters at their highest. The steepest face of this fault-block range faces north, toward the Atlantic, producing a rocky coast with numerous small, protected bays long used as fishing harbors. Extending to the east are the high Pyrenees that run along the border between Spain and France.

Moving farther east, the Alps—the highest and most famous European mountains—stretch from the French Riviera in an arc eastward, through Switzerland to Vienna on the bank of the Danube (fig. 2.4). The western Alps form the highest and most spectacular part of the range, with deeply incised valleys and impressive remnant glaciers. Mont Blanc, towering 4,813 meters above sea level, is the highest mountain peak in Europe. (By comparison, Mt. Whitney in California, the tallest peak in the contiguous 48 American states, is 4,421 meters above sea level.) Deep, sheer-sided U-shaped valleys sometimes have floors 2,750 meters lower than the adjacent peaks.

While impressive in appearance, the southern and western Alps never served as a true barrier to human movement. So many low passes exist through which invaders can move that the Italians, who live south of the mountains, sometimes refer to the range as the "magnificent traitor." The Carthaginian general Hannibal successfully moved a cavalry of elephants and 30,000 men through the southern Alps to attack Italy. Centuries later came various German tribes from the north, who slipped through to deal a deathblow to the Roman Empire. The ease of access through the western Alps

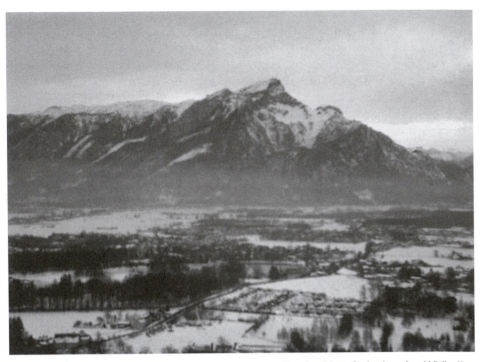

Figure 2.4.   The dramatic Alpine landscape near the Austrian-Swiss border. While the Alps appear formidable, low passes and water gaps make them relatively easy to traverse. (Photo by A.B.M., 1986.)

is attributable to low passes and streams that provide access into the heart of the range as they flow into the plains and hills beyond the Alps.

The Apennine Mountains, the backbone of the Italian Peninsula, branch out from the southern Alps in the Riviera region, arc gently to approach Italy's Adriatic shore, and then return to the western coast to form the toe of the Italian boot. Structurally, they reappear in the island of Sicily. The Apennines, narrow and low, offer many easy passes and have never presented much of a barrier to movement.

To the east of the Adriatic, the Dinaric Range begins where Italy, Slovenia, and Austria meet, and stretches southeastward along the Adriatic coast through the western Balkan Peninsula, continuing through to Greece. While not unusually high, the Dinaric Range is in many sections rugged and difficult to traverse, especially in areas of **karst topography**, where water filtering down from the surface dissolved permeable limestone, forming numerous large sinks or troughs that are used for farming. One of the few easy passages through the Dinaric Range is found in the extreme north, near the juncture with the Alps, where Pear Tree Pass allows access from the plains of Hungary into the Po–Veneto Plain of Italy. Both Hunnish and Gothic warriors poured through Pear Tree Pass to attack the Roman Empire. To the south, about midway through Albania, the Dinaric Range becomes more open and accessible, a condition that persists through Greece.

Figure 2.5.   A branch of the Sognefjord and an inhabited *vik* at its head. In the Norwegian Kjølen Range, only small agricultural areas occur. The fjords provide an excellent transportation facility. (Photo by T.G.J.-B., 1981.)

Just east of Vienna, across the Danube River in Slovakia, the Carpathian Mountains begin, almost as a continuation of the Alps. Their directional course inscribes a huge mirror-image of the letter C through southern Poland, a corner of Ukraine, and Romania, ending as they began on the shores of the Danube. The southern part of the Carpathians in Romania bears the name Transylvanian Alps. High elevations rarely occur in the Carpathians—few peaks are over 2,500 meters—and they form a narrow range with numerous low passes. To the east, the Crimean Mountains occupy the southern side of a large peninsula jutting into the Black Sea in Ukraine, and shelter the famous resort of Yalta from the east European winter.

There is one more significant mountain range found in Europe, namely the Kjølen Range, which forms the spine of the Scandinavian Peninsula in Norway and Sweden. With Hercynian roots, this range is not particularly high. However, its northern position means that it was heavily glaciated in the Ice Age, giving it an Alpine look. The range's western edge is deeply indented by fjords. One of the most spectacular is the long, narrow Hardanger Fjord ("Hair-String Fjord"). The Kjølen Range supports very few permanent dwellers, but at the upper end of most fjords, a small patch of flat, unflooded land known as a *vik* occurs, backed by a steep headwall and flanked by nearly perpendicular valley sides (fig. 2.5). Long ago the inhabitants derived their very name, *Vikings* ("people of the inlet"), from these small plains. Encouraged by the local terrain to look outward, down the fjord to the sea, the Vikings became famous as traders and sea raiders.

Closely linked to the mountain ranges of Europe, particularly in the south and on the island of Iceland, are the related phenomena of earthquakes, vulcanism, and

Figure 2.6. Earthquakes, vulcanism, and tsunamis in Europe, 1971. *Sources:* Kárník, V. 1971. *Seismicity of the European Area,* Dordrecht, NL: D. Reidel, II: 203; Simkin, T. et al. 1989. "This Dynamic Planet: World Map of Volcanoes, Earthquakes, and Plate Tectonics," Washington DC: Smithsonian Institution; data supplied by U.S. Geological Survey, National Earthquake Information Center website, http://earthquake.usgs.gov.

tsunamis (fig. 2.6). These phenomena are concentrated near the tectonic plate boundaries (fig. 2.2). Huge losses of life sometimes accompany European earthquakes, as was the case when 60,000 Sicilians died in an early-twentieth-century disaster, and when 25,000 Armenians died in 1988. The fatalities are often caused by the collapse of stone houses and tiled roofs, both common in southern Europe.

Volcanoes can also bring grief. The eruption of Vesuvius near Naples in 79 C.E. destroyed the Roman city of Pompeii, while on Sicily over 500 recorded eruptions of Mount Etna, the largest continental volcano in the world, have claimed an estimated 1 million lives over the past 2,500 years. The perpetually active volcano called Stromboli lies in the Aeolian Isles, north of Sicily. The most violent and powerful volcanic eruption ever known in Europe occurred on the small Greek Aegean island of Santorini—today merely a shattered, sea-flooded caldera. The island erupted and collapsed with incredible force about 1625 B.C.E. The noise was likely heard as far away as Scandinavia and central Africa; a huge tsunami, perhaps 200 meters tall, crashed against the shore of nearby islands; and the sky was soon blackened with falling volcanic debris. Parts of the large nearby island of Crete (*Kriti*) may have become temporarily uninhabitable as volcanic ash killed vegetation. Altogether, some 54 cubic kilometers of material were removed in the explosion, in the process probably giving rise to the legend of the lost continent of Atlantis.

On the mountainous island of Iceland, astride a tectonic plate divide at the opposite territorial extremity of Europe, vulcanism and earthquake activity occur frequently. Iceland, with 30 volcanic systems, has experienced over 250 eruptions in the past 1,100 years. Recently, a new island—Surtsey—appeared as a volcanic peak off Iceland's southern shore, and a massive eruption occurred on a nearby, older island, creating a natural harbor. Small wonder that this northern island is called "the land of fire and ice."

HILLS

A second terrain category includes the major hill areas of Europe. Hills dominate the European west and midsection (fig. 2.1), where faulting and folding connected with the formation and break-up of Pangaea was concentrated. Moving from west to east, hills dominate the west and north of the British Isles, confining the English Scarplands to the southeastern part of Great Britain. Cornwall is the hilly peninsula reaching southwest to Land's End, and the Cambrian Mountains occupy the larger part of the province of Wales. Geographer Estyn Evans aptly called the jagged coastlines where these and other western hills meet the sea "the tattered ends of Europe." The Pennine Chain forms the spine of Great Britain, blending into the Scottish Highlands to the north. The hills of the British Isles have been the primary refuges of the Celtic people, where they were, for a time at least, able to resist the Anglo-Saxon invaders and preserve their customs and language.

Moving to the mainland, among the more important hilly districts are Brittany (*Bretagne*) in western France, the Massif Central to the southeast, and a complex of Hercynian Hills extending from northeast France and southern Belgium, through central Germany, and into Czechia. The hills of this area carry different names, including the Ardennes of Belgium and Luxembourg, the Vosges of eastern France, the *Schwarzwald* (Black Forest) of Germany, and the Jura of Switzerland. Scattered among these hills are numerous small plains that long served as human population centers. The web-like gateways linking them have been routes of trade and invasion.

PLAINS

Europe's plains are concentrated in the north and east (fig. 2.1). A large, compartmentalized lowland extends from the foot of the Pyrenees in southwestern France, bending northward and eastward along the coast through Germany and Poland as far as the Baltic states. Many different sections can be distinguished, from the Basin of Aquitaine in the southwest (home to France's famous Bordeaux wines), through the Paris Basin and the communal delta of the Rhine–Maas–Schelde–Ems estuary in the Low Countries, to the vast North and East European Plains. In some places, the retreating glaciers left behind relatively infertile, poorly drained areas, but they also helped form some of the most fertile parts of these lowlands. Winds sweeping down from the ice mass picked up fine particles of earth and carried them to the southern edge of the plain, where the lowlands give way to a zone of hilly terrain. The forced ascent blunted the velocity of the winds, causing them to drop at the foot of the hills much of their load of dust. These wind-deposited, fine-textured parent materials, known as **loess**, weathered into fertile and easy-to-work soils.

Across the English Channel, in the southeastern part of the island of Great Britain, lies the English Scarplands. This area is in many respects simply a continuation of the Paris Basin. Just as the Paris Basin served as the nucleus of the French state, so the English Scarplands witnessed the initial nation building by the Saxon invaders of Britain.

Europe's north is dominated by the Fenno-Scandian Shield. Massively glaciated and underlain by ancient rocks, some of which lie exposed at the surface, the shield is centered in Finland and Russian Karelia. Two great **moraine** walls, formed at the foot of a retreating glacier, parallel the south coast of Finland and serve to dam up much of the interior, producing an intricate system of connecting lakes. The Finns and Karelians long used these waterways as their dominant mode of transportation, but in the age of highways, roads follow sinuous **eskers**—high ground laid down as the beds of ancient rivers flowing in hollows beneath the glaciers.

All of the other plains areas lie in the south, wreathed by the mountain ranges. Most are small, but some are of great economic significance. Again moving from west to east, the mountain ranges of Iberia divide that peninsula into a series of separate plains, each of which is home to people of a distinct subculture. The narrow Portuguese Lowland, which fronts the Atlantic coast of Iberia, and the Ebro Valley in northeastern Spain, are economic heartlands for Portugal and Spain, respectively. The interior plains of Iberia differ from others in Europe because they are elevated plateaus rather than lowlands, standing about 800 meters above sea level. The Central Sierras divide the plateau into two parts, Old and New Castile, the homeland of the people who have traditionally dominated and ruled Spain.

Proceeding east, France's gateway to the Mediterranean is the Languedoc Plain, a narrow coastal lowland reaching from the Pyrenees to the Riviera. In Italy, the Po–Veneto Plain is the one sizable plain area in the country. Glaciers moving down into the fringe of the Po–Veneto Plain from the north deposited moraines, which dammed up the mouths of tributary Alpine valleys, creating a chain of beautiful natural lakes, including Como, Maggiore, Lugano, Iseo, and Garda. South of the moraine dams is an infertile outwash plain, beyond which lies the greater part of the Po–Veneto Plain, an area of fertile, river-deposited soils. At the juncture of alluvium and outwash, the groundwater table reaches the surface, resulting in an east–west line of springs called *fontanili*. From ancient times the fontanili attracted human settlement, and today a row of cities, including Turin and Milan, traces the course of the spring sites. Still another line of cities, including Parma, Modena, and Bologna, lies along the southern edge of the plain, at the foot of the Apennines. The western, uppermost part of the plain served as the political nucleus of Italian unification in the nineteenth century, and today the same area contains the industrial heart of the nation.

An exception to the small scale of most southern European plains is the Hungarian Basin in the east, surrounded by the Alps, Carpathians, and Dinaric Range. The fringing mountains provide no isolation for the Hungarian Basin. The Italian lands are easily reached through the Pear Tree Pass, while the Black Sea lies beyond the so-called Iron Gate on the Danube, where the river severs the Carpathians. The diverse ethnic makeup of the basin today, including German, Hungarian, Slav, and Romanian, is the heritage of a long history of warfare, trade, and migration.

To the southeast, the Valachian Plain is a smaller lowland reaching eastward into the Balkan Peninsula from the Black Sea. Valachia has witnessed the comings and goings of a great variety of invaders and migrating peoples, including the Huns, Slavs, Magyars, and Mongols. Today, the Valachian Plain is the heartland of the Romanians, who have managed to preserve a language derived from the Roman armies, perpetuating an isolated eastern bastion of Romance speech.

Compartmentalization is a recurrent trait in the terrain makeup of Europe. The segmentation into numerous peninsulas and islands helps create this image, but it is heightened by the fact that most individual terrain units are small and possess individuality. The Basin of Aquitaine differs from its neighbor, the Paris Basin, and the western Alps differ from the eastern Alps. Rarely does homogeneity of terrain dominate a sizable area, and each small landform district possesses its own special character.

HYDROGEOGRAPHY

As we saw earlier, Europe's highly indented coastline causes most parts of the region to be within striking distance of the sea. Only eight sizable independent countries in Europe lack a coastline, as contrasted to 29 major states that enjoy access to the sea. Winter ice troubles only the Baltic and White Seas—and even there it is with decreasing frequency. The White Sea, linked to the Baltic by a canal, is an inlet off of the Barents Sea in Russia. It has historically been the center of much of Russia's maritime activities (including being the site of a major submarine base during the Soviet era).

Europe's flanking seas, named on the accompanying map (fig. 2.7), are linked by numerous strategic straits, facilitating a movement of people and goods around the perimeter of Europe. Control over the connecting straits has long been the goal of many competing European powers, and many of these waterways have often been militarily contested. The Bosporus and the Dardanelles, two narrows that join the Black and Aegean Seas, have alternately been controlled by the seagoing Greeks, most notably in the period of the Byzantine Empire, and by the land-based Turks, who presently control these strategic straits. Similarly, Arabs and Spaniards contested Gibraltar—a small part of the southern part of the Iberian Peninsula adjacent to the strait bearing the same name—before it fell to the British, who hold it as a vestige of their sea-based empire.

Figure 2.7. Hydrogeographic features. Europe is characterized by a highly indented coastline of surrounding seas and connecting straits. Key to connecting straits: **1** = Bosporus-Dardanelles; **2** = Otranto; **3** = Messina; **4** = "Waist" of the Mediterranean; **5** = Bonifacio; **6** = Gibraltar; **7** = Dover; **8** = North Channel; **9** = Saint George's Channel; **10** = Skagerrak; **11** = Kattegat; **12** = Øresund; **13** = The Belts; **14** = Åland; and **15** = Kerch.

On the Atlantic front of Europe, the most crucial strait is at Dover. Briefly, this white-cliffed passage and the adjacent English Channel served as the core of a Norman French state, but ultimately it became a natural moat and trade route for the British. Instead of joining the mainland to Britain, Dover came to separate them. Since 1994, France and the United Kingdom have been linked by the Channel Tunnel, or "Chunnel," which passes under the English Channel between Calais and Dover.

The great, navigable rivers of Europe lie disproportionately on the North and East European Plains. Flowing in a southeast-to-northwest direction, each has a major port city at its juncture with the sea. Canals interconnect these streams, providing a splendid waterway system. Most of eastern and southeastern Europe drains to the Black Sea, in particular through the great Danube, which, rising in southern Germany, passes through or borders nine independent states and is known by five different names along its course. The rivers of southern Europe, not being navigable, generally lack port cities at their mouths. The important European Mediterranean rivers include only the Ebro, Rhône, and Po.

HUMAN MODIFICATION OF LANDS AND WATERS

Europe's geomorphology and hydrogeography have been significantly altered by humans though time. One example of geomorphic alteration is terracing. This ancient practice, probably derived from the mountain fringe of the Fertile Crescent in southwest Asia, comes out of the effort to "level" mountains for agricultural use. In the Mediterranean lands, where level terrain is in short supply, terraced hillsides are common, especially in Greece.

People even build hills. On the North European Plain near Berlin, for example, stands the *Teufelsberg*, or "Devil's Mountain." Building material for the Teufelsberg came from the rubble of the war-destroyed German capital, and the peak reaches sufficient height to provide a ski slope in winter. In eastern Ireland, there are numerous small hills called **motes**, erected as fortifications by invading Normans in the Middle Ages. Similar artificial hills or mounds dot the delta plains on the approach to the ruins of Pella, the capital of the Macedonian empire in northern Greece at the time of Alexander the Great (fig. 2.8). If people build, they also excavate, forming open-pit mines that scar the landscape in many regions.

Figure 2.8.   A huge artificial mound at the ancient Danish capital of Jelling, on the Jylland Peninsula. Europe abounds in such anthropogeomorphic features, helping produce the image of a thoroughly humanized landscape of great antiquity. (Photo by T.G.J.-B., 1981.)

Many European rivers have been greatly modified by human action, both deliberate and accidental. Some seas and streams, in particular the Vistula River, are severely polluted—laced with heavy metals such as lead and mercury, coal-mine salts, and organic carcinogens. Others, such as the Dnieper River, have had their character greatly altered by reservoir construction. The Drin, a minor river of northern Albania, has been completely transformed from a gorge-cutting mountain stream to a stair step of three lakes, now open to boat traffic. Many rivers of the North European Plain have been channelized and canalized, with locks and small dams to enhance transport. The great rapids at the Iron Gate of the Danube, where the river cuts through at the Carpathian–Stara Planina juncture, have been dynamited away. River banks are often manicured and lined with facing stones, giving them an artificial appearance.

Marshes were once common in many parts of Europe, but the majority of wetlands have been drained and converted to agriculture. The fens in the English Scarplands disappeared in this way. Some marshes were created by human action, as in the Val di Chiana in Toscana, Italy. There, Etruscan forest removal in ancient times began **siltation**, which in time clogged the valley's drainage system, forming a large malarial marsh. Later, farmers drained the Val di Chiana marshes and made them productive. Human modification of marshes is common in Europe, as it is elsewhere in the world, but converting marshland can have negative consequences. First, marshes act as natural sponges during wet periods; their water storage capacity can prevent intense, rapid flooding of streams, which can cause erosion and loss of property. Second, marshes and other wetlands are good storage sinks for sediment. The small particles that cause streams to be murky also affect the habitats of many species of fish, and marshes and other wetlands act as natural filtration for the hydrologic system.

Coastal silting represents another device by which Europeans have modified Europe's physical character, especially on the three Mediterranean peninsulas. As a result of deforestation and certain types of agriculture, bays have silted up, rivers have become unnavigable, ports have been made landlocked, and islands near the coast have been joined to the mainland (fig. 2.9). Many of these changes have unfolded over long periods of time. The Greek geographer Strabo, writing about 2,000 years ago, noted that the Adriatic tides reached to Ravenna in northern Italy, a city 10 kilometers inland today. Palos de la Frontera on the Odiel River, from which Columbus departed on his voyage of discovery in 1492, is now silted up for 1.5 kilometers below the former docks. Even more impressive is the silting that occurred in the area of Monte Circeo, a mountain on the western coast of Italy. According to the Homeric epic *Odyssey*, Monte Circeo formed an island in preclassical times, and it retained that status even as late as 300 B.C.E. Several centuries later, siltation joined it to the Italian mainland. Where Ulysses once sailed, farmers labor today in fertile fields.

THE SPECIAL CASE OF THE NETHERLANDS

Nowhere has the scale and scope of human modification of the physical landscape been greater than in the Netherlands, where the Dutch live on the "wrong" end of a huge geomorphological seesaw. Their deltaic homeland in the Low Country has been

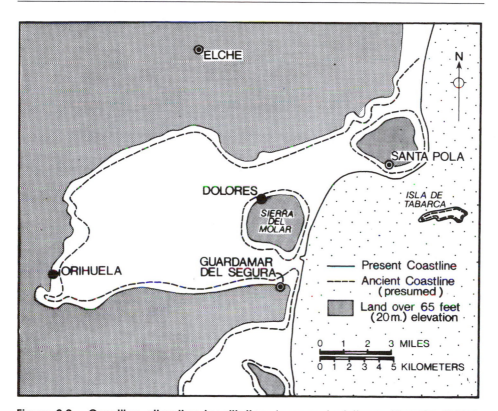

Figure 2.9.   Coastline alteration by siltation since ancient times, Alicante district, Mediterranean coastal Spain. Materials eroded from the adjacent Bética Range have filled a sizable bay and joined several islands to the mainland. Similar siltation occurred in other Mediterranean areas. *Source:* Smith, C. D. 1979. *Western Mediterranean Europe.* London: Academic Press, 332.

gradually sinking, at the rate of about 20 centimeters per century, coincident with an increase in elevation along the shores of the Baltic Sea. The elevation increase in the north is due to a process known as **isostatic rebound**, wherein a segment of the earth's surface that has been depressed by the weight of an ice sheet gradually returns to its former elevation after the ice melts. As that area rebounds, adjacent areas are sometimes pulled downward, and this is what has happened to the Netherlands. Since the end of the period of Pleistocene glaciation about 10,000 B.C.E., the coastal fringe of the Netherlands has sunk some 20 meters. Silt brought in and deposited by the Rhine, Maas, and Schelde Rivers has partially offset the sinking of the land, but without active human efforts, the coastline would have drastically deteriorated.

Before the encroachment by the sea began, the ancient Dutch coast had few indentations and was paralleled by a protective wall of sand dunes. The only breaks in the dunes occurred where the many distributaries of the Rhine, Maas, and Schelde cut through to reach the North Sea. As thousands of years passed and the level of some lands on the inland side of the dunes fell below sea level, parts of the Low Country flooded. Driven by storms, the North Sea broke through the sand dune barrier in the northern and southwestern Netherlands and permanently inundated large areas. This deterioration can still be seen today, especially in the north. The Friesche Islands, which lie in an east–west string along the northern coast, represent all that remains of the sand dune wall in that sector, and the shallow saltwater *Waddenzee*, which separates the islands from the coast, was once dry land. Besides the Waddenzee, the other major marine incursion helped create a huge flooded river mouth, or estuary, where the Rhine, Maas, and Schelde Rivers came to the sea on the southwestern coast.

Still, deterioration continued. Parts of the coastal margin of the Low Country fragmented into marshy tidal islands, and numerous lakes formed in depressions. From time to time, storm tides broke through to join some of these lakes to the sea. When the Romans came to this region, they found a large freshwater lake just south of the Waddenzee, fed and drained by a distributary of the Rhine, and called it the *Flevo Lacus*. A thousand years later the Roman lake became a saltwater embayment of the North Sea, when a series of storms about 1200 C.E. cut through the ribbon of dry land separating it from the Waddenzee. This created the shallow, saline *Zuider Zee* ("southern sea") to replace Flevo Lacus. Other freshwater lakes in the coastal fringe awaited their turn to be joined to the sea.

Another type of deterioration involved the slow eastward migration of what remained of the sand dune barrier. The prevailing westerly winds gradually moved the dunes inland, and the sea followed close behind. A fortress built during the Roman occupation on the landward side of the dunes was covered by drifting sands, disappeared, and was soon forgotten after the legions left, only to reappear during the Christmas season in the year 1520 on the *seaward* side of the dune wall. Soon thereafter the ruins were flooded by the advancing North Sea. This involved an eastward migration of about 3 kilometers in 1,500 years.

Human action to resist the environmental deterioration gained momentum over the last 1,700 years. At first, the early Dutch inhabitants did nothing more than pile up mounds of earth upon which to build their homes. These mounds, called **terpen** (in Dutch) can be seen today in parts of the Low Country and are generally still inhabited (fig. 2.10). During periods of high water, the terpen temporarily became little islands protecting the people in clustered dwellings on top. These mounds, 4 to 12 meters high, varied in area from 1.5 to 16 hectares. The terpen were built mainly from the third to the tenth centuries C.E., and the remnants of some 1,500 of them still survive. Somewhat later, in the 900s, the Dutch began placing obstructions along the coast to catch and hold accretions of sand and silt, and built walls to trap silt being washed down the rivers. In these ways they induced island building in the delta (fig. 2.11).

Dike building began about 900 C.E. in tidal marsh areas. The **dikes** protected lands above the low-tide level that were subject to periodic flooding, and sluice gates were opened at low tide to allow gravity discharge of the water that had accumulated through seepage. Such protected areas became known as **polders**, a term first used in 1138 in Flanders. Dike building and poldering spread northward into the province of Holland, where Count William "the Diker" directed poldering in an area of peat bogs, lakes, and marshes south of Amsterdam in the early 1200s. A peak of dike construction occurred in the 1300s to protect cropland from the unpredictable seas, lakes, and rivers.

Figure 2.10.   An ancient *terp* in the Dutch coastal province of Friesland. This artificial mound dates from the earliest period of the Dutch battle against the sea and today contains the church and cemetery of the village of Jelsum. Before the era of dike-building, the countryside all around the *terp* was subject to periodic inundation by the waters of the sea. (Copyright Marianne Dommisse, from Netherlands Information Service, used with permission.)

The development of polders in areas too low to be drained by gravity at low tide awaited the invention of a mechanical water lifter. The windmill, known in the Low Country at least since the late 1100s, initially served only as a grinder of grain; but in the year 1408 the windmill was first employed as a water lifter, and by the 1600s it had achieved general use for this purpose. The same westerlies that pushed the waters against the Dutch shores and caused the retreat of the protective sand dunes, were harnessed to reclaim the land. Within several centuries, nearly all of the marshes and bogs had been converted into polders, with a resultant increase in human population and food production.

Drainage of the numerous freshwater lakes dotting the coastal fringe of the Low Country represented the next advance in Dutch reclamation technology. Two centuries of experimentation with the windmill convinced engineers that sizable water bodies could be converted to agricultural use, and between 1609 and 1612 the combined work of 49 windmills laid dry a 7,300-hectare freshwater lake. Other small lakes were drained in quick succession. More powerful water lifters were needed to allow reclamation of large lakes and oceanic inlets, and for these the Dutch had to wait until the nineteenth and twentieth centuries, when steam- and, later, electric-engine pumps became available. Between 1840 and 1846, a dike was built around the 60-kilometer circumference of the freshwater Haarlemmer Lake, covering 17,800 hectares west of Amsterdam. Then three British-built steam-engine pumps worked continually for five

Figure 2.11. **Humans at work modifying the Dutch coastline, 1200–1950.** Both the advance of the North Sea and the subsequent work of humans to push back the waters are evident in these maps of the Rhine-Maas-Schelde Estuary in the Zeeland province of the Netherlands. The Delta Project is not shown. *Source:* 1963. *Westermanns Atlas zur Weltgeschichte.* Braunschweig, D: Georg Westermann, Part 2, 97.

years, from 1847 to 1852, to drain the lake. Haarlemmer was the largest water body yet to surrender to the Dutch at that time, but the greatest projects still lay in the future.

The treacherous Zuider Zee had been a menace to the Low Country ever since its formation. Its waters needed only a strong north wind to send them raging against the vulnerable sea dikes protecting the polderland to the south, and over the years the Zee had claimed many victims. A severe flood in 1916 finally prompted the Netherlands' government to take action on the Zuider Zee Project and actual work began seven years later. The key to the project, a huge sea dike called the *Afsluitdijk,* was completed seven years afterward, cutting off the mouth of the Zuider Zee from the ocean,

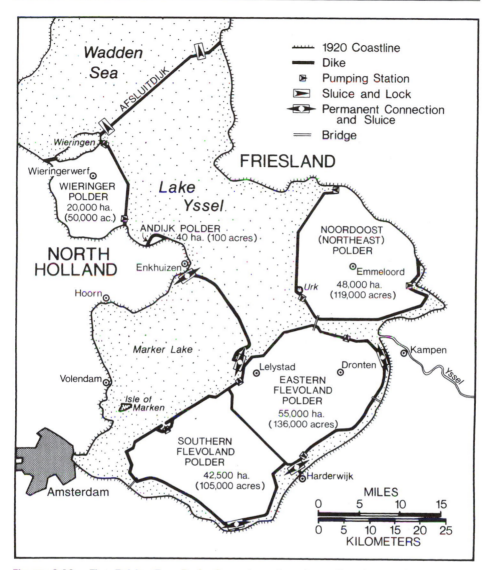

Figure 2.12.   The Zuider Zee Project produced a dramatic change in the Dutch coastline, as well as converting what remains of the old saltwater Zee into the freshwater Lake Yssel.

and greatly reducing the amount of protective dike exposed to the open sea by shortening the coastline (fig. 2.12). The streams flowing into the Zee soon flushed it clean of salt water, creating the freshwater Lake Yssel. The dike included sluices to allow for outflow of water, and locks to accommodate shipping. The name Zuider Zee disappeared from the map, and perhaps the only people who mourned its demise were the saltwater fishermen, mainly Frisians, whose livelihood was destroyed. The highway and railroad built on the new dike provided greatly shortened transport links between western and eastern parts of the Netherlands.

The second part of the project involved the diking and draining of four large polders from the floor of the old Zuider Zee. The Wieringer Polder in the far northern part was actually drained before the entire sea dike was finished, becoming dry in 1931. Experimentation established the best sequence of crops to remove salinity from the soils, and soon the Wieringer Polder was colonized by Dutch farmers. Settlement was completed in 1941, and the area is a fully integrated part of the Netherlands, largely indistinguishable from surrounding districts. The other major polders include the Noordoost, drained by electric pumps in 1936–1942 and colonized by the early 1960s; Eastern Flevoland, named for the ancient Roman lake and laid dry in 1957; and Southern Flevoland, pumped free of water in 1968 and today absorbing suburban spillover from the adjacent cities of Holland, as well as providing parkland. The remainder of Lake Yssel remains undrained, serving as a freshwater supply and recreational area.

With the Zuider Zee Project, the Dutch turned back the major marine encroachment on their northern coast. The other principal danger area lies in the southwestern province known as Zeeland, where the Rhine–Maas–Schelde estuary passes through six large gaps in the old sand dune barrier. This delta country was no stranger to storm floods from the sea, but the attention of the Dutch government was finally attracted by an especially severe disaster in 1953. Between January 31 and February 2 of that year, 160-kph winds from the northwest pushed river water back up into the estuary, breaking down dikes and spilling into the farmlands and towns of the islands in the estuary. More than 80 breaches were made in the dikes, and some 150,000 hectares were flooded with seawater. About 1,800 persons drowned, 100,000 were evacuated, and damage reached enormous proportions. The storm could easily have been even more catastrophic than it was. A strategic dike along the north bank of the Rhine–Maas channel called the Nieuwe Waterweg, protecting the densely settled heartland of Holland to the north, held—barely. Had it collapsed, the homeland of 3 million people would have been inundated and many more persons drowned.

To prevent such an occurrence in the future, the government approved the Delta Project (fig. 2.13). Four large new sea dikes closed off most of the mouths of the Rhine–Maas–Schelde estuary, with a freshwater lake on the landward side. The Nieuwe Waterweg remained open so as not to disrupt Rhine River shipping, but elaborate new water-diversion systems and storm-surge barriers directed the flow of the Rhine and Maas into the adjacent lake in case a storm tide backs up the river as in 1953. The lake can absorb the river flow for several days without spilling over its dikes, and the excess water can then escape through sluices to the sea when the storm subsides. The western Schelde estuary also remains open since it serves the major Belgian port of Antwerp, but dikes along the estuary shore were raised and strengthened. Little land reclamation occurred in the Delta Project, only about 16,200 hectares, for the goal was preservation rather than expansion.

More than any other part of Europe, then, the Netherlands has been human-made. Given all of this, the Dutch saying seems appropriate: "God made the world, but the Dutch made Holland." Without the effort of the inhabitants, the seacoast would lie far to the interior, and some of Europe's richest farmland and largest cities would be under water.

Figure 2.13.   The Delta Project was designed to protect the southern Dutch coast and prevent another catastrophic flood like the one in 1953. *Sources:* Wagret 1968; van Veen 1962.

Europe's Climate

Located to the north of the Eastern Hemisphere's great desert belt, Europe enjoys climates that are generally humid and mild, considering the rather high latitudes involved. These temperate, moist conditions favored the development of large population concentrations and helped Europe become one of the major homelands of humanity.

Why is Europe's climate predominantly humid and mild, and why does the mildness and humidity extend as far inland as it does? Addressing this fundamental geographical question requires consideration of a few basic aspects of the region's physical geography. Four phenomena are of particular significance: the **Gulf Stream**, the **North Atlantic Drift**, the seasonal movement of the **Azores anticyclone**, and the geographic arrangements of Europe's major mountain ranges.

The first two of these are related to fundamental forces that influence the movement of air and water in the northern hemisphere. The rotation of the earth in a counterclockwise direction when viewed from above the North Pole results in a dominant west-to-east movement of air masses. This means that the air masses moving into Europe, called westerlies, come off the Atlantic and bring an endless succession of cyclonic storms—centers of low pressure swept along in the wind belt known as the Gulf Stream.

Despite Europe's northerly location, the Gulf Stream passes over waters of moderate temperature as it makes its way into Europe. The presence of moderate water off Europe's west coast can be attributed to the clockwise rotation of ocean currents in the northern hemisphere. This rotation happens because anything moving in a straight line north of the equator is deflected to the right, due to the rotation of the earth below the moving object (the **Corriolis Effect**). The oceans are in constant flux, and the clockwise rotation of the North Atlantic moves water from the warm Caribbean to the north and east—producing what is known as the North Atlantic Drift. When the water from farther south and west reaches Europe's west coast, it has lost some of its warmth, but it retains enough to keep it from getting too cold during the winter months. But during the summer, the waters pushed along by the North Atlantic Drift become cool enough as they move north and west to keep ocean temperatures moderate. The air masses passing over the North Atlantic waters reflect the temperature characteristics of the water. The westerlies bring unsettled conditions into a significant part of Europe year-round, but they are not too cold in the winter and not too hot in the summer.

Not all of western Europe is affected year-round by the unstable westerlies coming off the Atlantic. The southern parts of the region are shielded from these effects during the summer months by the northward migration of something called the Azores anticyclone—the third fundamental force influencing Europe's climate. The Azores anticyclone is a product of global air circulation patterns that tend to produce downward drafts of air in bands at the northern and southern edges of the tropics. These bands are where the great deserts of the earth can be found, because downward drafts of air create zones of high pressure that push away unstable moist air masses. The high pressure ridge that lies off the northwest coast of Africa is called the Azores high, or Azores anticyclone, after the islands found in the region. The Azores anticyclone is not stationary throughout the year, however; it migrates north in the summer months and south in the winter as the position of the earth in its orbit alters which latitudes receive the most direct incoming solar insolation. The Azores anticyclone never moves far enough north to allow significant unstable air to penetrate into the Sahara Desert of northern Africa, but it does move far enough to keep the southern part of Europe quite dry during the summer months. As it retreats to the south in the winter, moister, more unstable air can find its way into areas bordering on the Mediterranean Sea.

A final basic influence on Europe's climate is a product of the arrangement of its mountains ranges. Unlike in North America, there is no north-south trending mountain range that causes moister air coming off the adjacent ocean to rise and lose much of its moisture, and then to descend and create dry conditions to the east of the mountains. Instead, as discussed previously, Europe's location in relation to colliding tectonic plates means that the region's major mountains extend west-to-east. As a result, there is nothing to block the inland penetration of the moderate, moist air coming off the Atlantic. That moderating influence is heightened by Europe's peninsular character. Moderating waters surround Europe well to the east of its western edge (the Mediterranean, the North Sea, and the Baltic); it is only in Europe's eastern reaches that land lies more than a few hundred kilometers from a surrounding sea.

Figure 2.14. Climate types. *Sources:* Köppen, W. et al. 1930–1936, *Handbuch der Klimatologie.* Berlin: Borntraeger; Wallén 1970; Flohn and Fantechi 1984.

The interaction of these influences shapes Europe's basic climate pattern. In broad brush, Europe is characterized by a zone of moderate, humid conditions to the north of the Pyrenees and Alps in the west—gradually giving way to more extreme conditions as one moves east and north. To the south of those mountain ranges, moderate, somewhat humid conditions dominate during the winter months, but hot humid conditions are found in the summer.

Mapping Europe's climate patterns requires grouping climate conditions into generalized regions. One of the most common approaches to this is shown in figure 2.14. It is useful to consider a few key characteristics of the principal regions shown on the map.

MARINE WEST COAST

Dominating Europe's western reaches to the north of the Pyrenees and Alps is the marine west coast region. The name describes both the region's location and an important property governing its character: the role of maritime air masses. As we have seen, the latter are moisture-laden and mild in winter, and not too hot in summer. They penetrate deeply into Europe—giving the marine west coast climate zone a significant eastward penetration. Temperatures remain mild all year, with cool summers and relatively pleasant winters. The coldest month averages above freezing and generally below 7°C. Temperatures do not differ greatly between winter and summer. Dublin, Ireland, averages only 10°C warmer in July than in January. The majority of January nights in London do not have frost. Even in the Shetland Islands, far to the north, snow is relatively rare.

Occasional bitter cold waves do occur in the marine west coast climate. London has recorded -16°C, and during one severe cold spell in February 1929, the temperature remained constantly below freezing for 226 hours in the British capital. A bitter cold spell struck western Europe again in December 1996 and January 1997, causing more than 200 deaths and freezing over the River Thames above London. Still, the appearance of a few palm trees at places along the southwest Irish coast suggests the overall mildness of the winters. It was not always so. During the colder climatic phase known colloquially as the Little Ice Age (1200 to 1800 C.E.), the marine west coast winters were more severe. The canals of Holland more often froze over, permitting the ice skating shown in the paintings of some of the Dutch masters.

Marine west coast summers are cool, with July averages generally below 21°C, and sweaters feel comfortable on many days. Heat waves, with temperatures above 32°C, do occur occasionally in parts of the marine west coast area. The record high temperature at Paris is 38°C. A number of severe heat waves have occurred in the marine west coast region in recent years. During an August 2003 outbreak of hot weather, in excess of 14,000 mainly elderly people were estimated to have perished in France of heat-related illnesses. During the summer of 2006, the British Isles endured an extended period of temperatures in the high 30s Celsius, and judges in the Royal Courts were allowed to remove their wigs in light of the heat. Most buildings in this region do not have air conditioning.

Because the marine air masses contain great amounts of moisture, the climate is quite humid, with adequate precipitation all year round. Normally between 50 and 100 centimeters fall each year, although relatively little precipitation typically falls on any given day. Gentle showers or drizzles are the rule. The cool temperatures retard evaporation, as does prevalent cloudiness, and precipitation is adequate to produce humid conditions. Stations situated at the western edge of hills and mountains receive considerably more precipitation as humid air masses moving from the west rise over hill and mountain barriers. In rising, the air mass cools, lowering its ability to hold moisture in an evaporated state. The excess is precipitated on west-facing slopes. This process is called the **orographic effect**.

In the marine west coast climate region, winds are generally gentle, although blustery conditions occur frequently in some coastal areas. In a few cases, winds come so regularly and from predictable directions as to have names. One of the best known is the *föhn* of southern Germany, a warm, dry wind from the south that results when a cyclonic storm moving north of the Alps in the winter draws drier, warmer winds over the mountains from the Mediterranean lands. A föhn blowing in midwinter can produce a sudden false springtime, with fair skies and pleasant temperatures, a delightful though short-lived respite from dreary, damp winter conditions.

MEDITERRANEAN

Southern Europe, in particular the three southward-reaching peninsulas of Iberia, Italy, and Greece, is dominated by the Mediterranean type of climate. Also included are the various European islands of the Mediterranean, southern coastal France, and the Adriatic coast of Croatia (fig. 2.14). The Mediterranean climate region is distinguished by the concentration of precipitation in the winter season, with exceptionally dry summers—a product of the seasonal movement of the Azores anticyclone. Generally, less than one-tenth of the annual precipitation falls in the quarter-year comprising the summer months of June, July, and August, and the month of July is almost totally rainless. Occasionally the summer drought expands to include the entire year, causing serious water shortages. Southern and central Spain suffered such a prolonged drought in the 1990s. Even the olives—hardy trees able to endure dry conditions—began to die. During the summer of 2007, Greece saw an unprecedented summer of hot and dry conditions, culminating in the worst fire season in many decades. At one point, forests were ablaze in half of the country, and many ancient ruins, including the site of the first Olympic games, were threatened by flames. The fires sparked an emotional debate over who was to blame for the extensive destruction: the government and its weak response in fighting the flames, or arsonists who perennially set forest land on fire to free up land for farming. Winter precipitation usually occurs as rainfall in the small lowland plains, but snow is common in the numerous mountain ranges concentrated in the Mediterranean climate region. Accumulated snow in the highlands is of crucial importance to farmers, because the runoff in spring and summer provides a source of irrigation water for the drought season.

Temperatures in the Mediterranean climate are warmer than those of the marine west coast area because of a more southerly location and a lower incidence of cloudiness. Summers are hot, with July averages usually in the 24° to 28°C range. Because the relative humidity in summer tends to be low, fairly rapid nighttime cooling occurs. A cool-summer subtype of the Mediterranean climate also appears in places, confined to the Atlantic **littoral** of Portugal and certain other windward coastlines (fig. 2.14). In these areas, warmest-month averages do not exceed 22°C.

Throughout the Mediterranean climate area, except in the mountain ranges, winters remain mild and extended periods of frost are unknown. Groves of citrus dot the lowlands of the Mediterranean, a good indicator of the absence of severe cold. Cloudiness is at a minimum, particularly in the summer, a striking contrast to the marine west coast region. Parts of Italy receive more than 2,500 hours of sunshine per year, almost twice as much as the British Isles.

The local winds of the Mediterranean reflect its location between the marine west coast and the desert. Winter storm centers moving through the basin draw cold, damp winds down from the north, including the **mistral** and the **bora**. The mistral blows with fury down the Rhône-Saône corridor into the Mediterranean coastal fringe of France and on beyond to the islands of Corsica and Sardinia, while the bora strikes the eastern coast of Italy from across the Adriatic Sea. From the opposite direction, dry, hot *sirocco* winds are drawn up from the Saharan region by cyclonic storms to afflict southern Italy and Greece. In Italy, the sirocco blows from 30 to 50 times annually, lasting 80 to 120 days per year and occurring most often from March through May and again in November. The Saharan winds are least common in summer, but when they do happen in that season, the searing heat is brutal and can be damaging to crops and orchards.

HUMID CONTINENTAL

The third of the major climate types found in Europe, the humid continental, dominates the eastern part of Europe, from southern Scandinavia to the eastern Balkans and deep into Russia (fig. 2.14). Here, as the climate's name implies, continental air masses, borne over the vast Eurasian interior and frozen Arctic Ocean, prevail over those of marine origin. These air masses display a great annual range of temperature, becoming very cold in the winters and surprisingly warm in the summers, producing a climate given to seasonal extremes. In particular, the winters are colder and become progressively more bitter toward the east. The disasters that befell the armies of Hitler and Napoleon in Russia were in no small part the work of numbing cold. January averages in the humid continental area range from about -12°C up to freezing, and low readings below -20°C are common. A blizzard in February 1999 produced heavy snowfall that cut off more than 200 villages and towns in Hungary. January 2006 saw another cold spell, with Moscow recording the longest stretch of days with temperatures dipping below -30° C since 1950.

The difference between January and July averages runs double or more the annual range of many marine west coast stations. Winter temperatures are low enough to cause a durable snow cover to develop, with usually at least one month in which the ground remains blanketed. In more eastern areas, the continuous snow cover can last for three or four months. Rivers, lakes, and shallow ocean inlets freeze over, including the Baltic Sea. Occasionally during winter in the East European Plain, the heart of the humid continental climate zone, cloudy and mild spells of weather occur.

Summer temperatures are remarkably similar to those in the marine west coast area. The July average at Moscow and Warsaw is identical to that at Paris, and most stations fall in the 16°C to 21°C range for the warmest month average. Only in the southern extremity of the humid continental area, in the Balkans and in an outlier in the upper Po-Veneto Plain, does a warm-summer subtype of the humid continental climate occur (fig. 2.14). In this zone, July averages exceed 22°C, and some summer days are unpleasantly hot. Throughout the humid continental climate region, precipitation is adequate if not abundant at all seasons, owing in part to the low evaporation rate associated with cool and cold weather. Between 48 and 65 centimeters of precipitation can be expected each year at typical humid continental stations, only slightly less than is the rule in marine west coast areas.

MINOR CLIMATE TYPES

The greater parts of Sweden and Finland lie in the subarctic climate zone, more severe than the humid continental (fig 2.14). Only one to three months average over 10°C, and the proximity to the pole in a continental location means bitter, dark winters. Summers are very cool and short, and winter is clearly the dominant season. In January 1987, a temperature of -45°C was recorded in Norway's Kjølen Range. The precipitation total is modest and comes mainly as snow, but the resultant climate is humid due to very low evaporation. At these high latitudes, darkness prevails in the winter months and daylight is fleeting. One of every ten Finns suffers Seasonal Affective Disorder (SAD), a depression caused by the prevailing darkness, and extravagant use of public lighting is employed to offset the problem.

Still more severe is the arctic climate zone, a region largely devoid of trees (fig. 2.14). It lacks a summer altogether, and the warmest month averages below 10°C. Surprisingly, the adjacent Barents Sea, part of the Arctic Ocean, does not freeze in winter, and the entire Norwegian coast and the Russian Arctic port of Murmansk remain open to shipping, thanks to the influence of the easternmost branch of the North Atlantic Drift.

The Dinaric Range and coastal portion of the Po-Veneto Plain are characterized by a humid subtropical climate, similar to the Mediterranean area in temperature but lacking the pronounced summer drought. Here the summers are hot with high humidity, and the July visitor to Venice may well be reminded of New Orleans or Brisbane.

Nearly all of Europe receives adequate precipitation, even if it is seasonal as in the Mediterranean. The only exceptions are some peripheral semiarid regions. In these places, the great desert belts of Africa and Eurasia gently touch Europe. Two minor types result: (1) the cold semiarid climate, typical of the lands north of the Black and Caspian seas that share the bitter continental winter, made all the more fierce here by the absence of trees to block the wind; and (2) the mild semiarid climate, sharing the temperatures of the Mediterranean winter but lacking its precipitation (fig. 2.14). The mild semiarid districts lie in Iberian rain shadow areas east of the Bética, Ibérica, and Cantabrica ranges, where the moisture-bearing westerlies are orographically drained of their moisture. Included are the Ebro Valley, the coastal *huertas* flanking the Bética Range, and the western reaches of the Meseta in Old Castilla.

The final type, the Alpine climate, occurs to some extent in all the mountain ranges of Europe, though shown in figure 2.14 only in the Alps. The key causal factor is elevation above sea level. Mountain heights cause the climate to be colder. The Alpine climate varies greatly from valley to valley and slope to slope, creating a pattern too chaotic to map on a small scale.

HUMAN ALTERATION OF THE ATMOSPHERE

Europeans have altered the climate, both on a local scale and more broadly. They live preponderantly in cities, each of which suffers in some measure from air pollution and experiences temperature alteration.

London's climate has been studied for centuries, and we know a lot about the human-induced changes there. As early as 1661, John Evelyn wrote in reference to London that "the weary traveler, at many miles distance, sooner smells, than sees the city." When the coal smoke poured through myriad chimneys, "London resembles the face rather of Mount Etna, the Court of Vulcan, Stromboli, or the suburbs of hell than an assembly of rational creatures." On October 15, 1880, *New York Times* concluded that "the fate of London is obvious and inevitable. It will be smothered in its poisonous and sooty fogs, while New York, which burns anthracite coal and never indulges in mixed fogs, will become the chief city of the earth." In more recent times geographers came to speak of London's **heat island**, a reference to the fact that temperatures are consistently higher over the built-up portion of the city than over the surrounding rural greenbelt. Minimum nighttime temperatures are at times 7°C higher over the central portion of London than in the greenbelt, and daytime maxima are also higher. This results from the inability of heat radiation from surfaces to penetrate the pollution haze that hangs over the city; the retention of heat by paved streets and buildings; and the heat produced locally by fuel combustion in vehicles, factories, and homes. At times, *isotherms*, lines connecting points with the same temperature, take on the same shape as the London urban area.

Human activity also influences rainfall and humidity characteristics of the London area. More thunderstorms occur over the city, more precipitation, and a distinctly higher absolute humidity than in adjacent rural areas. The cause lies both in the greater amount of thermal convection resulting from more surface heating, and in the superabundance of microscopic particulate matter associated with air pollution. Drops of condensation are built around such nuclei. A decrease in coal burning has lessened the degree of air pollution in London since about 1960, but the heat island persists. This same effect can be detected in many other areas of Europe. In fact, every city has a heat island, and severe air pollution remains a problem in many countries.

Ozone buildups, caused when emissions from automobiles and factories interact chemically in the presence of sunlight, have reached critical levels in the center of Europe. The corridor of worst air pollution, including not only ozone but also particulate matter, lies in the humid continental climate, along the southern margins of the North European Plain and in the Bohemian Basin, from eastern Germany and Czechia into Poland. This corridor, not coincidentally, also appears as the worst concentration of acid rain, a phenomenon best revealed by damage to forests (fig. 2.15). Various chemicals released into the air as a consequence of burning fossil fuels are cleansed from the atmosphere by precipitation. The resultant rainfall has a much higher than normal acidity, diminishing soil fertility, poisoning fish, and damaging vegetation. Air pollution extends to the outermost peripheries of Europe, as in the far north, where the phenomenon called *Arctic haze* occurs.

Figure 2.15. Percentage of forest area damaged or dead, 1998. Acid rain is a significant contributor to forest disease. Subnational data are shown only for Germany. *Source: Statistical Yearbook 1999 for Foreign Countries.* Stuttgart: Metzler-Poeschel, and various national statistical yearbooks.

Also found on a wide scale and likely the result of human activity is a pan-European warming of climate. According to the European Environment Agency (EEA) (http://www.eea.europa.eu/themes/climate), the global mean temperature has increased by 0.8 °C, and by slightly more than that in Europe since the mid-nineteenth century. Climatologists have established that eleven of the twelve years from 1995 to 2006 in Europe rank among the twelve warmest since records have been kept (1850). The EEA concludes, along with virtually all of the environmental agencies and climate research institutes in the world, that human activity, particularly the release of green-house gases such as carbon dioxide (CO_2), is to blame for this warming. As a result of warming, Atlantic cyclones have taken more northerly tracks, and sirocco-type winds off the Sahara have increased in both frequency and duration. Reflecting the increased warmth, Alpine glaciers lost one-third to one-half of their ice mass in the twentieth century. For example, the Aletsch glacier in Switzerland retreated almost 2 kilometers and lost about 100 meters of thickness in the 1900s. By contrast, the Icelandic and Kjølen glaciers have grown since 1950, but this is not inconsistent with climatic warming, since a hotter world is also wetter in places, providing the northern glaciers more snow while still not increasing temperatures to the melting point. At the lower latitudes, where the Alpine glaciers are found, snowfall has decreased markedly since the 1970s, not just in the Alps but throughout the temperate zone in Europe. The glaciers of the Caucasus have also retreated. Climate change entails a variety of impacts on the habitats of plants and animals, as well as on human activities. The EEA predicts that the ecosystems in Europe especially threatened by warming are mountain zones (due to the melting of glaciers and lower snowpack) and coastal zones, particularly coastal wetlands (largely due to sea level rise). Species are forced to adapt or migrate. It is predicted, for example, that climate change will likely raise the elevation of reliable snow conditions in Switzerland from its current 1,200 m to 1,800 m, which would make 56% of the country's famed ski areas unavailable for skiing during the winter. Sea level rise also threatens low-lying parts of the Netherlands and Belgium and the Po River delta region of Italy, as well as Venice.

Vegetation Patterns

Europe's vegetation pattern closely mirrors its climate regions (fig. 2.16). This is hardly surprising, given that climate has a major shaping influence upon plant life. So do people. In fact, Europeans have so massively altered the vegetative cover that we cannot know precisely what these biotic provinces were like in a natural state.

BROADLEAF DECIDUOUS FOREST

The part of Europe corresponding to all but the eastern and northern fringes of the marine west climate zone was once largely covered by a broadleaf deciduous forest, consisting of trees which drop their leaves during the dormant season in winter. Oaks served as the dominant species, and other common trees included the ash, linden, beech, and birch. Elms, maples, willows, and hornbeams were also well represented among the canopy trees. In the vegetative understory grew yews, hollies, and hazel shrubs, beneath which lay a groundcover of ivy, heather, anemone, ferns, bracken, primrose, and wild strawberry.

No fully intact broadleaf deciduous forest biotic system survives today, so pervasive has been the human influence. Clearing the forest for agricultural use led to widespread destruction of the deciduous broadleaf forest, a process begun in earnest about 500 C.E. by Germanic peoples. Charcoal burners also exacted a toll on the Atlantic woodlands, as in the Belgian province of Brabant, where in the place of the once-great *Silva Carbonaria* (charcoal forest), an unwooded plain meets the eye today. This devastation by farmers and burners continued unabated into the 1300s, when pestilence

Figure 2.16.   Floristic provinces. *Sources:* Jalas and Suominen 1972–1976; Polunin and Walters 1985.)

and warfare greatly reduced the population. The Hundred Years' War between France and England proved so destructive of human life in the Basin of Aquitaine, as to give rise to the local folk saying that "the forests returned to France with the English."

Following this respite, the broadleaf deciduous forests were subjected to a renewed attack by ax wielders. Population decline proved to be temporary, and a final phase in the clearing occurred in the 1500s and 1600s. To the renewed demands of an expanding farm population were added the needs of English, French, and Dutch shipbuilders, as well as other artisans. By 1550 England suffered from acute timber shortages, and France reached the same predicament a century later. Both came to rely on their American colonies to supply much-needed lumber. Considerable forests remained in Ireland during the late 1500s, for contemporary documents mention the difficulty of conducting military campaigns against Irish rebels in their woodland refuges. It seems

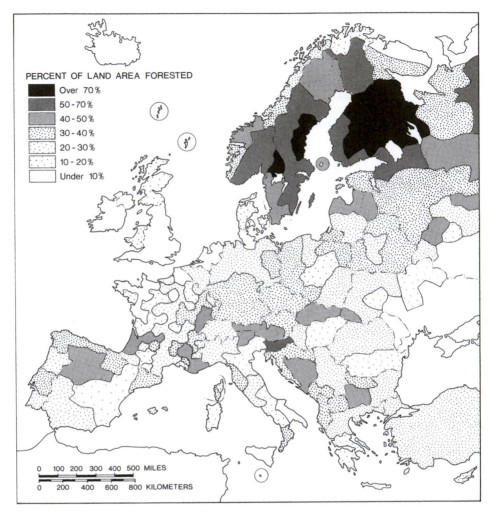

Figure 2.17.   Percentage of land forested. Deforestation is greatest in the west and south.

likely that the English felled many Irish woods for military reasons, to destroy these hideouts. Profit-hungry landlords completed the process of deforestation in Ireland in the 1600s, selling the timber abroad. By the year 1700, woodlands had vanished from the Irish scene, and oak virtually disappeared from the pollen record after that time. In England, similarly deforested, the word *wold* (as in Cotswold), which originally meant "forest," came to mean instead "an upland area of open country."

So catastrophic was the assault on the woodland that in several countries lying within the broadleaf deciduous forest zone, less than 10% of the land bears a forest cover today, and much of this meager woodland results from twentieth-century **afforestation**—the replanting of forests (fig. 2.17). Hill districts of the British Isles have been the scene of some of the most impressive afforestation projects, especially

Figure 2.18.   "The forest's in trouble on Wenlock Edge," according to an old English saying. Reference is to a ridge in the Scarplands of western England, near the border of Wales. Only the steep slopes of Wenlock Edge, unattractive to farmers, retain a forest cover. In contrast, the fertile vales below lie stripped of trees and well cultivated. The remnant forests resemble dark caps on the steep leading edges of a succession of great earthen "waves." (Copyright Aerofilms Limited, London.)

the Scottish Highlands and islands. However, trees planted in these projects tend to be commercially valuable exotics such as Douglas fir and Sitka spruce. The soil must be regularly limed, often by helicopter drop, to counteract natural acidity so that the desired exotic trees will survive.

Only scattered patches of forest containing native Atlantic trees remain. Some owe their existence to royal protection, as for example England's Sherwood Forest. In places, rough terrain, unattractive to farmers, sheltered a remnant of woods (fig. 2.18). The tiny vestiges of Atlantic woodland are today carefully tended, with heavy penalties for unauthorized cutting. Often these tidy groves resemble parks more than natural woodlands, particularly to the American eye. Western Europeans value remnant forests as recreational areas and have laid out a splendid network of hiking trails, and one rarely finds a forest area not open to the public.

Places such as the British Isles and Denmark have large expanses of treeless moor and heath. As a general rule, "heath" is the term used for hilly areas or undulating plains, whereas "moor" describes level surfaces. Both are covered with a variety of low shrubs, including heather, juniper, and gorse (reed-like, with abundant yellow flowers).

Figure 2.19.   Reduction of heath in the Jylland Peninsula of Denmark, 1800–1950. The land was reclaimed for agricultural use. *Source:* Thorpe 1957, 88.

Peat bogs abound. Some of these areas never had trees because they were insufficiently well drained. But there is evidence that some of these areas came about when human-set fires, used to create pastureland, produced a more open landscape.

Ironically, these heaths and moors are themselves now under human attack and rapidly declining in area. Afforestation projects are partly responsible, and one can still see the rock fences that once enclosed Scottish sheep pastures zigzagging through new forests of spruce and fir. In other cases, especially in Denmark, heath has been converted to agricultural use, especially improved pastures for dairy cattle (fig. 2.19). In other words, people first removed the forests in ancient times to produce rough pasture of heath, and then much later they destroyed the heath to obtain a better grassland. Clearly, the concept of natural vegetation is largely alien to Europe.

MIXED DECIDUOUS AND CONIFEROUS FOREST

As one moves to the east and north, the broadleaf deciduous forest zone gives way to a mixed broadleaf and deciduous forest. Here the beech was a dominant species, with many oak, larch, and hornbeam, but there are also abundant coniferous needle-leaf

Figure 2.20.   The retreat of woodland in central Europe, 900–1900 C.E. *Source:* Otto Schlüter, as reproduced in Darby 1956a.

evergreen trees such as fir, spruce, and the Scottish pine, especially in hilly, mountainous, and sandy regions. The understories are similar to those in the Atlantic forest, and orchids and sedges also abound.

While less catastrophically influenced by human activity, the mixed deciduous/coniferous forest of central Europe has also been greatly altered. As in areas farther west, Germanic farmers engaged in a great era of forest clearance during the Middle Ages to create new farming colonies (fig. 2.20). Often, evidence of the initial clearing survives in the present-day village and town names. In Germany, the common suffixes *-rod, -rot, -reuth,* and the like, as in Wernigerode, Heiligenroth, and Bayreuth, are all related to the modern German verb *roden,* which means "to root out," or "to clear." The German suffix or prefix *brand* indicates that the original clearing was accomplished by burning, for it derives from a Germanic root word meaning "fire."

Germanic forest removal typically began with small clearings. As populations grew, the settlers worked communally to push the perimeter of farmland outward at the expense of the forest, until finally the clearings of adjacent villages joined, sometimes leaving small isolated groves of trees at points farthest from the settlements (fig. 2.21). Less common, and confined mainly to valleys in central Germany and southern Poland, a second linear pattern of clearing began with a long, narrow cut along the valley to serve as a road. The colonists each received a ribbon-shaped farm stretching in a narrow strip back away from the road. In the absence of communalism, the more ambitious settlers rapidly cleared the forest toward the hinter portions of their land, while their neighbors lagged behind, producing an uneven linear swath of farmland advancing from the valley toward the adjacent ridge crest.

From the Germans, extensive clearance of the central European forests spread east to the Slavs, who had already made modest inroads before 500 C.E. Slavic forest

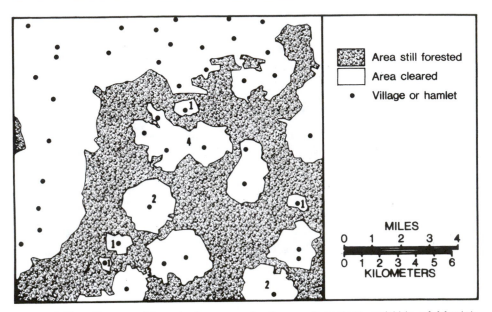

Figure 2.21. Stages of forest clearance in the southeastern outskirts of Munich, Germany, showing typical Teutonic clearance at almost every stage curiously preserved to the modern day. The smaller clearings **(1)** are suggestive of the early stage, while those marked **2**, almost perfectly circular, reflect a somewhat later stage. Symbol **3** indicates the earliest phase of coalescence of adjacent clearings, while **4** illustrates more mature coalescence. To the north and west, more complete clearing occurred. *Source:* Brunhes, J. 1920. *Human Geography.* Chicago: Rand McNally, 81.

removal is indicated by place names containing the word elements *kop, lazy,* and *paseky,* all of which specifically indicate "clearing."

A conservation movement arose in time to rescue substantial wooded areas in central Europe. As in the west, the nobility, anxious to preserve recreational hunting grounds, took the lead. An example, rare because it stands in the middle of a great city, is Berlin's *Tiergarten,* literally "animal garden," long the royal hunting preserve of the Hohenzollern family. It survived until the winter of 1945–46, when desperate inhabitants of the destroyed capital cut the trees for firewood. The Tiergarten has since been replanted and offers Berliners and tourists a peaceful respite from the urban bustle that surrounds it on all sides.

Much of the woodland standing in central Europe today consists of artificially planted tree farms. The science of forestry arose in eastern Germany in the late 1700s, but the result was single-species commercial forests. When traveling in Germany, it is common to see tree stands that have been planted in orderly rows, and the North American visitor is often struck by the lack of debris on the forest floor. This reflects the fact that most forests, particularly in the western part of the Germany, are cultivated commercially for timber and are maintained assiduously. Since the 1980s, the introduction of sustainable forestry practices have resulted in more mixed-species forests and unevenly aged stands, as scientists became aware that monocultural woodlands lack biodiversity and are not ecologically rich.

The most impressive remnant of the original central European woodland is the Bialowieza Forest on the eastern margin of the North European Plain, straddling the border between Poland and Belarus (fig. 2.16). It encompasses some 127,000 hectares; about 4% is preserved as a national park in Poland. Earlier, it enjoyed royal protection. The Bialowieza Forest houses at least 4,000 plant species, including immense specimens of hornbeam, spruce, and oak. Here, and only here, one can glimpse the great forest of the European heartland in something resembling its pristine condition, but access is carefully regulated.

MEDITERRANEAN FOREST

To the south, generally corresponding to the climate region of the same name, lies the Mediterranean forest zone. In its natural state this is an area of relatively open forests of broadleaf evergreen, live oaks, and olives, as well as Aleppo and stone pines, chestnuts, myrtles, walnuts, cypresses, and, in the mountains, firs. The dominant tree is the holm oak. Beneath and between the trees is an evergreen shrub layer of juniper, honeysuckle, heather, and spiny broom. The groundcover includes various grasses, especially esparto, as well as spurge and spleenwort.

This vegetative cover must withstand the pronounced summer drought of the Mediterranean region. Most trees and shrubs exhibit **sclerophyllous** features—an exceptional development of protective external tissue, as in the thickening of leaves and bark, in order to retard evaporation. This is well illustrated by the thick, deeply fissured bark of the cork oak and the stiff, leathery leaf of the olive. Also, leaves are small and the upper side is shiny, further retarding evaporation.

The destruction of the Mediterranean evergreen forest is virtually complete. Alteration began in prehistoric times, and the initial effect was probably to produce parkland in which live oaks were scattered in a grassland. Stretches of this sort of vegetation can still be seen in Extremadura, on the Meseta of southwestern Spain. In most cases, though, a far more complete alteration was achieved.

The process was well under way by Homer's time, some 3,000 years ago. He wrote of ongoing forest removal, both accidental and purposeful. In the rainless summers, "fierce fire rages through the glens on some parched mountainside, and the deep forest burns. The wind driving it whirls the flames in every direction." Shipbuilding also took a heavy toll, including the "thousand" ships launched for the sake of fair Helen of Troy. Timber also provided charcoal for smelting, particularly after the use of iron replaced bronze. The construction of buildings, including temples and palaces, demanded still more lumber, until finally a shortage of wood forced acceptance of stone as the primary Mediterranean building material. Considerable damage had already occurred by the 400s B.C.E., prompting the classical Greek writer Plato to compare deforested, eroded Attiki to "the skeleton of a sick man, all the fat and soft earth have been wasted away, leaving only the bare framework of the land" (fig. 2.22).

Figure 2.22.   Deforested, rocky landscape on the Aegean island of Patmos.
Thousands of years of grazing, accidental fires, and the need for lumber have left this Greek hillside denuded of forest, with much exposed rock. Tall stone fences have been built to separate adjacent herds of goats and sheep. Most of the Greek islands were once much more forested than they are today. (Photo by T.G.J.-B., 1971.)

People, then, using both fire and ax, assaulted the Mediterranean woodlands in ancient times and continued the destruction for many centuries. Unfortunately, the forest proved unable to reestablish itself after having been cleared, for two major reasons. First, most of the Mediterranean open forest occupied steep slopes, for mountainous terrain dominates southern Europe. With the trees removed from the slopes, the soil washed away with the winter rains, stripping the mountains to bare rocky skeletons unfit for reforestation. The second retarding factor in woodland regeneration was the lowly goat, a domestic animal of great importance to most Mediterranean rural people. Quite at home in the rugged terrain, the goat devours the tender young shoots of trees newly broken through the soil. Still, much timber survived in the classical period, as is indicated by the writings of numerous scholars of the time. Destruction continued in postclassical times. Venetian and Genovese merchant fleets and Byzantine, Spanish, and Portuguese imperial navies made the same demands on the forests as had their Greek and Roman predecessors. The craftsmen of Florence, Toledo, and Byzantium (modern Istanbul) needed charcoal as had their classical forerunners, and the ever-present herdsmen and farmers continued to regard the woodland as an enemy to be conquered.

Expanses of bare rock devoid of vegetation today represent the most extreme result of human activity in the Mediterranean (fig. 2.22). More common, however, are regions covered with thickets of evergreen shrub growth a meter or more in height. Such thickets served as hiding places for the French underground in World War II. Some limited afforestation has been accomplished in the Mediterranean, but often with exotics such as Australian eucalypts, now especially widespread in Portugal. As scientists have identified the Mediterranean zone as one of the ecosystems most threatened by climate change, it is likely that the nature of forests will continue to change dramatically in the future as current flora struggle to adapt to warmer, drier conditions.

SMALLER-SCALE VEGETATION ZONES

The steppe areas of Ukraine and southern parts of Euro-Russia were traditionally areas of tallgrass prairie. The prairie represents an extension of the expansive steppe grasslands that dominate the heart of Asia, reaching eastward to Mongolia and beyond. Pointed like an extended finger toward Europe, Eurasia's steppe corridor served repeatedly as a natural route of invasion by mounted nomad-warriors from the east, who found the treeless country suited to their mode of warfare and the abundant grasses excellent for their flocks and herds. For a thousand years and more, wave after wave of people passed this way—Hun, Bulgar, Magyar, Avar, Tartar. Some left, but most remained.

The great prairie that led the Asian nomadic tribes into Europe has largely vanished. The steppe proved too fertile to escape the plow, and today domesticated grasses, mainly wheat, grow in place of the natural grassland.

The *taiga* zone, sometimes called the *boreal forest*, lies in the European north. This is where the great coniferous evergreen woodlands are found. Dominant species include the Norway spruce, Scottish pine, and various firs. The downy birch, a broadleaf deciduous tree, also abounds, as does the gray alder and larch. In poorly drained places, abundant due to the heavy hand of glaciation, peat bogs and mires support a growth of mosses, grasses, and shrubs, while some hilly areas have heaths. The taiga remains thinly populated and a refuge for peoples speaking non-Indo-European languages. Most of the land retains a forest cover, as in Finland, which is 76% wooded (fig. 2.17). The taiga represents the last substantial forest in Europe, and is the focus of a large lumbering and paper-pulp industry (fig. 2.23). As a result, most of the taiga is no longer a natural forest but instead is planted and regularly harvested. Nor does this represent a new industry. For centuries, the northern lands have supplied lumber for the European core countries.

The final vegetation zone to note is the *tundra*, which occupies lands north of the tree line along the Arctic coast of Scandinavia and Russia, Iceland, in the higher elevations of the Kjølen Range, and above the limit of forest growth in certain mountain ranges such as the Alps. Tundra vegetation consists largely of lichens, mosses, sedges, rushes, dwarf beech and birch, stunted or creeping evergreen shrublets, and some grasses. Rarely do these plants exceed 30 centimeters in height, though in the transition zone between the tundra and taiga, scrub birch forests grow somewhat taller. The brief Arctic summer brings an outburst of flowery plants of unique coloring and beauty. *Permafrost,* or permanently frozen subsoil, occurs in some places, causing

Figure 2.23. Logs floating to Joensuu, Finland, in the taiga region of the Fenno-Scandian shield. The great needleleaf evergreen forests of the European north provide the basis for a large-scale wood-processing industry, dealing in lumber and pulp. (Photo by T.G.J.-B., 1985.)

waterlogging of the upper layers and a variety of surface soil hummocks. As a result, walking across the tundra in summer can be very difficult. The European tundra is an area of low human population densities. It serves as a refuge for the Sami people and other Finnic minorities.

THE IMPACTS OF ACID PRECIPITATION ON FORESTS

Of crucial significance to the fate of the remnant woodlands of Europe, whether natural or artificial, is **acid precipitation**, more commonly referred to as *acid rain*. Around 1975, forestry experts began to notice tree damage, especially in needle-leaf species. Then in the 1980s, as if some critical threshold had been crossed, the percentage of trees exhibiting damage increased rapidly. In western Germany, only 8% of the forest showed visible damage in 1982, in the form of leaf or needle loss or discoloration, but a year later the proportion had increased dramatically to 34%, and by 1984 to 50%. Switzerland's forest damage rose from 17% in 1984 to 40% by 1988 and 65% by 1998 (fig. 2.15). In Czechia, well over two-thirds of the woodland exhibited damage by 1988, a proportion that rose to 96% a decade later. The Black Forest (*Schwarzwald*) of southwestern Germany became another center of the phenomenon. Even peripheral lands such as Greece, Norway, the Kola Peninsula of northern Russia, and Estonia have damage in half of their forests. The culprit is rain that has a higher level of acidity because of a chemical reaction between water in the atmosphere and industrial pollutants. After this was discovered, there was widespread concern about an impending die-off of European forests (called *Waldsterben* in German). Those concerns now appear to have been exaggerated, but as figure 2.15 shows, acid rain has had a deleterious impact on forest health in many parts of Europe. Over the past decade, things have not gotten noticeably worse, but they have not improved much either.

Soils

Climate, vegetation, and parent materials combine to yield a variety of soil types in Europe, varying greatly in texture, depth, and fertility. Geographers recognize eleven or more major soil groups in Europe, displaying a highly complex spatial pattern. For our purposes, it is important simply to understand basic distribution patterns of soils of varying fertility (fig. 2.24).

Highly fertile soils encompass those derived from several different parent materials, including *loess*—wind-borne materials ground up by glaciers; *alluvium*—riverine deposits; and volcanic ash. Loess-derived soils occur in a fragmented belt from northern France to Ukraine, in plains and valleys beyond the southern margins of the glaciated lands. Over the millennia, loess has weathered into a dark-colored, fertile, fine-textured, deep, and easily filled soil *chernozem*, or "black earth," and the organic matter of decaying prairie grasses has added to its fertility. Loessial soils elsewhere, mainly on the Great European Plain, had a light forest cover, lacking the thick sod of the prairies, and attracted farmers from ancient times to the present day. Alluvial soils—or *fluvisols*—dominate the Low Countries and also occur in smaller pockets elsewhere, as in broad river valleys and certain Mediterranean lowlands. Dark volcanic soils, called *andosols*, occur too locally to be revealed on the map of Europe, but are highly fertile and attract dense agricultural populations to the environs of volcanoes in Italy and Greece.

A second category consists of moderately fertile soils found on parts of the plains in northern and eastern Europe. Limestone also weathered into moderately fertile soils in the three Mediterranean peninsulas. Highly infertile soils lie mainly in northern Europe. These *podsols*, meaning "white earth" or "ash-colored soils," are highly acidic and humus-starved. *Leaching*—the downward movement of plant nutrients to lower soil layers—is the cause of the humus deficiency. Before these sterile soils can yield harvests, a farmer must add lime and compost to counteract the acidity and infertility. Sandy areas such as outwash plains are also highly infertile.

The human impact on soils has been great. Deep plowing mixes soil layers—called *horizons*-and irrigation can cause surface deposits of salt or other sediments to accumulate. Soil erosion has also occurred widely, especially in the dry-summered Mediterranean. In Spain, about half of all farmland in some provinces is severely eroded, prompting land abandonment in places. Some Spanish fields lost up to a meter of soil through erosion.

The mix of geomorphology, hydrogeography, climate, vegetation, and soils provided substantial areas where European civilization could take root and flourish. In the past, some commentators have been tempted to attribute Europe's human character to the expanses of fertile land and moderate climate found in the region, but that

Figure 2.24.   Soil Regions. This simple classification conceals an incredibly complex pattern. Note the core/periphery pattern of fertility and infertility. *Sources:* F.A.O. UNESCO. 1981. *Soil Map of the World,* Vol. 5 (Europe), Paris, F: United Nations; F.A.O. UNESCO. 1988. *Soil Map of the World: Revised Legend.* Rome, I: United Nations; Garnett 1945.

interpretation is a simplistic example of environmental determinism. Nonetheless, the physical environment is an important part of the stage on which the European drama has played out, and it helps us understand everything from population concentrations to early patterns of industrial activity. We turn to the former of these in the next chapter.

Sources and Suggested Readings

Alexander, D. 1984. The Reclamation of Val-Di-Chiana (Tuscany). *Annals of the Association of American Geographers* 74 (4): 527–550.

Barr, B. M., and K. E. Braden. 1988. *The Disappearing Russian Forest: A Dilemma in Soviet Resource Management.* Totowa, N.J.: Rowman & Littlefield.

Barry, R. 2006. The Status of Research on Glaciers and Global Glacier Recession: A Review. *Progress in Physical Geography* 30 (3): 285–306.

Behncke, B., and M. Neri. 2003. Cycles and Trends in the Recent Eruptive Behaviour of Mount Etna (Italy). *Canadian Journal of Earth Sciences* 40 (10): 1405–1411.

Behre, K. 2005. Meeresspiegelbewegungen, Landverluste und Landgewinnungen an der Nordsee. *Siedlungsforschung* 23: 19–46.

Bennett, C. F. 1975. Human Influences on the Ecosystems of Europe and the Mediterranean. In *Man and Earth's Ecosystems: An Introduction to the Geography of Human Modification of the Earth*, ed. C. F. Bennett, 121–144. New York: Wiley.

Berz, G. 2006. Globaler Klimawandel: Werden die Alpen zum Katastrophengebiet? *Jahrbuch des Vereins zum Schutz der Bergwelt* 71: 51–60.

Bischoff, U. 1992. Der Scirocco—Untersuchungen Zur Haufigkeit und Dauer Uber Mittel- und Suditalien. *Erdkunde* 46 (1): 52–57.

Bishop, K. H. 1997. Liming of Acid Surface Waters in Northern Sweden: Questions of Geographical Variation and the Precautionary Principle. *Transactions of the Institute of British Geographers* 22 (1): 49–60.

Black, E., and R. Sutton. 2007. The Influence of Oceanic Conditions on the Hot European Summer of 2003. *Climate Dynamics* 28 (1): 53–66.

Brönnimann, S., E. Xoplaki, and C. Casty. 2007. Enso Influence on Europe during the Last Centuries. *Climate Dynamics* 28 (2/3): 181–197.

Chandler, T. J. 1965. *The Climate of London.* London: Hutchinson.

Cioc, M. 2002. *The Rhine: An Eco-Biography, 1815–2000, Weyerhaeuser Environmental Book.* Seattle: University of Washington Press.

Darby, H. C. 1956. The Clearing of the Woodland in Europe. In *Man's Role in Changing the Face of the Earth*, ed. W. L. J. Thomas, 183–216. Chicago: Published for the Wenner-Gren Foundation for Anthropological Research and the National Science Foundation by the University of Chicago Press.

———. 1968. *The Draining of the Fens.* 2nd ed., *Cambridge University Press Library Editions.* London: Cambridge University Press.

Embleton, C. 1984. *Geomorphology of Europe.* New York: Wiley.

Endlicher, W., and N. Lanfer. 2003. Meso- and Micro-Climatic Aspects of Berlin's Urban Climate. *Erde* 134 (3): 277–293.

European Environment Agency (EEA). 2005. Vulnerability and Adaptation to Climate Change in Europe, 84 pp.: EEA. Available from http://reports.eea.europa.eu/technical_report_2005_1207_144937/en/EEA_Technical_report_7_2005.pdf.

Gentilcore, R. L. 1970. Reclamation in the Agro Pontino, Italy. *Geographical Review* 60 (3): 301–327.

Goeldner-Gianella, L. 2007. Perceptions and Attitudes toward De-Polderisation in Europe: A Comparison of Five Opinion Surveys in France and the UK. *Journal of Coastal Research* 23 (5): 1218–1230.

Goudie, A. 1990. *The Landforms of England and Wales.* Oxford: Basil Blackwell.

Grenon, M., and M. Batisse, eds. 1989. *Futures for the Mediterranean Basin: The Blue Plan.* Oxford: Oxford University Press.

Haber, W., J. Reichholf, and C. Deigele. 2007. Natur und Mensch in Mitteleuropa im Letzten Jahrtausend. Paper read at Rundgespräche der Kommission für Ökologie, at München.

Heine, K., and H. P. Niller. 2003. Human and Climate Impacts on the Holocene Landscape Development in Southern Germany. *Geographia Polonica* 76 (2): 109–122.

Hulme, M., and E. Barrow. 1997. *Climates of the British Isles: Present, Past, and Future.* London: Routledge.

Ives, J. D. 1991. Landscape Change and Human Response during a Thousand Years of Climatic Fluctuations and Volcanism: Skaftafell, Southeast Iceland. *Pirineos* 137: 5–50.

Jalas, J. 1999. *Atlas Florae Europaeae: Distribution of Vascular Plants in Europe.* Helsinki: Committee for Mapping the Flora of Europe.

Jeftic, L., J. D. Milliman, and G. Sestini, eds. 1992. *Climatic Change and the Mediterranean.* New York: Routledge.

Jones, A., L. Montanarella, R. Jones, and E. Akça. 2005. *Soil Atlas of Europe.* Luxembourg: Office for Official Publications of the European Communities.

Koster, E. A., ed. 2005. *The Physical Geography of Western Europe.* The Oxford Regional Environments Series. Oxford: Oxford University Press.

Lambert, A. M. 1985. *The Making of the Dutch Landscape: An Historical Geography of the Netherlands.* 2nd ed. London: Academic Press.

Peterson, D. J. 1993. *Troubled Lands: The Legacy of Soviet Environmental Destruction, A Rand Research Study.* Boulder: Westview Press.

Pryde, P. R., ed. 1995. *Environmental Resources and Constraints in the Former Soviet Republics.* Boulder: Westview Press.

Raisz, E. 2000. Physiography of Europe. In *Goode's World Atlas,* eds. J. C. Hudson and E. B. Espenshade, 150–151. Skokie, IL: Rand McNally.

Roth, D., and J. Warner. 2007. Flood Risk, Uncertainty and Changing River Protection Policy in the Netherlands: The Case of "Calamity Polders." *Tijdschrift voor Economische en Sociale Geografie* 98 (4): 519–525.

Ryan, W. B. F., and W. C. Pitman. 2000. *Noah's Flood: The New Scientific Discoveries about the Event that Changed History.* 1st Touchtone ed. New York: Simon & Schuster.

Sigurdson, H., et al. 1985. The Eruption of Vesuvius in A.D. 79. *National Geographic Research* 1: 332–387.

Svenning, J., and F. Skov. 2005. The Relative Roles of Environmental and History as Controls of Tree Species Composition and Richness in Europe. *Journal of Biogeography* 32 (6): 1019–1033.

Thorarinsson, S. 1966. *Surtsey: The New Island in the North Atlantic.* New York: Viking Press.

Thorpe, H. 1957. A Special Case of Heath Reclamation in the Alheden District of Jutland, 1700-1955. *Transactions and Papers (Institute of British Geographers)* (23): 87–121.

United Kingdom. Treasury. 2007. *The Economics of Climate Change: The Stern Review.* Cambridge, UK: Cambridge University Press.

van Veen, J. 1962. *Dredge, Drain, Reclaim: The Art of a Nation.* 5th ed. The Hague: Nijhoff.

Wagret, P. 1968. *Polderlands.* Translated by M. Sparks. London: Methuen.

Wainwright, J., and J. B. Thornes. 2004. *Environmental Issues in the Mediterranean: Processes and Perspectives from the Past and Present, Routledge Studies in Physical Geography and Environment.* London: Routledge.

Wallén, C. C. 1970. *Climates of Northern and Western Europe, World Survey of Climatology, V. 5.* Amsterdam: Elsevier.

Williams, M. 1970. *The Draining of the Somerset Levels.* Cambridge: Cambridge University Press.

Zwingle, E. 2006. Meltdown: The Alps under Pressure. *National Geographic* 209 (2): 96–115.

CHAPTER 3

Demography

Hominids began arriving in Europe from Africa as much as a million or more years ago. By 130,000 years ago, a distinctive hominid known as **Neanderthal** had taken up residence throughout much of the region. About 30,000–40,000 years ago, the Neanderthal faced another Homo species arriving from Africa: **Homo sapiens**. For reasons that remain under debate, the Neanderthals disappeared by c. 24,000 years ago, leaving Homo sapiens as the sole hominid in Europe. With northern Europe still under ice produced by the most recent glaciation (known in Europe as Würm and in North America as Wisconsin), these early Stone Age peoples settled in the southern and central parts of Europe. The paintings they left behind on the walls of caves in southern France and Spain provide the earliest evidence of the artistic creativity of modern humans in Europe.

After the onset of the current interglacial period (known as the **Holocene**) a little over 10,000 years ago, Europe saw a gradual expansion of its human population, the movement of people into northern Europe, and the arrival of new peoples from the east and south. Between 8,000 and 5,000 years ago, agricultural communities started to develop—setting the stage for expanding populations in different parts of Europe and the rise of the classical civilizations of the Mediterranean. We will look at some of the cultural, social, and environmental legacies of these developments later in the book, but we begin our exploration of human Europe by examining its basic demographic character.

Demography is concerned with quantitative aspects of population: numbers, densities, growth rates, and the like. The geographical study of demography involves examining the distribution of such factors across space, and developing explanations of the circumstances that give rise to variations across space. Our focus in this chapter is on basic demographic patterns and the forces that have shaped them. We make reference to certain qualitative influences on Europe's demography (e.g., health, social circumstances), but central consideration of such variables will be deferred until later in the book (especially Chapter 11).

The Big Picture

Europe plays host to one of the greatest concentrations of people in the world. Some 715 million people live in Europe (including Eurorussia, Armenia, and Georgia)—more than any "continent" other than Asia. If Eurorussia, Ukraine, Belarus, Moldova, and the Caucasus states are subtracted, the remaining total, 530 million, is still one and three-quarters times the population of the United States.

A number of individual European states have substantial populations. Five have populations in excess of 50 million, including Eurorussia with 110 million; Germany, 82 million; France, 64 million; the United Kingdom, 61 million; and Italy, 58 million. Eleven other European countries have at least 10 million inhabitants. European Russia, if separate, would form the 10th most populous country in the world.

Even more remarkable than absolute numbers is the density of the European population. The 430 million people in Europe west of Eurorussia, Ukraine, Belarus, Moldova, and the Caucasus are crammed into just under 3.5% of the world's land area, giving the European core a population density of 105 people per square kilometer. This is one of the highest population densities on earth. At the global scale, it is rivaled only by parts of South and East Asia and a limited area along the eastern seaboard of the United States.

The distribution and density of Europe's population has changed dramatically over the last two millennia. At the beginning of the Common Era, about 33 million people lived in Europe, broadly defined, and most were concentrated in southern Europe. The disruptions associated with the collapse of the Roman Empire caused the total population to fall to only 18 million by the year 600. The Middle Ages witnessed great population growth, to about 70 million by 1340, as well as the development of much higher densities in favorable areas north of the Alps and Pyrenees. The ravages of the Black Death led to another population decline in the fourteenth century, but there was a rapid rebound after about 1450. The European population reached 100 million by 1650, 200 million by shortly after 1800, 400 million by about 1900, and 600 million by 1960.

Despite Europe's expanding population, the region's share of the world's population has declined dramatically over the last 100 years. At the beginning of the twentieth century, more than 20% of the world's people lived in Europe; that figure has now fallen to 10.8%. This is because Europe's population growth fell far below many other parts of the world during the course of the last 100 years.

As for the distribution of people within Europe, if everyone presently living west of the Urals and north of the Mediterranean were evenly distributed over the land, each square kilometer would contain about 75 persons. But this figure conceals the fact that population density varies greatly from one part of Europe to another, ranging from the totally uninhabited glaciers of interior Iceland to more than 500 persons per sq km in some districts. Among independent states, densities range from Iceland's 2.9 persons per sq km to Malta's 1,270 and Monaco's 18,000.

One way to display population distribution is through the concept of continuous and discontinuous settlement, the former including all areas in which habitations and transport routes form a dense network (fig. 3.1). Defined in this manner, Europe

Figure 3.1.   Europe forms one of the major clusters of "continuous" settlement in the world. "Continuous settlement" means that all habitations lie no more than 5 km from other habitations in at least six different directions and that roads/railroads lie no farther than 16 to 32 km away in at least three directions. In other words, the term describes a densely inhabited land, served by a transportation network. *Sources:* Adapted from Stone, K. A. 1993. personal communication; Stone. 1978. The World's Primary Settlement Regions, *GeoJournal* 2 (3): 196; Stone 1962, 1966, 1971.

stands somewhat apart, bounded by sparsely settled deserts and subarctic wastes, which serve to separate it from the peoples of sub-Saharan Africa and the great cultures of South and East Asia.

Measured and mapped in another way, as the number of persons per sq km, the pattern of population density in Europe presents a core-periphery configuration (fig. 3.2). Most densely populated districts—those having 100, 200, or more persons per sq km—lie in or near the center of Europe, whereas regions of sparse settlement, with fewer than 25 or 50 persons per sq km, usually appear around the perimeter, forming the transition into the deserts and boreal forests that border Europe.

What explains the variable density of the population revealed in figure 3.2? No single factor provides a complete answer, but there is a relatively good correlation

Figure 3.2.   Population density in Europe. A distinct core-periphery pattern is evident. A core area of over 200 persons per square kilometer reaches southeast from the Anglican Plain through the Low Country and Germany to Sicily, forming an English-Rhenish-Italian axis of dense population. Peripheral regions, especially the subarctic north, are far more sparsely settled. *Source:* 2006 ESRI data acquired from Michael Bauer Research GmbH and EuroGraphics.

between areas of high population density and **arable land**. Put simply, people settled historically where they could produce the food they needed, and the inertia of that settlement pattern is still evident today. Thus, at continental scale the areas with the highest population concentrations are generally in the parts of the European plains with good soils and ample rainfall, and in the valleys of the major rivers. This translates into a corridor of unusually dense settlement stretching across the North European Plain into England. Other areas of dense settlement include the river valleys of the Po, Rhone, Ebro, and Tagus. By contrast, European mountain ranges stand out as zones of sparser settlement. Also, settlement is much less dense in colder climates; the northern border of continuous settlement in Scandinavia follows very closely the line between humid continental and subarctic climate types.

To better understand the fundamentals of Europe's demography, we need to look at several interrelated factors that have influenced the region's population geography over time: the environment, rates of natural population growth, political-economic circumstances, and migration. We focus on patterns revealed at the scale of Europe as a whole, but at the end of the chapter we will consider how shifting the scale of analysis alters the analysis of population dynamics.

The Role of the Environment

We have already noted the role that arable land plays in shaping population patterns. Put simply, environments suitable for agriculture have favored the development of substantial population concentrations. So has the concentration of particular natural resources of value to humans. It is no surprise that in earlier times, humans concentrated around water sources, at places where game was abundant, or in areas where they had access to a valuable raw material. More recently, a shift in the distribution of England's population occurred in the early phases of the Industrial Revolution as economic opportunities opened up near areas with accessible coal deposits in northern England. Since then technological advances have altered the relative advantages of locations as places to live and work. For example, southeast England has recently experienced significant growth at the expense of older industrial areas in the north, as new economic opportunities have developed in the vicinity of London. But the natural environment has not become irrelevant. In today's affluent Europe, a noticeable shift in population has taken place in response to the perceived advantages of living in warm, dry climates. Higher population densities in favorable spots along the Mediterranean are a product of wealthy Europeans from farther north moving to what they regard as pleasant environments.

Another way of seeing the importance of the environment to demography is to reflect on the influence of Europe's changing climate on population distribution over a long timescale. As Homo sapiens moved into Europe, they colonized the southern areas because northern Europe was in the grip of the most recent glaciation. Only gradually did northern areas become more populated as the Holocene unfolded. Under the circumstances, it is no surprise that the first major civilizations in Europe developed around the Mediterranean.

Moving forward in time, the expansion of population in northern and western Europe was likely facilitated by the **Medieval Warm Period** (sometimes called the Medieval Optimum) that brought milder conditions between the ninth and twelfth centuries. Agricultural areas expanded, and Norse seafaring developed. Populations were sufficiently well established north of the Alps and Pyrenees to withstand the temperature downturn associated with the so-called Little Ice Age (c. 1200–1800), although far northern areas and Iceland experienced significant population losses during this period. Over the past 200 years, technological developments have allowed humans to expand into increasingly marginal areas and remain there when they become even more marginal. The Dutch case discussed in the previous chapter provides a particularly dramatic example. But modern technologies are also likely contributing to the recent round of climate change, which has produced substantial warming throughout much of Europe in recent decades. It is unclear whether human adjustment capacities can keep up with the changes that are likely to unfold in some areas—particularly low-lying coastal areas that are vulnerable to sea-level rise.

Disease is another environmental factor that has shaped Europe's demographic picture. As is true of recent climate changes, disease is not a purely environmental factor, in that humans play a significant role in creating the conditions that foster the spread of disease. But its roots are environmental, and its demographic impacts can be great. No example illustrates this better than the bubonic plague of the Middle Ages. Arriving in Constantinople (modern Istanbul) from the east in 1347, the plague spread quickly to Crete, Genoa, and southern France (fig. 3.3). In 1348 the bubonic plague

Figure 3.3.   Diffusion of the Bubonic Plague, 1347–1351. Before the century ended, the disease had killed perhaps 25 million persons in Europe, causing a major population decline. The political borders shown are modern. *Sources:* Adapted from Pounds, N. J. G. 1989. *Hearth and Home,* Bloomington, IN: Indiana University Press, 225; Charpentier, E. 1962. Autour de la Peste Noire. *Annales: Economies/Sociétés/ Civilisation,* 17: 1062–1092; McEvedy, C. 1988. The Bubonic Plague. *Scientific American* 258 (2): 121.

made major inroads in southern Europe, and it spread north the following year. Scandinavia and eastern Europe felt its effect by 1350, and epidemics recurred through much of the remainder of the fourteenth century. Some believe that the bubonic plague (sometimes called the Black Death) claimed 25 million victims in the 1300s, including two-thirds of the people living in parts of Italy. The English population is said to have declined from 3.7 million in 1350 to only 2 million by 1377. Graphs of population numbers throughout most of Europe show a noticeable downtick during the second half of the fourteenth century and early fifteenth century.

No disease in more recent times has rivaled the plague in its impact, although malaria had a significant impact in parts of southern Europe in the 1600s and 1700s. Malaria has been largely eradicated in Europe, but a recent plague of sorts has come in the form of HIV/AIDS, with noticeable demographic impacts in defined areas. Recent increases in infection rates in the eastern part of Europe are of concern, with some estimates suggesting that a half-million Europeans may be carrying HIV. The social and personal consequences of this are great, but the overall demographic impact has been small in comparison to the bubonic plague of the fourteenth century. Not surprisingly, the leading causes of death in contemporary Europe are circulatory and respiratory diseases, and cancer.

Rates of Natural Population Growth

A fundamental component of any demographic analysis is natural population growth. The natural increase of a population is the difference between the numbers of births and deaths during a given time period. Throughout the medieval and early modern periods in Europe, the death rate and the birth rate were both high, meaning that the rate of natural increase was low. It was even negative at times. But with improvements in diet and hygiene—most notably the use of soap—people began living longer. This brought down the death rate, but the birth rate remained high, leading to a rapid expansion in the size of the population. Then birth rates went through a gradual, persistent fall as well, producing what has come to be known as the **demographic transition** (fig. 3.4). The European population explosion had ended, ushering in a period of slow growth.

Europe's demographic transition occurred at different times in different places. Sustained fertility decline first appeared in France about 1820 (fig. 3.5). Ethnic minorities in France and people in other countries were initially slow to follow the French example, with the result that France fell behind major neighboring countries' population size. In the 1700s, when 1 of every 6 Europeans was French, and even as late as 1850, the French outnumbered the Germans, Italians, and British; by 1970 they had become the smallest of these four nations.

Eventually, sustained fertility decline spread, loosely tracking increasing prosperity and levels of urbanization (see the next section of this chapter). By 1900 about half of all European provinces had been affected (fig. 3.5), and today birth rates have become remarkably low throughout the area. Sustained fertility decline came last to the eastern areas of Europe (fig. 3.6), but a major decline in fertility began there after 1990.

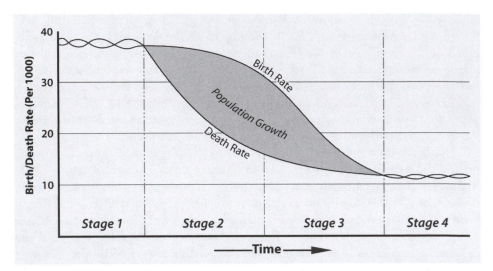

Figure 3.4.   Diagram of the Demographic Transition. All of Europe was in Stage 1 throughout the Middle Ages and Early Modern period. By the nineteenth century, parts of western Europe started to move into Stage 2, with most of the rest of Europe following by the end of the century—and western Europe beginning to move into Stage 3. By the closing decades of the twentieth century, most of Europe was moving into Stage 4, which is where almost all of Europe lies today.

In Russia, for example, the annual birth rate fell from 17.2 per thousand inhabitants in 1987 to only 10.9 in 2007. Czechia's birth rate declined from 11.1 in 1990, at the time of reunification, to only 5.1 as early as 1993. Nonetheless, some peripheral European areas continue to have fertility rates above the European average, as, for example, Iceland, the Arctic fringe, and Muslim sections of the Balkans.

The **total fertility rate** (TFR) of a population is a statistic indicating the number of children born per woman of child-bearing age. Without immigration, a TFR of 2.1 is needed to keep a population stable over time. In Europe, the TFR has fallen to around 1.5, a startling contrast to Africa's 4.7. The TFR in Europe as a whole had fallen to 1.69 as early as 1985 and in western Germany to 1.28. Russia experienced the latest phase of the demographic transition with surprising rapidity; deaths exceeded births by 200,000 there in 1992 and by 800,000 the following year, by which time the TFR had declined to only 1.4, where it remains today. The Czech Republic is at an even lower rank, with a TFR of 1.2. Not one European country today except Albania has a TFR as high as 2.1. Terms such as "demographic collapse" or "demographic crisis" are heard today in describing Europe. If it were not for substantial immigration from Africa and Asia, the population of Europe would already be in sharp decline.

Europeans achieved a remarkably low level of fertility through diverse techniques. In recent decades, modern contraception has been of greatest importance. In the formative stage in early nineteenth-century France, infanticide—the killing of the newborn—occurred. Abortion, early achieved with various folk medicines and later at modern, state-supported clinics, has also played a role, though it is

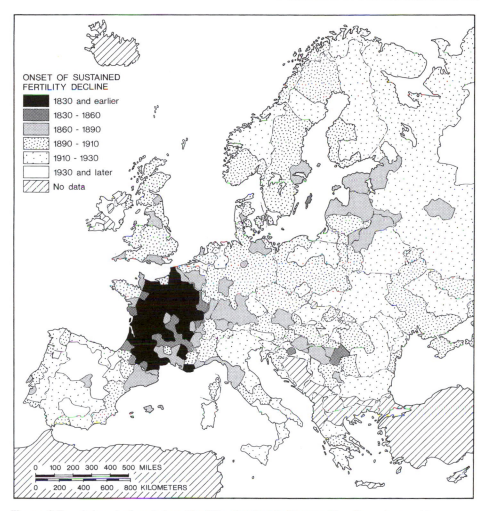

Figure 3.5.   Advent of sustained fertility decline in Europe. The French-speaking part of France provided the prototype for diminished fertility. People in other countries were slow to emulate the French, but diffusion to the various peripheries of Europe eventually occurred. Today, all areas have birth rates well below the world average. *Source:* Adapted from Coale and Watkins 1986, 484 et seq.

now in decline. During Communist times, abortion was particularly common in Eastern Europe. The number of abortions is declining throughout much of that region, but the annual number of abortions still exceeds the number of live births in Russia.

As we will see later in the book, the decline of the European population is a cause for concern. It has made Europe's population among the world's oldest. All but one of the 20 countries in the world having the greatest proportion of people aged 60 or older lie in Europe, led by Italy, Germany, Greece, and Sweden. Many provinces, especially in the European Union, have an aged population forming 16% or more of the total; a

Figure 3.6.   Annual natural population change, as a percentage of total population, by province. This rate is arrived at by comparing the number of births and deaths in a year, calculating the difference (either + or –), and taking it as a percentage of population. Faint core-periphery and east-west patterns can be detected. Gains or losses through migration are not reflected here. *Source:* 2006 ESRI data acquired from Michael Bauer Research GmbH and EuroGraphics.

few even exceed 20% (fig. 3.7). Major problems loom concerning provision of health and welfare services to an older population. This is shown by the low **potential support ratio** in Europe—a measure of the number of persons aged 15 to 64 years per one older person aged 65 years or older. In the early 2000s, the global average PSR was 9; in Europe it was 4.

In some countries efforts are being made to increase fertility through family-friendly policies. As we will see, these are having some positive effects, but the primary offset to fertility decline is migration, which raises other social issues and tensions. Looking forward, it seems clear that there will be few areas of significant population growth in Europe in the near future and that Europe's percentage of the global population will continue to decline.

Figure 3.7. Percentage of population aged 60 or older. Europe's population is far older than the world average. *Source:* 2006 ESRI data acquired from Michael Bauer Research GmbH and EuroGraphics.

Political-Economic Circumstances

Population growth rates reflect more than individual choice; they are also a product of political and economic circumstances. Consider, for example, the importance of inheritance laws in the pre-modern era. Traditionally southern Europe's legal systems derived from the Romans. Under the Roman system, landholdings and possessions were divided equally among all heirs. This meant that over the generations farms became smaller. Roman law thus tended to produce very dense rural settlement. In northern Europe, by contrast, Germanic law supported the principle of **primogeniture** or some other means of undivided inheritance. Land passed intact from parent to one child—often the oldest son. The landless children often emigrated or, in more recent times, moved to cities. This tended to depress population growth rates in rural areas dominated by Germanic law traditions.

More generally, significant population growth in pre-modern times occurred most frequently in areas of political stability and economic sufficiency, for these were the areas where death rates were the lowest. By contrast, areas of economic privation and political chaos had low or even negative population growth rates. Warfare had a particularly negative demographic impact. The Thirty Years' War, which raged from 1618 to 1648 in central Europe, provides a particularly dramatic example. The population of some German districts declined by two-thirds or more in that war, and major losses of life occurred in Bohemia as well (fig. 3.8). Warfare remained a source of demographic decline into the modern era. Well over a million French and almost two million Germans died in World War I. The French toll in World War II was lower, but German casualty figures were much higher, and Russia suffered extraordinary losses. The estimated 20 million casualties suffered in World War II by the Soviet Union represented about 10% of its inhabitants, causing a population decline that has only recently been overcome. Yugoslavia was deprived of fully 11% of its population, some 1.7 million persons.

Figure 3.8. Population loss owing to warfare and disease in central Europe, 1618–1648. The Thirty Years' War and associated epidemics drastically reduced the number of people in parts of Germany and Bohemia, producing a major change in population density and distribution. *Source:* After Franz and Keyser. 1956. In *Westermanns Grosser Atlas zur Weltgeschichte.* Braunschweig, West Germany: Georg Westermann, 107).

Wars remain a source of demographic decline, but the role of political and economic factors has changed to some degree in the modern era of generally low death rates. As the percentage of the population working in the agricultural sector shrank, people moved into cities, general prosperity increased, and birth rates fell dramatically. For the past 150 years, the areas with greatest political stability and economic prosperity have tended to be the places with the *lowest* population growth rates. The patterns shown in figure 3.6 bear this out. Those parts of Europe that were the slowest to develop and urbanize are the ones with the highest current rates of natural population increase. The reasons why development and urbanization produce declining birth rates are complex and a matter of some debate. Some point to the fact that children are more of an economic advantage in rural settings than in urban settings, but there is much to suggest that the decision to give birth is not simply an exercise in utility maximization. Instead, the decline of birth rates in prosperous urban areas is likely the result of a complex of economic, cultural, and psychological factors that come with living in a radically different material and social context.

The rise of strong state governments led to another political influence on demography in the contemporary era: government population policy. There are dark times in Europe's recent history when governments pursued policies of forced migration and extermination that changed the demographic picture. During the Nazi period, government policies of eugenics in Germany were designed to steer natural evolution by means of forced sterilization of the mentally or physically handicapped, and incentives were offered for racially "pure" couples to have children. In a more benign vein, governments have sought to promote increased growth rates. Governmental encouragement of large families in Eastern Europe during Communist times retarded the decline of birth rates for a time, especially in Romania. Farther west, France in particular has been engaged in an active effort to increase its birth rate. In the 1970s French President Valéry Giscard d'Estaing called on his countrymen to have "un troisième enfant pour la France" (a third child for France). It took some time before his call was answered, but by 2006 the TFR had increased to 1.94—second only to that of Ireland in western Europe. Some of this is due to relatively high fertility rates among immigrants, but France's social policy is likely playing a role as well. That policy provides for long maternity leaves, allowances for parents, and government-supported childcare. Such policies are unlikely to alter current demographic trends in any dramatic way, but they can have an impact. Britain introduced French-style measures in 2001 and had its highest birthrate in 13 years by 2006.

Governments can also influence demographic trends through policies on medical care. Access to high-quality, affordable medical care remains the rule in Europe. Doctor-patient ratios are low; the traditional epidemic and endemic diseases have been banished; and life expectancy, with some eastern European exceptions, exceeds 70 years. Only Russians, whose life expectancy is 66 years, and Ukrainians at 68, fall below this level. Andorra, Sweden, Switzerland, and Iceland rank highest, at over 80 years. These remarkable achievements in human health emanated from states in western and northern Europe and spread east and south—a diffusion completed in fairly recent times. In Greece, male life expectancy rose from 49 to 70 years in the half-century between 1930 and 1980.

The most revealing single indicator of health standards is the **infant mortality rate**. Indeed this index, which shows the number of infants per thousand that die before reaching the age of one year, is widely regarded as the best single measure not just of health, but of the overall standard of living (fig. 3.9). Within Europe, a pronounced east-west contrast in the infant mortality rate exists. Romania, Albania, and Bulgaria have the highest rates in Europe, ranging between 19 and 25. But even in eastern Europe, the rate remains good by world standards. In parts of Africa the infant mortality rate stands well above 100, and just across the Mediterranean and Aegean, one encounters rates such as 38 in Turkey, 39 in Morocco, and 29.5 in Egypt.

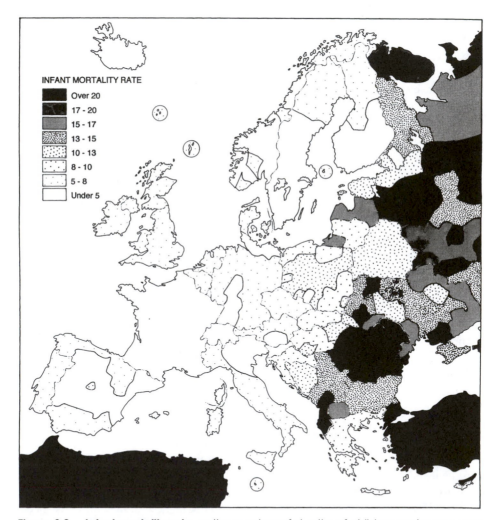

Figure 3.9.   Infant mortality rate, or the number of deaths of children under one year of age per 1,000 live births. Many experts feel that this rate provides the single best index of the standard of living. The east-west and Europe-Africa contrasts are notable. *Sources:* Eurostat and various national statistical yearbooks.

Migration

A further potent force influencing Europe's population over time is migration. There are several components to this: emigration, immigration, and internal migration. Viewed historically, the principal dynamic at work during the sixteenth to nineteenth centuries was external migration. A great many "push" and "pull" factors work to prompt the decision to leave one's home and seek another. From about 1500 to 1950, many millions of Europeans departed for Anglo-America, Latin America, Australia, New Zealand, South Africa, Israel, Siberia, and Algeria. Iberians began the exodus in the 1500s. Between 1600 and 1880, this tremendous emigration involved mainly northwestern Europeans of Germanic and Celtic background seeking better economic opportunity abroad. After about 1870 the exodus spread to southern and eastern Europe.

Some countries lost substantial parts of their total populations in this manner, causing major changes in densities. The island of Ireland provides a good example. In 1841 the census listed more than 8 million Irish, a density of nearly 100 per sq km. By the middle of the decade, the Irish population had reached an all-time high of almost 8.5 million. Then came the great famine of the mid-1840s, bringing death to hundreds of thousands, and in its wake a massive and persistent out-migration to Great Britain and overseas. In a five-year span from 1846 to 1851, some 800,000 Irish starved or perished from disease, and another million emigrated to foreign lands. Hardest hit was interior Ireland, where one county lost more than 20% of its population through emigration (fig. 3.10). A century later, a little more than half as many people resided in Ireland as in 1841. By the early twenty-first century, 9 times as many persons claiming Irish ancestry lived in the United States as remained in Ireland.

Germans, too, departed their native land in enormous numbers, settling mainly in the United States but also in southern Brazil, Canada, and South Africa. Persons of German ancestry constitute the largest national-origin group in the United States, numbering some 60 million in 1990, about 73% of the present population of Germany. Sweden and Norway experienced huge proportional losses. Between 20 and 25% of the total population of those two Scandinavian countries emigrated overseas in the nineteenth century.

By the second half of the nineteenth century, another migration dynamic was at work that was to greatly transform the European demographic picture. That was rural-to-urban migration, a process that greatly accelerated in the twentieth century and has not yet fully run its course everywhere. In 1900, the United Kingdom was the only country in Europe in which more than 50% of the population lived in cities. Now all European countries are dominated by urban dwellers. And as cities grew and transportation technology improved, urbanites began building new settlements around cities—giving rise to a wave of suburbanization in the second half of the twentieth century.

A disturbing piece of the story of internal European migration over the past 100 years has been forced migration. Most dramatically, in the short span of about 35 years between 1920 and 1950, an astounding 33 million Europeans were forced to

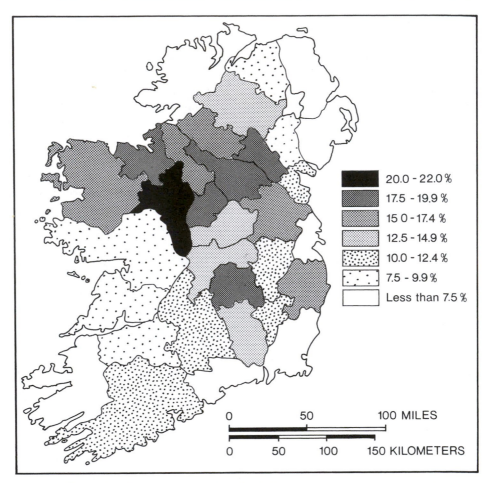

Figure 3.10.   Emigration from Ireland, 1846–1851, as a percentage of the 1841 population. *Source:* After Cousens, S. H. 1960. The Regional Pattern of Emigration During the Great Irish Famine, 1846–51. *Institute of British Geographers, Transactions and Papers* 28: 121; see also: Johnson, J. H. 1988. The Distribution of Irish Emigration in the Decade Before the Great Famine. *Irish Geography* 21 (2): 78–87.

leave their homelands without the right of return—violating what Albert Schweitzer called "the most basic of human rights." Dramatic changes in population density and cultural patterns resulted. The first step came in the early 1920s, following Greek liberation from Turkish rule. More than one million Greeks left Turkey in exchange for hundreds of thousands of Turks, Pomaks, and other Muslims. The next series of forced population transfers was carried out at the instigation of Nazi Germany. Contrary to what one might expect, some of the people involved were ethnic Germans who left Italy, Estonia, Latvia, Lithuania, eastern Poland, Croatia, Romania, and Hungary to move to the "homeland." The Nazis expelled even greater numbers of Jews, Poles, Russians, and other groups from their territories, and a great many of these populations perished in concentration camps. In the process, the Nazis brought about an immense restructuring of the ethnic geography of Eastern Europe.

As the Third Reich collapsed, large eastern territories were annexed by Poland and Russia. Between 1944 and 1951, in the largest forced migration ever to occur, 9 million people were expelled from these areas, amounting to 90% of the total population in an area the size of Pennsylvania. The effects of population density persisted for decades. Contemporaneously, Czechs expelled 3 million Germans, and exchanges of Slovaks and Hungarians and of Poles and Russians occurred. More recently, 260,000 Greeks and Turks suffered **ethnic cleansing** in Cyprus in the 1970s. The Balkan war of the 1990s brought renewed ethnic cleansing to Europe. Bosnians and Croats suffered most in this latest episode of forced migration, with the number of refugees totaling as many as 1 million.

The last 60 years have also seen significant population shifts as a result of migration spurred by differential economic opportunities in and around Europe. This began as an internal migration in Europe from periphery to core. Its prototype was perhaps the large-scale movement of Irish to Great Britain in the nineteenth century. Of far greater magnitude in the periphery-to-core shift was the south-to-north migration in the period from 1950 to 1975. Spain, Portugal, Italy, Greece, Croatia, and Slovenia became the major senders, with destinations lying mainly in France, Germany, Belgium, the Netherlands, and the Alpine countries (fig. 3.11). Some 5 million persons took part in this migration, including 1.7 million Italians, mainly from the impoverished southern part of that country, and 1.1 million Portuguese. As recently as 1970 in Germany, Yugoslavs and Italians ranked as the two largest immigrant groups. Portugal and Spain contributed disproportionately to France, and the Low Countries also received large contingents of Spaniards. Many Greek Cypriots came to the United Kingdom. Numerous southern European emigrants eventually returned to their native lands. The northern periphery of Europe, far more thinly populated than the south, could not send mass migration to the core. Even so, a sizable proportion of the northerners went south, most notably Finns from subarctic districts who sought employment opportunities in central and southern Sweden.

As early as the late 1950s, Europe's booming economy began attracting workers from farther afield. Moreover, growing affluence left many Europeans unwilling to engage in menial jobs and actively seeking cheap labor to fill those jobs. Among the immigrants drawn into Europe at this time were West Indians, Africans, and Asians, who came mainly to the United Kingdom, France, and the Netherlands. Many came at the invitation of national governments, who saw them as temporary laborers who would eventually return to their home countries. Hence, they came to be known as **guest workers**.

These extra-European guest workers were followed by some 1 million Muslims from the formerly French-ruled Maghreb countries of North Africa—Morocco, Algeria, and Tunisia (fig. 3.11). Following on the heels of numerous ethnic French fleeing Algeria after that country overthrew rule by France in 1962, the Maghreb Muslims came mainly to France. In addition, many Moroccans went to Belgium and the Netherlands. The Maghreb immigration to France peaked in the 1970s, after which Italy and Spain became their major destinations. Paralleling the Maghreb immigration,

Figure 3.11.   Migration within and to continental western Europe during the 1960s and 1970s. Prior to 1950, Europe lost more people through migration than it gained. Since then western Europe has become an immigration zone. The base of the arrows on the map are located in sending countries, and the points of the arrows are in receiving countries. The thickness of the arrows corresponds to numbers of migrants. *Source*: Rogers, R. 1985. Post-World War II European Labor Migration: An Introduction to the Issues, in R. Rogers, ed., *Guests Come to Stay: The Effects of European Labor Migration on Sending and Receiving Countries.* Boulder, CO: Westview Press, 4–11.

another 2 million persons or more entered Europe from Turkey prior to 1990; three-quarters of them headed to Germany (fig 3.11). Turks also became the largest non-European immigrant group in Switzerland and Sweden.

Since about 1990, this mass immigration has changed in character. The sources are now more diverse, reaching into sub-Saharan Africa and South Asia, though the Maghreb and Turkey remain important. In addition, much of the immigration of the past two decades has been illegal, with people crossing into Europe at Gibraltar, at the waist of the Mediterranean, and at the Strait of Otranto. Germany and Switzerland are among the favored destinations of legal and illegal immigrants alike. Fully 23% of

Switzerland's population now consists of foreign-born persons, about twice the proportion in the United States. Germany houses about 12.5 million foreign-born.

An anti-immigrant backlash has developed in many of the major destination countries. Certain right-wing political parties, such as France's National Front, Austria's Freedom Party, Belgium's Vlaams Belang, and the Swiss People's Party, openly oppose immigration, and in Austria this sentiment reached the highest levels of government in the year 2000. Some 500,000 illegal immigrants continue to enter the EU each year. Many Europeans feel threatened today, fearing being overwhelmed by masses of poor people from other regions. Germans and Austrians have coined the word *Überfremdung*, or "over-foreignization," to describe this perceived threat. Less stigmatized is another type of immigration. After the collapse of the Soviet Union in 1991, ethnic Russians and Germans residing in the former Central Asian Soviet Republics, particularly Kazakhstan, began moving to Russia and Germany, reversing a centuries-old diaspora and overwhelming the supply of jobs, housing, and social services for a time.

More recently, workers from countries in eastern Europe have moved to the west. Long dammed up by the Iron Curtain and Cold War, this new avenue of mobility opened in earnest in the late 1980s. Dire predictions of uncontrollable mass migration from the east appeared, including speculation that as many as 40 million Russians desired to move west. As early as 1989, about 1 million Eastern Europeans, excluding emigrants from East Germany, resided in Western Europe. Still, the predicted tidal wave of east-to-west migration has not materialized. The proportion of the workforce from eastern Europe is below 2% in all western and central European countries, and in only two of those countries (Austria and Ireland) does the percentage exceed 1%. Poland is the largest labor-exporting country, but many eastern European states have a larger volume of immigration than emigration. Barring total economic collapse in the east, migration seems unlikely to zoom out of control. However, the great disparity in wealth and living standards between the two halves of Europe will continue to exert a powerful westward pull, and an even more profound contrast along Europe's Mediterranean frontier will likewise produce continuing instability.

Scale Differences

So far we have concentrated on population patterns and processes that are evident when looking at Europe as a whole. An important geographic principle holds that the scale of analysis influences both what we see and the explanations we derive. In this general treatment of Europe, we can only suggest the insights that come from changing scales, but a few examples of localized influences on demography can serve as a reminder of the importance of thinking across scales.

Figure 3.12, a historical settlement map from a Swiss valley, reveals a completely different impact of the environment on demography from what is evident at the European scale. In the Alps of Switzerland, northern Italy, and Austria, south-facing slopes receive much more sunlight than do shadowy north-facing slopes. The local inhabitants long recognized this contrast and tended to cluster in the areas with the greatest

Figure 3.12.   Concentration of settlement in the Rhône Valley, Swiss Alps. The shaded area is in shadow at noon at the winter solstice. Villages and scattered dwellings are shown in black. Elevations are shown in meters. *Source:* After Garnett, 1935.

insolation. In some instances, social distinctions developed between those living on the sunnier and shadier sides of the river—complete with sense of superiority and even taboos against intermarriage. Elsewhere in Europe, other types of environmental influences on population geography are evident, ranging from the clustering of settlements in the hills of Tuscany away from malaria-ridden lowlands, to the abandonment of areas threatened by volcanism in Iceland and Sicily.

Turning to population growth and migration, an analysis that focuses solely on the European scale obscures local variations that can be both demographically significant and politically volatile. Some of the immediate suburbs around Paris have large immigrant populations with much higher rates of natural population increase than does the central city or more far-flung suburbs. These differences affect population densities, and place strains on infrastructure and housing supply. They are also highlighted by those seeking to draw attention to the growing presence of immigrant populations in France.

Population patterns around political boundaries provide an example of the impacts of political-economic circumstances on demography at more local scales. Particularly in places where borders are closed or difficult to cross, economies tend to stagnate, and people move out. In the former West Germany, the zone bordering Czechoslovakia and East Germany experienced steady population decline during the decades immediately after World War II. Only recently have these areas begun to rebound.

We could go on, but since our primary goal is to make sense of the larger European picture, we move on from basic demography to consider some of the cultural patterns that constitute the European landscape. Whether the subject is demography, culture, or something else, however, it is important to remember that different insights are gained when the scale of analysis changes.

Sources and Suggested Readings

Almagia, R. 1929. The Repopulation of the Roman Campagna. *Geographical Review* 19 (4): 529–555.

Anderson, B. A. 2002. Russia Faces Depopulation? Dynamics of Population Decline. *Population & Environment* 23 (5): 437–464.

Berezin, M., and M. Schain. 2003. *Europe without Borders: Remapping Territory, Citizenship, and Identity in a Transnational Age*. Baltimore: Johns Hopkins University Press.

Blotevogel, H., and A. J. Fielding. 1997. *People, Jobs and Mobility in the New Europe*. New York: Wiley.

Bucher, H., C. Schlömer, and G. Lackmann. 2004. Die Bevölkerungsentwicklung in den Kreisen der Bundesrepublik Deutschland zwischen 1990 und 2020. *Informationen zur Raumentwicklung* (3/4): 107–126.

Carter, F. W., and W. Maik. 1999. *Shock-Shift in an Enlarged Europe: The Geography of Socio-Economic Change in East-Central Europe after 1989*. Aldershot: Ashgate.

Casado-Diaz, M. A., C. Kaiser, and A. M. Warnes. 2004. Northern European Retired Residents in Nine Southern European Areas: Characteristics, Motivations and Adjustment. *Ageing and Society* 24 (3): 353–381.

Cole, J. P., and I. V. Filatotchev. 1992. Some Observations on Migration within and from the Former USSR in the 1990s. *Post-Soviet Geography* 33 (7): 432–453.

Compton, P. A. 1976. Religious Affiliation and Demographic Variability in Northern-Ireland. *Transactions of the Institute of British Geographers* 1 (4): 433–452.

Demko, G. J., G. V. Ioffe, and Z. A. Zaonchkovskaia, eds. 1999. *Population under Duress: The Geodemography of Post-Soviet Russia*. Boulder, CO: Westview Press.

Dorbritz, J. 2007. Demographischer Wandel in Mittel- und Osteuropa. Krisenreaktion oder Einstellungswandel? *Geographische Rundschau* 59 (3): 44–51.

Grigg, D. 1995. The Nutritional Transition in Western Europe. *Journal of Historical Geography* 21 (3): 247–261.

Hamilton, K. A., ed. 1994. *Migration and the New Europe*. Washington, D.C.: Center for Strategic & International Studies.

Johnson, J. H. 1990. The Context of Migration: The Example of Ireland in the 19th Century. *Transactions of the Institute of British Geographers* 15 (3): 259–276.

Joshi, H., ed. 1989. *The Changing Population of Britain*. Oxford, UK: Blackwell.

King, R., ed. 1993a. *Mass Migrations in Europe the Legacy and the Future*. London: Belhaven Press.

———, ed. 1993b. *The New Geography of European Migrations*. London: Belhaven Press.

———, ed. 2001. *The Mediterranean Passage Migration and New Cultural Encounters in Southern Europe*. Liverpool Studies in European Regional Cultures 9. Liverpool: Liverpool University Press.

King, R., and A. M. Warnes. 1998. International Retirement Migration in Europe. *International Journal of Population Geography* 4 (2): 91–111.

Leitner, H. 1997. Reconfiguring the Spatiality of Power: The Construction of a Supranational Migration Framework for the European Union. *Political Geography* 16 (2): 123–143.

Lesthaeghe, R., and P. Willems. 1999. Is Low Fertility a Temporary Phenomenon in the European Union? *Population and Development Review* 25 (2): 211–228.

Malkhazova, S. M. e. a. 1997. Public Health and Environmental Pollution in Russia. *Bulletin, International Geographical Union* 47 (1): 5–16.

Mead, W. R. 1951. The Cold Farm in Finland: Resettlement of Finland's Displaced Farmers. *Geographical Review* 41 (4): 529–543.

Monzini, P. 2007. Sea-Border Crossings: The Organization of Irregular Migration to Italy. *Mediterranean Politics* 12 (2): 163–184.

Noin, D., and R. Woods, eds. 1993. *The Changing Population of Europe*. Oxford, UK: Blackwell.

Oberhauser, A. M. 1991. The International Mobility of Labor: North African Migrant Workers in France. *Professional Geographer* 43 (4): 431–445.

Ogden, P. E., and R. Hall. 2004. The Second Demographic Transition: New Household Forms and the Urban Population of France During the 1990s. *Transactions—Institute of British Geographers* 29 (1): 88–105.

Penninx, R., M. Berger, and K. Kraal. 2006. *The Dynamics of International Migration and Settlement in Europe: A State of the Art*. Amsterdam: Amsterdam University Press.

Pounds, N. J. G., and C. C. Roome. 1971. Population Density in Fifteenth Century France and the Low Countries. *Annals of the Association of American Geographers* 61 (1): 116–130.

Preusser, H. 1976. Entwicklung und Raumliche Differenzierung der Bevolkerung Islands. *Geografiska Annaler. Series B, Human Geography* 58 (2): 116–144.

Prioux, F. 2003. Recent Demographic Developments in France. *Population* 58 (4–5): 525–558.

Range, P. R., and J. B. Pinneo. 1993. Europe Faces an Immigrant Tide. *National Geographic* 183 (5): 94–125.

Rodriguez, V., G. Fernandez-Mayoralas, and F. Rojo. 1998. European Retirees on the Costa del Sol: A Cross-National Comparison. *International Journal of Population Geography* 4 (2): 183–200.

Salt, J., and H. D. Clout, eds. 1976. *Migration in Post-War Europe Geographical Essays*. London: Oxford University Press.

Samers, M. 2004. An Emerging Geopolitics of "Illegal" Immigration in the European Union. *European Journal of Migration & Law* 6 (1): 27–45.

Sardon, J. P. 2002. Recent Demographic Trends in the Developed Countries. *Population* 57 (1): 111–156.

Schwab, O., and K. Toepel. 2006. Together Apart? Stocktaking of the Process of Labour Market Integration in the Border Region between Germany, Poland and the Czech Republic. *Zeitschrift für Arbeitsmarktforschung* 39 (1): 77–93.

Siirila, S., L. Hautamaki, J. Kuitunen, and T. Keski-Petaja. 1990. Regional Well-Being Variations in Finland. *Fennia* 168 (2): 179–200.

Stone, K. H. 1962. Swedish Fringes of Settlement. *Annals of the Association of American Geographers* 52 (4): 373–393.

Thorarinsson, S. 1961. Population Changes in Iceland. *Geographical Review* 51 (4): 519–533.

Thumerelle, J. 1992. Migrations Internationales et Changement Géopolitique en Europe. *Annales de Géographie* 101: 289–318.

Usher, A. P. 1930. The History of Population and Settlement in Eurasia. *Geographical Review* 20 (1): 110–132.

Vandermotten, C., G. Hamme, and P. Medina Lockhart. 2005. The Geography of Migratory Movements in Europe from the Sixties to the Present Day. *Belgeo* (1–2): 19–34.

Velikonja, J. 1958. Postwar Population Movements in Europe. *Annals of the Association of American Geographers* 48 (4): 458–472.

Walsh, J. A. 1991. The Turn-around of the Turn-around in the Population of the Republic of Ireland. *Irish Geography* 24 (2): 117–125.

Wild, T., and P. N. Jones. 1994. Spatial Impacts of German Unification. *Geographical Journal* 160 (1): 1–16.

CHAPTER 4

The Pattern of Languages

Since all societies function by communication, it follows that language is considered one of the basic components of society. Indeed, the ability to communicate is one way that a community sets itself apart from "outsiders." Language is so fundamental to the way we view society that the common origin of most of the major languages of Europe has served to bolster the idea that Europe is a distinctive culture area.

In this chapter, we explore the many different languages spoken (or once spoken) in Europe, their distribution, and the relationships among them. We also look at the social and political implications of language divisions.

Languages and Language Families

In Europe, including Eurorussia, nearly 100 recognizably separate, mutually unintelligible languages are spoken, plus countless local dialects. Moreover, the region's complex linguistic geography is ever-changing. Over the centuries and millennia, some languages spread and grew, others retreated to refuge areas, and still others vanished, leaving behind only a few words adopted into surviving tongues or perhaps merely a sprinkling of place names (fig. 4.1).

To grasp the essentials of the European language pattern, we need to understand how languages are defined and organized. Defining a language is no easy matter. We often think of languages as sets of mutually understood words and phrases that allow people to communicate with one another. **Dialects**, following this reasoning, are variants of languages. In practice, however, we generally refer to Chinese as a language even though there are at least five major variants of spoken Chinese that are mutually unintelligible. At the same time, we typically think of Norwegian and Danish as distinct languages even though a Dane could understand most of what was being said by someone speaking the form of Norwegian found in Oslo. Or consider another example. Many inhabitants of northern Switzerland think of themselves as speaking a separate language, *Schweizerdeutsch* or *Schwyzerdütsch* (Swiss-German). Swiss-German varies so greatly from the German of northern Germany that someone from Hamburg would

Figure 4.1.   Languages and selected dialects of modern Europe. Many forms of speech normally considered separate languages, such as Swedish or Ukrainian, are perhaps better regarded as dialects enmeshed in nets. *Sources:* Zaborski 2000, Straka 1979, Alinei 1983, Comrie 1994, Mackenzie 1994, and Murphy 1998.

be hard pressed to converse with someone speaking true Swiss-German. Yet most Germans consider Swiss-German to be a dialect of German, and most language maps take the same position.

These examples show that there is no neat distinction between a language and a dialect. What we generally refer to as a language is a dialect or set of dialects that has achieved recognition as such, often as a result of political events. Hence, it is only partly in jest that one can describe a language as a dialect with an army behind it. This general point is a good illustration of why geography matters. Language cannot be understood in isolation from the sociopolitical and environmental context in which it is situated.

When we seek to describe the language pattern of an area, we need to consider the relationships among languages and dialects. To do this, linguists look at the way languages are structured and their vocabularies. Those languages that share broad similarities among these features are grouped together into **language families**. Even greater similarities provide the basis for identifying broader and then narrower subfamilies and eventually individual languages. This approach means that language families can be diagrammed in tree form with the trunk representing the language family, the major branches representing broad subfamilies, and so on outward until one ends up with individual small branches representing discrete languages (fig. 4.2).

When one looks at the European linguistic kaleidoscope in these terms, it becomes clear that most of the major languages of Europe belong to a single language family, **Indo-European**. The linguistic kinship of the various Indo-European languages can be illustrated by comparing their vocabularies, especially words that describe commonplace things encountered in everyday life. Consider, for example, the word for *three* in various Indo-European tongues: *tre* or *tri* in Erse, Albanian, Italian, Swedish, Russian, Czech, and Serbo-Croatian; *tría* in Greek; *tres* in Spanish; *trei* in Romanian; *thrír* in Icelandic; *trzy* in Polish; and *trys* in Lithuanian. Contrast these to the words for *three* in non-Indo-European languages, such as *uç* in Turkish, *kolme* in Finnish, *három* in Hungarian, or *sahn* in Chinese.

Vocabularies are not a completely reliable guide to linguistic relationships because groups can borrow words from very different languages. Hence, linguists also look for similarities and differences in word order and the linguistic alterations that are made when, for example, a singular noun becomes plural. Indo-European languages generally employ the sentence structure of subject-verb-object. For example, "Jamie threw the ball." By contrast, languages in the Sino-Tibetan family employ a different word order, which is often verb-subject-object. Forming the plural of a word in an Indo-European tongue involves changing the ending. *Apple* becomes *apples*. In Swahili, however, one adds a prefix to form the plural.

Classifying languages is only a beginning. As geographers, we want to understand why a particular pattern of languages came into being. **Geolinguistics** is the study of language change over space and through time. Language families are thought to begin with a proto-language, or set of closely related tongues in a given area. Geolinguists use a combination of archeological evidence and words for animals and plants that languages in a language family share in common to figure out where the language family began. The next task is to understand the process of language diffusion. Geolinguistics

Figure 4.2.   The Indo-European Language Tree. The trunk of the tree represents the language family, the major branches are the principal sub-families, and the limbs are the major languages.

infer that major language subfamilies arise when groups of speakers move away from the area where the proto-language developed. Over time, the language of the separated groups evolves with the general assumption that greater distance and time apart yields greater differences.

The pattern of particular languages that follows geographical separation can be fundamentally influenced by writing, technology, and political organization. Writing is critical because texts are the primary means by which the evolution of language is slowed. Technology is important because it influences both the production of written

Figure 4.3. Maximum extent of the Roman Empire. The Roman Empire collapsed more than 1,500 years ago. In some places, little can be found today to remind us of the Empire, but its cultural imprint remains strong in the parts of continental western Europe where it held sway.

texts and their dissemination. Political organization is key because it affects what people have access to and which areas are in close contact with one another.

Armed with these insights, we can begin to make sense of the circumstances that produced a language pattern such as that found in Europe. First, various peoples speaking languages that were part of the dominant language family diffused into Europe. Then, the rise of larger-scale, more technologically sophisticated literate societies allowed certain languages to spread over larger areas. Most notably, by 2,000 years ago, Latin had successfully diffused over a significant part of Europe (fig. 4.3). This was possible because Latin was associated with a sophisticated political system that knit together large swaths of territory. When the Roman Empire collapsed, however, linguistic divergence took place.

Given the importance of writing, technology, and politics for the diffusion of languages, two developments in the late Middle Ages were of particular importance to the emergence of the modern language pattern: the invention of the printing press and the rise of relatively large states. The printing press was invented in Germany in 1588, and during the succeeding century, it spread to other parts of Europe and beyond. The printing press allowed for the mass production and dissemination of materials that helped to spread particular forms of what became the major languages of Europe. The form of writing and speech promoted by elites to foster communication across broad areas is known as the **standard** (or standardized) **language**. Many of the early printed texts that promoted standardization were religious. The Luther Bible played this role for German, as did the King James Bible for English. In later centuries, the media and schools played key roles in language standardization.

It follows that the spread of political authority was important to the rise of standard languages, for political leaders have a strong interest in fostering integration by bringing peoples together and exposing them to common linguistic influences. Thus, language became a tool through which the leaders of early European states such as England and Spain sought to consolidate their power (see Chapter 6). The expansion of political authority also explains why some European languages spread far beyond Europe. As the states with colonial empires expanded their influence, certain languages came to be spread over vast portions of the earth's surface (fig. 1.9).

To move beyond these generalities, we need to look at the circumstances that brought speakers of different language families into Europe. We begin with the region's dominant language family, Indo-European. After examining the pattern of Indo-European subfamilies and languages that emerged, we turn our attention to the pockets of non-Indo-European speech that also are (or were) found in Europe.

The Diffusion of Indo-European Tongues into Europe

The Indo-European language family is thought to have originated somewhere in the region of the Caucasus Mountains around 12,000 years ago. Archeological evidence suggests that its speakers were among the first farmers—that is, the people who initially domesticated plants and animals. Indo-European-speaking agriculturalists moved out of this area, both to the southeast and to the west, absorbing indigenous hunter-gatherers and producing a swath of Indo-European speech stretching from the Atlantic coast of Europe through South Asia. Great linguistic divergence occurred as speakers of the proto-language lost contact with one another, coined terms for new things they encountered, and borrowed words and phrases from other peoples. But recognizable similarities can still be found between the French spoken in northwestern Europe, the Farsi (Persian) spoken in Iran, and the Urdu spoken in Pakistan and India.

Indo-European speakers probably began moving out of the area around the Black Sea about 8000 B.C.E. As they became separated, different dialects developed due to linguistic drift and mixing with alien peoples. A **dialect net**, a linguistic continuum in which the speakers of each dialect could understand the neighboring ones but not those spoken farther away in regions with which they had no regular contact, formed. Further fragmentation into separate, mutually unintelligible tongues seems to have occurred whenever the dialect net was torn. That likely happened where the farming frontier, spreading slowly west and north from Turkish Anatolia at the rate of about a kilometer every 20 years, encountered physical geographic obstacles. Indo-European pioneer farmers branched around these obstacles. Some went one way; some went the other. When that occurred, the two groups lost contact with each other for centuries, and their speech drifted apart. Generations later, when they coalesced beyond the obstacle, they could not understand each other.

The first such tear of significance to Europe probably occurred about 6000 B.C.E. when one group of Indo-Europeans spread westward from Anatolia into the Aegean Isles and beyond onto the Greek mainland, while the other went north along the Black Sea's western coast (fig. 4.4). The split between western and eastern divisions of Indo-European may have been induced by the catastrophic creation of the Black Sea about 5600 B.C.E. Scientists recently determined that, prior to then, the Black Sea was a much smaller, interior drainage lake, lacking a connection to the Aegean and standing 120 meters below sea level. (See book by Ryan and Pitman in Chapter 2 readings.) The sea suddenly burst through the natural dam at what is today the Bosporos, spilling in and enlarging the Black Sea to its present size. In the process, the large lowland plain adjacent to modern Bulgaria, Romania, and Turkey was inundated, which very possibly gave rise to the story of the great biblical flood. The Indo-European farmers living in these lowlands fled in different directions. Some went toward Turkey and Greece; others went into the Balkans, likely ripping the dialect net. Whether caused by the Aegean water barrier or the Black Sea flood, this tear produced the divide between Western and Eastern (formerly called *Centum* and *Satem*) Indo-European. This divide would later extend all the way to the Baltic Sea.

Fragmentation continued. The Eastern branch perhaps divided at the Stara Planina with **Thracian** developing to the south among flood refugees in the Maritsa Valley (see fig. 2.1). In the north, perhaps even beyond the corridor of steppe grasslands on the margin of the East European Plain, the ancestral Balto-Slavs, descendants of others who fled the waters, arose. In their continued northward migration, they apparently divided around the Pripyat Marsh, separating the ancient **Baltic** and **Slavic** languages. The Slavs drove east and north, eventually populating a wedge between the 120-day growing season to the north and the steppes to the south, pushing agriculture as far as their prehistoric technology would allow (fig 4.4).

Equally profound tears in the dialect net happened at obstacles in the west. From Greece, where **Hellenic** speech developed, some Indo-Europeans migrated across the Strait of Otranto to Italy, apparently giving rise to the Italic-speaking group, while about the same time, others seem to have pressed north through the Vardar–Morava rift valley, a narrows that restricted contact with the Hellenes to the south. Emerging into the Hungarian Basin, they became the Danubian people. Later, at the northern foot of the Alps, the proto-**Celtic** culture evolved from the Danubian parent, and it eventually spread to dominate most of central and north-western Europe. Other Danubians went north into Scandinavia by way of the Jutland Peninsula of modern Denmark, crossing the infertile outwash plain and following a narrow strip of fertile land along the fjord-strewn east coast of Jutland (fig. 4.4). Those venturing north along this route after about 3500 B.C.E. became the **Germanic** peoples.

What happened in the Iberian Peninsula is less clear. The substantial survival of non-Indo-European languages there into historic times suggests a different linguistic order prevailed. Perhaps farmers speaking Afro-Asiatic tongues, belonging to a different language family, spread across North Africa, entered Iberia at Gibraltar, and continued northward until they met their fellow agriculturists, the Indo-Europeans, at the Pyrenees. Basque, apparently an indigenous language unrelated to either Indo-European or Afro-Asiatic (see below), could have survived along the contact zone of the two immigrant farming peoples (fig. 4.4).

Many geolinguistic changes have occurred in Europe since 3000 B.C.E. when the Indo-European diffusion had largely run its course. Yet some features have displayed remarkable durability, such as the western-eastern divide and the tenacious survival of

Figure 4.4.   *(See figure legend on facing page).*

minorities such as the Basques. One of the most notable changes, however, has been the continued tearing of several dialect nets to form the language subfamilies and individual languages of contemporary Europe.

The Three Major Subfamilies of Indo-European

At the dawn of the Roman Empire, much of western and central Europe was dominated by Celtic-speaking peoples with a zone of Italic speech in what is now Italy and southern and western France, and some non-Indo-European languages in the periphery. Over the ensuing 2,000 years, the situation fundamentally changed. Celtic speech was reduced to a small periphery as two major subfamilies of western Indo-European speech spread across western and central Europe, and one subfamily came to dominate the east. Now over 90 percent of all Europeans are accounted for by three Indo-European subfamilies: Germanic, Slavic, and Romance. Each of these, however, encompasses multiple languages (fig. 4.1).

ROMANCE LANGUAGES

The **Romance** languages, western Indo-European in affiliation, today dominate the western and southern edges of Europe (excluding the British Isles). Romance languages derive from the ancient Italic division of Indo-European (fig. 4.4). One Italic tongue, Latin, originally spoken only in the district of Lazio (Latium) around Rome, rose to dominance and achieved a remarkable dispersal. When a language successfully expands in this manner, its speakers possess some cultural or technological advantage. In the case of Latin speakers, this advantage came in the form of a highly developed political

Figure 4.4. Origin, diffusion, and fragmentation of the Indo-European languages. 8000 to 3000 B.C.E.: a geographical speculation. The dialect net was "torn" whenever the advancing Indo-European farmers split around an obstacle or fled a catastrophe, losing contact with their former neighbors. Such tears soon produced separate languages, due to linguistic drift in isolation. It is possible that other, now extinct Indo-European groups developed in southern France and the British Isles, due to the Alpine and English Channel obstacles. Residual non-Indo-European speakers survived best in border areas between languages and in harsh environments marginally suited to agriculture. Much of the map is speculative. Key to groups: **B** = Proto-Balts; **BS** = Proto-Balto-Slavs; **C** = Proto-Celts; **D** = Danubic; **G** = Proto-Germanic; **H** = Proto-Hellenes; **I** = Proto-Italic; **S** = Proto-Slavs; **T** = Proto-Thraco-Illyrians. Key to possible obstacles to migration: **1** = Vardar-Morava rift valley; **2** = Constriction between Carpathians and steppes; **3** = Pripyat Marsh; **4** = Jylland narrows, a wedge of good land between marshes and outwash plains on the west and south and the Schlei Fjord on the east; **5** = Cilician Gate, a passage through the Taurus Mountains; **6** = Danube water gap; **7** = Stara Planina. *Sources:* Krantz 1988; Ryan and Pitman 1998; Renfrew 1988, 1989, and personal communication 1999; all with very substantial modifications.

organization and technological sophistication, which permitted empire-building. Latin was the language of the Roman Empire. It spread with Roman victories. By about 100 C.E. the Roman Empire, with its Latin language, reached its greatest territorial extent (fig. 4.3). Latin was heard on the banks of the Thames, Rhine, and Danube Rivers, as well as in North Africa. Few of the cultural groups ruled by the Roman Empire successfully resisted linguistic assimilation, though the Greeks did because of their written language tradition and the respect the Romans accorded to it. In fact, many Greek words found their way into Latin. The Etruscans, a highly developed, non-Indo-European civilization just north of Rome, succumbed linguistically to Latin, but not before they gave the parent words for *people*, *public*, *military*, and *autumn*. In Iberia, the Romans likely achieved the decisive introduction of Indo-European, wresting it away from the Afro-Asiatic peoples and a scattering of Celts.

Even before the Roman Empire collapsed, Latin was mixing with other tongues throughout the Empire to form different variants. Romance languages are the result of the continued linguistic fragmentation that occurred in succeeding centuries. All had roots in Latin, but their vocabularies and forms of pronunciation evolved in different directions.

The fall of the Roman Empire led to some decline in the use of Romance tongues, but they survived remarkably well throughout the core of what had been the Roman Empire. Nonetheless, Germanic invaders brought their own language to Britain, the west bank of the Rhine, and the Alps (see below), while Slavs and Magyars surged into the Balkans, leaving a lonely linguistic outpost in Romania as a reminder of the former eastern extent of the Romans (fig. 4.1). In these forfeited areas, only place names survive today as remnants of the Latin tongue. In England for example, *-caster* and *-chester* suffixes, as in Lancaster or Manchester, derive from *castra*, Latin for "military camp." Later, when the Moors invaded Iberia beginning in the eighth century, the Afro-Asiatic languages, especially Arabic, regained a foothold there, though the Latin-derived Mozarabic tongue survived as the language of Christians under Moorish rule. The subsequent defeat of the Moors by the Spaniards and Portuguese reclaimed nearly all of Iberia for the Romance languages and completely extinguished Arabic. Only abundant place names and numerous loanwords survive as reminders of the former Arabic presence (fig. 4.5).

The fragmentation of Latin into many separate languages proceeded rapidly after the political and social institutions that had bound the Roman Empire together ceased to exist. All of the surviving Romance tongues in modern Europe represent the fragmented legacy of Latin, but they solidified and spread as Europe's political geography took shape. Today, the Iberian Peninsula is home to three of these languages. Dominating the nation of Spain from the Meseta interior is Castilian Spanish, which some 30 million people speak as a mother tongue. Speakers of the Catalan language, numbering close to 7 million, are found in the eastern coastal fringe of Spain, the Balearic Islands, a corner of southern France, and Andorra, and they also have a foothold on the Italian isle of Sardinia. Catalan is now the dominant tongue in Barcelona and all of Catalonia, an autonomous region in Spain. Even France, which historically extended few rights and privileges to linguistic minorities, permits bilingual French-Catalan road signs in its southern region, where Catalan is spoken. The Atlantic front

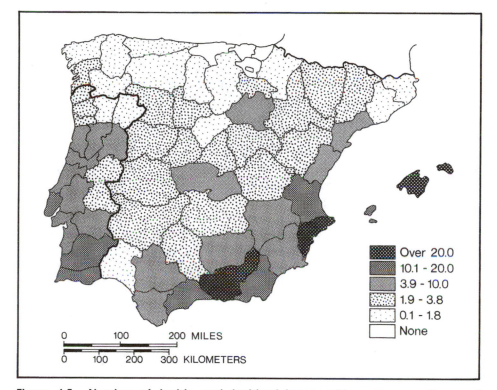

Figure 4.5. Number of Arabic and Arabized topographic names per thousand square kilometers in Iberia. "Africa begins at the Pyrenees," according to a traditional French saying, a reflection of the fact that, a thousand years ago, the Moors (Arabic-speaking Muslims from North Africa) were the dominant presence south of the Pyrenees. The subsequent Indo-European, Christian "reconquest" of Iberia led to their expulsion. A reminder of their presence is the many place names derived from the Arabic tongue. *Source:* After Lautensach 1954 and Sopher 1955.

of Iberia is home to Portuguese/Galician, a dialect net with almost 13 million speakers. The survival of Portuguese seems guaranteed by political independence, and Galician has achieved legal status in the autonomous Spanish province of Galicia, where it is the habitual language of daily use of a considerable majority of the population.

Northward from Iberia, beyond the Pyrenees, is found French, the speech of the large majority of France's population as well as of the southern Belgians, or Walloons; the western Swiss; and residents of the Valle d'Aosta in northwest Italy. All in all, it encompasses a total of some 57 million persons. The southern of two principal French tongues, *langue d'oc*, has gradually retreated before *langue d'oïl*, which was originally found only in the Parisian north. Occitan is the principal dialect in the *langue d'oc* region, and it is now being taught in some schools, ending two centuries of government suppression. Italian, at 60 million speakers, is spoken not only in Italy but also on the island of Corsica, which belongs to France; Canton Ticino in southern Switzerland; and parts of the Nice district on the French Riviera. The Tuscan dialect has become standard Italian speech, a heritage of the cultural significance of Florence. Italian has the third-largest number of speakers among the languages of Europe.

Along the northern fringe of Romance speech, sheltered in Alpine valleys, are found several minor tongues with diminishing numbers of speakers: Romansh with 40,000 speakers and two main dialects in eastern Switzerland; Ladinic in Italian South Tirol; and Friuli in the easternmost end of the Po–Veneto Plain. Collectively, these three constitute the Raeto-Romanic group. With about 1,850,000 speakers, Sardinian, distinct from Italian, survives on a Mediterranean island.

Romanian, an eastern outlier of the Romance languages, is separated from the larger western area by the interposed South Slavs. This language, spoken by a little over 22 million persons in Romania and adjacent Moldova, has survived in spite of invasions by Slavs, Magyars, and other groups, though the vocabulary is infiltrated with Slavic words. Closely related to Romanian is Vlakh, presumably derived from Valachia in southern Romania. Today, it is spoken by a few nomadic herding tribes in interior northern Greece and adjacent countries. The Vlakhs apparently descend from Romanians who migrated southward after the collapse of the Roman Empire to find refuge in the Dinaric–Pindhos mountain region. The seasonal shelters of Vlakh nomads may be seen at the foot of Mount Ólimbos in Greece and elsewhere.

The northern border of the Romance languages today, stretching from the English Channel to the head of the Adriatic Sea (fig. 4.1), displays a diverse character that relates to physical geography. Generally, where the border crosses plains, as in Flanders and the upper Rhône Valley of Switzerland, it tends to be unstable and mobile. French has advanced against Dutch in the former and retreated before German in the latter. But where the language border follows mountain ridges, as in the St. Gotthard Pass region in the western Alps, it has remained unchanged for more than a thousand years. To cross St. Gotthard going north today, as in the Early Middle Ages, is to leave Romance speech and enter the Germanic lands.

GERMANIC LANGUAGES

The second of the three major Indo-European subfamilies, also belonging to the western division, consists of the **Germanic** languages. These languages dominate in west-central and northern Europe (fig. 4.1).

The Germanic branch probably arose, as described earlier, in the isolation of Jutland (fig. 4.4), and, from there, it spread through the Danish Isles and into northern Scandinavia, absorbing a non-Indo-European race of hunters and fishers, a tall, blond people skilled in building longboats. They are sometimes referred to as *Nordish*. From them, the early Germanic people apparently adopted a sizable vocabulary, with the result that perhaps one-fourth or even one-third of all Germanic words today are not Indo-European in origin. *Bear* provides an example, for the parent Indo-European word for this animal was *urse*. (Compare modern French *ours* or Spanish *oso*.) The Germanic speakers, in the process, also took on some of the modes of livelihood of the indigenous hunter-fishers, including their seagoing practices. In the colder conditions of the north, their grain crops developed into faster-maturing varieties to accommodate the shorter growing season, but the Germanic advance apparently halted at about the northern limits of the humid continental and marine west coast climates. (Compare figures 2.14 and 4.4.)

There, in the north, the Germanic people remained for millennia on the outer margins of the agricultural, Indo-European world. Then, about 500 B.C.E., the climate of Scandinavia became colder, in a deterioration that continued to the beginning of the Common Era. Their response was remarkable. Nearly all Germanic people evacuated the north, boarding longboats and crossing the seas to resettle in the river valleys of northern Germany. These valleys, due to a pattern of springtime flooding that delayed planting and effectively shortened the growing season, had apparently remained largely uncolonized by the resident Celtic Indo-Europeans. The Germanic folk, with their fast-ripening grains, could occupy this riverine environment. Their southward advance continued, eventually displacing the Celts from Germany, leaving behind only a scattering of Celtic place names such as *Alp* (mountain), *Halle* (salt), and *Rhine* (river). With the collapse of the Roman Empire, Germanic tribes such as the Franks, Goths, Burgundians, and Lombards pressed far into Romance territory, but they usually failed to achieve a permanent implantation of their languages.

Elsewhere, the Germanic longboat invasions continued, bringing Anglo-Saxons to England, and, after warmer climatic conditions resumed, they accomplished much agricultural recolonization in Scandinavia. From there, Viking longboats eventually reached the Faeroes, Iceland, and Greenland. For 1,500 years, Germanic longboats assisted the dispersal of these peoples.

In central Europe, about 700 C.E., the Germans developed an innovative, more intensive form of agriculture known as the three-field system (see Chapter 7) and an effective system of organized government, the **feudal system**. Deploying those new arrangements to their advantage, they began expanding east at the expense of the Slavic peoples in about 800, pushing the German language frontier well into present-day Poland as well as eventually creating the eastern diaspora of Germans that eventually returned to Germany. Only a residue of Slavic place names survived in some parts of the North German Plain and Danube Valley as reminders of their former presence (fig. 4.6).

The single most important Germanic language, both in terms of the population of speakers and the number of countries where it serves as a mother tongue, is German. Close to 90 million people speak this language, including majorities not just in Germany, but also in Austria, Switzerland, Liechtenstein, and Luxembourg. In addition, German-speaking provinces can be found in Italy (South Tirol or Alto-Adige), eastern Belgium, and France (Alsace). German has the second-highest number of speakers in Europe, surpassed only by Russian. Until very recently, large German minorities remained in many eastern European countries, especially Russia, Hungary, Romania, and Poland, though all of these groups have been greatly depleted by recent **return migration** to Germany after an absence of centuries. During the six-year span from 1986 through 1992, the peak of the migration, over 1.5 million ethnic Germans departed from lands east of the former Iron Curtain, including the former Soviet Union, and went to Germany, where automatic citizenship awaited them. Romania's German minority dwindled from 360,000 in 1977 to only 17,000 by 1998. The

Figure 4.6.   An archaic language border in Germany. About the year 800 C.E., the Germanic-Slavic boundary in central Europe lay roughly along the line of the Elbe and Saale rivers. German-speaking settlers, in the 800–1300 period, surged eastward across this border, changing the linguistic pattern as they carried their speech far into Slavic territory. But even today, evidence of the old border remains in the form of Slavic place names. Villages with name suffixes such as *-itz, -in*, and *-zig* are of Slavic origin. Europe abounds with such archaic linguistic features.

German diaspora in eastern Europe has, for all practical purposes, ceased to exist, though many remain in Russia.

A standardized form of German based on Luther's Bible translation is understood and spoken throughout the German language region, but many dialects survive, some of which have become proper languages, unintelligible to speakers of standard German. Most notable are Letzeburgish, which is gaining increased usage in Luxembourg; Alsatian, the declining German dialect of eastern France; and Swiss-German, spoken by the majority in Switzerland.

Dutch, spoken by 20 million in the Netherlands, northern Belgium, and extreme northern France, also developed as a separate language out of the former German dialect net in the northern German region, but the difference is that its speakers never adopted standard German. Another offshoot is the Frisian language, spoken by about 300,000, mainly in the northeastern Netherlands.

The northern part of the Germanic language region is dominated by the Scandinavian dialect net (fig. 4.1). The standard language maps suggest that separate Danish, Norwegian, and Swedish languages exist, but, in fact, these are mutually intelligible dialects, even in the standard forms promoted by the three governments. For example, some 64 percent of Norwegians understand "all but a few words" of standard Swedish, and the same is true of 58 percent of all Danes concerning the Bokmål form of Norwegian, one of two government-recognized dialects in that country (fig. 4.1). In local areas along international borders within Scandinavia, mutual intelligibility is virtually universal. **Isoglosses**, or word boundaries, crisscross Scandinavia without regard to political borders.

Only Icelandic, where the Scandinavian dialect net was torn by the intervening sea, is a separate language if mutual intelligibility is the criterion. The Scandinavian dialect net encompasses a little over 20 million speakers, and Icelandic includes about 300,000 speakers. Faeroese, spoken in a small island group between Iceland and

Norway, should perhaps also be regarded as a separate Scandinavian language, but long rule by Denmark has altered the local speech to the extent that Faeroese probably fits better in the Scandinavian dialect net.

The Special Case of English

English, the closest Germanic relative of Frisian, is also a Germanic language, but with a twist. As a result of the Norman-French conquest of England almost a thousand years ago, English absorbed a great many Romance words, totaling perhaps 30% of the present English vocabulary. This mixing of Germanic and Romance, with the resultant richness of vocabulary, made English a **composite language**, one whose form was taken from more than one language. Of course, almost all languages are composite in the sense that they are influenced by other tongues, but, in the case of English, the influence was particularly dramatic.

The story of English begins in Britain in the beginning of the fifth century. The Roman Empire was losing its grip, and the ensuing vacuum facilitated the arrival of new Germanic-speaking peoples from farther east, including Jutes, Angles, Saxons, and Frisians. Within a couple of hundred years, the languages of the new arrivals came to dominate significant areas in Great Britain, particularly in the fertile Anglican Plain of the southeast where an Anglo-Saxon mix (referred to as Old English) held sway.

When the Norman-French leader William the Conqueror arrived on the southern coast of England in 1066, he encountered a largely Germanic-speaking population. He and his successors came to control much of southern Great Britain. The Norman-French conquerors were too small in number to change the essential character of the Germanic tongues that they encountered, but they introduced a new language that coexisted—and ultimately blended—with those tongues. As a result, English developed two words for many objects and actions. In English people are tired (Germanic root) or fatigued (Romance root). They seek help (Germanic root) or aid (Romance root). The animal in the field is called a cow (Germanic root), whereas the meat from that animal that is consumed at the dinner table is called beef (Romance root). These examples tell us something about the social structure of Norman England. Words that refer to basic things, for example, tired, help, and cow, reflect the language history of those at the lower ends of the social and political hierarchy. Words that refer to basic things—for example, tired, help, and cow—reflect the language history of those at the lower ends of the social and political hierarchy.

The so-called Middle English that evolved from the Germanic-Romance mixture was still fairly different from the English of today. One strand of Middle English centered in London evolved to the point where it began to take on a form more like modern English, and that strand came to be widely disseminated because it was institutionalized as the principal tongue of culture and government. Publications in the late sixteenth and early seventeenth century, such as the King James Bible and Shakespearean plays, played key roles in the standardization of English. The language continued to evolve, but more slowly. To this day, we can read works from the period with only modest difficulty.

The extraordinary reach of the British Empire brought the English language to the far corners of the globe. In some places, for example, parts of North America and Australia, it became the dominant tongue. In other areas, it provided a **lingua franca**, a common language that could be used as a means of communication among speakers of diverse tongues. Over the last 150 years, the rising power of the United States and the continued global influence of the United Kingdom have made English an increasingly common lingua franca around the world, including in Europe itself. French occupied that role throughout much of Europe in the seventeenth and eighteenth centuries, but English now dominates when Europeans who do not speak each other's language communicate with one another.

SLAVIC LANGUAGES

The third (and largest) of the three major Indo-European divisions consists of the **Slavic** languages, which belong to the eastern branch of the family. Slavic speech dominates throughout much of the eastern half of Europe.

The origins of the Slavic languages probably lie somewhere on the margins of the Pripyat Marsh (fig. 4.4) in dim prehistory. The proto-Slavs, who called themselves *Sorby*, established agricultural communities on the central section of the East European Plain. Slavic might have remained a minor and peripheral linguistic group if its speakers had not invented a new type of curved-blade plow in about the year 200 C.E. Equipped with a moldboard, it lifted the topsoil and turned it over. Mounted on wheels and pulled by multiple teams of oxen, this plow allowed the cultivation of heavy clay soils for the first time, and greatly increased crop production. With this innovation, the Slavs expanded west and south, entering the rich prairie regions of the North and East European Plain (fig. 2.1). When the Roman Empire collapsed, Slavic peoples pushed deep into the Balkans.

The Slavic region today is separated into a large northern part and a much smaller southern area, divided by a corridor of non-Slavic languages (fig. 4.1). In the north, Polish claims about 42 million speakers, the Czech/Slovakian dialect net 16 million, and the Russian dialect net about 165 million inside Europe. Most sources recognize Ukrainian, Belarussian, and Russian as three separate languages, and they are now being promoted as such for nationalistic purposes, but, linguistically, they are part of a single multi-ethnic Russian dialect net that encompasses virtually the entirety of the East European Plain. In 2005, the Russian component, formerly strewn widely through the Soviet Union, included about 12 million persons living outside Russia in newly independent European countries, more than two-thirds of them in Ukraine. Another 6 million or so Russian speakers still live in the former Soviet Central Asian republics, plus Azerbaijan.

A substantial return migration of Russian speakers to Russia from the former Soviet republics is occurring. Between 1989 and 1996, over 2 million people took part in this mass migration, and the flow continues, though at a lower volume. Many additional ethnic Russians departed Siberia, the Asian part of Russia, to return to Eurorussia in the 1990s. Russian is spoken by more people than any other language in Europe today.

Stretching from the Adriatic to the Black Sea in the Balkan Peninsula, the three southern Slavic languages are Slovenian with 2 million speakers, the Serbo-Croatian dialect net with some 20 million speakers, and the Bulgarian-Macedonian dialect net with close to 11 million speakers. Further complicating the pattern of Slavic languages is an alphabet divide, a fundamental cultural boundary in Europe that separates users of the Latin characters from those employing Greek or Greek-derived Cyrillic letters (fig. 4.1). This literary divide cuts right through the Slavic lands, both northern and southern.

Other Indo-European Languages

All of the other Indo-European tongues present in Europe are spoken by relatively small numbers of people, generally in peripheral locations. Some have experienced retreat, and a few face the possibility of extinction. The Celtic division of Western Indo-European clings to refuges on the hilly, cloudy coasts of northwestern Europe (figs. 4.1 and 4.7). Welsh, one of the surviving Celtic tongues, retains about 610,000 speakers in the hills of western Wales, a refuge area called the *Bro gymraeg*. As recently as 1911, Welsh had almost a million speakers, and the subsequent decline has caused some to predict "a land where children will not be able to pronounce the names of the places where they live." Indeed, some Celtic languages died in recent times, including Manx on the Isle of Man and Cornish in Cornwall. In the case of Welsh, the obituary seems to have been premature. The Welsh Language Act of 1993 gave the language legal equality with English, and the Welsh elite began insisting that their children study the ancestral tongue. It is a required language in state schools. A higher percentage of Wales' youth now can speak Welsh than is true of the population at large. The number of speakers stabilized and then began to increase in the 1990s. Welsh newspapers, radio broadcasts, and television channels are now available.

Breton, the Celtic language of western France, has a condition similar to Welsh, retaining a population of relatively fluent speakers estimated to be somewhere between 250,000 and 500,000. A Breton elite has mounted a linguistic revival movement in recent decades. In the 1990s, 34 Breton-only schools opened, a radical departure from the not-too-distant past, when French officials banned the language altogether in education and the number of speakers declined. It is not clear, however, that the revival is producing much growth in the number of Breton speakers.

The situation of Gaelic in the *Gaidhealtacht* refuge of the northern highlands and islands of Scotland has become desperate. Bilingual Gaelic/English road markers conceal the fact that only a little over 50,000 persons, mainly elderly, speak the language. Erse, or Irish Gaelic, has enjoyed governmental protection and support since the independence of Ireland in the 1920s, but it too has declined. Its *Gaeltacht* refuge area continues to shrink, and mandatory teaching of Erse in schools ceased in the 1980s. Only about 53,000 persons still use Erse as the language of the household, though anywhere from 500,000 to 1.5 million reputedly have at least limited ability in the language. Some Gaeltacht residents protest by defacing the English parts of bilingual signs (fig. 4.8). An Erse revival of sorts is underway in the cities of Ireland, all of which lie outside the

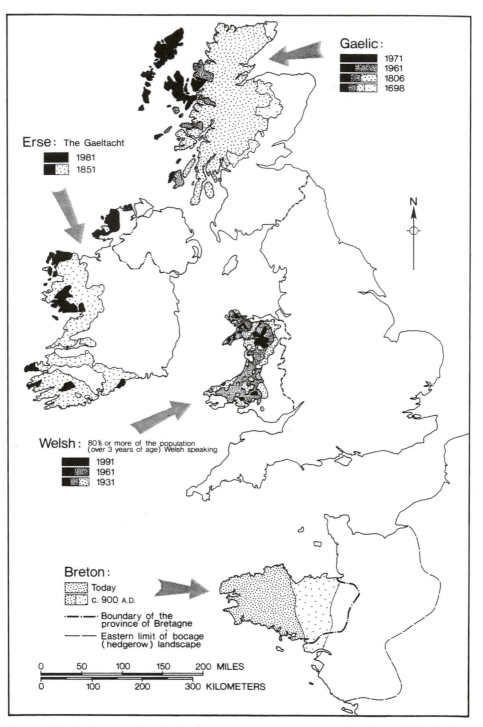

Figure 4.7.   Retreat of the Celtic languages, as represented by Erse (Irish), Breton, Scottish Gaelic, and Welsh. The rural refuge areas fragmented as the decline progressed. Today all but Scottish Gaelic are experiencing a revival, centered in the towns and cities, not in the rural refuges. *Sources:* After Withers 1984, 47, 81, 233, 234; Aitchison and Carter 1999; Hindley 1990).

Figure 4.8.   Defacing of English language on highway signs in the Connemara *Gaeltacht,* Republic of Ireland. The official bilingual policy of the republic is unpopular in both English and Erse areas. (Photo by T.G.J.-B. 1974.)

Gaeltacht. The first Erse television station began operating in 1996, and a few all-Erse primary schools were opened. Reputedly, just over 3% of Ireland's population uses Erse frequently in conversation.

The ancient **Hellenic** branch of the Indo-European languages is parent to modern Greek, which is spoken by a little over 10 million people in Greece and Cyprus. Minorities can be found in surrounding countries, such as Albania. While a minor tongue, accounting for less than 1.5% of all Europeans, Greek is not an endangered language. Greeks celebrate their tongue and take pride in the cultural achievements of their ancient ancestors. Greek Orthodox Christianity has also played a major role in the survival and vigor of Greek culture. Self-pride allowed the Greeks to preserve their language even during lengthy periods of rule by the Romans and Turks. Modern Greek is spoken in almost precisely the same region as in the Mycenean Age (1300 B.C.E.) and the area where the dialect net tear apparently produced proto-Hellenic some 8,500 years ago. The language changed. Modern Greek is roughly as different from Classical Greek as Italian is from Latin, but it remained astoundingly stable geographically.

Neighbors to the Greeks are the speakers of **Thraco-Illyrian** tongues, today represented only by Albanian. They number over 5 million and reside mainly in Albania, Kosovo, and western Macedonia. A scattering of Albanian villages can also be found in southern Italy and Greece. The ancestral Thraco-Illyrian linguistic subfamily, belonging to the Eastern Indo-European division, perhaps originated in the Maritsa Valley of Bulgaria (figs. 2.1 and 4.4), but the ancient geographical development remains poorly understood. Apparently, Thraco-Illyrian speakers were a mountain people, diffusing through the Stara Planina and Rodopi Range. This may have happened as early as the time of the Black Sea flood. They went over into Illyria, in the Dinaric Range, the present seat of the Albanian language. Eventually, Thraco-Illyrian died out altogether in the eastern Balkans, and modern Albanian occupies a refuge not unlike that of Celtic.

Another minor Eastern Indo-European group consists of the **Baltic** languages, Lettish (Latvian) and Lithuanian, spoken in two small independent states on the eastern shore of the Baltic Sea (fig. 4.1). Together, these languages have a little over 4 million speakers. Baltic speech survives close to its presumed area of origin, west of the Pripyat Marsh (fig. 4.4). Territory was later lost to both Germanic and Slavic languages, but the Balts have held out in a northern refuge. The achievement of political independence by Latvia and Lithuania bodes well for these two relatively small languages.

Romany, the eastern Indo-European speech of many or most of the 7 million or more Roma (or *gypsies* as they are popularly called), is spoken widely, especially in eastern Europe, though not in contiguous or sizable areas. Romania, with some 2 million, and Bulgaria with 750,000 Roma, house the largest numbers, representing about 11% of each country's inhabitants. Romany has split into three separate languages and 13 dialects, due to the wide distribution of the group and the largely oral status of the tongue. The Roma apparently entered Europe in the fourteenth century as a caste of itinerant Hindu peddlers from the Indus Valley of present-day Pakistan. In almost every European country, they are the objects of discrimination.

Non-Indo-European Languages

The non-Indo-European languages are both rare, accounting for only 5% of the population, and generally peripheral in location (fig. 4.9). On the northeastern margins of Europe live speakers of the **Uralic** language family, an indigenous group whose

Figure 4.9.   The non-Indo-European lands of Europe. Most lie at or near the European periphery, with the exception of Hungary.

ancestors retreated to cold, marshy refuges as the Indo-Europeans advanced. Today, they live in a chain of independent countries and autonomous regions from Finland and Estonia eastward through the Karelian and Komi republics of Russia, among others, as far as Mordvinia (fig. 4.9). These are peoples of the taiga. Many, particularly the speakers of Estonian (1 million) and Finnish-Karelian (6 million), adopted agriculture from the Indo-Europeans in ancient times and carried it into the taiga, but certain other Uralic groups, such as the Sami (or Lapps), with a present population of around 70,000, never became farmers. The Uralic peoples were historically closely connected to the forest, and their graveyards often take on a wooded, wild appearance. A formidable belt of marshes marks the Uralic-Indo-European border along the present Estonia–Latvia boundary, a line beyond which the Baltic speakers apparently never progressed.

Among the Uralic speakers, only the Hungarians, or Magyar, do not live in a peripheral area. Instead, 13.5 million strong, they occupy the heart of the structural basin that bears their name, close to the center of Europe (fig. 4.9). Most live in Hungary, but sizable minorities can also be found in Romania, Slovakia, Slovenia, northern Yugoslavia, and western Ukraine. By their own tradition and historical evidence, the ancient Hungarians, a herding people of the east, entered Europe as invaders in 895 C.E. and found a permanent foothold in areas where prairie vegetation had been created by earlier human activity in the central European biotic province. They largely replaced the Slavic peoples who had moved into what came to be known as the Hungarian Basin, completing the break between northern and southern Slavic.

On the southeast, the Indo-Europeans border the **Altaic** language family, mainly Turkic groups. The Osman Turks of Anatolia long ago attained footholds in Cyprus and north of the Bosporos–Dardanelles. In addition, the long rule of the Balkans left behind minorities in countries such as Bulgaria, where perhaps one in ten persons speak Turkish, in spite of three attempts in the past 150 years to expel them, most recently in 1989. Another 2 million Osman Turks reside as immigrants in Germany, and an additional 700,000 German citizens are of Turkish descent. Tataric, also a major Turkic language, is centered in Tatarstan, Bashkortostan, and, as a minority, Krym, the peninsular part of Ukraine (fig. 4.9). Altogether, about 6 million Tatars live in Europe. In small pockets of Moldova, Bulgaria, and southern Ukraine live over 200,000 Gagauz speakers, who are Christians and belong to the Oguz branch of Turkic. Europe abounds with such tiny minorities, most of which have not been mentioned here.

The **Caucasic** language family, including most notably Georgian, also bounds Indo-European on the southeast (fig. 4.9). To the south, across the Mediterranean Sea, **Afro-Asiatic** languages such as Arabic and Maltese mark the edges of Europe as conventionally defined.

The non-Indo-European periphery of Europe is completed by Basque, or Euskera, in the southwest, on the Pyrenean borders of Spain and France (fig. 4.9). With a little under 700,000 speakers, Basque long suffered decline, but a vigorous revival is presently underway. In Spain, establishment of the Basque Autonomous Province offers hope for the future of this unique language that faced considerable repression during much of the twentieth century. That repression served as a catalyst for a resistance movement that has pushed for independence for the Basque country—sometimes employing violence in support of its cause. The autonomous status of the Basque country has blunted the more extreme forms of Basque nationalism, but tensions remain between the Basques and the Castilian Spanish.

Closer inspection, then, reveals that at Europe's core three major Indo-European divisions prevail, surrounded by an inner periphery of smaller Indo-European groups and an outer periphery of altogether different tongues. Moreover, east-west linguistic contrasts are reflected in the major, most ancient division within the Indo-European family and two different alphabets. The Romance-Germanic divide and the split of Slavic into two geographically separate areas provide a significant north-south patterning.

For centuries, many smaller languages declined, and some perished, but recent decades have witnessed the revival of many endangered tongues. It is instructive to look more closely at these opposing trends.

Linguistic Decline and Revival

Why do some languages decline or even die? Why do revivals occur? Geographer Charles Withers, studying Scottish Gaelic, listed four basic processes, each directly or indirectly spatial, for decline. First is a **clearance model**, or decline caused by emigration of speakers to places outside the refuge area, leaving behind a smaller population to perpetuate the language. Second, a **changeover model** describes reduced linguistic viability due to the immigration of an alien population. A third process encouraging linguistic simplification is the **economic development model**. New modes of production, particularly industrialization, accompanied by urbanization, can break up the social structure needed to perpetuate a language. The transition from subsistence farming to working in a factory, even if made within the ethnic area, could be quite destructive in the linguistic sense, particularly if the language of the workplace was not that of the farm. In this context, geographer Keith Buchanan referred to the decline of the Celtic tongues as an example of "liquidation" carried out by the English in order to produce a loyal and obedient workforce for the mines and factories. Finally, a **social morale model** describes the process by which an ethnic minority, over time, loses pride in its language and voluntarily abandons it. An educational system using solely the majority language produced bilingualism and, indirectly, fostered illiteracy in the minority tongue. Depriving the language of legal and religious status helped convey the same message—that is, the minority tongue is inferior, and its use is socially degrading. Denying the language access to printed and broadcast media can hasten the process. All four of these processes were at work until the late twentieth century to diminish or destroy many lesser languages in Europe.

Recent decades have witnessed the opposite process—the revival of endangered languages. Welsh and Breton provide examples, as do numerous languages of the former Soviet Union. Partly, these revivals accompanied the collapse of the Soviet Empire, and have seen migration patterns reverse, counteracting the earlier clearance and changeover models. Russian speakers since 1990 emigrate from Latvia, for example, while Lettish speakers immigrate back to it. The social morale model is reversed as newly independent governments promote languages such as Lettish and stigmatize Russian.

But more is at work in linguistic revival than simply imperial collapse. The rise of a global economy and progress toward a united Europe also contribute. The more globalized and uniform European civilization becomes, the more people seem to want to anchor themselves in a regional or even local culture. An identity with place and region counteracts the trend toward oneness. Ethno-linguistic resurgence occurs.

This movement invariably has political consequences (see Chapter 6) and is a **postindustrial** phenomenon (see Chapter 9) (fig. 4.10). Indeed, the rapid

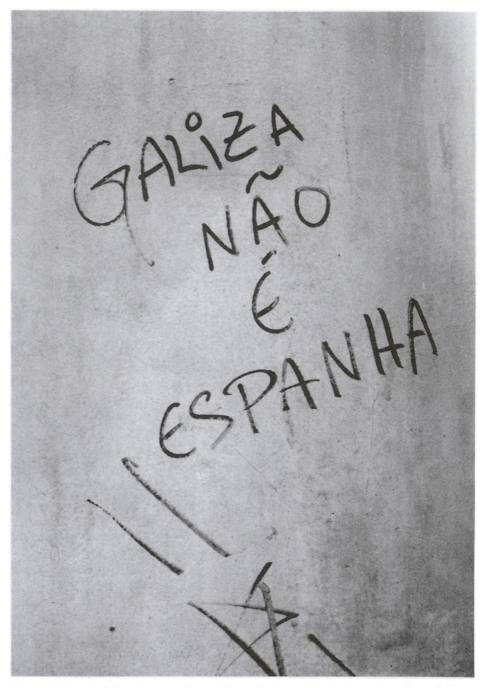

Figure 4.10.   Galician-language graffiti greets the visitor to the pilgrimage town of Santiago de Compostela, in the Spanish autonomous province of Galicia. Galician is undergoing a modest revival, following repression under the Franco dictatorship. The message is political—"Galicia is not Spain." (Photo by T.G.J.-B. 1999.)

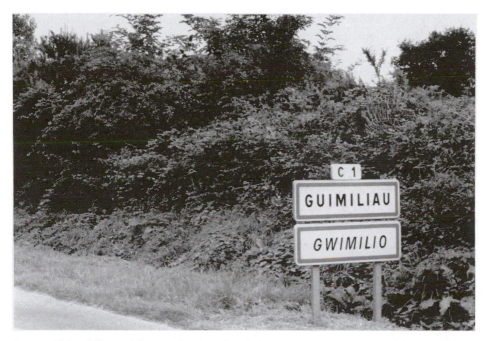

Figure 4.11. Bilingual French-Breton sign in Brittany, France. Breton "hid" in isolation behind hedgerows like the one seen here, for a thousand years, gradually retreating before French, but today this Celtic language is enjoying a modest revival. (Photo by T.G.J.-B. 1999.)

deindustrialization of Wales after about 1965, which witnessed the widespread closure of mines and factories, coincided with the Welsh revival movement. Buchanan's linguistic liquidation collapsed when the Celtic workforce became unemployed. Whatever the exact causal forces may be, modern Europe is witnessing the widespread rejuvenation of small languages as well as regional dialects (fig. 4.11). In the Netherlands, for example, radio broadcasts in the Limburgs dialect of the southeast can now be heard.

Multilingualism

Given the presence of many languages in Europe in close proximity to one another, it is not surprising that many Europeans put a high value on being able to speak more than one language. Recent surveys show that well over half of those living in the EU are able to hold a conversation in a language other than their mother tongue, and the figure rises to over 90% in countries such as Luxembourg, Slovakia, and Latvia. Perhaps even more remarkably, a little more than a quarter of the citizens of the EU claim they can carry on a conversation in two languages other than their mother tongue.

Nonetheless, multilingualism is much more advanced in some parts of Europe than in others. Most generally, those speaking major international languages (e.g., English,

Spanish, French) are less likely to know another language than those speaking tongues with less international standing (e.g., Swedish, Finnish, Slovak). It is important to note, however, that even among people who speak another language, most are anxious to preserve and protect their native tongues. Thus, all 23 of the main languages in the EU are treated as working languages, and extensive translation and interpreting services are maintained despite their considerable cost.

As noted above, English is increasingly becoming Europe's lingua franca. In countries such as Sweden and the Netherlands, over half of the population speaks English as a second language (fig. 4.12). In almost all EU countries, students are far more likely to study English as a second language rather than German, French, Spanish, or Italian. Even in eastern Europe, Russian and German have been overshadowed by English. This development has raised some concerns, particularly in France, where the government

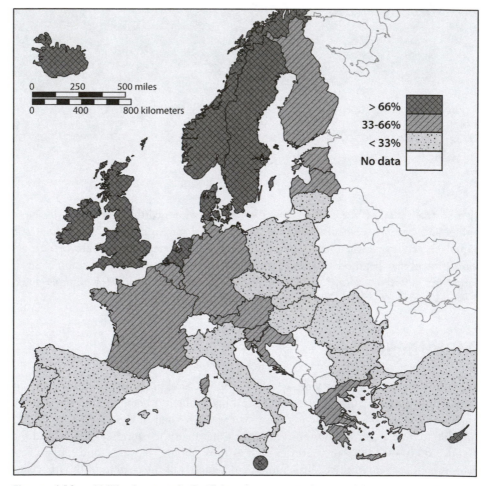

Figure 4.12.   Ability to speak English, as a percentage of total population, by national units and selected dependent territories. *Sources:* Eurobarometer and selected national statistical yearbooks.

has taken steps to purge the French language of English vocabulary. In other parts of Europe, serious questions are being raised about what might be lost if languages lose standing or are radically changed by the rush toward English. Others, however, see this as merely the latest phase in a process of linguistic evolution that is as old as humanity itself.

Controversies over multilingualism are also present in states with significant populations speaking more than one language. Despite the role of the state in spreading and standardizing languages, there are many places in Europe where the political and language boundaries do not coincide. As we have seen, some of these cases involve relatively small language groups fighting for their survival. In other cases, speakers of one major language spill across the border into adjacent countries (e.g., French speakers in northwest Italy, German speakers in Belgium and Italy). In yet other cases, a substantial population (more than 5%) in a state speaks a minority language (e.g., Catalan speakers in Spain, Hungarian speakers in both Romania and Slovakia, Swedish speakers in Finland). Given that states have historically sought to foster a common identity based on a single language, these situations are fraught with controversy. In many cases, active ethnolinguistic movements have developed that seek to ensure not just language rights, but some degree of political autonomy (see Chapter 6).

Multilingualism is a particularly important issue in Switzerland and Belgium, where sizable populations (greater than 30%) speak two or more languages in different parts of the country. Both states are officially multilingual, and the central governments have little say over language matters. Switzerland has a long tradition of multilingualism and an internal administrative structure that vests substantial power in cantons, units that are even smaller than language regions. Hence, language has not been a source of great controversy there. Belgium, by contrast, developed initially as a French-language state despite its majority Dutch/Flemish-speaking population, because the ruling elite in the nineteenth century was largely French-speaking. The legacy of attempting to create a single-language state, combined with an internal administrative structure that gives each major language group a single region, has turned language into a major source of social friction in that country. Controversies over relations between the country's two major ethnolinguistic groups have intensified to the point that some are questioning whether Belgium can hold together as a state.

Arguments over language serve as an important reminder that cultural phenomena are a product of the ideas and practices that develop in different places. They are, in other words, influenced by their geographical situation. If that is true of language, it is certainly true of religion, which is the topic of the next chapter.

Sources and Suggested Readings

Aitchison, J.W. and H. Carter. 1994. *A Geography of the Welsh Language, 1961–1991.* Cardiff: University of Wales Press.

———. 1999. Cultural Empowerment and Language Shift in Wales. *Tijdschrift voor Economische en Sociale Geografie* 90: 168–183.

Alinei, M., et al. 1983. *Atlas Linguarum Europae*, vol. 1. Assen, the Netherlands: van Gorcum.

Bellwood, P. 2005. *First Farmers: The Origins of Agricultural Societies.* Malden, MA: Blackwell.

Beynon, E.D. 1941. The Eastern Outpost of the Magyars. *Geographical Review* 31: 63–78.

Blomkvist, Y.E. 1985. Settlements of the Eastern Slavs. *Soviet Geography* 26: 183–198, 268–283.

Buchanan, K. 1977. "Economic Growth and Cultural Liquidation: The Case of the Celtic Nations." In *Radical Geography: Alternative Viewpoints on Contemporary Social Issues*, ed. R. Peet, 125–143. Chicago: Maaroufa.

Augusto, C., et al. 2003. Asserting Ethnic Identity and Power through Language. *Journal of Ethnic & Migration Studies* 29 (5): 865–883.

Chinn, J. and R. Kaiser. 1996. *Russians as the New Minority.* Boulder: Westview.

Coluzzi, P. 2006. Minority Language Planning and Micronationalism in Italy: The Cases of Lombardy and Friuli. *Journal of Multilingual & Multicultural Development* 27(6): 457–471.

Comrie, B. 1994. "Northern Asia and Eastern Europe." In *Atlas of the World's Languages*, eds C. Moseley and R. E. Asher, 219–244. London: Routledge.

Cornish, V. 1936. *Borderlands of Language in Europe and their Relations to the Historic Frontiers of Christendom.* London: Sifton.

Cvijic, J. 1918. The Geographical Distribution of the Balkan Peoples. *Geographical Review* 5: 345–361.

Dominian, L. 1917. *The Frontiers of Language and Nationality in Europe*, Special Publication No. 3. New York: American Geographical Society.

Dugdale, J.S. 1969. *The Linguistic Map of Europe.* London: Hutchinson University Library.

Fernández-Armesto, F., ed. 1994. *The Times Guide to the Peoples of Europe.* London: Times Books.

Geipel, J. 1969. *The Europeans: An Ethnohistorical Survey.* London: Longmans.

Goetschy, H., and A-L Sanguin, eds. 1995. *Langues Régionales et Relations Transfrontalières en Europe.* Paris: Harmattan.

Gordon, R.G. 2005. *Ethnologue: Languages of the World*, 15th ed. Dallas: SIL International.

Greenberg, J.H. 2000. *Indo-European and its Closest Relatives: The Eurasiatic Language Family.* Stanford: Stanford University Press.

Grüll, J. 1965. Entwicklung und Bestand der Rätoromanen in den Alpen. *Mitteilungen der Österreichischen Geographischen Gesellschaft* 107: 86–103, 117.

Hindley, R. 1990. *The Death of the Irish Language: A Qualified Obituary.* London: Routledge.

Jones, P., and M.T. Wild. 1992. Western Germany's "Third Wave" of Migrants: The Arrival of the Aussiedler. *Geoforum* 23: 1–11.

Kirk, J.M., S.F. Sanderson, and J.D.A. Widdowson, eds. 1985. *Studies in Linguistic Geography: The Dialects of English in Britain and Ireland.* London: Croom Helm.

Krantz, G.S. 1988. *Geographical Development of European Languages.* New York: Peter Lang.

Lautensach, H. 1954. Über die Topographischen Namen Arabischen Ursprungs in Spanien und Portugal. *Die Erde* 6: 219–243.

Lundén, T. 1988. Language, Geography and Social Development: The Case of Norden. In *Language in Geographic Context*, ed. C.H. Williams, 47–72. Clevedon: Multilingual Matters.

MacGiolla Chríost, D., and J.W. Aitchison. 1998. Ethnic Identities and Language in Northern Ireland. *Area* 30: 301–309.

Mackenzie, J.L. 1994. Western Europe. In *Atlas of the World's Languages*, eds. C.R Moseley and R. E. Asher, 245–261. London: Routledge.

Makkay, János, and J. Jamieson. 2003. An Archeologist Speculates on the Origin of the Finno-Ugrians. *Mankind Quarterly* 43(3): 235–272.

Mallory, J.P. 1989. *In Search of the Indo-Europeans: Language, Archaeology, and Myth.* London: Thames & Hudson.

Murphy, A.B. 1988. *The Regional Dynamics of Language Differentiation in Belgium: A Study in Cultural-Political Geography.* Chicago: University of Chicago, Geography Research Paper No. 227.

————. 1998. "European Languages." In *A European Geography*, ed. T. Unwin, 34–50. Harlow, Essex: Addison Wesley Longman.

Nash, C. 1999. Irish Placenames: Post-Colonial Locations. *Transactions of the Institute of British Geographers* 24: 457–480.

O'Luain, C. 1989. The Irish Language Today. *Europa Ethnica* 46(1): 1–10.

Orton, H., and N. Wright. 1974. *A Word Geography of England.* London: Seminar Press.

Pryce, W.T.R. 1975. Migration and the Evolution of Culture Areas: Cultural and Linguistic Frontiers in North-East Wales, 1750 and 1851. *Transactions of the Institute of British Geographers* 65: 79–108.

Renfrew, C. 1988. *Archaeology and Language: The Puzzle of Indo-European Origin.* Cambridge: Cambridge University Press.

————. 1989. The Origins of Indo-European Languages. *Scientific American* 261(4): 106–114.

Sanguin, A-L, ed. 1993. *Les Minorités Ethniques en Europe.* Paris: Harmattan.

Schwartz, L. 1991. USSR Nationality Redistribution by Republic, 1979–1989. *Soviet Geography* 32: 209–248.

Sopher, D.E. 1955. Arabic Place Names in Spain. *Names* 3: 5–13.

Straka, M. 1979. Karte der Völker und Sprachen Europas unter besonderer Berücksichtigung der Volksgruppen. Graz: Akademische Druck- u. Verlagsanstalt.

Vanhaeren, M., and F. d'Errico. 2006. Aurignacian Ethno-linguistic Geography of Europe Revealed by Personal Ornaments. *Journal of Archaeological Science* 33(8): 1105–1128.

Wilkinson, H.R. 1951. *Maps and Politics: A Review of the Ethnographic Cartography of Macedonia.* Liverpool: University Press.

Withers, C.W.J. 1984. *Gaelic in Scotland, 1698–1981: The Geographical History of a Language.* Edinburgh: Donald.

————. 1988. *Gaelic Scotland: The Transformation of a Culture Region.* London: Routledge.

Wixman, R. 1980. *Language Aspects of Ethnic Patterns and Processes in the North Caucasus.* Chicago: University of Chicago, Department of Geography, Research Paper No. 191.

————. 1981. Territorial Russification and Linguistic Russianization in Some Soviet Republics. *Soviet Geography* 22: 667–675.

————. 1984. "Demographic Russification and Linguistic Russianization of the Ukraine, 1959–1979." In *Geographical Studies on the Soviet Union*, eds. G.J. Demko and R.J. Fuchs, 131–156. Chicago: University of Chicago, Department of Geography, Research Paper No. 211.

CHAPTER 5

The Geography of Religion

Of all the human traits mentioned in Chapter 1 that have been used to define "Europe," the one that stands out most prominently across the sweep of time is religiosity. In the centuries preceding the Age of Exploration, Europe and Christianity were viewed as nearly synonymous. Christian Europeans had been engaged in armed conflict with Muslims in the Mediterranean for centuries, strengthening their sense of collective identity based on religion. European colonialism led to the diffusion of Christianity to the far corners of the globe, but the idea of Europe as the center of Christianity was never lost. Pope John Paul II, in 1982, claimed that European identity "is incomprehensible without Christianity," that the faith "ripened the civilization of the continent, its culture, its dynamism, its activeness, its capacity for constructive expansion on other continents." That same impulse led some of the framers of a draft Constitution for the European Union in the early 2000s to call for a reference to Europe's Christian heritage in the document's preamble. They were unsuccessful, but the proposal and the debate that ensued provided a clear reminder of the historical role of Christianity in Europe's development.

From the perspective of the early twenty-first century, the foregoing point is easy to overlook because a dramatic turn toward secularism has occurred in Europe. Yet it is important to remember that Christianity is at the heart of much of what came out of Europe—both good and bad. Much of its great art, literature, music, and philosophy were inspired by Christianity. One cannot imagine European culture devoid of the magnificent cathedrals, altarpieces, crucifixes, and religious statuary. The *Commentaries* of Saint Thomas Aquinas, Leonardo da Vinci's *Last Supper,* Michelangelo's *David* and Sistine Chapel, the Kremlin in Moscow and the cathedral at Chartres, Dante's *Inferno* and Milton's *Paradise Lost* were all products of Christianity. Yet some of Europe's most intractable wars, its genocides, inquisitions, and colonial endeavors, were also inspired by Christianity.

However one views the Christian legacy, it is important to understand its foundations and geographical expression. This means focusing attention on the diffusion of Christianity in Europe, and its fragmentation into different branches (fig. 5.1). It also means situating Christianity within the context of other religious traditions that have been part of Europe's story.

Figure 5.1.   Religious groups in Europe. Significant minority religions within each country are shown by lowercase abbreviations (**c** = Catholic; **o** = Orthodox; **p** = Protestant; **i** = Islam) followed by the percentage of adherents to the minority religion found in each country. The figures for Russia are for Eurorussia, as defined in the Preface. *Sources: Eurobarometer*, Eurostat, and various national statistical yearbooks.

Pre-Christian Europe

Christianity was not native to Europe. In pre-Christian times, European religions were principally **polytheistic**—worshipping multiple divinities. Most groups practiced **animism,** which imbued objects such as rocks, heavenly bodies, mountains, forests, and rivers with souls.

A bewildering array of spirits, gods, and goddesses ruled over war, fertility, woodlands, high places, caves, harvests, death, lightning, navigation, earthquakes, volcanoes, moon, sun, winds, and a hundred other domains. The Germanic Thor hurled thunderbolts, the Greek Aphrodite governed love and fertility, and the Roman Mars assisted in warfare. Thousands of shrines and altars dedicated to these divinities dotted the ancient landscape of Europe, many of which remain today as ruins (fig. 5.2). Some pre-Christian deities achieved more importance than others, often gaining acceptance over fairly large areas. A mother-fertility-love goddess, referred to by the Romans as *Magna Mater*—the great mother—was widely venerated throughout the Mediterranean lands, and *Mithras,* a male god originating in Persia, achieved widespread worship among the Roman military class. Especially strong in Greece, the *Mystery Cults* had a main center at Eleusis near Athens. In the western and northern fringes of Europe, astronomy-based religions of early Indo-European origin held sway, leaving us megalithic ruins such as Stonehenge, which is believed to have been a rather sophisticated observatory.

In other words, pre-Christian Europe was religiously divided and complex. That most of Europe should have been converted to a radically different, **monotheistic** faith—Christianity—seems amazing. Originally, the worship of a single male divinity

Figure 5.2.   Templed promontories of the ancient Aegean. The seagoing Greeks placed great importance upon promontories, both as hazards to sailing and as landmarks. Temples both heightened the visibility of the promontories and allowed placation of the relevant gods. *Source:* Semple 1927.

had been confined to Afro-Asiatic nomadic herders of the Near Eastern deserts. This tribal Semitic shepherd-god seemed ill-suited to the agricultural, polytheistic Indo-Europeans.

Diffusion of Christianity

The key figure in the remarkable diffusion of Christianity to Europe, the Apostle Paul, bridged the Semitic and Greek cultures; he presented monotheism in terms that were understandable and appealing to Europeans. Throughout the centuries of conversion, Christianity also proved adept at absorbing elements of the native religions of Europe. *Sun*day, devoted to a Roman god of the sun, became the Christian Sabbath; many of the old multiple divinities survived as saints; the Virgin Mary annexed the devotion afforded to the Mediterranean Magna Mater; Jehovah replaced the old king of the gods, Zeus/Jupiter/Odin; and the Mystery Cult promise of eternal life was honored by Christianity. The veneration of Mary remains strongest in the Mediterranean lands even today (fig. 5.3).

Pagan places of worship typically became Christian shrines and churches. For example, a rural church in Scotland stands atop a prehistoric artificial mound venerated since ancient times; the Alvestra monastery in south-central Sweden abuts standing stones dating from pre-Christian antiquity; and Canterbury Cathedral, seat of the Church of England, rests on the foundations of a solar-oriented pagan temple (fig. 5.4). Sacred groves from pagan times still stand protected alongside Greek monasteries, and springs holy to the pre-Christian Irish continue to be pilgrimage sites today.

Christianity largely destroyed the animistic belief that humans were part of nature, replacing it with the doctrine that God had given his people dominion over the environment. By removing the animistic sacredness of nature, some people believe that Christianity opened the way for the massive environmental modification that has so altered Europe's physical environment. Others, however, see these changes largely as the product of modernization and industrialization.

Initially, Christianity spread from city to city in the Roman Empire, leaving the intervening rural areas pagan. (The Latin word *pagus,* meaning "rural district," is the root of both the word *pagan* and *peasant.*) Similarly, the isolated, unconverted dwellers of the heaths gave rise to the word *heathen.* Christianity in Europe was, at first, an urban faith.

Perhaps one key to the concentration of the first European Christians in the cities of the Roman Empire lies in the Jewish **diaspora**. Early in the Christian era, the Romans dispersed most Jews from Israel in an attempt to quell their rebellions against imperial authority. Jews came as refugees to almost every Roman city throughout the Empire, and they clustered in ethnic neighborhoods. Evidence now suggests that those very neighborhoods often housed the first Christian congregations. In other words, certain Jewish people in their diaspora, already monotheists whose holy scriptures formed half the Christian Bible, may have become the earliest Christians in Europe, though many or even most Jews did not convert.

Figure 5.3.   Proportion of pilgrimage shrines dedicated to the Virgin Mary in modern Europe. Marian devotion is greatest in the Mediterranean lands, where the *Magna Mater* was venerated in pre-Christian times. Spain alone has some 22,000 Marian shrines. Catholic shrines dedicated to Christ and various saints are most common in the North and Alpine lands. *Source:* Nolan and Nolan 1989, 121.

Whatever the case, the spread of Christianity remained slow until 313 C.E., when the Roman emperor Constantine issued an edict of toleration for Christianity, which led eventually to its status as a state religion. In the centuries that followed, two major centers directed the diffusion of Christianity into Europe from its Mediterranean base: Latin Rome and Greek Byzantium (later Constantinople, and now Istanbul). The Roman Church spread rapidly in the western Mediterranean during the 4th and 5th centuries C.E. Before the fall of the empire, significant areas in what are now Italy, France, and Spain became converted, and many members of the Germanic tribes who subsequently overran these areas quickly accepted Christianity. From the western Mediterranean core, Roman missionaries spread far to the north. Patrick arrived in Ireland in 432, and a major cultural flowering occurred among the Celtic converts there. Many of the peoples of Britain, missionized from both

Figure 5.4. Kildrummy Church positioned atop an ancient artificial mound in the northern Scottish Highlands where pagans worshipped. Such juxtapositions occur frequently in all parts of Europe. (Photo by T.G.J.-B. 1992.)

Ireland and the continent, converted from the 400s through the early 600s C.E. (fig. 5.5).

Christianity lost ground in parts of western Europe with the disintegration of social and political institutions following the fall of the Roman Empire. However, missionary activity—often from peripheral locations in the British Isles and what we now call France—began to reclaim territory for the religion. The pagan tribes of Germany received missionaries beginning in the early 600s, and the Germans in turn carried the church to Scandinavians and Slavic Poles by about 1100. The pivotal event in Poland occurred in 966, when the principal local ruler allowed himself to be baptized, an event duplicated in Hungary in 973. The European work of Roman missionaries ended in 1386 with the conversion of the Balts in distant Lithuania. In carrying Christianity to the north, missionaries also took the Latin alphabet, and the zone of Roman mission work is fairly well indicated even today by the use of Latin characters.

The impressive gains in the north were partially offset by losses to Islam in the south. North Africa, where the Christian church had been well established, became permanently Muslim in the 700s, and much of Iberia fell under the control of Muslims for many centuries. The *Moors* (Islamicized Arabs) who came into Iberia respected those religions that possessed a written book of beliefs, so Christianity survived.

Figure 5.5.   Diffusion of Christianity to 1400 C.E. The faith spread in the early centuries by moving from city to city, while bypassing rural areas.

Greek Christians, centered in the Byzantine Empire, initially converted the Slavic tribes that had spread south of the Danube River into imperial territory. Mission work north of the Danube was hindered by repeated invasions of Asiatic tribes entering Europe through the steppe corridor and Valachian Plain between 550 and 1050 C.E. (fig. 5.5); but finally, in 988, Ukrainians and Russians became Christian. Missionaries working among the Slavs developed the Cyrillic alphabet, derived from the Greek characters, and the distribution of this script today, with some exceptions, parallels the extent of their church in Europe. Greek Christianity, like its Roman counterpart, lost ground in the south while winning converts in the north. Soon after 1200, the Byzantine Empire collapsed under Turkish pressure, eventually causing the loss of Asia Minor, and even the Christian center at Constantinople, to Islam.

Christian Fragmentation

Europe may appear to have been unified by Christianity, but this façade conceals major internal contrasts. Monolithic Christianity never existed in Europe. From the very first, the more ancient contrast between Greek and Roman civilizations dictated fragmentation. The claim of the Latin bishop of Rome to leadership of all Christendom never gained unqualified acceptance by the Greeks and the bishop of Byzantium. The subsequent split of the Empire into western and eastern halves presaged a major religious schism. In a separation made formal in 1054 C.E., the western church became Roman Catholicism, whereas the Byzantine Church became Eastern Orthodoxy. The dividing line between Catholicism and Orthodoxy remains the most fundamental religious border in Europe today (fig. 5.1). It has changed little in a thousand years, and provides the basis for important contrasts between west and east in Europe.

The second great schism occurred in the 1500s, when western Christianity split, the southern lands remaining Catholic and the north becoming Protestant (fig. 5.6). Protestantism arose in different places over several centuries in an attempt to bring about reforms within the Roman church. The pivotal event, the challenge to the church issued by Martin Luther at Wittenberg, Germany, in 1517, evolved into successful secession. The new church quickly spread through northern Germany and the Scandinavian lands, supported by the rulers of individual states. John Calvin furthered the Protestant cause in the mid-1500s from his base in Switzerland, dispersing a set of ideas that gave rise to Puritanism in England, Presbyterianism in Scotland, the Reformed Church in the Netherlands and Germany, and the Huguenot faith in France, as well as lesser groups of Calvinist followers in eastern Europe. Also in Switzerland, Ulrich Zwingli led a Protestant movement in the German-speaking cantons. A number of Anabaptist Protestant sects also arose, including the Mennonites in the Netherlands. These people rejected infant baptism and offered the rite only to adult believers. An additional breakaway from Roman Catholicism came in 1534, when King Henry VIII created the Church of England, also known as the Anglican Church.

Henry VIII's initiative was not simply a matter of differing beliefs; it reflected a desire on the part of the English monarch to free himself and his domain from the influence of Rome. This same desire led political leaders in other parts of northern Europe, including some states within the German Empire, to adopt Protestantism as the official religion. The spread of Protestantism was not simply a product of individual conversion, then; in many cases it was imposed from above by state leaders. To this day, many northern European countries have an official state religion, even though freedom of religious practice is guaranteed.

The Protestant breakaway reinforced a significant north-south cultural divide in Europe. The religious border between Catholicism and Protestantism had pretty much stabilized by 1570, though the dreadful Thirty Years' War between Catholics and Protestants still lay ahead (compare figs. 5.1 and 5.6). As a result of the two Christian schisms, Europe acquired three major religious regions: a Roman Catholic region, a Protestant region, and an Eastern Orthodox region.

Figure 5.6.   Diffusion of Protestantism to 1570 C.E. The Reformation spread from several different nuclei to influence most of Northern and Central Europe.

ROMAN CATHOLICISM

About 230 million Europeans are practicing or nominal Roman Catholics today, roughly 32% of the total population. **Roman Catholicism** is practiced across a huge region, stretching from Iberia and Italy in the south to Lithuania in the north, and from Ireland in the west to Croatia and Hungary in the east. In some countries, such as Spain, Catholicism is overwhelmingly prevalent, but many regions, particularly along the contact zones with Protestantism and Orthodoxy, exhibit considerable denominational variety.

Roman Catholicism remains a relatively united church oriented toward the papacy, and Vatican City is the seat of a highly centralized administration (fig. 5.7). At the same

Figure 5.7. **St. Peter's in the Vatican City,** the papal seat and center of European and world Roman Catholicism. The Roman Catholic Church retains a viable central authority, based here in a small independent state. (Photo by T.G.H.-B. 1989.)

time, regional differences exist. Irish Catholicism is not the same as Italian or Lithuanian Catholicism, and the church has encouraged national patron saints and other regional qualities to persist. Individual districts and valleys often boast their own patron saints and shrines. For example, in the Bética mountains south of Granada in Spain lies the highly distinctive region of Las Alpujarras, where the town of Ugijar proudly houses the sanctuary of Our Lady of the Martirio, "patroness of Las Alpujarras." In this manner, Catholicism heightens, and draws strength from, a local sense of place.

Catholicism has certainly shaped the landscape over time. Geographers speak of **cultural landscapes**—the visual, varied trace of human presence as revealed in the assemblage of tangible physical and human characteristics making up an area—and significant parts of Europe can be said to display a Catholic landscape. Among the most obvious religious contributions to the landscape are sacred structures, especially the church buildings. Europe exhibits many regional contrasts in church size, building material, and architectural style. In Catholic areas, the church structures tend to be large and visually inspiring, in part because the Roman church places great value on visible beauty. Catholic landscapes gain additional distinctiveness from the numerous roadside shrines and chapels that dot the countryside.

Catholicism also influenced the names people gave to places and physical features. In Catholic countries, the custom of naming towns for Christian saints was common. Often, saintly suffixes were added to pre-existing settlements, as in Alcazar de San Juan in Spain. The frequency of such sacred names decreases to the north in Europe, and they are rarely found in Protestant lands. In Germany, some three-quarters of the towns and villages bearing the saintly prefix *Sankt* lie in the Catholic-dominated southern part of the country, including 21% in the province of Bavaria alone. Cross the religious divide into Protestant Germany, and saints largely disappear from place names.

Catholicism has also left a distinctive economic imprint on its part of Europe. For example, the Catholic tradition of avoiding meat on Friday and on numerous church holidays greatly stimulated the development of the fishing industry. The church encouraged the use of fish during periods of fasting and penitence, as well as on Friday. Seashore Catholics, such as Basques, Bretons, Galicians, and Portuguese, are among the greatest fishing peoples of Europe. Saint Peter, the original Christian fisherman, holds a place of special veneration in the fishing villages of Catholic Europe. The importance of the Catholic Church to fishing is suggested by the economic crisis in English fishing communities when Catholic dietary restrictions ended as a result of the Anglican breakaway in the 1500s. Many fishermen were obliged to become sailors, perhaps leading to the great era of English naval exploration, piracy, and overseas colonization.

Pilgrimages

An even more profound economic influence of Catholicism results from the Church's enduring practice of religious pilgrimages. Favored holy sites have long derived considerable financial benefit. In Catholic Europe, tens of millions of pilgrims travel to thousands of holy places each year. Pilgrimage sites vary in importance, ranging from small shrines that attract only the faithful from the immediate surroundings, to internationally known places sought out by Catholics from all over Europe and the Americas. Pilgrimage sites are unevenly distributed in Europe, even within Catholic areas (fig. 5.8). In France, for example, pilgrimage sites devoted to the Virgin Mary lie mainly in the south and west, with a few isolated clusters elsewhere in the country (fig. 5.3).

Vatican City draws millions of Catholic visitors to Rome each year, adding to the already important tourist trade based on antiquities. As recently as the 1700s, most long-distance travel of people within Europe involved pilgrims going to Rome and a few other religious centers. Many roads developed mainly for pilgrim traffic, complete with hospices at difficult places such as mountain passes. Monks built bridges along these routes.

The major present-day pilgrimage sites, in addition to Rome, include Lourdes, a French town at the foot of the Pyrenees in the Basin of Aquitaine where the Virgin Mary supposedly appeared in a vision; Fátima, north of Lisboa in Portugal; Czestochowa, where the greatest icon of Polish Catholicism, the miraculous Black Virgin, is housed; Medjugorje, in the Croatian Catholic district of Bosnia-Herzegovina, where the faithful believe the Virgin Mary appeared repeatedly beginning in 1981; and Santiago de Compostela in Spanish Galicia, a medieval site associated with St. James (fig. 5.8, 5.9). Fátima alone attracts over five million pilgrims annually, as does Lourdes. In the centennial year of the miracle at Lourdes in 1958, an astounding 8 million visitors came to

Figure 5.8.   Pilgrimage shrines in Western Europe. Each dot represents a shrine that is the most important in its diocese and/or draws at least 10,000 pilgrims per year. In the shaded areas, remarkable concentrations of lesser shrines occur. Pilgrimage is largely a Roman Catholic phenomenon, as the distribution suggests. Only a small selection of eastern European shrines is shown. Key to symbols for most famous shrines: **B** = Beauraing; **C** = Czestochowa; **F** = Fátima; **K** = Knock; **L** = Lourdes; **M** = Medjugorje; **R** = Rome; **S** = Santiago de Compostela. *Source:* In part from Nolan and Nolan 1989, 29, 31, 32.

the area. Small wonder that this small provincial town ranks second in France only to Paris in number of hotels.

PROTESTANTISM

Protestantism is the traditional faith of the European north, centered in the lands around the shores of the North and Baltic seas (fig. 5.1). Some 110 million Protestants live in Europe, forming roughly 15% of the total population.

In marked contrast to Catholicism, the most profound geographical feature of European Protestantism is its fragmentation into separate denominational regions, a

Figure 5.9.   Pilgrims at Santiago de Compostela, the greatest of the shrines in Spain and a goal of pilgrims since the Middle Ages. It lies in Galicia. (Photo by T.G.J.-B. 1999.)

splintering present from the very first due to the work of multiple Reformation leaders (fig. 5.6). Lutheranism has the largest geographical distribution, including the Scandinavian countries, Iceland, Estonia, Finland, Latvia, and half of Germany (figs. 5.1, 5.10). No central Lutheran authority exists in Europe, and the faith is divided into a series of independent national churches.

The Anglican denomination remains the official established church in England, with lesser branches in the other British provinces, as well as in Ireland; and Presbyterianism, derived from Calvinism, enjoys the status of official Church of Scotland, with some 2 million adherents. The United Kingdom also has an array of so-called *free churches*, which lack official status but are nevertheless traditional denominations of long standing. The largest of these is Methodism (with some 800,000 adherents), with lesser numbers of Baptists and many others. The Dutch Reformed Church, another Calvinist-derived body, is centered in the northern Netherlands. In 2004 it merged with the Evangelical Lutheran Church to form the Protestant Church in the Netherlands—with some 2.3 million adherents. In Switzerland, the Protestant majority belongs to a church that combines Calvinist, Lutheran, and Zwinglian influences. About all that remains of the work of Jan Hus, the first Reformation leader, is a community of some 120,000 Brethren in Czechia.

All of these traditional Protestant groups in Europe have experienced sharp declines, particularly since 1900. Neo-Protestantism provides an exception. In the past several decades, evangelical-fundamentalist groups, often based in the United States,

Figure 5.10. **A rural Lutheran church** in southwestern Iceland. This modest, Gothic-influenced structure is typical of the Protestant cultural landscape in Iceland, a European outpost in the North Atlantic. (Photo by T.G.J.-B. 1971.)

have begun actively missionizing Europe, both in the Protestant north and the formerly Communist east (fig. 5.11). Pentecostals, Jehovah's Witnesses, Seventh-Day Adventists, and Baptists have been especially active. Ethnic minorities, such as the Sami of the far north and South Asians in the United Kingdom, have been particularly attracted to neo-Protestantism, but the phenomenon is widespread. Cultural links with Latin America brought charismatic Evangelical groups to Roman Catholic Spain. These neo-Protestant communities are predominantly concentrated in urban centers. Romania, perhaps typical of Eastern Europe, now has about 550,000 converts. In Russia, neo-Protestantism won many new members after the collapse of the Soviet Union.

As a result of the diversity of European Protestantism, no single religious land-scape has been produced. As a rule, however, Protestantism is less visible than Catholicism. Church buildings tend to be smaller and less ornate, pilgrimage places are absent, and no wayside shrines line the roadsides (fig. 5.10). Some Protestant groups traditionally rejected all visible ostentation, rendering their presence almost invisible. For example, the modest Methodist chapels of Wales, lacking steeples and stained glass, often prove difficult for the uninitiated even to identify as places of wor-ship (fig. 5.12).

Instead, Protestant influences manifest themselves in other aspects of European cul-ture. Individualism, so central a trait in modern European culture, may have its roots in the Protestant Reformation. The far-reaching **Industrial Revolution** (see Chapter 8),

Figure 5.11. Neo-Protestant church in southern Sweden. The church buildings are humble in appearance. Evangelical Christians have won many converts in Scandinavia and Finland. (Photo by T.G.J.-B. 1989.)

which so profoundly reshaped European culture, also has ties to Protestantism. The inherently dynamic character of Protestantism, the willingness of its adherents to accept change and strive for self-improvement, coupled with the Protestant ethic of hard work and the rejection of Catholic restrictions on lending money for interest, provided necessary social precedents for the Industrial Revolution. Modern industrialism arose in Protestant lands and only belatedly spread into Catholic and Orthodox areas, though nonreligious factors such as the location of coal deposits help explain some industrial origin and dispersal. Earlier, Catholic persecution of French Calvinists (or Huguenots) and Protestant Flemings, including many skilled artisans, caused an emigration of these craftsmen to England, northern Germany, and Holland. The Protestant countries thereby gained a valuable industrial impetus, while the Catholic lands, particularly France, lagged behind.

Given such attitudinal and cultural contrasts, it is not surprising that the Protestant-Catholic border, helping divide Europe into north and south, witnessed much strife over the centuries. The Thirty Years' War (1618–1648), a Protestant-Catholic contest for possession of the core of Europe, devastated large areas of Germany and Czechia and caused enormous loss of life. Two centuries earlier the Hussite war, a similar contest, also caused much grief. Most of the religious border has since fallen quiet, and the two groups learned to live in peace. Only in Northern Ireland, where the population is fairly evenly divided between Protestants and Catholics, does the feud persist—and

Figure 5.12.   This Methodist chapel in the Lleyn Peninsula of Celtic Wales reflects the architectural simplicity preferred by British "free" churches. (Photo by the T.G.J.-B. 1974.)

this has as much to do with nationalism as it does with religion. An intrusive British-Protestant conquest and colonization occurred in Northern Ireland in the 1600s, followed by centuries of overlordship and attempted conversion of native Irish Catholics by the Protestants. During the second half of the twentieth century, the province suffered from terrorist activity by extremists of both religious groups, with the result that Protestants and Catholics became increasingly segregated (fig. 5.13). Over the past two decades a set of agreements between the British and the Irish have served to reduce tensions, and in 2006 significant powers were formally given to a Northern Ireland Assembly (seated in 2007) with representation from both communities. Nonetheless, residential segregation remains high, particularly among the middle and lower classes, although public spaces and institutions are becoming more integrated.

EASTERN ORTHODOXY

As its name implies, **Eastern Orthodox** Christianity prevails in the eastern part of Europe, especially in Greece, most of the Balkans, Ukraine, Belarus, Georgia and Russia (fig. 5.1). Some 150–200 million Europeans profess this faith, roughly 20–28% of the total population of Europe. The Eastern Church, steeped in mysticism and communalism, retains more of the qualities of the original Christianity, unaltered by the Renaissance, Reformation, and Enlightenment.

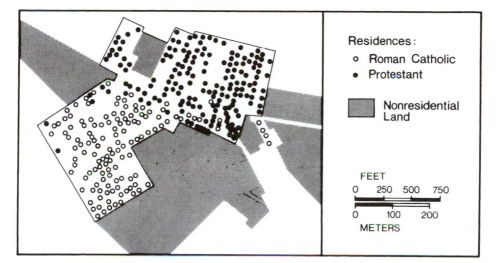

Figure 5.13.   On the Protestant-Catholic divide, in Belfast, Northern Ireland. Only here does strife continue on the great north-south religious border in Europe, with the result that people have become residentially segregated along denominational lines. *Source:* Boal 1969, 37.

The Patriarch of Constantinople, nominal leader of Orthodoxy, enjoys none of the central authority of the Roman papacy. Orthodoxy long ago began splintering into an array of national churches, including Greek, Serbian, Bulgarian, Romanian, Russian, Cypriot, Estonian, Georgian, and two Ukrainian Orthodox groups. The leadership at Constantinople, or Istanbul, was permanently weakened when this capital of eastern Christendom fell to the Turks in 1453. Only a few thousand Christians remain in Istanbul today. In 1996, the Russian Orthodox Church severed all ties to the Patriarch.

Splintering extended still further. In Russia, the ultraconservative Old Believers separated from Orthodoxy in the late 1600s, and some 10 million followers lived in different parts of Russia by 1910. Today, only about 70,000 remain, centered in Belarus, Latvia, Lithuania, and Russia, though a revival appears to be underway. Another conservative splinter group, the *Molokans,* dating from the 1700s, once had over a million followers; today surviving parishes can be found in the Caucasus, south Russia, Ukraine, and Moldova. In 1991, the splintering continued when the Free Orthodox Church broke away from established Russian Orthodoxy.

The Orthodox religious landscape shares with that of Catholicism a beauty and vividness, while at the same time being both highly distinctive and regionally varied. Balkan church buildings, borrowing from the colorful and decorative Byzantine architectural style of the south, attract the eye with abundant reds and yellows. Russian churches and monasteries display their own style, often built of wood with distinctive onion-shaped domes (fig. 5.14).

The Orthodox Church today is experiencing something of a revival in the Slavic north, after eight decades of governmental oppression. In Russia and Ukraine, hundreds

Figure 5.14.   A venerable wooden Russian Orthodox church, in the town of Suzdal, east of Moscow. Eastern Orthodoxy produces distinctive regional religious landscapes. (Photo by T.G.J.-B. 1999.)

of churches and cathedrals have been restored or built anew. A mass campaign was organized throughout Russia to rebuild the cathedral of Christ the Savior in downtown Moscow, which was razed on Stalin's orders in 1931. During the 1990s, when the Russian economy was in shambles and people were struggling to eke out a living, almost one billion dollars was collected from Russian citizens for the restoration of this spectacular structure, which now occupies a significant place in the cityscape of the Russian capital (fig. 5.15).

The contemporary Orthodox Church in Russia encompasses a range of beliefs and practices, but a close tie has developed between one wing of the Church and ardent Russian nationalists. Many nationalists believe that Orthodoxy is at the heart of Russian culture and has played a fundamental role in the development of the Russian state. Some worry that the Orthodox Church will come increasingly under the sway of the more extreme variants of Russian nationalism.

The East-West Divide

The western border of Orthodoxy remains the most fundamental internal cultural divide in Europe. In the Orthodox realm, east of this line, individualism, personal freedom, and materialism are only weakly developed, whereas communalism is strong. This may help explain why concepts of democracy and the market economy have shallower historical roots in the east than the west.

The border between Eastern and Western Christianity is both stable in location and well-marked on the cultural landscape. Perhaps the best place to observe this ancient divide is the small Russian town of Pechory, situated directly on the Estonian border, a remarkable outpost of the Greco-Russian religious world. An impressive and beautiful Orthodox monastery, itself a pilgrimage destination, dominates Pechory, announcing visibly this perimeter of the Orthodox realm (fig. 5.16). A scant few kilometers away lies Estonia, belonging to the Western Christian tradition.

A very short distance from Pechory stands the ruined stone fortress of Izborsk, built over a millennium ago to fend off invaders from the west. Just beyond Izborsk, towards the provincial city of Pskov, is the venerated place where the Russian hero-prince, Aleksandr Nevsky, met and crushed a German Catholic military order, the Teutonic Knights, on the ice of frozen Chudskoye Lake in 1242—a victory commemorated by a huge statue and monument. Nevsky's defiant words, "Who comes here bearing a sword will die by the sword," are still remembered by Russians.

For a thousand years and more, then, this segment of the great European cultural divide has been marked and defended. All who would understand the multiplicity of European culture should come to this place. Go stand on this same line much farther south, in the Balkans. Listen, with author Michael Ignatieff, to a Serbian militiaman— a representative of the Orthodox east—as he explains how the neighboring Catholic Croats (who speak the same language, Serbo-Croatian) differ from Serbs. "Those Croats, they think they're better than us. Think they're fancy Europeans." The guns of war fell silent over a half-century ago at Pechory, but in the Balkans the east-west war flared anew at the end of the twentieth century.

Figure 5.15.   The Cathedral of Christ the Savior in Moscow. The church, shown under construction here, was completed in 2000. (Photo by T.G.J.-B. 1999.)

Figure 5.16.   The great monastery at Pechory, in far western Russia, is an Orthodox outpost on Europe's main religious divide. (Photo by T.G.J.-B. 1999.)

Uniate and Armenian Churches

A fourth, minor division of European Christianity consists of the **Uniate** Church, centered in western Ukraine and adjacent parts of Romania, Slovakia, Hungary, and Poland. Also referred to as Greek Catholic or Ukrainian Catholic, this church claims about 6 million adherents. It is that rarest of hybrids—an attempted merging of Eastern and Western Christianity, along the religious divide. The Uniate Church derives from the long Catholic Polish and Austrian rule of an Orthodox area. The Catholic monarchs demanded that their Orthodox subjects acknowledge the authority and supremacy of the Roman pope. Beneath that façade of Catholicism, the Uniate church retained most Orthodox rites and practices, such as a married priesthood. When Polish and Austrian rule ended, Uniate Christians suffered persecution by Russian czarist Orthodoxy and, later, Communists. When freedom of religion was restored in 1990, the church reemerged vigorously in the western part of Ukraine, becoming one statement of national identity. Some 2,000 parishes reopened, and the future of the revitalized Uniate Church seems secure.

The **Armenian Orthodox Apostolic Church**, founded by apostles Thaddeus and Bartholomew, is officially a branch of Eastern Christianity. Yet it has an independent status because it never acknowledged the supremacy of the Patriarch at Constantinople. Its liturgy is close to Latin rites, and priests below the rank of a bishop can marry before ordination. This autocephalic ethnic church, with about 2 million adherents, is one of the oldest branches of Christendom and today survives in independent Armenia, at Europe's southeastern edge.

Dechristianization

A substantial part of the European population is secularized. Terms such as *dechristianization* and *post-Christian* have been used to describe modern Europe. More than a quarter of Europe's total population does not profess belief in any religion. The geographical pattern of dechristianization is complicated (fig. 5.17). In some regions, especially in the north and east, over half of the population is secularized, as in most of Scandinavia, Euro-Russia, the United Kingdom, the Netherlands, and Czechia. Eastern Germany—the formerly communist area—is thoroughly dechristianized, as are significant parts of France and Bulgaria. If measured by national units, the most thoroughly secular countries are Estonia, with over 72% of its population claiming to be unreligious, agnostic, and/or atheist; Czechia 60%; Russia 50%; France 48%; Denmark 42%; the Netherlands 41; Germany 29% and the United Kingdom 23.2% (fig. 5.17). Attendance at mass among Catholics has declined drastically just within the last three decades: to only 10% in the Netherlands, 12% in France, 15% in Germany and Austria, 18% in Spain, and 25% in Italy. Of course attendance at religious services does not indicate a lack of religious belief. In Russia, 66% of those who identified themselves as "believers" have never attended a religious service. But the trend away from religion is marked. Even in Ireland, once a bastion

Figure 5.17. Population in European countries that is secular (percentage). *Secular is defined as a combination of those who regard themselves as "atheist," "agnostic," "unreligious," "no religious faith," and "never attend church." Sources: Eurobarometer 2005; U.S. Department of State. 2005. International Religious Freedom Report.*

of Catholic strength, more than 40% of the population today claims no religious faith.

Within Euro-Russia, the northern regions are clearly the most disaffected. By contrast, refuge regions of surviving Christian vitality include a belt from Poland through western Ukraine to Romania, nearly all of Greece, southern Italy, western Iberia, the Irish west, and an area overlapping parts of the Alps and the Po-Veneto Plain. In Greece, 98% of the people claim to be religious, and in Portugal 85% claim to be. Moreover, active efforts are being made to promote religion in some areas. For example, in the German province of Bavaria, part of the Alpine zone of religious intensity and a center of Catholicism, the parliament in 1995 passed a law requiring crucifixes to be hung in all school classrooms, defying a Supreme Court ruling against this practice and citing "the historical and cultural character of Bavaria."

The decades-long persecution of the church under Communist regimes in the east clearly helps explain the dechristianization pattern there, though it does not address the issues of how Polish Catholicism, Romanian Orthodoxy, or the Ukrainian Uniate Church so successfully resisted that oppression, or why Scandinavia and Britain are so secular. Of the three main divisions of Christianity, Catholicism clearly resisted secularization most successfully, whereas Protestantism has suffered the greatest losses. In formerly Lutheran-dominated Latvia, only 5% of the people claim to be actively involved in a church, while in the United Kingdom some 40% of the adult population never attends church.

Some dechristianization may be a reaction against established churches, particularly since these churches often have official status and are supported by tax revenues. It can work the other way, too. Professed devotion to the church can be a reaction to governmental suppression, as happened in Poland during the Communist era. For these reasons, a better measure of secularization in a Christian realm might be the proportion of the population that prays at least once a week. By this measure, Poland at 74% and Portugal at 66% appear fairly religious, but not as much as one might expect. By contrast, religiosity as measured by regular prayer appears to be quite low in Sweden (17%) and Czechia (15%).

Though many Europeans hold secular views, the influence of a Christian heritage still permeates the culture of Europe. An entire mindset, a way of thinking and viewing the world, was shaped by Christianity. That cornerstone of European culture is unlikely to disappear. True, some say that secularized Europe lives on "old capital" inherited from Christianity, its basic institutions supported only by inertia, but others counter that agnostic intellectual freedom, unfettered by religious dogma, represents the logical culmination of the European experiment in reason and individualism.

Sects and Cults

Dechristianization during the twentieth century has left the door open to other ideologies. Some argue that Communism spread as rapidly as it did because it was positioned to fill the void. Indeed, Communist ideology incorporated some precepts associated with Christianity, such as the victorious proletariat ("the meek shall inherit the earth"), spreading the Revolution (missionizing the world), and the almost God-like status of Marx and Lenin (presented as new Russian icons, or holy images). For others, nationalism became the new faith, as in Nazi Germany.

Others have turned to New Age sects and cults. In Britain, Druids have reappeared and now make regular pilgrimages to ancient sites such as Stonehenge. Nearby Glastonbury has become the focus of several New Age cults. The French government has identified 172 sectarian movements with some 400,000 followers. Their activities have sometimes raised concerns. In the mid-1990s, the Order of the Solar Temple, active in both Switzerland and France, conducted two mass suicides. In response, French authorities tightened their scrutiny and regulation of sects, but these initiatives have raised concerns about religious freedom in some circles. Religious freedom is also an issue in Germany, where Scientologists claim to be the object of discrimination and oppression. Germany does not recognize Scientology as a religion, and the governments of both France and Germany have brought legal charges against the group for fraud and tax-evasion.

Non-Christian Minorities

ISLAM

The diffusion of Christianity through Europe proved almost complete, leaving little in the way of minority religions. Today, the only substantial non-Christian presence consists of Muslims, or **Islamic** peoples. For the past 1,200 years, the southern and southeastern borders of the Europe have coincided with the Christian-Muslim religious divide, a boundary that has shifted back and forth in the face of frequent warfare (fig. 5.1). In recent times, the border has taken on socio-economic meaning—with the Christian-Muslim divide often representing a fault line in prosperity, living standards, and population growth rates. This has helped to fuel an "us versus them" dynamic between those of Christian and Muslim heritage.

As is true of nearly every cultural border, there is no sharp geographic divide between Christians and Muslims. Only the Strait of Gibraltar offers a clear-cut division, achieved by systematic ethnic cleansing centuries ago. Excluding Russia, nearly 23 million Muslims reside in modern Europe, and an additional 14–19 million Islamic adherents can be found in Russia. Most of Europe's Muslims live in ancient homelands, including parts of Bosnia, Albania, Kosovo, southern Bulgaria (the Pomak area), the Caucasus (Chechens, Ingushis, Dagestanis, Balkaris, Cherkessians, Abkhazis, and Adzhars), and on the southeastern margins of Russia's East European Plain and the Crimean Peninsula of Ukraine (Turkic Tatars and Bashkortis) (fig. 5.18).

Of the areas with long-standing Islamic populations, Islam is most notably on the rise in Russia. Between 1991 and 2003, the number of Islamic communities increased from 914 to 3,445. Since the fall of the Soviet Union, the number of mosques has increased from a mere 90 to some 4,000. These are concentrated mainly in the republics of Tatarstan and Bashkortostan, and the North Caucasus. Kazan, the capital of Tatarstan, located on the confluence site of the Volga and Kama rivers, was one of the first places where a grandiose Muslim mosque arose after the collapse of the Soviet Union. The mosque was built in the very heart of the Kazan Kremlin—hovering above the Russian Orthodox Church.

Looking farther west, some 12 million Muslims are the product of recent immigration streams to Europe, particularly from Turkey, North Africa, and Pakistan (fig. 5.18). France has approximately 6.1 million Muslims, largely Arabs; Germany has 3.2 million, mainly Turks and Kurds; and Great Britain, has 1.6 million, mainly from the Indian subcontinent. The French port city of Marseille alone has 200,000 Muslims in its population of 1,400,000, as well as some 50 mosques.

Europe's immigrant Muslims have faced considerable prejudice, hatred, and worse. Muslims have been attacked, and some mosques have been targets of vandalism,

Figure 5.18.   Muslim population in European countries (percentage). Europe's Muslim population has swelled in recent decades, first as guest workers came at the invitation of state governments, and then as their families and other immigrants followed.

including the large Paris mosque in 2005. Even though two-thirds of the North African Muslims of France no longer practice the faith and only 10% are devout, the government in 1999 banned Islamic headscarves for schoolgirls. One French political extremist declared Islam to be "incompatible with our civilization and our laws." Turks and Kurds face similar prejudice in Germany.

Sensitivities surrounding the Islamic presence in Europe were very much on display in 2006 when Pope Benedict XVI made reference to the comments of a fourteenth-century Byzantine emperor who described Islam as "evil and inhuman" and argued that jihad was "contrary to God's plan and to reason." Even though the Pope's apparent motive was to show how Islam had been viewed in the past rather than to endorse the Byzantine view, his words aroused strong reactions. Islamic communities were outraged that the Pope would draw attention to such views, while the European ultra-right applauded. The Italian Prime Minister, Silvio Berlusconi, weighed in with a comment that incited passions further—calling Benedict's remarks "an open, a positive provocation, and so for this reason he is a great pope, with a great intelligence." Given such attitudes, can Muslim immigrants ever be accepted as Europeans?

Hostility toward Islam in Europe is directed not just toward recent immigrants, but also toward Muslim peoples living in their ancestral homelands. Catholic Croats and Orthodox Serbs battered Bosnian Muslim enclaves in the 1990s with a ferocity reminiscent of the Crusades. On Europe's southern cultural frontier, Armenians recently warred against Muslim Azeris, Georgians against Abkhazis, and Greek Cypriots against Turkish Cypriots (fig. 5.17). Muslim Chechens defy Russian rule today, but at great human cost, and other Caucasus Islamic minorities could follow Chechnya's example. Serbian leaders tried to cleanse Kosovo of Albanian Muslims; and Bulgaria, in 1989, expelled hundreds of thousands of Muslim Turks, most of whom later returned. Earlier, in 1877–1878, many Muslims were expelled from Bulgaria, causing it to become a Christian majority country. Tensions between Orthodox Greece and Muslim Turkey never completely relaxed, and the two countries fought a war in the 1920s. Clearly, Islam has given focus to European cultural identity over time, even as many today see it as a threat to that identity. Against this backdrop, it is not difficult to see why Turkey's application to join the European Union has met such resistance (see Chapter 12).

Of course hostility does not run in only one direction. Europe has been a seedbed for Islamic extremism. Terrorist cells in Germany were implicated in the September 11, 2001, attacks on the United States, and in the early 2000s Europeans faced major terrorist bombings by self-described Islamic militants in London and Madrid. Some mosques in Britain, Spain, and Germany have been recruiting grounds for disaffected Muslims, who are encouraged to think of Europeans of Christian heritage as the enemy. And of course this all fuels a widening divide along religious lines.

There are some hopeful signs, though. In the mid-1990s a European Monitoring Centre on Racism and Xenophobia was established to document, and draw attention to, instances of discrimination and harassment against Muslims. Reconstituted as the European Agency on Fundamental Rights in 2007, the organization has released high-profile reports documenting the challenges faced by Muslims in Europe. Efforts to educate people about the nature and diversity of Islam are being actively pursued, and in some instances legal protections have increased. Nonetheless, prejudice persists.

Contrary to the popular perception of some, Islamic fundamentalism and revival have generally not caught hold among most European Muslims. Indeed, Bosnians and Albanians had become secularized, even before the arrival of Communism in the 1940s. Incredibly, recent history has seen dechristianized Europeans battling secularized Muslims in the name of religious heritage and identity.

Islam's presence is certainly evident in the European landscape. In parts of southeastern Europe, the minarets of mosques pierce the sky as aggressively as the spires of Christian churches (fig. 5.19). In Iberia, reminders of the past Islamic presence are found in mosques that were converted into churches (fig. 5.20). In other parts of western Europe, mosques were relatively scarce before the 1960s, although the Grand Mosque of Paris, which opened in 1926, was long a notable exception (fig. 5.21).

Many new mosques have sprung up in western Europe over the last several decades as a consequence of the influx of migrants from North Africa and Southwest Asia. Some of these have been the object of controversy. The city of Cologne (Köln), which Pope Benedict XVI declared to be "the Rome of the North," has witnessed a heated debate about plans to build the largest mosque in Germany. Home to the largest number of Muslims in the country, Cologne already has 30 small mosques, but the local Muslim residents want a prestigious place of worship in the center of the

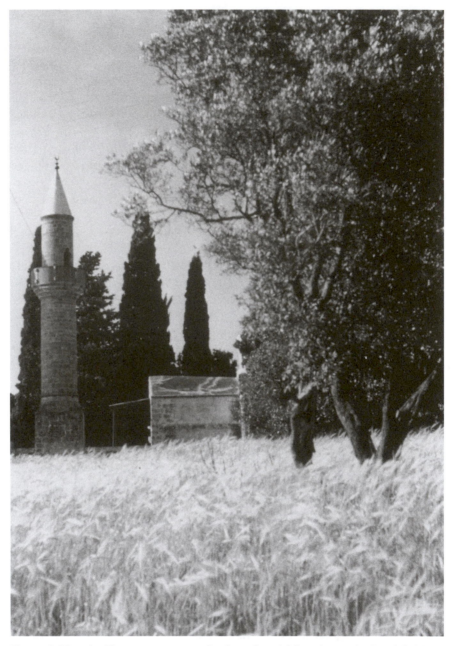

Figure 5.19.   A village mosque and minaret amid the ripened wheat fields of Rhodes announce the presence of the Muslim minority on this Greek Aegean Island. Rhodes is an area where Christians and Muslims co-exist peacefully. (Photo by T.G.J.-B. 1971.)

Figure 5.20. The Giralda, a tower on the Roman Catholic cathedral at Seville in southern Spain, was originally the minaret of the Great Mosque when the city was Arabic and Muslim. After the Christian "reconquest" and forced expulsion or conversion of the Muslims, victorious Christians added the bell chamber to the top. In this manner, a Muslim element was retained in the religious landscape. (Photo by T.G.J.-B. 1986.)

Figure 5.21. The Grand Mosque of Paris. The mosque was erected after World War I as a sign of gratitude for the Muslim military recruits from French colonies in North Africa who had fought along the French during the war. (Photo by A.B.M. 2000).

city—just across the Rhine from Cologne's grandiose, world-renowned, 700-year-old Gothic cathedral. As expected, strong opposition to the idea has come from ultra-right political groups, but the plan has also caused a stir in the broader community. The German-Jewish writer, Ralph Giordano, called the proposed mosque "an expression of creeping Islamicization of our land." Mosques have been erected in major German cities such as Berlin, Manheim, and Duisburg, but the scale of the new proposed Islamic structure in Cologne marks a dramatic change in the traditional European cityscape. Underlying much of the opposition to the structure is a concern that Europe is developing what some have called a "parallel Muslim society," in which new generations of immigrants opt not to assimilate but to create their own detached, if not always antagonistic, society (see Chapter 11). Such thinking is echoed by journalist Henryk Broder, who argues that "a mosque is more than a church or a synagogue. It is a political statement."

In an effort to counter such concerns, the Islamic community in some places has sought to keep landscape changes to a minimum. When a former Methodist church in the small town of Clitheroe, Lancashire, was sold to a local Muslim community to serve as a mosque, the cross was taken down. But no minarets were added, so that the familiar silhouette of a Christian edifice would remain a part of the town's historical landscape. As the leader of the local Muslim community explained, "There will be no external call to prayer. What matters is what goes on inside."

JUDAISM

The other sizable religious minority in Europe consists of adherents to Judaism, today numbering only about 1,500,000. Their fate at the hands of Europeans in the twentieth century is a grim reminder of the devastation human communities can visit on one another. As recently as 1939, Europe was the world's principal Jewish home, and the population stood at 9,700,000—about 60% of all Jews. In 1880, prior to the great Jewish migration to America, some 90% of all Jews in the world resided in Europe. Not only was Europe the principal home of Judaism, but Jews such as Albert Einstein, Felix Mendelssohn, Benjamin Disraeli, Sigmund Freud, and Heinrich Heine had contributed greatly to European history and civilization. It mattered little. Jews, in the mindset of Nazis, were not permitted to be Europeans and were murdered by the millions. Only 3,900,000 remained in Europe by the end of World War II—over half of whom have since emigrated.

France has more Jews in its population today (just under 500,000) than any other country, having received 220,000 Jews from Morocco and Algeria when those French colonies became independent in the 1950s and 1960s. French Jews live mainly on the Mediterranean coast and in Paris. The United Kingdom has just under 300,000 Jews, most of whom reside in greater London. Russia and Ukraine together retain only about 300,000 Jews. The number of Jewish religious communities, including synagogues and rabbinic schools, increased from 34 to 262 between 1991 and 2003, but the Jewish population in Ukraine has shrunk due to emigration. Remarkably, many of these Jews go to Germany, whose Jewish population has risen from 30,000 in 1970 to 115,000 today, in spite of the fact that anti-Semitic crimes continue to occur with some regularity. In 2006, the country's first and only rabbinic seminary after the Holocaust opened in Potsdam.

The Jewish presence in Europe, now so horribly diminished, had ancient roots. Jews reached Mediterranean Europe in Roman times, after their forced dispersal from Palestine. One major early concentration developed in Muslim Arabic Iberia, where Judaism won toleration, flourished, and eventually claimed perhaps one-fifth of the population. These Iberian Jews, or **Sephardim**, later faced eviction or forcible conversion to Roman Catholicism after the Christian reconquest, leaving behind only "secret Jews" (*Marranos*), and empty *judarias* (ghettoes). Their synagogues became churches. To the present day, in certain mountain towns of northern Portugal, Marranos still practice Jewish ritual while outwardly adhering to Roman Catholicism (fig. 5.22). Many Sephardic Jews fled Iberia and found new homes, particularly in Protestant countries such as Britain and the Netherlands.

Another major Jewish concentration developed in medieval times in western and southern Germany, where the German-derived Yiddish language originated. These became known as the **Ashkenazim**, the second major division of European Jewry. In the late Middle Ages, Ashkenazic Jews, responding to an edict of tolerance and invitation to settle by the Kingdom of Poland, began the migration that created the great concentration in Eastern Europe. This "Jewish Pale," as it came to be called after Russia annexed it and forced the Jews to remain within set borders,

Figure 5.22.   The non-Christian periphery and former Jewish diaspora. Islam and Judaism both present Europe with a perceived challenge to the very essence of its culture. Both minorities have faced prejudice and marginalization. *Sources:* Roth, C. 1974. *A History of the Marranos*, 4th ed. New York: Hermon Press, 368–373; King, R. D. 1992. Migration and Linguistics as Illustrated by Yiddish, in *Reconstructing Languages and Cultures*, eds. Edgar C. Polomé and Werner Winter, Berlin, D: de Gruyter, 419–439.

became the principal focus of Jewish life and culture in the entire world (fig. 5.17). The Lithuanian city of Vilnius, within the Pale, was at one time the unrivalled center of Jewish culture, the "Jerusalem of the North," with 100 synagogues, libraries, and a population that was 40% Jewish. The Nazis utterly destroyed the Pale and its inhabitants.

Sadly, anti-Semitism is not just a thing of the past. During the past decade, Jewish cemeteries and synagogues have been desecrated in France and Germany, and hate crimes are not infrequent. At the same time, many European speak out fervently against anti-Semitism. In 2005, a German cardinal, Walter Kasper, addressed the Organization on Security and Cooperation in Europe with the following admonition: "Anti-Semitism cuts through the roots of Christianity and has no place in the Church. The struggle against it means a struggle for human rights and engagement for peace." But when the larger Jewish experience in Europe is taken into consideration, it becomes clear that this small, creative religious minority has faced extraordinary intolerance. Any self-claim of Europe's cultural superiority—and these are not hard to find—must be measured against the treatment Europeans have afforded religious minorities over the centuries.

Conclusion

European Christianity faces many dilemmas in the twenty-first century. The traditional Christian churches have lost their mass appeal, and are facing dwindling attendance and memberships. In the *European Values Study*, published in 2003, only 21% of Europeans indicated that religion is "very important" to them. The parts of Europe that have experienced the highest degree of secularization are not just in the east, where religious practice was suppressed for decades, but also in the Protestant north, as well as significant parts of Catholic Europe. At the same time, new trends are afoot, including the growing popularity of charismatic Evangelical or Pentecostal denominations, especially among the younger generations, and the resurrection of historic denominations and religious communities in Russia, Ukraine, Moldova, and other former communist states.

Europeans today have to deal with increasingly pluralistic, multi-cultural, and multi-faith realities. The growing Muslim presence is presenting particular challenges. According to some public polls, Europeans have begun to address differences with their Muslim compatriots bluntly, especially as they relate to issues such as gender equality and free speech. Yet the events of 9/11, and the subsequent bombings in London and Madrid, have fostered feelings of distrust and fear. Immigrants from North Africa and Turkey and their descendents were long thought of as ethnic minorities; today, many think of them first and foremost as Muslims. In the process, a religious divide has once again become a significant cultural fault line in Europe. Differences between Muslims and non-Muslims were highlighted in the early 2000s, when a Danish newspaper published cartoons that cast the founder of Islam, Muhammad, in an unfavorable light. Many Europeans of Christian heritage saw this as an act of free speech. Yet one Belgian woman who is married to a Muslim man commented that "no amount of explanation about free speech could convince her husband that the publication of cartoons lampooning Muhammad in a Danish newspaper was in any way justified."

Yet efforts to encourage inter-religious and inter-cultural dialog are growing. In 2004, more than 2,000 Christian, Muslim, and Jewish leaders met with European Union officials in Russia to discuss ways of promoting constructive interaction among faiths in the aftermath of the massacre of school children in Beslan, North Ossetia. That same year, six Balkan presidents met in Albania and called for the "celebration of people's religious heritage" as a profound part of their identities. Such meetings and their resolutions remind us that, even as Europe has played host to appalling inter-faith conflicts, hope lies in the humanistic values of European civilization: human rights, democracy, pluralism, and equality.

Europe, then, reveals sharp, ever-changing religious contrasts. These contrasts have been shaped through time by social forces, but also by the political organization of space. It thus makes sense to turn in the next chapter to the evolution of the European political pattern.

Sources and Suggested Readings

Anderson, J. 1980. Regions and Religions in Ireland: A Short Critique of the Two Nations Theory. *Antipode* 11: 44–53.

Bar-Gal, Y. 1985. The Shtetl—the Jewish Small Town in Eastern Europe. *Journal of Cultural Geography* 5(2): 17–29.

Boyer, J.-C. 1996. La Frontière Entre Protestantisme et Catholicisme en Europe. *Annales de Géographie* 105: 119–140.

Byrnes, T. A. and P. J. Katzenstein, eds. 2006. *Religion in an Expanding Europe.* Cambridge: Cambridge University Press.

Connell, J. 1970. The Gilded Ghetto: Jewish Suburbanization in Leeds. *Bloomsbury Geographer* 3: 50–59.

Doherty, P. 1989. Ethnic Segregation Levels in the Belfast Urban Area. *Area* 21: 151–159.

Doherty, P. 1993. Religious Denomination in Northern Ireland, 1961 to 1991. *Irish Geography* 26: 14–21.

Donkin, R. A. 1978. *The Cistercians: Studies in the Geography of Medieval England and Wales.* Toronto: Pontifical Institute of Medieval Studies.

Duocastella, R. 1965. Géographie de la Pratique Religieuse en Espagne. *Social Compass* 12: 253–302.

Gay, J. D. 1971. *The Geography of Religion in England.* London: Duckworth.

Girardin, P. 1947. Les Passages Alpestres en Liaison avec les Abbayes, les Pèlerinages et les Saints de la Montagne. *Geographica Helvetica* 2: 65–74.

Greely, A. M. 2003. *Religion in Europe at the End of the Second Millennium: A Sociological Profile.* New Brunswick: Transaction Publishers.

Gustafsson, B. 1957. *Svensk Kyrkogeografi, med Samfundsbeskrivning.* Lund: Gleerup.

Hannemann, M. 1975. *The Diffusion of the Reformation in Southwestern Germany. 1518–1534.* Chicago: University of Chicago, Department of Geography, Research Paper No. 167.

Hard, G. 1965. Eine Topographie der Pilgerwege von Deutschland nach Santiago in Spanien aus dem 15. Jahrhundert. *Erdkunde* 19: 314–325.

Ignatieff, M. 1998. *The Warrior's Honor: Ethnic War and the Modern Conscience.* New York: Henry Holt.

Jouret, B. 1968. L'influence du Protestantisme dans l'Économie Douroise. *Revue Belge de Géographie* 92:61–74.

Jurkovich, J. M. and W. M. Gesler. 1997. Medjugorje: Finding Peace at the Heart of Conflict. *Geographical Review* 87: 447–467.

Kilpadi, P., ed. 2007. *Islam and Tolerance in Wider Europe.* Budapest: Open Society Institute.

Kotin, I. Y. and A. D. Krindatch. 2005. Religious Revival in a Multi-Cultural Landscape. In H. Knippenberg, ed. *The Changing Religious Landscape of Europe.* Amsterdam: Het Spinhuis: 145–173.

Knippenberg, H. 2005. The Netherlands. Selling churches and Building Mosques. In H. Knippenberg, ed., *The Changing Religious Landscape of Europe.* Amsterdam: Het Spinhuis: 88–106.

Knippenberg, H. and S. de Vos. 1989. Spatial Structural Effects on Dutch Church Attendance. *Tijdschrift voor Economische en Sociale Geografie* 80: 164–170.

Knudsen, J. P. 1986. Culture, Power and Periphery—The Christian Lay Movement in Norway. *Norsk Geografisk Tidsskrift* 40: 1–14.

Krindatch, A. D. 1996. *Geography of Religions in Russia.* Decatur, Georgia: Glenmary Research Center.

Lambert, E. 1943. Le Livre de Saint Jacques et les Routes du Pèlerinage de Compostelle. *Revue Géographique des Pyrénées et du Sud-Ouest* 14: 5–33.

Lehmann, S. G. 1998. Inter-Ethnic Conflict in the Republics of Russia in Light of Religious Revival. *Post-Soviet Geography and Economics* 39: 461–493.

Luxmoore, J. and J. Babiuch. 2005. *Rethinking Christendom: Europe's Struggle for Christianity.* Leominster: Gracewing.

Martyniuk, J. 1993. Religious Preferences in Five Urban Areas of Ukraine. *Radio Free Europe/Radio Liberty Research Report* 2(15): 52–55.

Newman, D. 1985. Integration and Ethnic Spatial Concentration: Changing Spatial Distribution of Anglo-Jewish Community. *Transactions of the Institute of British Geographers* 10: 360–376.

Nolan, M. L. 1983. Irish Pilgrimage: The Different Tradition. *Annals of the Association of American Geographers* 73: 421–438.

Nolan, M. L. and S. Nolan. 1989. *Religious Pilgrimage in Modern Western Europe.* Chapel Hill: University of North Carolina Press.

de Planhol, X. 1962. L'Islam dans la Physiognomie Géographique de la Péninsule Iberique. *Revue Géographique des Pyrénées et du Sud-Ouest* 33: 274–281.

Richard, J. 1996. Géographie Religieuse et Géopolitique en Biélorussie du XVIe Siècle a Nos Jours. *Annales de Géographie* 105: 141–163.

Rinschede, G. 1985. The Pilgrimage Town of Lourdes. In M. Buttner et al., eds. *Geographia Religionum, 1. Grundfragen der Religions-Geographie.* Berlin: Dietrich Reimer: 1–61.

Rinschede, G. 1992. Pilgerzentrum Fátima/Portugal. *Geographie Heute* 106: 15–22.

Schwartz, L. 1991. A Note on the Jewish Population of the USSR from the 1989 Census Data. *Soviet Geography* 32: 433–435.

Semple, E. C. 1927. The Templed Promontories of the Ancient Mediterranean. *Geographical Review* 17: 353–386.

Sidorov, D. 2000. The Resurrection of the Cathedral of Christ the Savior in Moscow. *Annals of the Association of American Geographers* 90: 548–572.

Stanislawski, D. 1975. Dionysus Westward: Early Religion and the Economic Geography of Wine. *Geographical Review* 65: 427–444.

Vertovec, S. and C. Peach, eds. 1997. *Islam in Europe.* London: Macmillan and St. Martin's.

Walker, E. W. 2005. Islam, Territory, and Contested Space in Post-Soviet Russia. *Eurasian Geography and Economics* 46: 247–271.

Waterman, S. and B. Kosmin. 1988. Residential Patterns and Processes: A Study of Jews in Three London Boroughs. *Transactions of the Institute of British Geographers* 13: 79–95.

Whelan, K. 1983. The Catholic Parish, the Catholic Chapel, and Village Development in Ireland. *Irish Geography* 16: 1–15.

Whelan, K. 1988. The Regional Impact of Irish Catholicism, 1700–1850. In W. J. Smyth and K. Whelan, eds. *Common Ground: Essays on the Historical Geography of Ireland.* Cork: Cork University Press: 253–277.

CHAPTER 6

The European State System

In previous chapters, we looked at a variety of maps that provide insight into Europe's physical and cultural characteristics. Yet when most people think of Europe's geography, they think of a map showing France, Germany, Italy, and so forth. In one sense this is remarkable, for most of the units on the typical political map of Europe did not exist 200 years ago, and none of them was around a thousand years ago. Yet the social and economic significance of the modern state became so great over the past two centuries that it came to dominate the geographical imagination. For every question that is asked about what is going on in the North European Plain or the Douro River Basin, thousands are asked about Germany, France, Spain, and Portugal.

The modern state is such a dominant influence in the contemporary world that it is difficult to talk about economic and social developments without reference to it. Hence, we focus on the emergence of the European state pattern before we turn to developments in the rural and urban sectors. There is a certain awkwardness to this ordering, because consideration of topics such as rural land use and urbanization require us to reach farther back in time than the emergence of the modern state system. Yet some understanding of the political partitioning of Europe over the past several hundred years provides a critical framework for understanding the changing geography of rural and urban life. The European state is now being challenged to some degree by the move toward European integration. We discuss that development at the end of this chapter. We begin, though, with the division of Europe into the spaces of governance that have had such a profound effect in recent times on how people define their identities and lead their lives.

The General Picture

Europe is splintered into no fewer than 47 independent states (fig. 6.1). These countries, in turn, contain many autonomous regions and territories, some of which harbor separatist sentiments. Geographer Richard Griggs has counted 130 culturally distinct peoples in Europe, only some of which have a state of their own.

Figure 6.1.   The independent countries of Europe with selected dependent territories. Excluding Turkey, Europe now encompasses almost 50 independent states, although the status of Kosovo is in dispute.

To gauge the magnitude of Europe's fragmentation, consider that the region, broadly defined, contains almost exactly the same amount of land area as the United States. Imagine the complexity that would exist if every state within the United States were independent. At the Russian border, this fragmentation abruptly gives way to the largest independent state in the world in land area, suggesting to some that Europe ends at that boundary. But of course others disagree.

So severe is the political splintering of Europe that a number of micro-states exist, some so small as to be invisible on a map of Europe as a whole. These include Andorra, Liechtenstein, Monaco, San Marino, and Vatican City. Most mini-states have turned their size to advantage, offering services not always available in their larger neighbors, such as the gambling casino in Monaco, the duty-free shops of Andorra, the postage stamp sales of San Marino, and the corporate headquarters lured to Liechtenstein by tax inducements.

Not only is Europe politically fragmented, but the level of internal division has increased markedly during the twentieth century. In the year 1900, Europe exclusive of Turkey had 23 independent states; in 1930, 31; in 1985, 34; and by 1993, 46, double the total at the beginning of the century. The breakup of several great imperial states as a result of World War I, most notably the Austro-Hungarian and Ottoman Turkish empires, yielded many new countries. The collapse in 1991 of Europe's last surviving empire, the Soviet Union, coupled with the almost simultaneous disintegration of two smaller multiethnic states, Yugoslavia and Czechoslovakia, produced many more independent European states. Against this trend, the reunification of Germany offered the only anomaly.

Nor has fragmentation necessarily run its course. Separatist movements of widely differing levels of intensity continue in Europe (see chapter 11). Before we turn to such matters, however, it is important to gain some understanding of how the pattern of European states came into being, and the role that pattern has played in the creation of patterns of identity in Europe.

The Emergence of the European State Pattern

During the Middle Ages, political territories were complex and overlapping throughout much of Europe. Few people had a sense of identity that was broader than a local commune or fief. The exception was a small ruling elite, most of whom functioned in royal and/or ecclesiastical territories with indistinct, frequently changing boundaries.

By the late Middle Ages, the feudal order began to erode. Increasingly autonomous cities sprang up in northern Italy and in Flanders (see Chapter 10), and rulers in the far western part of Europe began to consolidate power over larger territories—most notably in what we now call northern France and southern England. As these early states grew, they came into conflict with one another. (England controlled significant territories in what is now France—a legacy of the Norman invasion of England.) These conflicts, in turn, gave rise to larger-scale senses of identity. The concept of the **nation** was born. Many peoples now think of the terms *nation* and *state* as synonymous, but nation originally referred to a group of people with a shared sense of culture and history, and a desire to control its own affairs. In early modern Europe, the growing French and English states served as incubators for the development of national sensibilities, as did the states on the Iberian peninsula that came into being in the wake of the expulsion of the Moors. England, France, Spain, and Portugal are thus sometimes considered to be the original **nation-states** (in the original sense of the term, states associated with particular ethnic nations) (fig. 6.2). Of course these early nation-states encompassed many minorities, but each was based on the idea that the state was the homeland of a particular nation.

These early states grew up around a core area, which served as a power center and a crucible for the cultural norms that came to dominate the state (fig. 6.3). Such core areas generally possessed some measure of natural defense against the encroachments of rival political entities, a fairly dense population (at least in comparison to surrounding regions), and a prosperous agricultural economy that produced a surplus

Figure 6.2.   Types of states in Europe based on their territorial and ideological foundations. The different political-territorial circumstances that produced Europe's political pattern unfolded over many hundreds of years, but most modern European states are less than 200 years old.

capable of supporting a sizable military establishment. Perhaps most important of all, the core area required a government headed by ambitious leaders, skilled in the military and diplomatic arts and bent on territorial aggrandizement. During the process of accretion, the core often retained its status as the single most important area in the state, housing the capital city and the cultural and economic heart of the nation. An example would be Paris and the Île de France, which lie nearly in the middle of France. But in some instances, territorial accretion occurred mainly in one direction, leaving the core in a peripheral location. Wessex, the nucleus of the United Kingdom, became eccentric, as did the region in Spain from which the **reconquista** was mounted.

The European state system is grounded in two fundamental territorial concepts. One we have already introduced: the nation-state. The other is **sovereignty**—a concept

Figure 6.3.   Core areas and the evolution of European states. Many modern independent countries evolved gradually from core areas. Others celebrate an area deemed to be the historic heartland of a national culture, even if it did not play a direct role in the creation of the modern state. The Osman statelet was the core area of the Ottoman Empire and modern Turkey. *Sources:* Based in part upon Pounds/Ball 1964 and McManis 1967.

that emerged out of developments within the German Empire of the sixteenth and seventeenth centuries. During that time, the German Empire was comprised of hundreds of small states or principalities. The Wars of Religion (see Chapter 5) brought these entities into intense conflict with one another. A settlement, known as the Peace of Westphalia, was finally reached in 1648. Under the terms of the agreement, the religion of each of the territorial units making up the German Empire was to be the religion of the ruler of that unit—and no unit had the right to impose its religious ideas on its neighbors. This gave birth to the idea that states should be able to control their own affairs without outside interference.

The Peace of Westphalia ushered in a period of stability within the German Empire that lasted almost a century. By the middle of the eighteenth century, the German

Figure 6.4.   Europe in the eighteenth century. Only at Europe's western edge does the eighteenth-century political pattern look like that of today.

Empire was still carved up into multiple units, although internal conflicts had begun to develop. Elsewhere in Europe, the modern political pattern had only taken shape at the western edges of Europe (fig. 6.4). The original nation-states continued to function as relatively large-scale, autonomous political units—and they had grown increasingly powerful as a result of their colonial activities. The northern provinces of the Low Countries had also successfully thrown off external rule, giving rise to another independent state that is a clear predecessor of a modern state: the Netherlands. The Netherlands too set itself up as an early colonial power, and had developed financial and trading networks that gave it a position of enormous influence by the seventeenth century.

Outside of Europe's western fringe, the political map did not look much like the one we know today. What we now called Belgium was controlled from outside. The territories occupied by the modern states of Italy, Germany, and Austria were fragmented. To the east and north of the German and Italian realms, empires were the norm. The Kingdom of Hungary represented a partial exception, as a state-like entity had come into being there—albeit in a territory that was considerably larger than the present state of Hungary. Another exception was in the Alps, where a set of cantons had developed a loose alliance in an effort to ward off outside influence, giving rise to an entity that we now call Switzerland.

The rulers of the mix of political territorial units found in eighteenth-century Europe were primarily hereditary monarchs. However, the idea of the nation that had been forged in the early western European states gave rise to a growing sense that rulers should serve the interests of the nation, not vice versa. Spurred on by the excesses of the monarchy, this idea gained particular potency in France. It eventually led to the violent French Revolution of 1789, which was undertaken in the name of **nationalism** (a notion rooted in the glorification of a particular ethnic nation, and an insistence on the right of that nation to control its own affairs). The French Revolution ushered in Europe's *Age of Nationalism*, a period during which the ideal political form was seen to be a sovereign nation-state.

France was the key catalyst for the Age of Nationalism. The country entered a tumultuous period in the wake of its revolution, but order was restored for a time when Napoleon Bonaparte took control of the state in the name of the French nation. Napoleon's expansionist activities helped to spread the concept of the sovereign nation-state throughout the region—giving rise to a long century of independent state formation (from c. 1815–1925) that was to bring into being the modern political map of Europe. The states that emerged came about primarily as a result of two types of nationalism: **unification nationalism** and **anti-empire nationalism**—although the territorial cores of the dismantled empires also became states (fig. 6.2).

Unification nationalism was the product of an effort to bring together, within a single state, peoples who were thought to share a common culture and history. Unification movements developed in both Germany (based on the notion that the lands of the German Empire encompassed one people) and Italy (based on the notion that the peninsula at the core of the old Roman Empire was the homeland of a single people) (fig. 6.2). The German and Italian domains encompassed considerable cultural diversity as a result of centuries of political fragmentation, but the ideas of a German nation and an Italian nation were of sufficient appeal that the movements eventually were successful. They emerged from core areas (fig. 6.3), but only in the German case would the core become the power center of the newly independent state.

The different relationships between nation and state in the original nation-states, as opposed to the states that were the products of unification nationalism, are suggested by figure 6.5: a map of Europe's main post roads in 1850 (fig 6.5). A quick glance at the map shows that a country such as France is immediately evident from the road pattern. All roads lead to Paris. This reflected a centuries-long project, in which the political organization of territory promoted a growing sense of being French among relatively diverse peoples. The territory helped to create the nation (in the original sense of the term). In contrast, it is difficult to find Germany on the map because it had no history of unity. In the German case, an idea about nation created the territory.

Anti-empire nationalism occurred in places where a sense of nationalism took root among peoples who considered themselves to be under the control of outsiders. Peoples with a distinctive sense of culture and history wanted a sovereign nation-state of their own. Anti-empire nationalism took two forms: (1) movements to split off from states that were viewed by peripheral minority populations as empires because they had

Figure 6.5.   Main post roads in Europe, 1850. Note the highly centralized pattern in France and the lack of a dominant focal point in central Europe. This map clearly shows that France had functioned as a single territorial unit for some time, whereas Germany had not yet been unified. *Source:* Hoffman, G. W. ed. 1969. *A Geography of Europe,* 3rd ed. New York: Ronald Press, 107.)

expanded to encompass territories where groups with a distinct sense of ethnic identity were found, and (2) movements to break up avowedly multi-ethnic empires. The classic examples of the first kind of anti-empire nationalism are Ireland and Norway, both of which split away in the early twentieth century from countries that had come to rule them (the United Kingdom and Sweden, respectively) (fig. 6.2).

The second type of anti-imperial nationalism is associated with the disintegration of the explicitly multi-ethnic European empires of the nineteenth and twentieth centuries: the Ottoman Empire, the Austro-Hungarian Empire, and the Russian Empire. These empires began to disintegrate late in the nineteenth century, and the former two were fully dissolved at the end of World War I. Most of the states that emerged from them had a clear ethnic nationalist base, even if their borders did not necessarily correspond very well with ethnic distributions (fig. 6.2). Under the guise of the Soviet Union, Russia expanded its territorial reach during the twentieth century, but by the end of the century anti-empire nationalism led to the creation of independent states along the eastern edge of the empire.

As Europe's empires were dismantled, the political centers of the old empires also became part of the political map (fig. 6.2). Sweden was the old core of the Swedish Empire, Russia of the Russian Empire, and Turkey of the Ottoman Empire. Austria and Hungary each went their own ways—a reflection of political-territorial arrangements in pre-imperial times.

Even though the Age of Nationalism saw the disintegration of Europe's internal empires, it led to the solidification and expansion of the overseas colonial ventures of various European powers. In an atmosphere of increased competition among European states anxious to establish themselves as major powers, efforts to control resources and territory outside of Europe intensified. Long-standing colonial states such as France, the United Kingdom, the Netherlands, and Portugal were joined by Belgium, Germany, and Italy in a land grab in Africa that led to the partitioning of that continent near the end of the nineteenth century. Colonial control was also solidified over interior areas of Asia, and on selected islands and territories in other parts of the globe. Colonialism entered its most ruthless stage, with devastating impacts on many colonized areas. Within Europe, power disparities grew as some colonial countries successfully exploited the system at the expense of other colonial powers and non-colonial countries.

The Age of Nationalism culminated in a conflict of global proportions in 1914 that led to the final disintegration of Europe's central and southeastern empires. The immediate catalyst for World War I was a contest over territory and influence in southeastern Europe. In many senses, the war represented the high-water mark for nationalism in the region. It took an enormous human toll; the length of the list of war dead on the monuments of every small French town tells the story. Out of the ashes came a political pattern that bears a strong resemblance to the contemporary map of European states (fig. 6.6). There were exceptions. The area that came to be known as Yugoslavia (called the Kingdom of the Serbs, Croats, and Slovenes until 1929) was a multi-ethnic mix, and Czechoslovakia brought together two increasingly self-conscious ethnic nations and several smaller groups within one state. Both would break up in the closing decade of the twentieth century. Moreover, Germany controlled significant territories in the east—territories that were lost after the second horrendous European conflict of the twentieth century ended in 1945.

The Twentieth-Century European State

The European state that emerged in the early twentieth century was very much a product of the historical and geographical circumstances described above. Most states regarded themselves as nation-states, and the link between nation and state had become so naturalized that the two terms came to be seen as interchangeable—a troubling development for the many ethnic minorities that existed within European states. Moreover, the idea of territorial sovereignty was widely accepted, although for some sovereignty had come to mean the right of regimes to do whatever they wanted, including (if seen to be necessary to protect the national interest) seeking to influence developments beyond the boundaries of the state. This notion of sovereignty was at the

Figure 6.6. Europe at the end of World War I. The break-up of the Ottoman and Austro-Hungarian empires produced a map of states that, for the first time, looked much like the one that exists today.

heart of Nazi expansionism at the end of the 1930s, but was largely abandoned after the horrors of World War II in favor of a notion of sovereignty more in keeping with the principles set forth in the Peace of Westphalia.

Internally, states sought to integrate their territories economically and socially and encourage commitment to national norms through the expansion of state-funded education. The majority of states were **unitary** in administrative structure, with power concentrated in a central government (fig. 6.7). This was the default model in cases where states developed as power spread out from a core. Many of those core areas contained the capital of the state, which sometimes was also a **primate city**—one that contained by far the largest population and greatest concentration of economic and cultural functions (e.g., Paris and Athens). Yet the capital was sometimes removed from the original core, a relocation prompted by any one of several factors. In some instances, the capital was relocated to the frontier of most active territorial expansion. Sofia replaced Bulgarian capitals farther to the east as that state expanded south and west at the expense of the Turks; Lisbon and Madrid displaced northern capitals as the

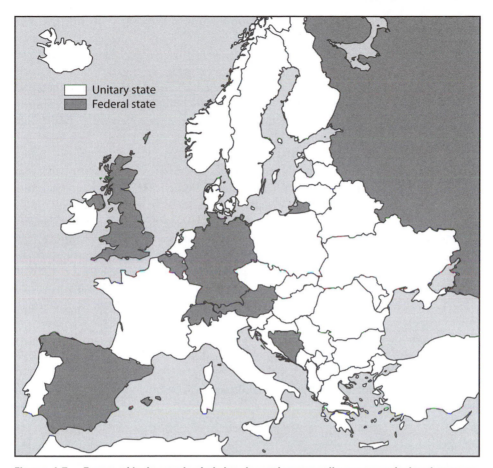

Figure 6.7. Types of independent states, based upon unitary versus federal governments. In those states shown as federal, all powers that are not explicitly granted to the central government reside with the units that make up the state.

Portuguese and Spaniards pushed the Moors southward in Iberia. Similarly, capitals were sometimes relocated to take advantage of commercial and cultural contacts. St. Petersburg replaced Moscow as the Russian capital for a time, when the czars desired closer cultural contacts with Europe; and Oslo replaced Trondheim in Norway as a result of its closer proximity to Sweden and Denmark, which ruled Norway for centuries.

An alternative to the unitary state is the **federal state**, in which internal states or provinces retain considerable power, or even autonomy. Europe had few of these early in the twentieth century, but the number has grown (fig. 6.7) as states such as Spain, Belgium, Russia, and the United Kingdom looked to federalism to accommodate the demands of regional ethnic minority groups for greater control over their own affairs. Switzerland represents the most disaggregated form of federalism; the country did not even have a national capital until the mid-nineteenth century.

Modern states are also characterized by international borders. Many of these borders are declining in significance (see below), but they are still marked in some way. Even the peaceful, uncontested Sweden-Norway frontier is marked by a swath cut through the forest, and by diverse official signs of varying age (fig. 6.8). The first acts of newly independent Estonia and Latvia included severing many connecting rural roads with trenchers, erecting street barriers within border towns, and establishing manned crossing points. Their mutual border, previously a largely invisible line between Soviet republics, sprang vividly into the landscape.

The policies and legislation of independent states often have a homogenizing effect within their borders, with the result that significantly different economic, social, and material landscapes can be found on either side of borders. An example is the Rhine River border between France and Germany. On the French side lies the province of Alsace, and on the German side, Baden. Both Alsace and Baden are traditionally German-speaking and predominantly Roman Catholic, and yet significant differences developed between the two provinces. Prosperous Baden underwent rapid industrialization after 1945, absorbing numerous refugees from ceded eastern German territories, while Alsace stagnated economically. In part, the economic malaise of Alsace was caused by repeated boundary changes when the province passed back and forth from German to French rule in 1871, 1918, 1940, and 1945. Yet many lay part of the blame for the depressed condition of peripheries such as Alsace on the highly centralized French government. Baden, as part of a much less centralized federal state, fared better. Federal funds generously assisted resettled refugees in Baden, causing a boom in housing construction and renovation. Rural population density is now much lower on the Alsatian

Figure 6.8.   Swedish-Norwegian border near Torsby, Sweden. The border is clearly marked by a strip cleared through the Finnskog, or "Finns' Forest." (Photo by T.G.J.-B.1985.)

side, and the prosperity of Baden causes many French citizens to commute to jobs on the German side of the Rhine. The two provinces also differ in the configuration of rural village suburbanization, a process under way in both due to the growth of nearby cities such as Strasbourg and Freiburg. Partly as a result of differences in national planning legislation, the suburbs being added to villages in Baden tend to be compact, with apartment dwellings most common, whereas Alsatian villages sprawl loosely across the countryside due to the dominance of freestanding, single-family suburban houses.

This differentiating effect of borders can be found even where the borders themselves no longer exist. The northern border of the Roman Empire ran through the modern German state of Hessen. As we saw in Chapter 3, the Roman system of law required that inheritances be divided among all heirs, in contrast to the tradition of the neighboring German tribes, which favored primogeniture. After the empire collapsed and the political border ceased to exist, the boundary separating the different inheritance systems persisted into the modern era (fig. 6.9).

Traditional inheritance form requiring partition among heirs

400 or more ownership parcels of land per 100 hectares of agricultural land

Figure 6.9.   Inheritance systems and land fragmentation in the German province of Hessen, 1955. In the southern and western parts of Hessen, the tradition, dating to Roman times, was to divide the farms among the various heirs. As a result, the farms there became ever smaller over the centuries, with excessive fragmentation of the holdings. Northern and eastern Hessen, by contrast, clung to the ancient Germanic custom of primogeniture, by which the farm passes intact to the eldest son. *Source:* Adapted from Ehlers, E. 1977. Land Consolidation and Farm Resettlement in the Federal Republic of Germany, in R. C. Eidt, et al., eds., *Man, Culture, and Settlement.* New Delhi, IND: Kalyani, 124.

Case Studies

Beyond the general forces and trends that shaped the European state system lies a multitude of particular circumstances at play in individual cases. To gain some appreciation of the historical and geographical differences that have shaped the European state system, as well as the ethnic diversity that lies behind the nation-state concept, it is useful to look at a few specific cases.

FRANCE: THE QUINTESSENTIAL UNITARY STATE

Though linked by language and religion to the Mediterranean, France owes both its origin and name to a Germanic tribe, the Franks, who moved into the power vacuum following the collapse of the Roman Empire. When this short-lived Frankish Empire fragmented in 843 C.E., the westernmost part—a loose feudal federation known as the Kingdom of the West Franks—became the embryonic France.

After about 1000 C.E., the kings of France, based in Paris, began a program of conquest and annexation to convert the federation, over which their rule was largely ceremonial, into a unitary state under royal domination. In this process, the so-called Île de France—the original, small domain of the kings in the center of the Paris Basin—served as the core area of the evolving unitary state (fig. 6.10). The Île de France enjoyed splendid natural defensive advantage, sheltered behind **cuesta** escarpment walls.

From their Paris Basin fortress, the French kings undertook three prolonged campaigns of expansion: southward to reach the Mediterranean and the Pyrenees; westward to dislodge the English from the Atlantic coast, where they ruled Normandy and Aquitaine; and eastward, at the expense of Bourgogne and other German states, to the banks of the Rhine. By 1650, France had reached more or less its present territorial limits. The city of Paris, the Île de France, and the Paris Basin never lost their early dominance. A unitary state with a powerful central government based in Paris has always characterized France.

The boundaries achieved in French expansion had two advantages. First, belts of mountains and hills parallel the border in many places, including the Pyrenees, Alps, Jura, Vosges, and Ardennes (fig. 6.10). Also, most of France's territory was relatively easily accessible from the fairly centrally located capital. Still, the resultant France was no nation-state in the original sense of the term. As late as 1790, half the population spoke a language other than the Parisian form of French. In 1793, the government mandated elimination of regional languages and dialects. This policy had considerable success, but even today ethnic minorities are found in many of France's peripheral regions (fig. 6.10). These include the German-speaking Alsatians in the east, the Dutch speakers around Dunkerque in the north, the Celtic Bretons of Bretagne, the Basques of the western Pyrenees, the Catalans of the south, and the Italian-speaking Corsicans. In addition, France had the task of uniting a Germanized north with a Mediterranean south. The northern French, occupying the Paris Basin, descended in large part from Germanic tribes—not only the Franks, but also Normans (Vikings),

Figure 6.10.   France, selected geopolitical features. Growing from the Île de France, a core area in the Paris Basin, France attained a hexagonal shape and "natural" borders such as the Alps and Pyrenees, but annexed numerous peripheral ethnic areas in the process, as well as the more Romanized south.

Burgundians, and others. While these tribes abandoned their ancestral languages and adopted French, they remained Germanic in many other ways. Their houses, villages, and farm field patterns are Teutonic in appearance and origin; their Germanic diet relies heavily on bovine dairy products, including butter for cooking; and their dialect of French, *langue d'oïl*, is distinctive.

The lands annexed in the south, sometimes called *Occitania*, retain a much stronger Roman and Mediterranean imprint, with minimal Germanic influence. This can be detected, for example, in the cultivation of grapes for wine, the use of olive oil in cooking, and the distinctive tongue known as *langue d'oc*. These are merely signs of a deeply rooted, distinctive southern regional culture.

The French reaction to these challenges of ethnic peripheries and regional culture was to develop an all-powerful unitary state, based in Paris, and to impose the will and culture of the north on both the south and the restive peripheries. This strategy largely succeeded. Over the past 30 years, France has devolved some power to its outlying regions, but it remains fundamentally a unitary state and no province has a substantial degree of autonomy from Paris.

GERMANY: FEDERALISM IN THE EUROPEAN CORE

Just as France represents the legacy of the collapsed Frankish Empire in the west, Germany descends from the east Frankish Kingdom of 843 C.E. For the initial millennium of its existence, the German realm, unlike France, remained a loose federation of feudal states whose emperor had little authority outside his home statelet. Federalism, verging on virtual disunity, has been the German norm. Potential core areas from which ambitious emperors might have forged a unitary state certainly existed, such as the fertile Börde beyond the Ruhr River on the North European Plain, or the hill-ringed Upper Rhine Plain between Frankfurt-am-Main and Basel, but no such process developed. By the 1600s, the Holy Roman Empire of German-speaking principalities encompassed some 300 virtually independent states.

The loose-knit German Empire did succeed in expanding eastward, into ancestral Slavic tribal lands, following the path of German agricultural colonists and forest clearers spreading east on the North German Plain and along the Danube. In each of these two lobes of eastern expansion, within the territory of the German Empire, a powerful state and ambitious royal family arose: Prussia (German *Preussen*) in the North European Plain, which grew from a core area in Brandenburg, and Austria, which expanded from the *Ostmark* (Eastern March) around Vienna. These two new states both continued to function as part of the Empire, even though some of the territories they annexed lay beyond its bounds. Once they consolidated their holdings in the east, Prussia and Austria (by then called *Österreich*, or the "Eastern Empire") began competing with one another for control of the original, politically fragmented western part of the Empire, each attempting to create a unitary German-speaking state under their rule. This contest lasted for centuries, but Prussia eventually emerged victorious in 1866.

Five years later, the German state was born, a union of Prussia and western Germany. The Prussian capital, Berlin, was named the imperial capital, and the Prussian kings became the German *kaisers*. Federalism persisted, and member states such as Bavaria and Sachsen retained their own monarchs and postal systems (fig. 6.11). Austria, the defeated rival, found itself excluded from Germany. In the 1930s the Nazis seized power and imposed the first dictatorship Germany had known. Unitary rule

Figure 6.11.   Germany, occupying much of the European core, has always struggled to unite north and south, east and west, lying astride these two European cultural fault lines.

quickly replaced the traditional federalism; not merely Germany, but all of Europe, felt the dire consequences. Nearly a half-century, marked by defeat and foreign military occupation, passed before the unified, federal Germany could be re-established. Modern Germany emerged only in 1990, when the Federal Republic, which had arisen in the military occupation zones of the Americans, French, and British, annexed the German Democratic Republic, the old Russian occupation zone. In 1999, Berlin regained its status as the capital of Germany.

An essential feature of the German state—one that helps explain its federalism and repeated fragmentation—is that while it occupies the core of Europe, it also straddles the east-west and north-south divides that characterize Europe. The north-south divide is ancient, going back 2,000 years to the time when southern Germany was part of the Roman Empire, while the north was controlled by various Teutonic tribes. Rome placed its cultural imprint on the south, and such influences never completely disappeared, even after many centuries. Thus the German south remains Roman Catholic, while the north is Protestant. The country is home to some 25,000,000 Protestants and 26,000,000 Catholics—about as even a split as could be imaginable. Dialects of the German language also separate south from north.

The east-west division within Germany is also deeply rooted. A thousand years ago and more, German peoples lived only in lands west of the Elbe and Saale rivers.

Slavic tribes possessed what is now eastern Germany, and only gradually did the Teutonic peoples spread east, absorbing the Slavs. In the process, they became considerably Slavicized. This colonial eastern German culture remained feudal, its landless peasants working on manorial estates owned by the aristocracy. Prussia, the political expression of eastern German culture, remained entirely confined to the east as late as the 1790s. When German unification was realized in the 1870s with the Prussian royal family in charge, the east-west contrast did not weaken.

The distinctiveness of eastern Germany was powerfully reinforced between 1945 and 1990, when it was a communist country under Russian domination, while West Germany belonged to the democratic, capitalist part of Europe. In spite of reunification in 1990, the old "Iron Curtain" border has far from disappeared. *Ossis* ("easterners") and *Wessis* ("westerners") still differ sharply in standard of living and political ideology. The prosperity divide between the two parts of Germany remains profound. The East, with 18% of the population, generates only 8% of Germany's tax revenues and has more than twice the level of unemployment. In an effort to mitigate this problem, the German government annually transfers billions of euros into the troubled eastern provinces.

The German state has struggled, then, to create a political core. Modern Germany pursues this task by structuring itself as a federal state, in which considerable powers are vested in the individual provinces and the central government is relatively weak.

THE UNITED KINGDOM: CORE-PERIPHERY TENSIONS

If Germany's quixotic task has been to bridge east, west, north, and south, the United Kingdom has struggled to link together peoples with diverse histories and cultures. Ultimately, this union proved untenable, and the Republic of Ireland broke away in the 1920s—the culmination of a revolt that had endured for centuries. The Irish secession occurred along one of several natural and cultural dividing lines that cut across the country's territory (fig. 6.12).

The United Kingdom was the creation of Germanic tribes, particularly the Saxons, Angles, and Normans, who came as waves of invaders from across the North Sea and English Channel, eventually mixing with indigenous groups and each other to become the English people. Their new state, England, arose in Wessex, in the lowland plains that form the southeastern part of the island of Great Britain (fig. 6.12). Once the English had unified the lowlands, they turned to the second great task—conquering and annexing the hilly lands on the west and north, inhabited by the Celts. One by one these Celtic refuges—Cornwall, Wales, and Scotland—fell to the English. Even before these conquests were completed, the English began their third, and final, major expansion—in Ireland, another Celtic land, lying across a narrow sea to the west. In this way, the two British Isles came to be a single country, the United Kingdom, ruled by the English from their base in London and the surrounding lowlands.

While outwardly successful, the expanded United Kingdom never fully absorbed the conquered Celts. Cultural and natural borders snaked through the country's territory, always threatening a rift. These included not only the environmental divide

Figure 6.12. The United Kingdom, originating as the Saxon state of Wessex, early came to encompass the Scarpland plains and began to claim territory in the Celtic refuges. At its peak, the U. K. ruled all the British Isles, but ultimately it failed to hold together.

between fertile lowlands and barren hills and the separation into two major islands, but also the borders between Anglo-Saxons and Celts, Protestants and Catholics, rich and poor, industrial and rural. It was along the Protestant/Catholic divide that the United Kingdom fragmented, though some Catholic counties in Northern Ireland remained under English control. The "Troubles" that plagued Northern Ireland for decades were the result. Recent power-sharing agreements have raised hope for a more stable future, but the situation remains fragile.

On the larger island, Great Britain, other divides continue to plague the United Kingdom. The independence movement in Scotland has many supporters, and the Scots in 1999 established their own separate parliament, as did the Welsh. "Rise up and be a nation again" implore bumper stickers in Scotland, a message carried forward by the Scottish Nationalist Party.

The future of the United Kingdom remains uncertain. Will Northern Ireland explode again into violence? Will Scotland opt for independence? The United Kingdom is an ancient and largely stable state, and further disintegration seems unlikely. But the balance is delicate in a state that has extended its reach into areas where it was not always welcome.

ITALY: ROMAN LEGACY

Like the United Kingdom, Italy struggles to unite segments of the European core and periphery. Unlike Britain, Italy is a relatively new state by European standards, but resting upon the memory of ancient greatness. The Roman Empire collapsed more than a millennium-and-a-half ago, and what is now Italy fell into political fragmentation; but the memory of Roman glory and unity persisted. In the nineteenth century, a unification movement arose which reassembled Italy from an array of weak, small states ruled by feudal lords, princes, and popes. Although the unification movement originated in the north, the ancient legacy demanded that Rome be the capital (fig. 6.13).

Although the ancient Roman legacy served as a unifying source, the peninsula was very diverse in the cultural sense, as it was even in Roman times. To unify Italy over 2,000 years ago, the tribes of *Latium* (modern Lazio)—a district surrounding Rome and the origin of the word "Latin"—had to conquer in the north both the Etruscan peoples of Tuscany and the Celts of the Po–Veneto Plain, then called *Cisalpine Gaul*. Then they had to annex the Greek-inhabited lands of south Italy.

These ancient minorities never completely vanished. To complicate matters more, new invaders settled the peninsula after the fall of the Roman Empire. Germanic tribes, especially the Lombards, seized the Po–Veneto Plain, while Arabs, Crusaders, and Catalans ruled much of the south, including the large island of Sicily. Then, in the 1400s and 1500s, northern Italy gave birth to a great awakening of culture—the Renaissance—and with it an era of prosperity based in trade and manufacturing, while the south—the *Mezzogiorno*—remained mired in impoverished feudal bondage.

The modern Italian state has struggled to hold the north and south together. Some of the resultant internal pressure was relieved by the mass migration of poor southerners to factory jobs in the north after 1950. In addition, the central government transfers enormous amounts of northern wealth to the south as subsidies, relief, and developmental funds. But tensions persist. Many prosperous northerners express disdain for southern Italians, and some even speak of *Padania*—an independent northern Italy (fig. 6.13). A political party, the Northern League, favors secession. In addition, inhabitants of the German-speaking part of Alpine Italy—the South Tirol or *Alto Adige*—have agitated for a half-century for autonomy, or even to be joined to adjacent Austria.

Figure 6.13.   Italy, though seemingly provided with a natural framework by the peninsula and the Alps, consists of very different regions. A prosperous North contrasts with the Mezzogiorno.

SPAIN: A MULTIETHNIC STATE

Spain, in common with Italy, has historically struggled to hold together north and south, but its internal stresses are far more complicated than this simple twofold division. The Spanish state had its beginnings in far northern Iberia in the Christian resistance against the Moors, who had invaded from Africa in the 700s C.E. In particular, two Christian statelets, Castilla and Aragon, led the resistance, and when they united

Figure 6.14.   Spain, though a very old state, encompasses restive ethnic peripheries and other internal contrasts.

in the 1400s, Spain was born (fig. 6.14). The defining deed of Spanish national identity was successful warfare against the Arabs, pushing them southward back into Africa, a process completed only after 700 years, in 1492.

The resultant Spanish state included the far greater part of the Iberian peninsula, excluding only Portugal in the far west. In common with Italy, the peninsula housed diverse peoples, speaking different languages and possessing strong regional allegiances. Portugal was one of these and soon succeeded in escaping Spanish rule. Others were incorporated, more or less against their will. The Castilians—the people of central Meseta—built and ruled Spain, establishing the capital city, Madrid, in the center of the elevated interior plains. Ethnic minorities in the peripheries—Basques, Catalans, and Gallegans—were dominated by the Castilians in a unitary state. Too, the cultural legacy of the Moors and Africa remained strong in southern Spain, particularly in the province of Andalucía.

Southern regionalism today finds its expression in poverty, aristocratic landed estates, secularism, and socialist political leanings (fig. 6.14).

These tensions almost tore Spain apart in a civil war in the 1930s, but the outcome was a Castilian-run fascist dictatorship that endured into the 1970s, perpetuating the traditional strong-handed rule from Madrid. In a radical shift, Spain then adopted a federalist democracy and extended sweeping freedoms to the provinces and ethnic minorities. These initiatives have not proven entirely successful, as both the Basques and Catalans continue to exhibit strong separatist sentiments, but the situation is far less volatile than it once was.

SWITZERLAND AND BELGIUM: ASTRIDE A LANGUAGE DIVIDE

One of the most important language borders in western Europe separates the Romance-speaking south from the Germanic-speaking north (Chapter 4). Switzerland and Belgium both straddle this border, but only the Swiss have achieved relative stability.

Switzerland has enjoyed considerable success in joining different linguistic and religious groups in a multinational country. Almost two-thirds of the Swiss speak German, 18% French, and one tenth Italian, in addition to a tiny Romansh minority. Religiously, Switzerland is 42% Catholic and 35% Protestant (fig. 6.15). The Alps cut directly through the country, dividing much of Switzerland into separate valleys, each with its own identity and desire for autonomy. In spite of these challenges, Switzerland has existed for over 700 years as an independent state.

The origins of the Swiss state can be traced to a core area in the 1200s around the eastern shores of the *Vierwaldstättersee* (Lake of Four Forest Cantons or Lake Luzern), at the northern approach to St. Gotthard Pass, the principal land route between Italy and Central Europe in the Middle Ages. Feudal lords there banded together in 1291 for mutual defense, and gradually over the centuries increased their autonomy within the loose-knit German Empire, strengthened by their control of the strategic pass (fig. 6.15). In its formative stage, the state remained wholly German in speech, Catholic in faith, and centered on the lake that afforded easy communication among the member cantons. From the first, Switzerland formed a very loose federal state, or *confederation*, a framework that successfully accommodated subsequent linguistic and religious diversity as the country continued to grow from its tiny core area.

In the 1400s and 1500s, the confederation seized control of other strategic Alpine passes and also Rhine River crossings, in the process incorporating Italian-and French-speaking districts. In more recent times, Switzerland achieved prosperity and demonstrated an isolationist ability to avoid wars, accomplishments that greatly enhanced the value of Swiss citizenship.

Switzerland has faced its share of internal problems over the centuries, including at least five civil wars and, recently, ethnic tensions which led the French-speaking part of Canton Bern to break away and form Jura, a new Francophone canton. But all things considered, Switzerland must be regarded as an astounding success in an improbable setting. It helps that much of the power is held at the cantonal level, and that there are

Figure 6.15.   Switzerland, territorial development and ethnic diversity. The Swiss state is a classic example of gradual expansion from a core area. It includes a mixture of Roman Catholics and Protestants, and four major linguistic groups. *Sources:* Fleure 1941 and Schib, K. 1965–1970. Territoriale Entwicklung der Eidgenossenschaft, in *Atlas der Schweiz*. Wabern-Bern, CH: Verlag der eidgenossischen Landestopographie, 21.

multiple cantons where the majority speak one of the major languages or practice one of the major religions. This means that the position that a given canton takes on a national issue is not necessarily interpreted as the stance of a religious or linguistic group.

Belgium, also astride the Germanic-Romance linguistic border, encompasses the Dutch (Flemish) speakers of Flanders in the north and the French speakers of Wallonia

Figure 6.16.   Belgium. The ethno-linguistic divide between north and south has raised growing questions about the viability of the Belgian state in the twenty-first century.

in the south—as well as a small German-speaking area in the east (fig. 6.16). A much newer state than Switzerland, Belgium dates only from 1830, when its Catholic population, with approval and encouragement from the Great Powers of Europe, broke away from the Protestant-dominated Netherlands. At its inception, the Belgian state was not viewed as a union of two major language regions. The term *Wallonia* was not even coined until later in the nineteenth century, and in 1830 Flanders meant the old medieval Flanders (the western part of present-day Flanders and adjacent parts of the Netherlands and France). Moreover, northern Belgium in particular was riven with deep dialectical divisions. No one at the time conceived of the north and south as discrete ethnic territories.

Language came to be politicized in Belgium as a result of the decision to construct a unitary state in which French was the language of power and governance. What followed was an effort to impose French throughout the country, and this led to a reaction that brought together the diverse dialectical communities of northern Belgium. As tensions grew between the two linguistic groups, and also between the French-speaking elite in Brussels and the French speakers of southern Belgium, the pressure to decentralize Belgium mounted. Belgium's struggle with that pressure during the middle of the twentieth century led to the establishment of an internal political structure that reflected emerging senses of ethnolinguistic identity. Significant powers were given to Flanders and Wallonia, as well as to Brussels—an officially bilingual third administrative region. Eventually Belgium became a loose federation made up of regions based explicitly on ethnolinguistic criteria.

Other paths to federalism could have been followed. Powers could have been devolved to the old provinces, in which case northern and southern Belgium would each have had four or five administrative regions. Each region would surely have had a single dominant language. But decisions on cultural, economic, and social issues would have produced different alignments of regions—focusing attention on divisions that transcend language. The decision to partition Belgium along ethnolinguistic lines, however, guaranteed a constant reinforcement of the idea that Belgium is made up of two ethnolinguistic communities. As a result, Belgium's continued viability as a state is frequently called into question.

The contrast between Switzerland and Belgium highlights the importance of viewing political geography as more than the memorization of place names. The different political-geographic arrangements that took shape within these two countries have profoundly influenced their internal cultural and political development.

YUGOSLAVIA: FRAGMENTATION IN THE BALKANS

Belgium's problems astride a major cultural divide pale in comparison to the geopolitical fate of Yugoslavia, the "land of the South Slavs." Formed following World War I when peacemakers appended various territories to previously independent Serbia (fig. 6.6), the new state joined shards of diverse former empires—Roman, Byzantine, Turkish, Austrian, and Hungarian—each of which had left indelible cultural residues. Largely Serbo-Croatian in speech, Yugoslavia inherited three major faiths—Catholicism, Orthodoxy, and Islam; two alphabets; and a territory running from the Hungarian Basin to the Adriatic coast, but split by the rugged Dinaric Range.

The Serbs dominated Yugoslavia from the first. Belgrade, the Serb capital, became the national capital, and street signs there remained exclusively in the Cyrillic alphabet. No meaningful steps toward federalism were taken in the 1920s and 1930s. Serbs saw themselves both as defenders of the Orthodox faith and of European civilization at large. Catholic Slovenes and Croats, as well as the Muslim Bosnians, though fellow south Slavs, became second-class Yugoslav citizens. Croats took advantage of the German occupation during World War II to contest their status, but also committed various atrocities against the temporarily weakened Serbs.

In addition, major economic disparities developed among the various provinces of Yugoslavia, with Slovenia and Croatia becoming relatively prosperous while Macedonia and parts of Serbia fell behind (fig. 6.17). When one considers that both Croatia and Bosnia-Herzegovina harbored memories of medieval independence, the challenges that faced this multi-ethnic state become clear.

The state was held together by a charismatic leader, Josip Tito, in the post-World War II era, but the rise to power of an uncompromising Serbian nationalist leader in the late 1980s sealed its fate. In the early 1990s, four provinces seceded from

Figure 6.17. The disintegration of the former Yugoslavia. Seven successor states emerged in the 1990s and 2000s: Slovenia, Croatia, Bosnia and Herzegovina, Macedonia, Montenegro, Serbia, and Kosovo. The latter did not declare independence until 2008. It has been recognized as an independent state by a number of European countries, as well as the United States, but Serbia, Russia, and several other countries insist that its declaration of independence is illegitimate. Hence, the long-term status of Kosovo remains in some doubt.

Yugoslavia and achieved independence—Slovenia, Croatia, Macedonia, and Bosnia-Herzegovina (fig. 6.17). In the early 2000s, Montenegro split off as well. Later in the decade Kosovo, a quasi-autonomous region within Serbia inhabited by an overwhelming majority of Albanians, followed Montenegro's lead. The dismantling of Yugoslavia was accomplished only with great bloodshed on all sides—primarily in Serbia, Croatia, and Bosnia-Herzegovina. The Serbian leadership undertook a program of ethnic cleansing in its territory. Croatia expelled hundreds of thousands of ethnic Serbs from its territory. And multi-ethnic Bosnia-Herzegovina was drawn into the vortex and disintegrated into a long civil war.

Traditionally in the Balkans people had identified with territories, regarding themselves as "Bosnians," "Kosovars," "Herzegovians," "Dalmacians," and such. In other words, they had regional rather than ethnic identities. Embedded in this mosaic of regions were scattered small areas of relative ethnic homogeneity. Serbia Proper was one of these. In those nuclei, nation-states developed beginning in the late nineteenth century, and as each expanded, ethnically mixed populations were annexed. As identity shifted from region to ethnicity, the stage was set for conflict. Political boundaries rarely matched ethnic borders, and most districts had a high degree of mixing. The nation-state principle, applied to such a situation, resulted in ethnic cleansing.

Of the successor states to the former Yugoslavia, Slovenia is arguably in the strongest position since it stood aside from the subsequent troubles and, in any case, had only a tiny Serb minority. Croatia, confronting an awkward territorial configuration and significant minorities, made matters worse by opting for a French-style unitary state that could not easily accommodate minority rights. Even some ethnic Croatian districts grew restive. In Istria, the westernmost part of Croatia, many people feel a greater loyalty to province than to state.

Landlocked Macedonia is a mere fragment of the former territory by that name, which laps over into Greece and Bulgaria and once housed a population of Bulgars, Pomaks, Turks, Greeks, and Albanians. Even the remnant independent Macedonia retains sizable Albanian and other Muslim minorities.

Bosnia-Herzegovina was, upon becoming independent, almost as diverse as the former Yugoslavia at large, a microcosm of that failed state. The partition that ended the civil war produced the Srpska Republic, now populated and ruled predominantly by Serbs. Its territory is very awkwardly shaped, with two areas barely joined at the strategic Posavina Corridor (fig. 6.17). The remainder of Bosnia-Herzegovia is made up of the "Muslim-Croat Federation," but in fact the Croat districts form the shadow "Herzeg-Bosna" Republic. Lying in Herzeg-Bosna is the major Croat religious pilgrimage town of Medjugorje, a place possessing enormous emotional importance to all Croats.

The condition of the remnant core of Yugoslavia—Serbia—was no more stable. Serb atrocities in Kosovo during the mid-1990s led its Albanian-Muslim population to declare their independence. Serbia has rejected the claim, but it seems unlikely that Kosovo can be reunited with Serbia. Vojvodina, the northernmost province of Yugoslavia, has a mixed population including many ethnic Hungarians, whose loyalty to a Serb-dominated nation-state is questionable. Also potentially troublesome is the Sandzak region on the border with Montenegro, peopled predominantly by 250,000 Slavic-speaking Muslims. The Yugoslav case shows that dismantlement of multiethnic states does not guarantee stability, as people are rarely distributed in ways that make line-drawing easy, and minorities are found almost everywhere.

RUSSIA: NATION-STATE OR EMPIRE?

In many respects, Russia presents a political anomaly in Europe. It is the only state to establish enduring unity over a sizable portion of Europe within the last millennium, causing eastern Europe to assume a very different political character from the West. Even in its greatly diminished post-Soviet size, Russia remains by far the largest independent state in Europe—and the entire world—while retaining aspects of empire long after the collapse of Europe's other imperial powers.

Muscovy—modern Moscow—was one of many competing principalities to emerge from an expansive Kiev-centered East Slav Kingdom whose demise in the thirteenth century was hastened by Tatar-Mongol invasions (fig. 6.18). Decisive in Muscovy's

Figure 6.18. Territorial evolution of Russia. Russia grew from a core area, the Principality of Muscovy around Moscow, to encompass a huge empire, which collapsed only in 1991. Its influence has at times extended deep into Europe and even more profoundly into Asia, but the East European Plain has always provided the spatial and physical focus of Russia.

development as the political focus of Russia was a succession of leaders who skillfully coop-erated with the Tatar-Mongols against competing Russian princedoms. Muscovy grew from its core area to dominate the East European Plain—traditionally called "European Russia"—and facing no natural barriers to the east, expanded unabated into Siberia, and then into the Caucasus and Central Asia. Following the Russian revolution and civil war, the Bolsheviks managed to reassemble much of the Czarist Empire by promising many important non-Russian populations territorial autonomy within the new communist state.

When the Soviet Union disintegrated in 1991, Russia faced a difficult transition. An empire traditionally under despotic, unitary rule, post-communist Russia evolved painfully and perhaps abortively toward nation-state status and federalism. In the polity that emerged from the collapsed empire, about 80% of the people were Russian and no single ethnic minority made up even 4% of the population. Increasingly, Russian nationalists have come to regard the country as a nation-state and emphasize its Eurasian—as opposed to European—character.

Federalism aims to accommodate ethnic minorities in autonomous republics. Yet Russia's territorial integrity has been tested as various Turkic, Caucasic, and Muslim minorities have sought, with greater or lesser fervor, autonomy or independence. Chechnya declared independence in 1991 and since then has undergone two periods of warfare with Moscow. Oil-rich Tatarstan, a Turkic Muslim republic lying on and beyond the Volga River in the southeastern reaches of the East European Plain, declared "sover-eignty" in 1990 and enjoyed considerable autonomy for the remainder of the decade. So did neighboring Bashkortostan, also Turkic and Muslim. In recent years, amid Moscow's recentralization of the Russian Federation, these aspirations have been muted.

Other republics and districts pose an array of challenges. Karelia, in the northwest, is a republic designated as the historic homeland of a Finnish-speaking people, but eth-nic Russians form the large majority of its population. The Kaliningrad District, on the Baltic Sea, presents a special problem to Russia. This territory was never a part of Russia before 1945, when it was taken from a defeated Germany, nor did any Russians live there. The German population was expelled and replaced by Russians. Moreover, Kaliningrad is an exclave, separated from the rest of Russian territory. In some ways, Kaliningrad is beginning to function like a separate Baltic republic, based on its status as a free-trade zone and smugglers' haven.

Another issue confronting Russia is the status of Belarus, one of the Soviet republics that became an independent state in 1991. Belarus did not actively seek independence, achieving that status by default when the USSR's central government was abolished. Many Belarusians identify as Russians, but there is a basis of Belarusian ethnicity. The Belarusian language, though closely related to the Russian tongue and spoken by only a minority in Belarus, is usually regarded as a distinct language. "Belarusian" often—but inaccurately—is translated as "White Russian," implying that they are a sub-ethnic group of a greater Russian people. But Belarusians also have much in common with Poles and Lithuanians, who controlled the isolated marshlands inhabited by the Belarusians until the late eighteenth century. Poverty-stricken and burdened with a corrupt, strong-armed dictator, Belarus represents a potential liability for Russia. A proclaimed federa-tion of the two countries lacks any real substance, but no noteworthy nation-building has occurred in Belarus, nor is public support for continued independence strong.

UKRAINE: FROM BORDER PROVINCE TO INDEPENDENT STATE

Ukraine, the second largest country in Europe in geographical area and the sixth largest in population, resembles Belarus in some ways. Its independence occurred in the same manner as that of Belarus, not as the result of a separatist movement, and many Ukrainians, especially the 12 million or so who are ethnic Russians, remain ambivalent about its independence.

Unlike Belarus, Ukraine contains huge areas of fertile soils and large mineral deposits, especially coal. It is a potentially rich country, and its present poverty is a reflection of political difficulties, both internal and external. Although "Ukraine" means "border province," commemorating its position along the battle lines between Russians and their historical enemies, the Tatar-Mongols, Turks, and Poles, the country has a distinguished history. The initial unification and Christianization of Russia emanated from Ukraine and its capital, Kiev.

The strongest nationalist sentiment in Ukraine is found in the western half of the country, sometimes referred to as the "European" part. Long ruled by Poland and Austria-Hungary, the western Ukrainians came under the influence of Roman Catholicism, giving rise to the Uniate Church (see Chapter 5)—a hybrid of Catholic and Orthodox faiths. The revived Uniate Church provides one major basis of Ukrainian nationalism today.

The eastern part of Ukraine, more heavily Orthodox and Russian, does not share this nationalism. The peninsula of Krym, jutting into the Black Sea and peopled dominantly by Russians and Crimean Tatars, recently was granted the status of autonomous republic in an effort to defuse separatist sentiment. The most heavily Russian district north of the peninsula, Kharkov (now renamed *Karkhiv* by Ukraine), is also restive. The westernmost part of the country, the *Zakarpats'ka* District, lies west of the Carpathian Mountains and has no history prior to 1945 of belonging to Ukraine. There, too, Ukrainian nationalism has not taken root, though no separatist sentiment has arisen.

A potential problem for Ukraine also exists in Transdnistria, a fertile, dominantly Slavic sliver of adjacent Moldova. A separatist movement exists there, but Transdnistria is small and unlikely to emerge as an independent state. Were it to secede from Moldova, the area might logically join Ukraine, but such a transfer might lead to a major boundary dispute, involving also Romania, which regards itself as Moldova's protector, given the two countries' shared language and Latinized culture.

European Integration

At the end of World War II, Europe found itself in ruins after a second devastating conflict in less than 50 years. Many Europeans felt that the only hope for the future lay in making some fundamental adjustments to the way Europe functioned politically. Yet this was difficult to do. The concept of the nation-state and the supporting doctrine of nationalism were deeply embedded principles in the European geographical imagination. Moreover, when the war ended, many state leaders focused their attention internally, adopting protectionist measures to help rejuvenate national economies. Even as the political map of

Europe had been changed somewhat by the war, it looked for a time as if the principles underlying the pre-war political geographic order would reemerge unscathed.

Nonetheless, a group of visionaries began calling for change—promoting the idea of a more integrated Europe. Few were ready to consider proposals for a United States of Europe, but by the 1950s the leaders of a core group of countries were willing to entertain tearing down some of the economic barriers that divided one country from another. The catalysts for moving forward were several. First, there was a recognition that it would be harder for countries with closer economic links to go to war with one another. Second, the increasing solidification of Soviet control over Eastern Europe prompted concerns about fragmentation in the West. Only by presenting a more united front, it was thought, could Western Europe hope to stand up to the increasingly unified and potentially threatening East. Third, the United States, which flooded Europe with redevelopment assistance under the Marshall Plan, pushed Western Europe toward a more unified stance in an effort to head off further internal conflict and promote solidarity in the face of the Soviet-dominated East. Finally, there was a sense within Europe that the world was increasingly being dominated by large superpowers. During the course of the prior 50 years, Europe had gone from being a major global player to an increasingly weakened and fragmented region. Only by working together, it was argued, could Europe regain some of its former standing.

The Low Countries provided a template for a possible way forward. Harkening back to a pre-war arrangement, in 1944 the governments in exile of Belgium, the Netherlands, and Luxembourg entered into the Benelux Customs Union, which created a free trade area among the three countries. Inspired in part by this example, in 1951 France, West Germany, and Italy joined the Low Countries in an agreement to create a "common market" in coal and steel: the European Coal and Steel Community (ECSC). By 1957, these same six countries decided to broaden greatly the scope of what they were doing—establishing the European Economic Community (EEC), which was designed to bring into being a common market in agricultural and industrial goods. These countries also founded a cooperative agency focused on nuclear energy: the European Atomic Energy Community (EURATOM).

Of the three "communities"—ECSC, EEC, and EURATOM—the EEC was clearly the largest and most important. Hence, the roots of the European unity project are often traced to the EEC and the agreement that brought it into being: the Treaty of Rome. (European treaties are often named after the place where they are negotiated and signed.) What started with six countries expanded in subsequent decades to include 9, then 10, then 12, then 15, then 25, and most recently 27 countries (fig. 6.19). The scope and significance of the integration project has also grown over time. That growth is reflected in changes to the name given to the formal European integration project. The EEC became the EC (the European Community), which in turn became the EU (European Union).

Broadly, the integration process unfolded through five periods. The first period, stretching from the founding of the EEC through the early 1970s, saw the establishment of basic institutions and remarkable success in tearing down tariff trade barriers between countries. Brussels emerged as the administrative center—a brilliant choice given that it lies at the center of a country straddling the Romance-Germanic language divide. Designating Brussels as the administrative capital also meant not having to choose between the two major powers in the early EEC: France and Germany. Even though the executive

Figure 6.19. The European Union. From a six-country nucleus in the 1950s, the EEC/EC/EU has grown to include much of Europe.

arm of the EEC was located in Brussels, a desire not to concentrate too much power in one place led to a decision to locate the major judicial functions in Luxembourg and to house the parliament, when meeting in general session, in Strasbourg—a city in France, but one that sits along the German border, that was traded back and forth between France and Germany over the centuries, and that has an indigenous population speaking a Germanic dialect. During the first period of European integration all tariffs were eliminated within the EEC, and the economies of the Member States became increasingly interlinked. By the late 1960s, the institutions of the three European communities were formally merged. Hence, the EEC became subsumed within something known as the European Communities, which soon came to be referred to simply as the European Community (EC). The success of economic integration and the growing willingness of the founding states to admit others led to the addition of three new Member States in 1973: Denmark, the United Kingdom, and Ireland (fig. 6.19).

The second major period in the European integration project stretched from late 1973 to the mid-1980s. Initiating this period was a major global economic recession. With economic growth slowed, countries within the EC began looking for ways to protect their industries. Tariffs were no longer an option, but in violation of the spirit of the European integration project, some turned to non-tariff trade barriers (e.g., regulations and taxes that impede the exchange of goods between countries). Many of these were struck down by the administrative and judicial arms of the EC, but the late 1970s through the early 1980s was a period of stasis for the EC in general. No great forward strides were taken, but the institutions were sufficiently robust to keep things from sliding back too far. Only one new country joined the EC during this period: Greece, in 1981 (fig. 6.19). Greece was less well off than the other EC members, but it was an appealing candidate both because of its historical legacy as the crucible of European civilization, and because membership was seen as a way to ensure that communists did not gain the upper hand in the country.

The third major period of European integration stretched from the mid-1980s to 1993. This was a significant period in the expansion of the administrative competence of the EU (known in Euro-speak as *deepening*), and led to the establishment of what could increasingly be regarded as a single economic space within the EC. By the mid-1980s it became clear that something fairly dramatic was needed to end the stagnation that had characterized the late 1970s and early 1980s. A series of meetings culminated in the adoption of the Single European Act in 1986, which called for the elimination of all non-tariff trade barriers by 1992 and paved the way for greater political cooperation. Around the same time, a number of Member States signed the so-called *Schengen Agreement*, which called for the elimination of border controls between participating countries. By the early 1990s, the project of eliminating non-tariff trade barriers was successful, and the EC was becoming increasingly powerful in arenas beyond the purely economic. The EC took on growing responsibility, for example, in the environmental policy and regional development arenas. This period also saw further territorial expansion of the EC (known as *widening*), with Spain and Portugal joining in 1985 with a multi-year phase-in given the economic disparities that existed between those two countries and most other parts of the EC. What had been East Germany came into the fold as part of an enlarged Germany after reunification in 1990 (fig. 6.19).

Building on the momentum of the third period, the fourth period of integration was ushered in by the signing of the Maastricht Treaty in late 1993. Also known as the Treaty on European Union, this treaty transformed the EC into the European Union (EU). The treaty institutionalized greater cooperation in law enforcement, judicial matters, and immigration; it gave greater power to the European parliament; it expanded the EU's role in social matters; and it paved the way for a common currency in Europe (the euro). The treaty was contested in some parts of Europe, and was only adopted after two votes in Denmark and special opt-out provisions on social matters were worked out for the United

Kingdom. But its general impact was to further the momentum of European integration. Within a few years, the Amsterdam Treaty gave the EU a greater role in foreign policy and, by 1998, a European Central Bank had been founded. Then in the early 2000s, the euro came into use throughout much of the EU (fig. 6.20). Three other states joined the EU near the beginning of this period: Sweden, Finland, and Austria (fig. 6.19).

The latest period in the European integration project is associated with the extraordinary territorial expansion of the EU in May 2004 to encompass eight new Member States in the eastern part of Europe (Estonia, Latvia, Lithuania, Poland, Czechia, Slovakia, Hungary, and Slovenia), as well as two Mediterranean islands (Cyprus and

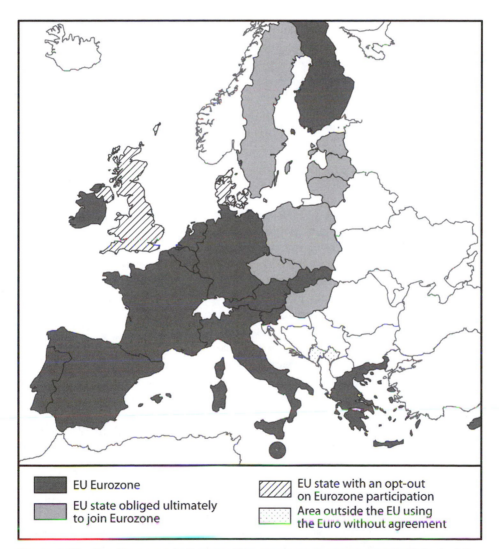

Figure 6.20. The Eurozone in Europe. The common currency was instituted at the beginning of the twenty-first century. A number of countries in the European east are hoping to join the euro zone, but the citizens of the United Kingdom and Denmark are not anxious to sacrifice their national currencies.

Malta)—followed by the addition of two more Member States in 2007 (Romania and Bulgaria) (fig. 6.19). The 2004 expansion alone added 77 million people and over 700,000 square kilometers to the EU. The expansion was driven by a sense of obligation in the European west toward the peoples and countries that had long been under Soviet domination, and by the desire to promote stability in Europe as a whole. Expansion has brought some economic gains—particularly for the new entrants—but it has also greatly complicated the integration process. The depth of the complications is clearly symbolized by the defeat of a proposed Constitution for the newly expanded EU at the hands of French and Dutch voters in 2005. The EU continues to function under a set of treaties, but the future is somewhat murky given growing concerns about how the EU will function in its enlarged form, about whose interests will be served, and about how far the EU should expand.

We will be in a better position to address where the EU stands and where it is going after we have examined the economic and social foundations of contemporary Europe. Hence, we will return to these matters at the end of the book. For present purposes, there are several important things to note. First, whatever questions are now being asked about the future of the EU, European integration has had an extraordinary impact on the economic and political geography of Europe. Europe has taken far more significant steps toward integration than anywhere else in the world. The greatest steps have been taken in the economic arena. The EU is, in important respects, a unified economic space, although there are certainly aspects of the economy—especially labor—that do not move seamlessly across national borders. Perhaps more remarkably, European integration has done something that would have seemed unthinkable 70 years ago: create a political and social environment that makes warfare between EU Member States almost unimaginable. Identification with Europe as a political space has grown, and a traditional map of European states is increasingly regarded as an insufficient representation of the region's political geography.

None of this means that the European state is about to disappear, however, or that the path ahead for European integration will be smooth. To the contrary, state nationalism is very much alive and well in Europe, and as we will see in chapters 11 and 12, migration and the prospects for further expansion of the EU are serving to intensify those feelings in some quarters. Moreover, many Europeans regard the EU as a bureaucratic maze, and with important decisions being made by political appointees rather than directly elected representatives, there is considerable concern about what some term a democratic deficit in the EU. Finally, the challenge of incorporating the disparate economies and peoples of the newest member states within the EU has given rise to considerable anxiety about the future of Europe's experiment with integration.

Supranational Military Engagements

Although EEC/EC/EU has reshaped economic, and to some extent political, space in Europe, extrastate military-security matters in Europe have been vested primarily in a different supranational organization: the North Atlantic Treaty Organization (NATO). Founded in 1949, NATO has been dominated from the first by the United States. During the four decades of the Cold War, NATO was effectively a military alliance confronting the Soviet Bloc, which controlled the eastern half of Europe (fig. 6.21). Weakened by World War II, Europe had become a zone of confrontation between the United States and the Soviet Union, and NATO provided the security umbrella within which the EEC/EC/EU developed.

With the collapse of the Soviet threat after 1990, NATO expanded into several former Soviet satellite states. Poland, Czechia, and Hungary joined in 1999, followed by Estonia, Latvia, Lithuania, Slovenia, Slovakia, Bulgaria, and Romania in 2004 (fig. 6.21). A number of other European countries have expressed interest in

■	Original member, 1949	⊠	Enlargement, 1999	
▨	Enlargement, 1950s	▨	Enlargement, 2004	
▨	Enlargement, 1982	⋯	Invited, 2008	
▨	Enlargement, 1990	★	Applicant state	

Figure 6.21.   NATO expansion, 1949 to present. Long dominated by the United States, NATO is a holdover from the Cold War, searching for a new *raison d'être*. Some applicant countries fear a revival of Russian imperialism.

joining, including Albania, Croatia, Macedonia, Georgia, Montenegro, and Ukraine. The purpose of NATO has also changed. It has become a military force employed to intervene in local and regional conflicts. In Bosnia-Herzegovina, NATO forces have served as peacekeepers. In Kosovo, the alliance undertook an eleven-week bombing campaign against the former Yugoslavia.

In the wake of the terrorist attacks on the United States on September 11, 2001, and the subsequent invasion of Afghanistan, NATO took command of the International Security Assistance Force (ISAF) in that country. Tensions between parts of Europe and the United States, over the U.S.-led invasion of Iraq and U.S. efforts to build a missile defense system in Europe, have raised growing questions in Europe about the region's role in an organization that is seen as being increasingly dominated by the United States. In response, there are ongoing efforts to strengthen the EU's European Security and Defense Policy and to create a military force that can deal with European crises. A significant step was taken in 2004 when a European Union Force (EUFOR) took over leadership of the mission in Bosnia and Herzegovina from NATO. Foreign policy differences among EU states may well work against a significant role for EUFOR outside of Europe, but it is already making a difference within Europe itself.

There is much more to say about Europe's changing political geography, but let us turn first to the ways Europeans have carved out a living, and the landscapes and socioeconomic patterns they have created in the process. We begin our exploration in the rural sector—the focus of the next chapter.

Sources and Suggested Readings

Agnew, J. 2007. No Borders, No Nations: Making Greece in Macedonia. *Annals of the Association of American Geographers* 97 (2): 398–422.

———. 2003. Territoriality and Political Identity in Europe. In *Europe without Borders*, eds. M. Berezin and M. Schain, 219–242. Baltimore: Johns Hopkins Press.

———. 1995. The Rhetoric of Regionalism: the Northern League in Italian Politics, 1983–94. *Transactions of the Institute of British Geographers* 20: 156–172.

Akinwumi, A. E. 2006. Changing Spaces, Emergent Places: Transborder Regionalism in the 'New' Europe. *Political Geography* 25 (7): 850–859.

Berezin, M., and M. Schain. 2003. *Europe without Borders: Remapping Territory, Citizenship, and Identity in a Transnational Age.* Baltimore: Johns Hopkins University Press.

Browning, C. S. 2003. The Region-Building Approach Revisited: The Continued Othering of Russia in Discourses of Region-Building in the European North. *Geopolitics* 8 (1): 45–71.

Brubaker, R. 1996. *Nationalism Reframed: Nationhood and the National Question in the New Europe.* Cambridge: Cambridge University Press.

Clem, R. S. 2006. Russia's Electoral Geography: A Review. *Eurasian Geography and Economics* 47 (4): 381–406.

Clem, R. S., and P. R. Craumer. 2005. Shades of Orange: The Electoral Geography of Ukraine's 2004 Presidential Elections. *Eurasian Geography and Economics* 46 (5): 364–385.

Hall, D. 2001. Albania in Europe: Condemned to the Periphery or Beyond? *Geopolitics* 6 (1): 107–118.

Hooghe, L., and G. Marks. 2003. Unraveling the Central State, but How? Types of Multi-Level Governance. *American Political Science Review* 97 (2): 233–243.

Houtum, H. v., O. Kramsch, and W. Zierhofer, eds. 2005. *B/Ordering Space.* Burlington, VT: Ashgate.

Hudson, R. 2000. One Europe or Many? Reflections on Becoming European. *Transactions—Institute of British Geographers* 25 (4): 409–426.

Jeffery, C., ed. 1999. *Recasting German Federalism: The Legacies of Unification.* New York: Pinter.

Jones, A. 2006. Narrative-Based Production of State Spaces for International Region Building: Europeanization and the Mediterranean. *Annals of the Association of American Geographers* 96 (2): 415–431.

Jones, A., and J. Clark. 2003. From Filière to Territoire: Changing Rural Policy in the Languedoc. *Modern & Contemporary France* 11 (3): 335–347.

Jönsson, C., S. Tägil, and G. Törnqvist. 2000. *Organizing European Space.* London: SAGE Publications.

Kaplan, D. H., and J. Hakli, eds. 2002. *Boundaries and Place: European Borderlands in Geographical Context.* Lanham: Rowman & Littlefield.

Klemencic, V. and R. Genorio. 1993. The New State of Slovenia and its Function within the Frame of Europe. *GeoJournal* 30: 323–333.

Lefebvre, E. L. 2003. Belgian Citizenship: Managing Linguistic, Regional, and Economic Demands. *Citizenship Studies* 7 (1): 111–134.

Mau, S. 2006. Politics and Borders: Processes of Demarcation and Political System-Building in the European Union. *Berliner Journal fur Soziologie* 16 (1): 115–132.

Meleshevich, A. 2006. Geographical Patterns of Party Support in the Baltic States, Russia, and Ukraine. *European Urban and Regional Studies* 13 (2): 113–129.

Paasi, A. 2002. Regional Transformation in the European Context: Notes on Regions, Boundaries and Identity. *Space & Polity* 6 (2): 197–201.

Perepechko, A. S., V. A. Kolossov, and C. ZumBrunnen. 2007. Remeasuring and Rethinking Social Cleavages in Russia: Continuity and Changes in Electoral Geography 1917–1995. *Political Geography* 26 (2): 179–208.

Roper, S. 2007. Cross-Border and Local Co-Operation on the Island of Ireland: An Economic Perspective. *Political Geography* 26 (5): 554–574.

Rumford, C. 2007. Does Europe Have Cosmopolitan Borders? *Globalizations* 4 (3): 327–339.

Sassen, S. 2006. *Territory, Authority, Rights: From Medieval to Global Assemblages.* Princeton: Princeton University Press.

Trenz, H.-J. 2007. Reconciling Diversity and Unity. *Ethnicities* 7 (2): 157–185.

Walters, W. 2004. The Frontiers of the European Union: A Geostrategic Perspective. *Geopolitics* 9 (3): 674–698.

CHAPTER 7

Land and Life in the Rural Sector

The vast majority of Europeans today live in cities, but until recently most people lived in rural areas and made their living by farming, herding, fishing, and harvesting natural resources. To comprehend both the legacy of the past and the ongoing agrarian sector Europe, it is important to consider how people have lived and worked in rural Europe. This means paying particular attention to **primary economic activities**, meaning those involved in extracting resources from the earth and seas (e.g., agriculture, mining, fishing, and lumbering). Because agriculture is the most important of these, we will emphasize it in this chapter, together with the land and settlement patterns that went along with it.

Traditional Agriculture

The origins of European agriculture lie in prehistory in the same hearth that gave Europe Christianity, Indo-European speech, and the political state. The domestication of plants and animals—the **neolithic revolution**—occurred in the Near East and entered Europe later, apparently borne by proto-Indo-Europeans. For that reason, the maps of linguistic and agricultural diffusion largely match (compare figs. 4.4 and 7.1). Both language and agrarian technology advanced from southeast to northwest over a period of about 4 millennia. Agriculture came first to Greece and arrived last in the lands beyond the North and Baltic Seas.

The advent of agriculture seems to have occurred in two ways. In southeastern and Central Europe, agriculture made a sudden intrusion, producing a sharp break in the archaeological record, as hunters were displaced by farmers (fig. 7.1). Elsewhere, the advent of farming occurred more gradually. Indigenous groups, such as the Etruscans in Italy and Uralic speakers in the north, often adopted agriculture rather than being displaced or absorbed. Transitional economies based both upon farming and hunting/gathering became typical, blurring the distinction between mesolithic and neolithic.

The earliest neolithic crop complex included wheat, barley, lentils, peas, and flax. Other crops came later, after the neolithic diffusion had reached Europe. Europe's

Figure 7.1.   Neolithic origins and the diffusion of agriculture in Europe. Domesticated plants and animals reached Europe from the Near East. The map is based upon archaeological finds but nevertheless remains speculative and controversial in detail. *Sources:* Chapman, J. and J. Müller. 1990. Early Farmers in the Mediterranean Basin. *Antiquity* 64: 128; Breunig, P. 1987. *14C-Chronologie des Vorderasiatischen, Südost- und Mitteleuropäischen Neolithikums*, Köln, D: Böhlau; Zilhão 1993; Renfrew 1989 and Krantz 1988, both cited in Chapter 4; Ryan and Pitman 1998, cited in Chapter 2; Sokal et al. 1991, cited in Chapter 5; Thorpe 1996.

garden vegetables and orchard trees belong among these later introductions from the Near East by way of Anatolia. Grapes may first have been made into wine in Georgia, a European outpost in the Caucasus region.

Domestic herd animals also came from the Near East. Cattle, pigs, sheep, goats, donkeys, and horses all first entered Europe by way of Anatolia, as did poultry. The basic tools of agriculture, such as the hoe and plow, the technique of terracing, and irrigation technology also came from the Near East by way of Anatolia. In the formation of early agriculture, then, Europe borrowed from higher civilizations to the east and south.

Spreading through Europe, and adjusting to different environments and cultures, agriculture fragmented into traditional regional types. The major ancient and traditional agrarian systems were the following: (1) Mediterranean agriculture; (2) three-field farming; (3) hardscrabble herding/farming; (4) shifting cultivation; and (5) nomadic herding (fig. 7.2). The basic understanding of Europe's physical geography outlined in Chapter 2 helps us understand why different agricultural activities came to dominate in different parts of Europe.

MEDITERRANEAN AGRICULTURE

The rural peoples of Cyprus, Greece, the eastern Adriatic coast, peninsular Italy, the Languedoc Plain, and southern Iberia traditionally practiced a distinctive agrarian system, appropriately referred to as **Mediterranean agriculture**. This system came more or less unaltered from the neolithic hearth to the east. Agriculture had arisen in an eastern extension of the Mediterranean climate zone, and the southern European peninsulas offered a sufficiently similar setting such that few adaptive changes were necessary.

By the time of classical Greco-Roman civilization, Mediterranean agriculture consisted of a threefold system of field agriculture, horticulture, and pasture, beautifully adapted to the unique climate and rugged terrain of Southern Europe. The Mediterranean climate has a long summer drought and mild, rainy winters. The field was devoted to the winter cultivation of small grains. These thrived in the cool, wet season without irrigation. Wheat and barley, sown with the arrival of the first autumnal rain showers, grew slowly through the winter months and reached maturity in the warm, sunny days of late spring. Harvesting occurred before the annual drought tightened its grip on the land. The great harvest festivals of the Mediterranean folk accordingly came in the spring rather than the fall. Farmers typically employed a two-field rotational system, cultivating the land only every other year to prevent soil exhaustion. Wheat was generally the more important of the two grain crops, but barley achieved greater importance in drier areas with poor soils since it is hardier than wheat. In the middle 1900s wheat and barley still accounted for 40% of all tilled land in Italy and 50% in Greece. Many classical farmers also raised millet, a hardy grain that tolerates heat, drought, and poor soils.

Horticulture provided the second element of the traditional Mediterranean agricultural trinity. Of particular importance were orchards and vineyards of drought-resistant

Figure 7.2.   Ancient and traditional types of agriculture. The division between wheat and rye as the dominant bread grain, as of about 1900 C.E. Ancient and traditional systems gave way at widely different periods in the various parts of Europe.

perennials native to the Mediterranean region and able to withstand the summer dry season. From the vineyard, Mediterranean farmers derived table grapes—raisins dried after the late summer harvest before the onset of rain—and wine. Southern Europeans have a long and close relationship with wine. About 1000 B.C.E., in the Greek lands, a cult devoted to the god Dionysus arose, in which wine and alcoholic intoxication served as aids to religious experience. The cult, not surprisingly, became very popular among the common folk, and by the sixth century B.C.E. it had gained governmental approval. Dionysus and wine spread to the western Mediterranean with the Greek colonists, and the Romans subsequently accepted the cult, renaming the wine god Bacchus. After Christianization of the Roman Empire, wine retained its ancient Dionysian sacredness by finding a place in the Eucharist as the symbolic blood of

Christ. Vineyards grow both on terraced hillsides and on alluvial valley floors. The vine produces a crop of high value on a wide variety of surfaces and soils, including steep slopes, without irrigation.

The olive is another important element of Mediterranean horticulture. Olive trees are long-lived and drought-resistant, but not tolerant of a hard frost. The olive tree yields a crop only in alternate years, blossoming in the first year and bearing fruit in the next; harvesting is accomplished by hitting the branches with a pole. While Mediterranean peoples eat many olives, the principal value of the olive tree, both in ancient times and today, is as a source of cooking oil. Butter has never been produced in Southern Europe, and olive oil provides a needed substitute.

Other orchard trees of the classical Mediterranean included the fig, which is also drought-resistant, native to the area, and suited to hillsides; the pistacio; the carob; and the pomegranate, a small tree that yields a tasty acidic flesh from the outer coating of its numerous seeds. While horticulture and field agriculture typically occupied different areas within the village lands of the Mediterranean, intertillage also occurred. In this system, wheat and barley were sown among the widely spaced orchard trees (fig. 7.3). While not technically an element of horticulture, the cork oak also played an important role in some Mediterranean regions. Every eight to ten years, the outer bark of this wild tree can be stripped, producing a commercially valuable item of trade (fig. 7.4).

Figure 7.3.   Intertillage of wheat and olives in an alluvial valley in Greece. Two typical Mediterranean crops share the same field on the island of Crete. The wheat has only recently been reaped by hand and tied into bundles to be carried in for threshing. Intertillage is common in traditional Mediterranean agriculture. The month is May, the time of grain harvest before the drought of summer. Olives from these young trees will be ready for harvest in autumn. (Photo by T.G.J.-B., 1971.)

Figure 7.4.   Cork newly stripped from the trunks of cork oak trees in Portugal. It takes about ten years for the bark to regenerate to a point where the tree can be stripped again. The numbers on the tree correspond to the last digit of the year in which the trunk was stripped. (Photo by A.B.M., 1986.)

The third element of traditional Mediterranean agriculture consisted of the pasture. Village herders raised mainly small livestock, particularly sheep, goats, and swine. These animals survived on the scanty forage offered by the rugged highland pastures and mountain oak forests of southern Europe. Goats and sheep moved with agility through the rocky landscape, and pigs thrived on the mast of the native live oak forests. Sheep, the most numerous livestock, provided wool, hides, and some meat—though the Mediterranean diet remained heavily vegetarian. Goats yielded mohair, milk, and hides, and to a certain extent they took the place of dairy cattle in Southern Europe. The cheeses produced in Mediterranean districts come from goat's milk or, more rarely, from sheep's milk, as in Roquefort.

The Mediterranean pasture remained largely divorced from field agriculture and horticulture. No crop harvests went as feed or fodder for the herds, and animal manure was not collected as fertilizer for the fields or orchards. In fact, livestock often ranged very far from villages, under the care of migrant shepherds and swineherders. In the dry, hot summer, sheep and goats moved to high pastures in the mountains, where grass grew more abundantly, and during the winter they migrated down to marshy parts of the alluvial lowlands. The herders went with them, in a system called **transhumance**, and often months passed between the herders' visits to the home village. The beast of burden of the traditional Mediterranean agriculture was the donkey—though some farmers did not own one, making do instead with only human labor.

This, then, was the agriculture of classical times. All three of the basic enterprises were practiced on most farms, though one or another might have been emphasized. From the diverse unspecialized trinity of small grains, vine and tree crops, and small livestock, nearly all of life's necessities could be obtained, including woolen and leather clothing, bread, beverages, fruit, cheese, cooking oil, and even a cork for the leather wine container.

THREE-FIELD FARMING

North of the Mediterranean, in fertile lands beyond the mountains and centered in the Great and East European plains and the Hungarian Basin, a second traditional agricultural system once prevailed: **three-field farming** (fig. 7.2). In this system, found mainly among Germanic and Slavic peoples living in the marine west coast and humid continental climate regions, grains were raised on a three-field rotation, in which the land was cropped two out of every three years. In this succession, any particular field was planted first to a summer crop, next to a winter grain, and then allowed to lie fallow for a year. At any given time, one-third of the land was at each stage in the cycle.

The grains differed somewhat within the area of three-field farming. In southern and western areas, including England, France, and northwestern Iberia, wheat was the principal and preferred bread grain. Rye, the second great bread grain, dominated the north, in Germany, Scandinavia, Poland, and Russia, where dark bread was preferred. Poland and Russia together produce nearly half of the world's rye today. Rye has greater resistance to cold and more tolerance for acidic, sandy soils than does wheat, allowing it to succeed better in northern and eastern regions. Oats share the hardiness of rye and grow, usually as a summer grain, throughout the three-field area, providing oatcakes, gruel, and—most important—the major livestock feed grain of the system. The fourth major grain, barley, provided beer, the northern substitute for wine, but was also raised primarily as a feed grain.

Oats and rye apparently joined the ancient Indo-European agrarian system as it spread north into colder lands. Earlier, these two grains had apparently grown only as weeds in the wheat and barley fields of early agriculturists in the south and east. Rye and oats may be the only crops domesticated within Europe. Flax, one of the original Near Eastern crops, made the transition northward to find an important place in three-field farming as the major fiber crop. Linen garments are made from flax. Still today, the old three-field countries, led by Russia, produce much of the world's flax.

Horticulture also survived the northward diffusion into colder lands, though a different array of fruit trees from those of the Mediterranean prevailed. In place of the olive, almond, fig, and pomegranate came the apple, pear, peach, cherry, and plum, all of Asian origin but also able to grow in the north. The grapevine eventually struggled northward, but reached its climatic limits roughly along the line of the Seine, Rhine, and Danube rivers. Even there, it thrived best on south-facing, sunny slopes.

Another basic part of three-field farming, the cutting of hay from meadowland, provided additional sustenance for livestock during the winter season. In our modern urban society, the meanings of "meadow" and "pasture" have come to be treated as synonymous. Traditionally, livestock grazed pasture but not meadow, from which hay was to be cut. As the famous nursery rhyme admonishes, "sheep's in the meadow" was a state of affairs to be corrected. During much of the winter season, the livestock remained in stalls to consume hay and feed grains. At the opposite season, they grazed fallow fields, pastures, and remnant forests, which usually lay toward the periphery of village lands.

Livestock played a much greater role in three-field farming than in Mediterranean agriculture, supplying a larger part of the rural diet. Cattle, the dominant animals, provided meat, dairy products, manure for the fields, and, as oxen, power to pull the bulky plow characteristic of the Germanic and Slavic lands. In more mountainous areas, transhumance was practiced. In much of Central Europe, including Germany and Poland, swine were a more important source of meat than cattle, and pork is still a mainstay of the diet there. The unique value of swine is their ability to convert even the least savory garbage and waste into high-quality meat. Few areas lacked flocks of sheep, but only in areas of poor quality, such as the Lüneburger Heath of northern Germany, did they serve as the most important livestock.

Perhaps the key difference between three-field farming and Mediterranean agriculture was the close relationship in the former between crops and livestock. The Mediterranean farmer raised both plants and animals, but there was little or no tie between the two, and animal husbandry remained separate from tillage. In the three-field system, crops and livestock were inseparable, for the animals provided the manure used to maintain soil fertility and the power for plowing the fields. In turn, much of the produce of the cropland, particularly the barley and oats, went to feed the livestock, and meadow and pasture occupied extensive acreage.

HARDSCRABBLE HERDER-FARMERS

Separating and surrounding the favored lands of the three-field farming and Mediterranean agriculture lay **hardscrabble belts**, afflicted with broken terrain, excessive cloudiness, and/or sterile soils (fig. 7.2). In these regions, open-range livestock herding constituted the dominant traditional activity, with crop farming minor and secondary in importance. From ancient times, stable village-dwelling farmers of the Mediterranean and Germano-Slavic lands both vilified and romanticized the herders of the peripheries—Celts, Vikings, Basques, Berbers, Vlakhs, and others.

In common with Mediterranean shepherds, the herder-farmer hardscrabble folk relied heavily upon transhumance, shifting their herds seasonally. While these shifts usually occurred between highlands in the summer and lowlands in the winter, other patterns also developed. For example, in Las Marismas, the great marsh at the mouth of the Guadalquivir River in Spain, Iberian longhorn cattle entered the core of the wetlands in the dry summer and then retreated to the peripheries of the marsh as the floods of winter turned the area into a huge lake. In Somersetshire, England, an expanse of low wetlands also provided the summer pastures. (The word Somerset means "summer pastures.")

Cattle were the favored animals of the herder-farmers, and a milking culture-complex characterized most of these areas. Alpine areas, even before the beginning of the Common Era, exported cheese, and by about 1100 C.E., a distinctive high-mountain system of dairy cattle herding developed among the Walser people there, involving transhumance, hay cutting, winter stall-feeding, milk products, and sheep raising. (Think of the lifestyle depicted in the famous story of Heidi.) Sheep dominated most of the other hill and mountain areas and were the favored animal of the Vlakhs, Basques, and Dinaric folk. In response to the demands of late medieval and Renaissance woolen textile industries, as well as the mechanized woolen mills of the Industrial Revolution (discussed in Chapter 8), many highland herding areas shifted from cattle to sheep.

The role of crops in this traditional system, while secondary, was still significant. In most areas, an infield-outfield system was practiced, involving a small, continuously cropped area close to the farmstead, the "infield," surrounded by a much more extensive "outfield." Only a small part of the outfield was planted at any given time, and a lengthy fallow period of a decade or more was needed to restore fertility after several crops.

SHIFTING CULTIVATION OF THE NORTH

In the subarctic expanse of taiga with poor soils, Finnic peoples of the forests practiced another traditional farming system called **shifting cultivation** (fig. 7.2). They cut down trees in small clearings, allowed the dead vegetation to dry, burned it, and then sowed rye and barley in the fertile ashes among the stumps (fig. 7.5). After a year or two, shifting cultivators (or burnbeaters as they were sometimes known) abandoned the clearing and made another. Shifting cultivation made the infertile, acidic soils of the virgin taiga highly productive for one crop year. Farmers cut or girdled trees in the early spring of the first year and allowed the wood to dry until midsummer of the third year and then set fire to the clearing. They then planted rye, which came to harvest in the fourth summer, after which the field was abandoned. The system must have offered the spectacular sight of flaming tree trunks being rolled over the ground by soot-blackened men and women. Shifting cultivators also kept cattle herds in the woods, and many relied as much on hunting and fishing as upon agriculture for livelihood. So successful was their system that the Swedish crown introduced Finnish shifting cultivators into interior Scandinavia as colonists after about 1575. In the long run, however, population pressures made shifting cultivation untenable in northern Europe, and it has not been practiced since about 1920.

NOMADIC HERDING

In the outermost peripheries of Europe the climatic extremes of cold, infertility, or aridity worked against the introduction of agriculture. In the dry Asian steppe, only the herd animals, not the crops of the ancient Near East agricultural hearth, were part

Figure 7.5.   Finnish farmers in the interior of their country practicing a traditional form of shifting cultivation that required the repeated clearing and burning of woodland. The fields were used only for one or two years before being abandoned. (Photo by T.G.J.-B., 1985, at the Kuopion Museum in Kuopio, Finland.)

of the mix. The Asiatic herders moved from place to place, seeking fresh pastures for their animals. The steppe corridor of the southeast and the Hungarian Puszta received wave after wave of such **nomadic herders**, who raised horses, sheep, goats, and cattle. Among them were the Magyars, Avars, Bulgars, Tatars, and many others, driving their flocks and herds westward in a competition for land.

A unique group of nomadic herders, the Sami, inhabited Sapmi (Lapland) in the far north. None of the Near Eastern herd animals could survive in the arctic tundra, but the Sami observed their linguistic cousins, the Finns, herding cattle. Following that example, they or some neighboring tundra people domesticated the reindeer, which became the sole basis of their herding system (fig. 7.6). The Sami had no other animals and no crops at all. Like the Finns, they also engaged in hunting and fishing, but Sami herders acquired many of the necessities of life from the reindeer: meat for food, skins for housing and clothing, and bone for tools and instruments. They spent the summer herding stock on the tundras of the hilly interior and northern Scandinavian coastal fringe, including some islands off the coast of Norway. In wintertime, the reindeer migrated into the protective coniferous forests adjacent to the tundra, which afforded shelter from the bitterly cold winds of the open tundra. Autumn and spring were spent en route to and from the summer pastures on the tundra. The Sami had no awareness of international boundaries and moved freely through what is today Norwegian, Swedish, Finnish, and Russian territory.

Figure 7.6.   Reindeer herds belonging to the Sami in northern Scandinavia. The formerly nomadic system has evolved into ranching today. (Photo by T.G.J.-B., 1985.)

Traditional Land and Settlement Patterns

Before the modern era, a landed aristocracy dominated a tenant peasantry in both the Mediterranean and three-field faming regions of Europe. Most agriculture was carried out on small plots. It was unspecialized and subsistence based—designed to produce the basic necessities of life. The fields of the Mediterranean region were divided into countless block-shaped parcels, forming a complicated patchwork of fragmented holdings. In districts colonized during Roman times, a more rigid checkerboard pattern survives in places, a legacy of the imperial land survey system (fig. 7.7). The Roman period also saw the establishment of some large grain farms in fertile parts of Sicily, northern Italy, and more far-flung areas to serve the needs of the expanding empire. Once the empire came to an end, however, the nobility took over control of large estates—called **latifundia**—which were divided into small units and farmed by indentured peasants. Because of a shortage of flat land in the Mediterranean, terraces were built on the hillsides of slopes throughout the region. Many of these continued to be farmed through the nineteenth, and into the twentieth, century, but most have now been abandoned.

As in the Mediterranean farming region, the lands devoted to three-field farming were controlled by an aristocracy that dominated a tenant peasantry. Nonetheless, field patterns north of the Alps and Pyrenees were quite different from their counterparts to the south. In most cases the land was divided into long, narrow strips (fig. 7.8). The strip field accommodated the massive moldboard plow of the three-field farmers, a

Figure 7.7. Field patterns exhibiting Roman influence, in the Campania north of Naples, Italy. Fields in the Mediterranean areas, dominated by the use of the small plow, take on a rectangular shape. In this instance, the rectangularity has been made even more pronounced by the survival of the Roman rectangular survey system.

device that cut deeply into the earth and turned the soil over, creating a furrow. Invented by the Slavs and later adopted among the Germanic peoples, the moldboard plow was pulled by teams of oxen. It was difficult to turn around. By laying the fields out in long, narrow strips, the number of times the plow and team needed to be turned was minimized.

An additional north-south difference in the traditional European agricultural landscape was produced by the different inheritance systems of Germanic and Roman Europe discussed in Chapter 3. Here the important dividing line was not the Alps and

Figure 7.8. Fragmented, long-lot landholdings in Lorraine. Small strip fields typical of three-field farming survived in the irregular clustered village of Seichamp, near Nancy in northeastern France, into the twentieth century. The 132 separate strips belonging to one sample farm are shown. *Source:* Demangeon, A. 1946. *La France,* Paris, F: Armand Colin, with modifications.

Pyrenees but the northern limit where traditions developed during Roman times held sway. In that part of Europe, which encompassed both the southern part of the three-field farming area and the Mediterranean region, the practice of dividing the land equally among offspring resulted in a high degree of land fragmentation over time (fig. 7.8). By contrast, where the Germanic tradition of primogeniture dominated, larger land parcels tended to remain intact because the oldest son of each generation would inherit the entire parcel.

Turning to settlement patterns, most rural inhabitants lived in clustered or semi-clustered villages and hamlets (fig. 7.9). The farmers then traveled to their fields. Clustering was a response to social needs and family ties in an era when transportation was limited to walking or a cart pulled slowly by an animal. Clustering traces its roots to time immemorial, but it was perpetuated under the manorial system of feudalism. In

Figure 7.9. Forms of rural settlement. *Sources:* Uhlig 1961; Schröder and Schwarz 1969; Roberts, 1979; Thorpe 1961; Demangeon 1939; Otremba 1961; Wagstaff 1969; Wilhelmy 1936.

areas of limited water availability, it was also encouraged by the need to live in close proximity to sources of water. It also served defensive needs in areas where outlaws, raiders, or political instability made the countryside a dangerous place.

Throughout much of Europe's southern and western areas, clustered villages were highly irregular in form. These villages grew, without planning, over many centuries, and often in places with defensive advantages (fig. 7.9). Paths chosen for convenience, called **desire paths**, gradually solidified into streets bordered by houses built close to the streets for ease of access. To stroll through them is to walk the streets of antiquity. The process of cutting a desire path, such as you might see where people have trampled through the grass on a college campus or in a city park, is the same process that shaped how many rural communities in Europe look today.

In parts of eastern and northern Europe, farmers lived in villages of a more regular layout. Whenever regularity is a feature of the landscape, some of kind of planning took place. The most widespread form of regularity can be found in **street villages**, in which the farmsteads lay on either side of a single road (fig. 7.10). These were probably of Slavic origin, linked to cultural preferences and transportation efficiencies, and they are found throughout much of eastern Europe—including eastern Germany where groups of German agricultural settlers moving eastward beyond the Elbe and Saale rivers after 800 C.E. abandoned the irregular clustered village form they had known and adopted the Slavic street village. A less common form of irregular settlement, the **green village**, developed in parts of the North European Plain, from lowland Britain to Poland (figs. 7.9 and 7.10). The houses in these villages were grouped around a central green or commons that served as a market place, a festival ground, and a protected enclosure for livestock. In

Irregular clustered village

Checkerboard village

Street village

Green village

Figure 7.10.   Major types of rural settlement in Europe. For the distribution of these types, see figure 7.9. *Sources:* Wilhelmy 1936; Demangeon 1939; Mayhew 1973; Schröder and Schwarz 1969; Thorpe 1961.

districts colonized during Roman times, a more rigid rectilinear pattern survives in some **checkerboard villages**, a legacy of the imperial land survey system (figs. 7.9 and 7.10).

Although clustered rural settlement is the norm in the more populous parts of Europe, dispersed settlement is found in the north, in mountainous areas, and in scattered agriculturally marginal regions. Dispersal tends to be found in areas where there is the following: (1) insufficient productive arable land to support groups of people living in close proximity to one another, (2) a widespread availability of water (so that people do not need to cluster near water sources), (3) an absence of the need for defense, and (4) no political obstacles to colonization by individual pioneer families. These are the conditions that prevailed in places such as the Alps, northern Scandinavia, and interior Ireland (fig. 7.9).

The traditional building styles evidenced in various parts of Europe very much reflected available building materials (fig. 7.11). The typical Mediterranean farmstead

Figure 7.11.   Traditional rural building materials. *Sources:* Vidal de la Blache, P. 1926. *Principles of Human Geography.* New York: Henry Holt, Meirion-Jones 1982; Smith 1988.

was built of stone or, less commonly, mud-brick and covered with a heavy tile roof. Because of deforestation, wood for construction had largely disappeared, leaving only earth and rock as building materials. In plan, the Mediterranean farmstead was multi-storied, with the ground level and cellar devoted to food storage and cheese- and wine-making. The upper stories contained the living quarters. Many such farmsteads survive to the present day, as do the venerable villages, lending a traditional charm to the southern European countryside.

In place of the stone farmsteads of the south, wooden buildings dominated the three-field region. Where wood was particularly plentiful (in the north and east), buildings were made of logs or sawn lumber. In transitional areas farther to the west, half-timbering was common. Half-timbering consists of a heavy framework of oaken beams, bound together and left exposed as the skeleton of the structure (fig. 7.12). The spaces between the beams are filled in with brick or, more commonly, with *wattle-and-daub*, a wickerwork of sticks daubed with clay and plastered. The folk architecture of these farmsteads was also distinctive. Typically, the stead consisted of multiple build-ings, grouped tightly around a central courtyard, a type closely associated with the Franks, a German tribe influential in spreading both the farmstead and three-field farming itself.

Peoples living in certain areas closer to the European periphery used building materials that were easily available and useful. In parts of southeastern Europe, con-structions made of turf, sod, and adobe brick were common (fig. 7.11). Along the southern shores of the North and Baltic seas, soils rich in clay favored the use of bricks in construction. The Sami of the far North lived in skin tents. The British Isles played host to several different types of construction. Half-timbering was popular in the southern, more productive agricultural lowlands, whereas stone construction was com-mon in the mountains and in northerly or poorly drained areas.

Little survives today of traditional agricultural systems. Here and there in remote hill areas of rural Europe one can occasionally glimpse archaic elements of the older, largely vanished ways, but for the most part, pervasive change meets the eye. These changes occurred in the types of crops raised, land tenure, field systems, levels of com-mercialization and specialization, intensity of land use, and the proportion of the pop-ulation working in agriculture.

New Crop Introductions

Two enormously significant diffusions brought exotic crops to Europe during the past two millennia, radically altering agriculture. The first wave came from the Ara-bic Muslim lands across the Mediterranean, bearing the citrus fruits, which had apparently been unknown to the classical Greeks, though the mythological eleventh labor of the mythical Hercules had been to obtain the "golden apple" from the Garden of the Hesperides, a probable reference to the orange. Hercules' quest took him into the warm lands to the south, where the orange in fact grew in the irrigated gardens of Arabia. He failed to get the job done properly, but the Arabs brought citrus into Europe when they conquered Iberia and parts of Italy in the

Figure 7.12.   Hessian half-timbering, or *Fachwerk,* adds a distinctive appearance to the cultural landscape in this farm village on the Lahn River in Germany. (Photo by T.G.J.-B., 1991.)

Middle Ages. Citrus quickly became a basic part of Mediterranean horticulture, though these fruits lacked drought resistance and required extensive development of irrigation. The Arabs also added apricots and sugar cane, as well as sorghum, cotton, and rice.

The second revolutionary introduction of crops came from the Americas as a result of the Age of Discovery. Two distinct diffusions occurred. The first involved the Mesoamerican food complex of maize (corn), chili peppers, squash, beans, and pumpkins, to which was appended the turkey and perhaps the tomato. Improbably, this food complex did not reach Europe directly, by way of the Spaniards in Mexico. Indeed, Iberians largely rejected these foods. Instead the complex of Mexican domesticates accompanied the Portuguese around Africa to India and from there to Turkey, gaining acceptance at every stop. All spread into Balkan Europe with the Turkish conquests, and adoption of the Mesoamerican complex remains greatest there, even to the present day. Taste the paprika in Hungarian food, observe the expansive tomato fields of Bulgaria, watch stick-wielding Peloponnesian women drive flocks of turkeys through the streets, see the festival corn decorations of the South Slavs, consider that cornmeal mush served as a main Romanian food staple, and you will grasp the extent to which Balkan agriculture has been reshaped in a Mesoamerican image.

Andean Indians of highland South America provided the other major New World crop, the so-called Irish potato. It spread to Europe by an altogether different route. Arriving in Spain from Peru in 1565, the potato quickly reached Spanish-ruled Belgium. Within two centuries it gained acceptance throughout most of the three-field farming region and the herder-farmer hardscrabble periphery, completely revolutionizing both. The potato provided four times as much carbohydrate per hectare as wheat and became the principal food crop of most peoples living north of the Alps and Pyrenees. It yielded large amounts of food from small fields, even in a cloudy, cool climate. Temporarily, at least, the potato ended famines wherever it gained acceptance. Hunger returned again only when the potato itself became blighted in the 1840s.

Modern Agricultural Systems

Even more radical changes in European agriculture occurred after about 1850 as a result of the urbanization and industrialization of Europe. Farmers moved away from subsistence agriculture, no longer content merely to provide their own needs and have a small surplus left over to sell. Instead, the large urban markets prompted them to focus on production of commodities for sale.

Subsistence breeds diversity, whereas market orientation usually leads to **specialization**. No longer would the Mediterranean farmer pursue a threefold system; no longer would three-field agriculture retain its multiplicity of crops and livestock. Small aspects of the traditional diversified systems would become the only agricultural pursuit. Specialization remains an ongoing process in Europe, increasing decade by decade. As a result, the map of agricultural types in Europe has been

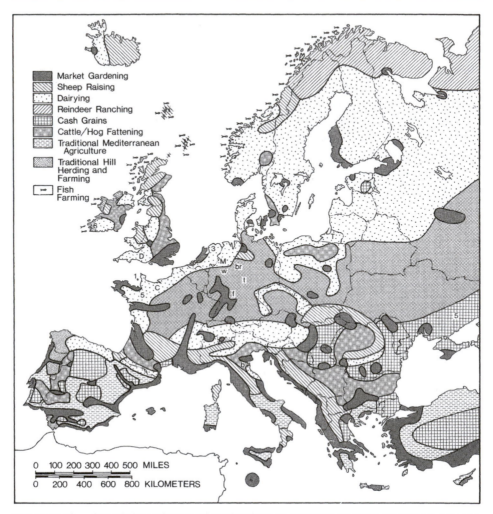

Figure 7.13.   Specialized types of agriculture in modern Europe. Numbers refer to source regions of selected dairy breeds: **1** = Guernsey and Jersey; **2** = Ayrshire; **3** = Friesian; **4** = Holstein; **5** = Maine-Anjou; **6** = Kerry. Capital letters refer to the place of origin of selected generic cheeses: **C** = Camembert; **D** = Cheddar; **G** = Gruyère; **M** = Muenster; **T** = Tilsit. Lowercase letters refer to the origin of selected generic meat products: **b** = bologna; **br** = braunschweiger; **f** = frankfurter; **w** = westphalian ham. *Sources:* Kostrowicki 1984; Fry 1971.

almost totally redrawn, with a focus on individual cash products replacing the older, many-faceted systems (fig. 7.13). In Mediterranean Europe, specialization was usually achieved by elevating horticulture to the principal agricultural pursuit. Grain fields and pastures shrank, crowded out by the expansion of orchards, vineyards, and vegetable fields—often made possible by expanded irrigation. The result was a modern, specialized type of agriculture called **market gardening** or truck farming.

MARKET GARDENING

Mediterranean specialization centered not merely upon horticulture, but upon specific elements within it. A farmer might choose to produce olives or oranges, wine grapes or garden vegetables. Entire districts focused upon a single orchard or vineyard product. The Languedoc Plain, for example, became one huge sea of grape vines stretching as far as the eye can see; the irrigated *huertas* of eastern coastal Spain developed specialized citrus cultivation and gave the name to the Valencia orange; whereas Andalucía, the Adriatic coast of Italy, and the Riviera achieved fame for their olives. Northern Sicily and the area around Naples also became noted for citrus, and the valley of the Douro River in Portugal expanded production of the famous port wines. One of the most remarkable agricultural sights in the Mediterranean lands is the view from adjacent mountain heights of the olive-clad expanse of the once-sacred Plain of Krissa, near Delfi in Greece. This plain, now one solid olive orchard to the almost complete exclusion of other trees or crops, gives the appearance from above of a gray-green embayment of the adjacent Gulf of Kórinthos.

The older, diversified Mediterranean system has not completely disappeared. Rougher, interior districts, poorly endowed with irrigation water or sufficient flat land, retain relics of the older system. Fine examples of traditional Mediterranean agriculture can be seen in such districts as the southern flank of the Pyrenees in Spain, in the mountains of Crete in insular Greece, or in the Cinque Terra area along Italy's northwest coast. In effect, two quite different agricultural types developed in Southern Europe, one preserving the traditional system and the other evolving into market gardening. In places, the juxtaposition of traditional Mediterranean farming and modern agribusiness is quite startling. For example, the district called Las Alpujarras, south of Granada in the Spanish Bética Range, displays an almost unaltered ancient agrarian system. Tiny fields and orchards, laboriously won from mountainside and flood plain, yield a variety of Mediterranean crops, while sheep and goats graze high above. Machines are few, with the necessary labor provided by people and donkeys. Journey a very short distance southward toward the Mediterranean shore, over the Sierra de Gádor, and you enter the altogether different agricultural world of the flat Campo de Dalías. Most of these plains are covered with huge sheets of white plastic, beneath which grow irrigated winter vegetables in one of the most impressive market-gardening enterprises anywhere in the world. Perhaps nowhere else in the world do such contrasting types of agriculture coexist in such a small area.

Market gardening also emerged north of the Alps, mainly in small pockets of the old three-field region. Each sizable city there acquired a surrounding "halo" of farms producing fruit and vegetables for the nearby urban market (fig. 7.13). Other local districts of northern market gardening appeared in climatically favored places where one or another crop thrived particularly well. For example, Bretagne in France today specializes in apples and cider; nearby Picardie produces potatoes; Holland is a center for flowers and bulbs; Bulgaria is known for tomatoes; and cherries thrive on the shores of the Bodensee in southern Germany. Modern technology has facilitated the expansion of market gardening even into areas where the climate is not conducive to the production of fruits and vegetables. One example is hothouse market gardening near

Figure 7.14.   Wine grape monoculture in the Bordeaux area of southwestern France. The specialization and commercialization of European agriculture produced such landscapes. (Photo by A.B.M., 1991.)

Reykjavik in Iceland, where all sorts of warmth-loving crops such as bananas grow beneath glass.

The most impressive and lucrative northern example of market gardening is found in the wine-producing vineyards of the Bordeaux region, Champagne, Bourgogne, the middle Rhine Valley, Austria's Weinviertel (wine region) north of Wien (itself named for wine in Roman times), and certain other favored districts (fig. 7.14). Traceable to monastic settlements of the fourth century, founded to produce sacramental wine, northern viticulture expanded rapidly to supply growing urban and export markets.

DAIRYING

Milk cows enjoyed importance in several traditional agricultural systems, especially in the three-field system and highland herding-farming of Scandinavia, the Alps, Celtic fringe, Massif Central, and the Pyrenees. When specialization and commercialization became popular, many of these districts elevated bovine dairying to their only major activity. Cropland was converted to pasture and meadow, herd size increased on each farm, and an elaborate network of milk processing plants, creameries, cheese factories, and milk transport systems developed. As a result, the great European **dairy belt** took shape around the shores of the North and Baltic seas, including much of northern Russia, the British Isles, coastal France, the Low Country, northern Germany, and the

Scandinavian lands. An outlier exists to the south, in the Alps of Switzerland and Austria (fig. 7.13). The dairy belt occupies the cloudiest, coolest part of northwestern Europe, a land better suited to pasture and the raising of hay than to field crops such as wheat. Similarly, the rugged mountain terrain of the Alps is more easily adapted to the raising of grasses, and hay can be mown on the steep slopes where crop tillage would be difficult.

The trend toward specialized dairying can be traced to the Middle Ages in some parts of northern Europe. In England, the counties of Essex and adjacent East Suffolk, on the North Sea coast northeast of London, became known for dairying in the late Middle Ages. In the 1600s, the shires of Hertford and Buckingham north of the British capital adopted the same agricultural specialty, as did certain districts in the English Midlands. Generally the more peripheral dairy areas produced cheese, which was less perishable. Also in the 1600s, the French provinces of Normandie on the English Channel and Brie near Paris became famous as dairy areas, as did parts of the Low Country. In the nineteenth century, commercial dairying spread to its present limits, displacing grain farming in countries such as Denmark. Dairying now enjoys overwhelming importance in the belt devoted to it. In Finland, for example, milk production accounts for 40% of the total agricultural income of the country, while meadow, pasture, and silage crops cover a third of the arable land.

Every major breed of dairy cattle in the world today derives from the European dairy belt, and the breeds bear names indicative of their origin. The Jersey and Guernsey commemorate the names of two of the Channel Islands, which lie between France and England; the Ayrshire breed reminds us of a Scottish county; the Holstein-Friesian comes from Friesland in the Netherlands and the north German province of Holstein; the Brown Swiss was originally bred in the canton of Schwyz in central Switzerland; the Maine-Anjou breed honors two old provinces of western France; and the Kerry breed reveals its Irish county of origin. The famous cheeses and butters of the world often have the names of towns, cities, or provinces in the European dairy belt, including Edam (Netherlands), Münster (Germany), Camembert (Normandie), Gruyères (Switzerland), Cheddar (English Somerset), and many others. In Russia, "Vologda" butter, bearing the name of a province north of Moskva, is synonymous with the highest quality product.

Pronounced regional contrasts exist within the European dairy belt, both in type of produce and intensity of farming. Denmark, which specializes in butter production and contributes a substantial percentage of all butter entering international trade, exemplifies highly developed dairying. The Danish farmers banded into local cooperatives, mainly for purposes of marketing but also for the construction of creameries. Land and livestock remain privately owned. Each package of butter bears a stamp with the code number of the cooperative and the individual farmer so that customer complaints concerning quality can be directed to the farmer responsible and fines levied. This system produces the highest-quality butter found anywhere, supplemented by fine pork and bacon from swine fattened on skim milk, a by-product of the butter-making process. In the Netherlands, attention is focused on milk and high-quality cheeses. Another advanced dairy country, the United Kingdom, has farmers specializing in fluid milk. The rise of specialized dairying brought a profound change

Figure 7.15.   A modern, isolated dairy farmstead on the coastal plain of southwestern Iceland. Dairying tended to disperse the rural population from villages and hamlets, in the American manner. The farmstead retains no traditional architectural elements. (Photo by T.G.J.-B., 1994.)

to the rural landscape. In many areas, villages and hamlets disappeared and were replaced by scattered farmsteads, standing apart from each other in the American manner (fig. 7.15). The field patterns of the older land-use systems were completely obliterated, replaced by pasture expanses.

CATTLE/HOG FATTENING

Another element of traditional three-field farming that survived into the modern age of commercialization and specialization is the breeding and fattening of cattle and hogs. Most of the protein in the Germanic and Slavic diet comes from these sources. As a result, an elongated belt of commercial cattle/hog-fattening farms now stretches from the Paris Basin through Germany, Poland, and Ukraine into Russia (fig. 7.13). Feeder specialization began at least as early as the 1600s in parts of England, particularly in East Anglia northeast of London and Leicestershire in the Midlands. Similar developments occurred about the same time in parts of Germany and the Netherlands, but most such developments awaited the growth of urban markets in the 1800s.

Throughout the cattle/hog fattening belt, more land is devoted to livestock feed than to crops for human consumption. A pronounced regional contrast developed in the choice of crops, however. South of a rather sharp line across the neck of the Balkan

Peninsula, the Alps, and on through central France, maize is the principal feed crop used to fatten livestock, as in the American corn belt, but north of the line small grains and root crops dominate, including barley, oats, potatoes, and sugar beets. In Germany, 70% or more of the potato harvest goes for livestock feed.

SHEEP RAISING

A great portion of the hardscrabble regions originally devoted to herding with secondary crop farming is now engaged in specialized sheep raising. The Celtic fringes of the British Isles, Massif Central, Dinaric Range, Carpathians, and Iceland all contain important sheep-raising districts today (fig. 7.13). The market that prompted this specialization lay in the woolen textile districts, especially in Great Britain. In the 1700s and 1800s, landlords in the British highlands converted the far greater part of their estates to sheep pasture. Raising sheep required only a small resident population of herders. Most of the tenant farmers pursuing the traditional agricultural system became superfluous and found themselves cruelly evicted from the land in a long series of "clearances," their houses pulled down stone by stone and their stored food destroyed to make sure they could not return. Many perished. Others fled to Australia or North America, leaving behind hilly homelands devoted almost solely to sheep raising. Cattle largely disappeared from these areas, as did crops.

CASH GRAIN FARMING

In some regions, the grain field prevailed in the age of specialization and commercialization (fig. 7.13). Wheat became the most common cash grain and today dominates the former nomadic herding region in the steppes of Ukraine and Russia, forming Europe's greatest wheat belt. Large wheat farms also appear in parts of the Castilian plateau and in the Paris Basin, served by migratory harvesting crews using giant American-made combines. Tall grain elevators now compete visually with Castilian church spires in local market towns, and much of the landscape has taken on the appearance of Kansas or Saskatchewan. The Seine River port of Rouen exports huge amounts of wheat.

REINDEER RANCHING

Not even the Sami, in the remotest northern fringes of Europe, have been immune to the far-reaching changes in the agricultural economy. Traditional nomadic herding by the Sami has been destroyed. Beginning in 1852, certain borders closed to their international migration, forcing the Sami to accept citizenship in one or another country and disrupting many routes of seasonal movement. An agreement allowed some Swedish Sami to use summer tundra pastures in Norway in exchange for the use of Swedish forests for winter refuge by Norwegian Sami, but border crossings became rare. Another significant change involved range fencing, separating the herds of adjacent groups and ending the traditional open-range system. The Sami have lost large areas that once belonged to them, particularly in Finland, where dairy farmers pushed far to the north. Moreover, commercial lumbering, utilizing large machines and clear-cutting techniques, damaged woodlands that once supported large herds. Those who remain herders have adopted new, different methods. Snowmobiles replaced skis in reindeer herding, and the stock receives less frequent attention nowadays, owing to the fencing of ranges and the reduction of predators. Herders now belong to cooperatives, which operate much like collective farms. Most Sami abandoned herding altogether, accepting employment in fishing, mining, and other industries.

FISHING AND FISH FARMING

In the seas that flank Europe on the south, west, and north, a great variety of commercially valuable fish is found. These are exploited in part by peoples of the less-industrialized periphery of Europe, particularly Norwegians, Icelanders, Færoese, Portuguese, Greeks, Dalmatian Croats, and Basques. Norway, with one of the smallest populations in Europe, accounts for 2.5% of the total world catch of fish each year, and Iceland is also a major fishing country. Fishing occupies a very sizable segment of the labor force in Iceland and the Færoe Islands.

The types of fisheries vary from one peripheral sea to another in Europe. Mediterranean fishermen go after tuna, sardines—which are named for the Italian island of Sardinia—and sponges, found particularly in the Aegean Sea. The Black and Caspian seas yield sturgeon, from which caviar is obtained, while the North Sea, Arctic Ocean, and Norwegian Sea fishers specialize in cod, herring, mackerel, and haddock. The less saline Baltic Sea is important for flounder and eels, in addition to cod and herring. Oysters and sardines provide the principal take in the Bay of Biscay and other Iberian Atlantic waters.

Fish farming is also of growing importance. In the past four decades, northern Scotland, parts of Ireland, western Norway, and the Færoe Islands have become fish-farming centers, an enterprise that grew out of the traditional importance of fishing (fig. 7.13). Fish farming focuses mainly upon salmon, raised in anchored cages moored in the saltwater inlets, bays, and channels of peripheral northwestern Europe. In the same region, trout grow to maturity in freshwater ponds, often providing a second income on sheep farms. These valued fish find a ready market in the urban areas of Europe and now offer significant competition for the fishing industry.

The modern period in Europe has also brought a significant expansion in the growth of crops that can be used as bio-fuels. Rapeseed in particular, with its bright yellow spring flowers, has dramatically altered the visual landscape of parts of Europe north of the Alps. The modernization of the rural sector has involved more than new crop introductions and the rise of specialized, market-oriented pursuits, however. Radical changes in land consolidation and land tenure are also of great importance.

Land Tenure in the Modern Era

As we have seen, crop farming systems in Europe traditionally took place on fragmented holdings. Farmers had many different fields, at varying distances and directions from the village or hamlet. Such a field system put European farmers at a distinct disadvantage in producing cash crops. As a result, all governments took steps to bring about **land consolidation**, redrawing property lines to reduce or eliminate the fragmentation of holdings.

Land consolidation began in the United Kingdom, where the process was completed by the late 1700s. Scandinavian countries followed the British example, and in the twentieth century most other western European countries followed suit. The process was slow, however. In western Germany, only half of all agricultural land had undergone consolidation by the middle 1970s, but there are increasingly few vestiges of the old system. Eastern Europe experienced an altogether different process in the elimination of fragmented holdings. Under Communism, large fields suited to **collective agriculture** abruptly replaced private farms, radically and suddenly altering the rural landscape (fig. 7.16).

In recent decades, land consolidation in western Europe has not been driven by government policy, but by the rise of large-scale **agribusiness**. The commercialization of agriculture and the opening of markets have favored large-scale production. Corporate agricultural concerns have emerged that buy up adjacent smaller holdings to put

Figure 7.16.   A collective farm in the Hungarian Basin. Many such large-scale farms were broken up after the fall of communism, but some were taken over by large agricultural concerns and run as modern, commercialized farms. (Photo by A.B.M., 1973.)

Figure 7.17.   A commercial sunflower farm in southwest France. Small French farms can still be found in parts of France, but large concerns now control a significant portion of French agriculture. (Photo by A.B.M., 1991.)

together mega-farms (fig. 7.17). These are particularly common in the agriculturally productive lowlands of Europe found in parts of France, the Low Countries, and Germany. The competitive advantages of large-scale farming in a capitalist environment make it very difficult for smaller farms to stay in business.

This brings us to the matter of farm ownership. Traditionally, almost all of rural Europe belonged to a landed aristocracy. The peasantry labored as tenants, required to pay a share of their produce as rent (this practice is called **sharecropping**). Only the shifting cultivators and nomadic herders escaped this pervasive bondage. In a few regions, large landed estates survive to the present day, as in southern Iberia, parts of southern Italy, and some British Highland areas. Elsewhere, agrarian **land reform** took place. In most of western Europe, a steady move toward peasant landownership occurred between about 1650 and 1850 with a gradual elimination of the landed aristocracy. This transition occurred in various ways, but the sequence of events in the Po Valley of northern Italy is illustrative. Landlords there by law had to pay outgoing peasant tenants for any improvements made during their terms as renters, and failure to do so forced the owner to renew the lease at no increase in rent. These improvements included clearing of woodland, marsh drainage, or even irrigation development, for which the landlords were hard pressed to pay, and typically they allowed the lease to be renewed. The rent thus remained constant while inflation lowered its relative cost, until eventually the peasant could buy the land. In Greece, the successful rebellion against Turkish rule had the side effect of destroying the landed aristocracy, composed primarily of Turks. Typical of present conditions is the Greek island of Kriti, where 96% of the farmers owned their land by 1960.

In eastern Europe the landed aristocracy persisted, and few farmers gained possession of the fields they worked. Some aspects of medieval bondage even survived into the 1900s in Slavic Europe and eastern Germany. A more drastic and violent solution came there—liquidation of the landed aristocracy under Communist rule. Typically, the Communists won early peasant support by promising the farmers landownership. In 1946, for example, such a campaign occurred in Soviet-occupied East Germany under the slogan "aristocrats' lands in farmers' hands." After a brief period of peasant ownership, the state confiscated the land and established collective and state farms. Collectives involved farmers operating as a unit, more or less in business for themselves as a group, paying rent to the state and splitting profits. In the less-common state-farm system, the farmers labored as salaried state employees for a fixed wage on huge super-farms, turning all produce over to the government. Collective and state farms became dominant in most Communist countries.

Since the collapse of Communism, land tenure has once again undergone fundamental changes in Eastern Europe. Every formerly Communist country is presently experiencing privatization of the agricultural sector, with differing results and rates of progress. Some commonalties exist. In the majority of countries, most state and collective farms have been replaced with cooperative farms, owned and operated by the workers, who no longer answer to state planners. The ancient peasant collectivism of eastern Europe replaced the state-owned enterprises. In the process, almost everywhere, production levels fell, and many farm workers left the land.

In Russia, some collectives made the transition directly to agribusiness, when farm directors from the Soviet era seized ownership and became capitalistic entrepreneurs. Even so, private farms have grown in number, and by 2003 private farms accounted for 14.4% of Russia's total grain production. The greatest strides toward privatization occurred in the fertile black-earth belt of southern Euro-Russia. Farm production declined in the 1990s, and today nearly half of all food grown in Russia comes from garden lands, especially in the urban peripheries, where many city dwellers own or rent plots of land.

Ukraine possesses the richest farmlands of Europe. Until recently all land was tilled by private farmers who were not allowed to control more than 100 hectares each—too little to be commercially viable. Recent reforms are beginning to change the picture, but inefficient private collectives prevail in Ukraine. Estonia, a Baltic republic, made the transition to private farm ownership, but in the process agricultural production fell by 56% between 1990 and 1997, and it is only recently beginning to rebound. In all of Estonia, only a few farms are operating at a competitive level. Neighboring Latvia seems to have made the transition to private, family-operated farms more smoothly, and agricultural production began to increase again in the middle 1990s, following an abrupt decline. In Latvia, 95% of all farms are now privately owned.

In Romania, nearly half of all parcels had passed into private hands as early as 1991, but the average size of such farms today is around three hectares. Most are seriously undercapitalized and unable to achieve more than a subsistence production. The state-owned cooperative farm, a compromise between socialistic and capitalistic enterprise but retaining far more of the old system, remains important in Romania. Neighboring Bulgaria allowed each state collective to oversee its own dissolution, dividing land and fixed assets as fairly as possible.

By contrast, in Czechia, Slovakia, and Hungary, most land reverted to private ownership but was then promptly pooled into cooperatives or rented to agribusiness enterprises. Many people own land while the number of renters is small. Hungary reached a similar solution, allowing the old collectives to survive as cooperatives. About a third of Hungarian farmland in cooperatives is privately owned, with most of the balance collectively owned. Slovakia has favored cooperatives over agribusiness enterprises.

In the former East Germany, yet another solution was found. The 4,500 state-owned farms in 1990, at the close of the Communist period, gave way to some 20,000 corporate and private enterprises by 1993. Corporate agribusiness now owns more than 80% of all East German livestock. In the process, the farm population plummeted. The restoration of rural property to private owners is complete, but most East German landowners are absentee and lease their property to corporate agribusinesses.

Productivity Patterns

The commercialization of European agriculture over the past two centuries was part of a larger move toward industrialization and modernization that we will examine in the next chapter. It was fueled by the dominant position Europe came to play in the developing world economy, which in turn was a product of its colonial and imperial reach. Increased intensity of land use in the European core began in England in the 1700s and then spread to adjacent parts of the continent. One of its first victims was the traditional three-field system. Fallowing one year in three disappeared from the three-field rotation, greatly increasing the acreage and production of feed crops. Fallowing had always been something of a problem, because the field quickly became choked with grass and weeds in the idle year unless the farmers continually cultivated it. In many areas, turnip crops replaced the fallow, with repeated hoeing employed to keep the weeds out. The amount of pastureland declined, and many old grazing areas became cropland. The net result of the changes was a marked increase in the amount of feed available for livestock, and the numbers of animals rose accordingly. Stall-feeding became all-important, for many stock were kept penned rather than roaming about in pastures and forests. Increased confinement of animals also allowed a more complete collection of manure, which in turn aided the elimination of fallowing. The changes occurred in a spiral: the elimination of fallowing, an increase in yield of feed crops, more livestock per farm, more manure per farm, increased fertility of fields, increased yields of feed crops, and so on. Chemical fertilizers, invented by the Germans, assisted the upward spiral, as did agricultural machinery of various kinds. Later, in the twentieth century, pesticides further enhanced productivity. Increased attention to selective breeding produced better-quality livestock and hybrid seeds.

The two world wars during the first half of the twentieth century represented significant setbacks for European agriculture, and food shortages were common. Hence, one of the early goals of the European Economic Community (now the European Union) was to ensure a stable food supply. The chief policy instrument for achieving this goal was the Common Agricultural Policy (CAP). Begun in the late 1950s, the CAP was designed to boost productivity by subsidizing farmers to produce specific crops. The CAP contributed to specialization and also greatly boosted productivity. By the 1980s, however, the CAP had led to large surpluses of certain products and charges were made that certain countries—particularly France with its large agricultural sector—were receiving a disproportionate share of the benefits.

Significant reforms to the CAP have been introduced over the past two decades. Farmers are no longer paid simply to produce certain crops. They now receive aid but must look more to the market in making production decisions. Also, the CAP began offering special supports for environmentally friendly farming and has become an instrument that is used to encourage broad-based regional development initiatives. The program remains somewhat controversial, however, as it is expensive and its benefits go disproportionately to states with a significant agricultural sector. With the enlargements of the European Union to include most of the countries in eastern Europe, vast amounts of new agricultural land were added to the CAP. Instead of extending the same benefits that, for example, an Austrian farmer might receive to a new member such as Slovakia (just across the border), the EU has curtailed benefits in new entrant states. There have also been benefit cuts in places such as France and Germany to finance the added expense of the CAP caused by a larger EU. As in many places, agriculture as a way of life is a cultural issue in Europe. Some see the CAP in its new form as something that continues to push Europe in the direction of large-scale commercialized agriculture and away from smaller-scale, potentially more sustainable farms. Not surprisingly, then, the CAP has come in for significant criticism.

Whatever the merits of such criticisms, one thing is clear: the CAP and other agricultural developments have made Europe a major player at the global scale. Europe is one of the major agricultural exporters in the world, particularly of processed food items. (Beverages, cereals, fats and oils, fruits and vegetables, and meat dominate the export picture.) At the same time, it is a major importer of agricultural products—many coming from former colonies in the developing world, as well as the United States, Canada, Japan, Australia, and New Zealand. Europe is thus in a powerful position to influence global prices for agricultural products and to shape the global exchange of agricultural goods. This is why Europe so often figures in the disputes and agreements that govern production and trade in the agricultural sector around the world.

Within Europe, agricultural productivity follows a rather pronounced core-periphery pattern. Land use intensified throughout Europe in the modern age. This happened earliest and most profoundly, however, in the central regions closest to the industrial complexes and growing cities (Chapters 8 and 10). Any number of statistical measures reveal the agrarian core-periphery pattern of Europe, including grain productivity per hectare, percentage of land cultivated, livestock density, amount of fertilizer applied per hectare, value of agricultural produce per capita, and the distribution of economically distressed rural regions (fig. 7.18). Some of the environmental consequences of this spiral—including nitrogen-infused groundwater, declining organic matter in the soil, and soil erosion—are raising concerns about the long-term viability of modernized agriculture.

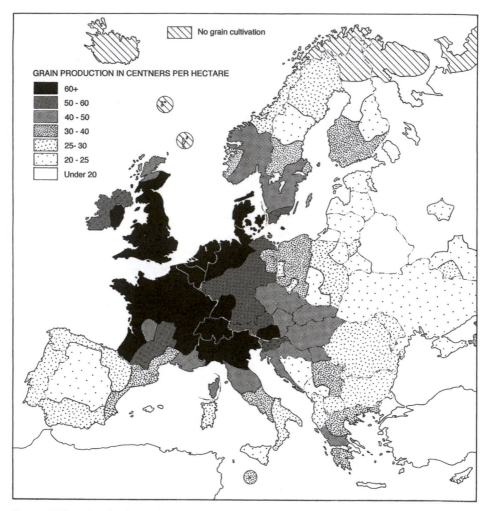

Figure 7.18.   Production of all grains per hectare. A classic core-periphery pattern is revealed, a recurring geographical configuration in Europe. Anomalies include the cultivation of irrigated rice in some small Mediterranean districts and maize in the Balkans, which yields far more per unit of land than the European small grains. *Sources:* Eurostat and national statistical yearbooks.

But for the moment the head start enjoyed by England and adjacent areas of the conti-nent has given the part of Europe that lies north of the Alps and Pyrenees, and west of the old Iron Curtain, a significant lead in terms of agricultural productivity.

At the scale of the state, a few countries dominate the European agricultural pic-ture. In the east, Ukraine and Russia have vast agricultural lands, and crop production represents an important element of their economies. Within the European Union, the amount of arable land differs greatly from country to country. France leads the list with over 18 million hectares. Spain, Poland, and Germany are next with around 12 million hectares. Then comes Romania at 9 million, Italy at 8.7 million, the United Kingdom at 5.4 million, and Hungary at 4.5 million. All other EU countries fall below 3.5 million. When productivity and crop value is put into the mix, France, Spain, and Italy emerge as the agricultural superpowers within the EU.

Rural Depopulation

Another profound agricultural change in Europe during the past two centuries has been the flight of people from the land. Today only a small minority of Europeans still work in agriculture, constituting in some districts of less than 2% of the labor force (fig. 7.19). The decline of farm population has been absolute as well as proportional, and flight to the cities continues today.

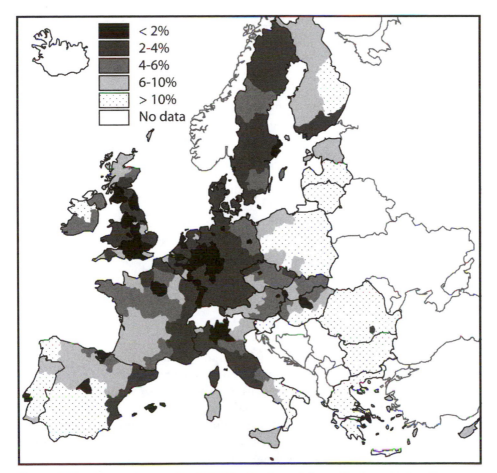

Figure 7.19. Percentage of workforce employed in agriculture in the European Union. The pattern is complicated, revealing north-south, east-west, and core-periphery elements. *Sources:* Eurostat and national statistical yearbooks.

In large part, economic circumstances explain the emigration of rural people. Europe's small farms simply could not effectively compete on the world market when the commercialization of agriculture occurred. Moreover, mechanization reduced the labor needs on larger farms. At the same time, growing cities offered jobs at salaries allowing a higher standard of living. One of the criteria defining economically depressed regions in Europe today is a higher-than-average proportion of the workforce in agriculture. Those who remain in farming often take second jobs to augment their income. Increasingly, people left in the countryside are elderly. Aging of the agricultural population guarantees that the numbers engaged in farming will continue to dwindle.

The map showing the proportion of the labor force working in agriculture reveals several basic geographical patterns that should by now be familiar. A core-periphery arrangement appears, in which the lands bordering the North Sea rank lowest in percentage employed in farming (fig. 7.19). The eye also detects north-south and east-west contrasts.

Emigration from the countryside caused both a decline in the number of farms and an increase in their size. In western Germany, for example, the number of farms declined by 57% between 1949 and 1986, and by half in Finland between 1960 and 1990. A third of all French vineyards have disappeared since 1960. In every country, the agricultural contribution to the national economy has declined sharply. Some countries, most notably Norway, provide subsidies designed to keep people working the land, with results readily visible when one crosses the Norwegian/Swedish border, but the trend nevertheless continues.

Partly as a consequence of rural depopulation, farmland of marginal quality has gone out of production. Recreational land use of one type or another, including tourism, has taken over much of Europe's abandoned farmland, a trend likely to continue. Many Europeans own second homes in the countryside, often converted farmhouses purchased cheaply from departing agriculturists. Others who have stayed in rural areas commute to cities for work. As a consequence, the distinction between rural and urban has significantly eroded.

Preserving Rural Landscapes

As European agriculture changes, the venerable villages, hamlets, and farmsteads that provide beauty and charm to the countryside stand at risk. Were the traditional landscape to disappear, Europe could lose much of its aesthetic appeal. Europeans in many countries have responded to the endangerment of their rural landscapes with effective, subsidized preservation programs. In the Netherlands, for example, some 43,000 features of the cultural landscape were listed and protected by the middle 1980s, including 5,300 farm buildings, 1,000 mills, and an array of other objects such as wayside shrines. In various countries, rigorously enforced building codes restrict the demolition of traditional structures and regulate their renovation. Beneath the façade of a seventeenth-century farmhouse may lie a modern suburban home equipped with central heating, modern appliances, and a jacuzzi. New buildings often must be architecturally compatible with traditional ones. In short, many countries have inventoried their rural landscapes, passed protective legislation, implemented preservation, aggressively resorted to rural land-use zoning, and subsidized these enterprises with tax monies.

In this chapter we have emphasized the primary economic activities that are at the heart of rural life. But some manufacturing has always accompanied farming, fishing, and lumbering. Throughout much of European history, **secondary economic activities** such as weaving, blacksmithing, and grain grinding had only modest impacts on the landscapes of rural Europe, but they laid the foundations for a set of economic developments that gave rise to the urbanization of Europe and, in more recent times, served to break down the distinctions between rural and urban. We turn to these developments in the next chapter.

Sources and Suggested Readings

Agnew, J. 2007. No Borders, No Nations: Making Greece in Macedonia. *Annals of the Association of American Geographers* 97 (2): 398–422.

Agnew, J. A. 2003. Territoriality and Political Identity in Europe. In *Europe without Borders*, eds. M. Berezin and M. Schain, 219–242. Baltimore: Johns Hopkins Press.

Akinwumi, A. E. 2006. Changing Spaces, Emergent Places: Transborder Regionalism in the "New" Europe. *Political Geography* 25 (7): 850–859.

Berezin, M. and M. Schain. 2003. *Europe without Borders: Remapping Territory, Citizenship, and Identity in a Transnational Age.* Baltimore: Johns Hopkins University Press.

Browning, C. S. 2003. The Region-Building Approach Revisited: The Continued Othering of Russia in Discourses of Region-Building in the European North. *Geopolitics* 8 (1): 45–71.

Brubaker, R. 1996. *Nationalism Reframed Nationhood and the National Question in the New Europe, Nationhood and the National Question in the New Europe.* Cambridge: Cambridge University Press.

Clem, R. S. 2006. Russia's Electoral Geography: A Review. *Eurasian Geography and Economics* 47 (4): 381–406.

Clem, R. S. and P. R. Craumer. 2005. Shades of Orange: The Electoral Geography of Ukraine's 2004 Presidential Elections. *Eurasian Geography and Economics* 46 (5): 364–385.

Crowley, W. K. 1993. Changes in the French Winescape. *Geographical Review* 83: 252–268.

Hall, D. 2001. Albania in Europe: Condemned to the Periphery or Beyond? *Geopolitics* 6 (1): 107–118.

Hooghe, L. and G. Marks. 2003. Unraveling the Central State, but How? Types of Multi-Level Governance. *American Political Science Review* 97 (2): 233–243.

Houtum, H. v., O. Kramsch, and W. Zierhofer, eds. 2005. *B/Ordering Space.* Burlington, VT: Ashgate.

Hudson, R. 2000. One Europe or Many? Reflections on Becoming European. *Transactions— Institute of British Geographers* 25 (4): 409–426.

Jeffery, C., ed. 1999. *Recasting German Federalism: The Legacies of Unification.* New York: Pinter.

Jones, A. 2006. Narrative-Based Production of State Spaces for International Region Building: Europeanization and the Mediterranean. *Annals of the Association of American Geographers* 96 (2): 415–431.

Jones, A. and J. Clark. 2003. From Filière to Territoire: Changing Rural Policy in the Languedoc. *Modern & Contemporary France* 11 (3): 335–347.

Jönsson, C., S. Tägil, and G. Törnqvist. 2000. *Organizing European Space*. London: SAGE Publications.

Kaplan, D. H. and J. Hakli, eds. 2002. *Boundaries and Place: European Borderlands in Geographical Context*. Lanham: Rowman & Littlefield.

Lefebvre, E. L. 2003. Belgian Citizenship: Managing Linguistic, Regional, and Economic Demands. *Citizenship Studies* 7 (1): 111–134.

Mau, S. 2006. Politics and Borders: Processes of Demarcation and Political System-Building in the European Union. *Berliner Journal Fur Soziologie* 16 (1): 115–132.

Meleshevich, A. 2006. Geographical Patterns of Party Support in the Baltic States, Russia, and Ukraine. *European Urban and Regional Studies* 13 (2): 113–129.

Paasi, A. 2002. Regional Transformation in the European Context: Notes on Regions, Boundaries, and Identity. *Space & Polity* 6 (2): 197–201.

Perepechko, A. S., V. A. Kolossov, and C. ZumBrunnen. 2007. Remeasuring and Rethinking Social Cleavages in Russia: Continuity and Changes in Electoral Geography 1917–1995. *Political Geography* 26 (2): 179–208.

Roper, S. 2007. Cross-Border and Local Co-Operation on the Island of Ireland: An Economic Perspective. *Political Geography* 26 (5): 554–574.

Rumford, C. 2007. Does Europe Have Cosmopolitan Borders? *Globalizations* 4 (3): 327–339.

Sassen, S. 2006. *Territory, Authority, Rights: From Medieval to Global Assemblages*. Princeton: Princeton University Press.

Trenz, H.-J. 2007. Reconciling Diversity and Unity. *Ethnicities* 7 (2): 157–185.

Valdes, A., C. Csaki, and A. Fock. 1998. Estonian Agriculture in Efforts to Accede to the European Union. *Post-Soviet Geography and Economics* 39: 518–548.

Woodruffe, B. J. 1990. Conservation and the Rural Landscape. In David Pinder, ed. *Western Europe: Challenge and Change*, 258–276. London: Belhaven.

Zilhão, J. 1993. The Spread of Agro-Pastoral Economies across Mediterranean Europe. *Journal of Mediterranean Archaeology* 6: 5–63.

Manufacturing and Industry

Primary economic activity lies at the heart of rural life, but Europe's modern urbanized landscape is first and foremost a product of the secondary sector. That sector—traditionally termed manufacturing—is concerned with processing the materials collected by primary industries into finished products. Ore is converted to steel, fibers made into cloth, textiles and steel become clothing, automobiles, machines, and the like. The importance of the secondary sector has declined in recent years as manufacturing has moved overseas, but the story of modern Europe's rise as a global economic and political power is inextricably tied to the development of large-scale secondary industries.

Historical Overview (Pre-Eighteenth Century)

The rise of secondary industries can be traced to the time of the Bronze and Iron Ages—named for the tools human communities created from natural resources. The origins of Europe's secondary sector lie in prehistory in the same Near Eastern culture hearth that gave Europe agriculture, Christianity, Indo-European speech, the city, and the political state. Initially, secondary industries were centered in Mediterranean Europe, particularly in Greece. By the golden age of Greece, the cities of Athens and Corinth led in manufacturing, boasting cloth makers, dyers, leather workers, potters, weapon makers, jewelers, metalworkers, stonemasons, and shipwrights to keep the great Greek merchant fleets and navies afloat. The Hellenic leadership in artisanry passed temporarily to the Romans, only to return to the Byzantine Greeks. Constantinople (modern Istanbul) was in time rivaled by Moorish Spain, where Toledo developed a reputation for high-quality steel and Cordoba produced fine leather goods.

Then came the rise of northern Italy as a center of manufacturing and of Mediterranean **mercantilism**. Above all, the Italian blossoming resulted from the dominant position achieved by its merchants, who ranged from China to England. Cities such as Genoa, Milan, Florence, and Venice acquired widespread fame for their silks and other textiles, cloth dying, brassware, weaponry, glass, and shipbuilding. At its peak, Venice housed 16,000 shipwrights, who turned out an average of one galleon per day, using prefabricated parts in an early form of assembly-line production. By 1300, artisans of the city of Florence fabricated 100,000 pieces of cloth per year, and Milan became the chief European center of weaponry manufacture. A system of free, prosperous craftsmen facilitated the northern Italian achievement, a major departure from the classical tradition of slave artisans.

Manufacturing-commercial leadership next shifted north to Belgium, Switzerland, and southern Germany in particular, where Italian skills were in some instances transplanted. Other Italians founded the silk industry of Lyon, in France. The most important manufacturing district of the north lay in Flanders, where the first major developments occurred in the 1100s. Flanders, like northern Italy, acquired its manufacturing importance partly as a result of a favorable trade location. A fortunate concentration of river, road, and marine trade routes allowed the inhabitants of the region to achieve the same dominance in northern Europe that the Italian towns had in the Mediterranean. Cloth making was centered at Ypres, Ghent, and Bruges, which drew on the wool of England and Spain as the primary raw material. In the 1400s, linen joined wool as a major product of the Flemish towns and attained an importance that persisted into the nineteenth century.

Carried by emigrant artisans, the influence of Flanders was instrumental in the industrial development of the Netherlands beginning in the 1400s. Flemish tradesmen skilled in woolen-textile manufacture also migrated to England, particularly Yorkshire, as early as the 1300s. The Netherlands rose to commercial dominance in the seventeenth century, and northern Germany also experienced growth. The wealth and influence of this part of the world was rooted in an economic system that, as it developed and grew, was characterized by several distinct features: the right of manufacturers to own (and by extension buy and sell) the property and materials that were part of the production process, the payment of wages to laborers, and the right of individuals to hold and reinvest the profits that came from selling goods. These, of course, are the foundations of modern **capitalism**.

The gradual northward shift of secondary economic activity and corresponding decline in southern Europe meant that manufacturing became increasingly identified with Germanic, Protestant areas and less with Roman Catholic, Romance-language countries. Some commentators have suggested that certain social characteristics of Protestantism, including approval of change and veneration of work, proved more conducive to economic development. Persecution and expulsion of Huguenot merchants and artisans by the Catholic-backed French government and similar pressure on Protestant Flemings by the Spanish rulers contributed materially to the rise of the Netherlands, northern Germany, and England as manufacturing centers.

Advances in manufacturing facilitated the development of far-flung trade routes, which in turn paved the way for the establishment of far-reaching colonial empires. With some Europeans becoming rich from the exploitation of distant goods and people, the capital was available for further expansion of the manufacturing sector, and the ground was laid for more far-reaching changes in Europe's secondary economic sector. Before turning to those developments, it is useful to consider the types of traditional manufacturing systems found in Europe.

TRADITIONAL MANUFACTURING SYSTEMS

Traditional European manufacturing was carried on in two different systems: **guild** and **cottage**, the former based in towns and cities, the latter largely rural. The guild was a professional organization of free artisans skilled in a particular craft. The skills were passed from generation to generation through an apprenticeship system. A boy served as apprentice, for example, to a cooper, potter, mason, ironworker, glassblower, silversmith, sculptor, or master weaver and worked for years as a helper. At the end of apprenticeship, the young man demonstrated his skill before an examining board composed of members of the particular guild. Approval allowed the apprentice to be a member of the guild and begin practicing the trade on his own. In larger cities, each major guild had a house on the main municipal square, and some of these survive today in well-preserved towns such as Ghent, Bruges, and Antwerp in Belgium.

Many relics of the guild system remain today, and craft shops are still surprisingly numerous, even in highly industrialized countries such as Germany. In that country scores of registered crafts still exist, represented by thousands of local guilds, including tailors, bakers, knifesmiths, sausage makers, and others. The same high standards for membership typical of medieval times survive to the present day.

A much more common traditional system of manufacturing, the cottage industry, remained confined to European farm villages, generally practiced as a sideline to agriculture. A village might have a cobbler, weaver, miller, and blacksmith, who spent part of the time farming and the remainder, during slack periods in the fields, working at the household trade. The abundance of people today with surnames such as Smith, Miller, Potter, and Weaver, suggest the former abundance of village crafts. Little formality surrounded the passing on of skills, and sons most commonly learned from fathers and daughters from mothers simply by observing the work being done. Cottage trades survive today in some parts of Europe, particularly if they attract buyers from beyond the village community. On islands off the west coast of Scotland, for example, women still weave the famous Harris Tweed on looms in their individual cottages.

The Industrial Revolution

In Britain during the 1600s, some skilled craftsmen began moving to rural areas to escape the confining, formal control of the urban guilds, which acted to keep membership and production low, while the quality of goods and prices remained high. By fleeing to villages and small towns, they acquired the freedom to increase output and cheapen products, thereby enlarging the market. Simultaneously, some workers engaged in cottage industry began increasing their output and selling wares in a larger territory, abandoning farming altogether. Among such proto-industrial villagers—fugitive guildsmen and, particularly, cottagers—in a small corner of England, a series of revolutionary manufacturing innovations occurred in the 1700s, forever changing England, Europe, and the entire world.

Both primary and secondary industry, both guild and cottage manufacturing systems, were fundamentally altered by this **Industrial Revolution**. Collectively, the associated inventions represent the most rapid and pervasive technological change in the history of the human race. Two fundamental modifications accompanied the revolution. First, machines replaced human hands in extracting primary resources and in fashioning products. The word manufacturing ("made by hand") became technically obsolete. No longer would the weaver sit at the hand loom and painstakingly produce each piece of cloth; instead, huge mechanical looms were invented to do the job faster and more economically. In many industries the machine made possible the use of interchangeable parts and the assembly line. A second change involved the rise of inanimate power, as humans harnessed water, steam, and eventually electricity, petroleum, and the atom. The new technology did not appear overnight but in bits and pieces over many decades and centuries. Nearly all of the interconnected developments of the formative stage of the Industrial Revolution, from about 1730 to 1850, occurred in back-country Great Britain. That is, the Industrial Revolution arose in a peripheral part of Europe. Innovations often occur in such peripheries, where orthodox thinking and behavior are weaker. It was much more likely that the Industrial Revolution would emerge out of the relatively informal environment of northern England than in cities under the tight control of guilds.

The textile industry first felt the effect of the Industrial Revolution. Beginning in the 1730s, major advances led to mechanical spinning and weaving devices driven by waterpower and operated by semiskilled labor. These technological breakthroughs occurred in village and small-town areas, where cottagers had long favored quantity of goods over quality and low price over high. The lower price of goods expanded the market available for manufactured cloth. The textile revolution unfolded in the small towns and villages of dominantly rural areas in England such as Lancashire, Yorkshire, and the Midlands (fig. 8.1). New mechanized factories soon appeared wherever waterfalls and rapids could power the machine looms, particularly on the eastern and western sides of the Pennines, where some traditional textile making had long been centered. In Yorkshire, on the eastern flank, a woolen textile center since late medieval times, the same streams that had long provided the soft water for cleaning wool now turned the waterwheels that drove the new machine looms. Lancashire, on the western Pennine flank, applied the power loom to cotton textile manufacture. To a lesser extent the Midlands and, somewhat later, the Scottish Lowlands shared the water-powered textile boom. By 1830, the tiny island of Great Britain produced some 70% of the world's cotton textiles.

Waterpower dominated the early textile phase of the Industrial Revolution, but not for long. James Watt and others perfected the steam engine in the 1760s, and the first steam-powered cotton textile mill went into operation shortly thereafter. General acceptance followed in the 1790s. The steam engine required fuel, but Great Britain, an almost totally deforested land, had an inadequate supply of wood. The island fortunately possessed an even better fuel: coal. The mining of coal represented the second major industry to be affected by the Industrial Revolution. Coal presented a problem, though. It was bulky and expensive to transport any great distance, especially at the turn of the nineteenth century, before the railroad, internal-combustion engine, and bulk-carrying ships had been developed. Consequently, the industries

Figure 8.1.   The concentrations of primary industry and traditional heavy manufacturing, about 1960. Major manufacturing districts: **1** = Lancashire, **2** = Yorkshire-Humberside, **3** = English Midlands, **4** = Scottish Lowlands, **5** = South Wales, **6** = Newcastle-Tyneside-Tees, **7** = Greater London, **8** = Sambre-Meuse-Lys, **9** = Ruhr, **10** = Upper Slask, **11** = Bohemian Basin, **12** = Saxon Triangle, **13** = Saar-Lorraine, **14** = Lower Sachsen, **15** = Randstad Holland, **16** = Upper Rhine Plain, **17** = Greater Hamburg, **18** = Paris-Lower Seine, **19** = Upper Po Plain, **20** = Swedish Central Lowland, **21** = Bergslagen, **22** = Swiss Plateau-Jura, **23** = Rhône-Alps, **24** = Greater Moskva, **25** = Greater St. Petersburg, **26** = Donets Basin-Lower Don, **27** = Kryvyy Rih-Dnipro Bend, **28** = Ploeşti, and **29** = Kiruna-Gällivare. Key for the fishing areas: **C** = cod, **F** = flounder, **H** = herring, **M** = mackerel, **O** = oysters, **S** = sardines, **Sp** = sponges, **St** = sturgeon, and **T** = tuna.

that relied upon coal as fuel were drawn to the coalfields, just as the earlier factories had been attracted to waterfalls and rapids. The Midlands, Lancashire, and Yorkshire, as well as the Scottish Lowlands, possessed noteworthy coal deposits, allowing a smooth transition from water to thermal power with a minimum of factory relocations. In addition, substantial reserves of coal occurred along the coastal fringe of southern Wales and in the region of Newcastle on the North Sea coast near the Scottish border (fig. 8.1).

A distinctive trait of the Industrial Revolution had become evident: the spatial concentration of industries in areas close to the natural resources used in production. Mechanized production focused on a small number of cities and districts, which attracted large populations. Gravitation to the coalfields accelerated the spatial concentration of industry, causing great increases in population in favored districts and substantial emigration elsewhere.

Metallurgical industries, including the making of iron and steel, also felt the effects of the Industrial Revolution. Throughout most of history, the smelting of iron remained a primitive process, and few who practiced it had any valid understanding of what happened chemically. Iron ore was simply heated over a charcoal fire, and the charcoal's carbon combined with the ore's oxygen to free the iron. The Industrial Revolution brought major changes. The pivotal early developments occurred in Coalbrookdale, a town and valley in the Midlands (fig. 8.1). There, in 1709, coke (purified coal that burns at a high temperature) was first substituted for charcoal in smelting, a process that caused steelmaking to become cheaper and permitted the use of lower-grade ores. By 1790, Coalbrookdale produced almost 50% of Britain's iron. Acceptance of coke drastically changed the geographical distribution of steelmaking. The industry abandoned countless scattered small forges and, out of necessity, relocated in the coal districts, where coke could be obtained most cheaply. Iron and steel thus contributed to the accelerating **nucleation** of industries in small coalfield districts.

Other technological changes in steelmaking followed. The traditional hammer and anvil gave way to the rolling mill as the final processing stage, blast furnaces supplanted small ovens, and metallurgical science arose. Through such innovation and change, the steelmakers of Britain achieved world leadership in the nineteenth century. In other developing British manufacturing areas where both ore and coal occurred, additional concentrations of steel mills soon developed, as in the Newcastle-Tyneside-Tees district, where the legendary coal of Newcastle supplemented iron ore from the nearby Cleveland Hills, in South Wales, and in the western part of the Scottish Lowlands (fig. 8.1).

Another industry forever changed by the Industrial Revolution was the ancient and honored craft of shipbuilding. Traditionally, ships had been small, wooden, and powered by wind or oars. The Industrial Revolution created demands for larger, faster ships to transport bulky raw materials and finished products, and provided the technology needed to produce such vessels. Iron barges first appeared in the late 1700s, and experimental steam navigation began about the same time. Steam-powered steel ships arose in the 1830s, and wooden sailing vessels disappeared a generation later. By the 1890s, British shipyards produced 80% of the world's seagoing tonnage, and Britannia ruled the waves.

Textiles, coal mining, steelmaking, and shipbuilding formed the core of the Industrial Revolution, but other industries were also involved. The shift to machinery gave rise to an entire new engineering industry specializing in the manufacture of machines and machine tools. Both of the raw materials of this industry lay in the coalfields, and as a result, the machine makers located there too. As machines became more numerous and complex, the industry that supplied them grew steadily.

Another basically new industry arose, devoted to the large-scale manufacture and processing of various chemicals, including dyes, paints, fertilizers, drugs, explosives, soap, and, eventually, products such as synthetic fibers. Many such items could be salvaged from by-products of the coking process, and, partly for this reason, many chemical factories developed in the coalfields. Other industries besides shipbuilding and machine making used finished steel as a raw material, and these often located near steel mills: manufacturers of cutlery, surgical instruments, locks, locomotives, automobiles, and weaponry. Similarly, textile-using industries, such as the making of clothing, found it advantageous to be situated near the textile factories.

The snowballing accumulation of a great variety of industries in the coalfield districts of Britain caused hundreds of thousands of people to migrate there, seeking factory employment. In short order, the British population massed in a small number of clusters. These concentrations in turn attracted still other manufacturers, primarily those that needed to be close to the consumers of their products, such as bakers, brewers, meatpackers, and other food processors.

The importance of coal as a locational factor in the formative stages of the British Industrial Revolution was so great that all but one of the major industrial districts developed on the coalfields. London provided the only exception (fig. 8.1). Remote from coal deposits, it had no significant natural resources other than a navigable river, yet London developed into the largest single industrial center in the United Kingdom. Its advantages were several. First, London had already accumulated a large population before the Industrial Revolution, reaching perhaps a half million by the late 1600s. This population offered both market and labor supply when industrialization came. Second, London served as the center for commerce and trade of the country, handling in its harbor three-quarters of the nation's overseas trade by 1700. As a result, a concentration of banks, insurance firms, and shipping brokerage houses developed, which in turn stimulated the process of growth. Industries that depended on foreign areas either as suppliers of raw materials or as consumers of finished products found advantage by locating in London. Third, the large, well-to-do merchant class of the city controlled a huge amount of capital that was needed for investment in industrial activities. Consequently, London thrived in the Industrial Revolution. Its diverse industries eventually ranged from clothing and food processing to oil refining, various engineering and electronic industries, printing, and automobile and aircraft manufacture.

On a far more modest scale, coastal Northern Ireland—the part of the island settled by Protestants from Great Britain—followed London's example and industrialized in the absence of coal (fig. 8.1). Linen textiles and shipbuilding became the principal industries of cities such as Belfast and Londonderry.

Diffusion of the Industrial Revolution

As in Britain, manufacturing on the European mainland tended to localize in small coalfield districts. The first mainland area to feel the effects of the British innovations, the Sambre-Meuse-Lys valley, straddled the Belgian-French border (fig. 8.1). Long before the Industrial Revolution, textile manufacture was well established, especially in the basin of the Lys River. Even before 1800, British textile technology began to be adopted. Traditional metalworking industries had long lined the region's rivers, and in the Middle Ages, copper, brass, and iron came from towns such as Dinant, Namur, and Huy. Around Namur in the mid-1500s, 120 forges and furnaces supported the activities of 7,000 charcoal burners in the surrounding forests. A district of adjacent Brabant became known as the "forest of the charcoal makers."

Coal in the Sambre-Meuse area occurs on the Great European Plain at the foot of the belt of Hercynian hills, in this case the Ardennes. Some use was made of the coal as early as the 1500s, but large-scale mining activities awaited the nineteenth century. A coke-fired blast furnace operated at Liège by 1823; within two decades 45 of 120 furnaces used coke. Expansion of coke production outstripped any other mainland industrial district. Sambre-Meuse craftsmen served as leaders in adopting British techniques, remaining ahead of better-endowed districts in Germany until the mid-1860s. Textile production became centered in Lille, France, known for cottons, linens, and woolens; in Verviers, Belgium, where woolens dominated; and in the southern Netherlands.

One mainland manufacturing district, the Ruhr in Germany, eventually surpassed all the others in importance and even eclipsed the British parent districts (fig. 8.1). Also situated at the juncture of the Great European Plain and the Hercynian regions to the south, it lies in an area underlain by huge deposits of accessible high-grade coal (fig. 8.2). Small amounts of coal had been chipped away from surface outcroppings in the Ruhr valley at least as early as the thirteenth century—mainly to provide heat for local houses. In medieval times, a significant iron and steel industry developed at the town of Solingen. Linen textiles made from locally grown flax were similarly well established. As late as 1800 the textile weavers and steelmakers continued to function in the

Figure 8.2.   The Ruhr industrial district, Germany, about 1950. The southern part of the coalfield had been largely mined out, and mining migrated steadily northward. Steel mills remained concentrated between the Ruhr and Emscher rivers, whereas textiles were manufactured at Wuppertal and in the cities west of the Rhine. *Source:* Pounds 1952.

traditional way. Little or no suggestion of the Industrial Revolution sweeping Britain was visible in the Ruhr, with the minor exception of steam pumps installed in 1801 to combat water seepage in some of the small coal mines. Urban growth had not been rapid, and guilds still dominated the manufacturing system.

Things began to change in the middle of the nineteenth century. Mechanized, steam-powered textile mills arose by 1850 in Krefeld and the twin cities of Mönchen-Gladbach, west of the Rhine. The textile guilds and cottage weavers rapidly gave way to the new technology. These early industrial developments paved the way for a radical change that, by the end of the 1800s, made the Ruhr area the most important European industrial center. Annual coal production increased by 33 times. The mines grew from small enterprises scratching at the surface of the earth to sizable establishments employing hundreds or thousands of workers and utilizing sophisticated mining machinery. The manufacture of iron and steel shifted primarily to the coalfield, and large plants using coke supplanted the charcoal-burning guilds of Solingen. The small, local iron-ore deposits proved inadequate to supply the demand, and the Ruhr reached out to Sweden, Spain, and Lorraine for additional ore, exporting, in exchange, large amounts of coking coal. The Rhine River forfeited much of its romantic character to become the major transport route linking the Ruhr to the rest of the world. Barges bearing coal and ore came to dominate the riverine scene at the foot of the Lorelei Cliffs, as progress shoved aside poetry.

The population of the Ruhr exploded, as towns became sprawling industrial cities. A line of urban centers developed from Dortmund in the east through Bochum, Essen, and Oberhausen to Duisburg on the Rhine in the west (fig. 8.2). Essen, which had a population of only 4,000 within its medieval town walls in 1800 and still only 10,000 at mid-century, became a city of 200,000 by 1900. The local agricultural population proved inadequate as a labor supply, and workers immigrated from other parts of Germany, as well as from Belgium, the Netherlands, Italy, and the Slavic lands of the east. A melting pot of peoples assembled, giving the Ruhr a distinctly different ethnic character from the rest of Germany. A gray pall of smoke settled over the district, blackening buildings and human lungs, and blotting out the sun. With the smoke, however, came a prosperous, powerful Germany, which, by the turn of the twentieth century, rivaled Great Britain as an industrial and military powerhouse.

During the second half of the nineteenth century, industrialization spread to other parts of Europe that had the advantage of accessible coal deposits and the ability to obtain raw materials either locally or by use of Europe's waterways. Among the key areas to industrialize were the Upper Slask, an area in what is now southern Poland, where the North European Plain joins the hills and mountains of Central Europe; the Saxon Triangle, with apexes at the cities of Chemnitz (the "Saxon Manchester"), Halle, and Dresden; the Saar-Lorraine area, which straddles the present border between Germany and France, and also including parts of southern Luxembourg; the northern part of the province of Cechy that became the core of the modern Czech Republic; and far to the east the Donets Basin in eastern Ukraine where a combination of coal iron ore deposits permitted development of one of Europe's most important centers of heavy industry (fig. 8.1). Many of these places had been centers of smaller-scale manufacturing in the pre-industrial period, and governments played a key role in bringing industrialization to all of them.

SPREADING BEYOND THE COALFIELDS

In most areas not endowed with coal deposits, the nineteenth century witnessed slow industrial growth, or even decline in the face of competition from the coal-rich areas. Some urban centers with sizable populations in the pre-Industrial Revolution period imitated the success of London in attracting industries on the basis of a large, ready-made labor force and market. In this category were places such as Paris, Hamburg, Vienna, and Rotterdam-Europoort. Paris, for example, developed two basic industries: high-quality luxury items such as fashion clothing, cosmetics, and jewelry, distributed in small workshop factories around the city; and engineering industries, dominated in the present century by automobile manufacture and concentrated in the suburb towns.

A few areas in a strategic position to capture trade also became targets of industrialization. The Upper Rhine Plain of southwestern Germany and French Alsace, including cities such as Mannheim and Frankfurt-am-Main, is a prime example (fig. 8.1). This area lies on an ancient route between the Mediterranean coast and the North European Plain, and many cities had a heritage of guild industries. In the 1800s, new industries moved here, especially those producing textiles and chemicals. Ludwigshafen, founded in the nineteenth century on the Rhine River, became the site of the famous Farben chemical works, and the Frankfurt suburb of Höchst developed a similar industry. In the twentieth century, the Upper Rhine and nearby Neckar Valley acquired important automobile factories, including the Daimler-Benz works at Stuttgart and the Opel plant at Rüsselsheim near Frankfurt. Alsace played host to early textile mills developed at waterpower sites along the foot of the Vosges.

Hydropower, converted into electricity, helped revive the former industrial greatness of northern Italy, particularly in the area between Milan and Turin in the upper reaches of the Po River Plain (fig. 8.1). Milan became the first European city to have electric lights, in 1883. The government provided added subsidies and incentives to industrialization, and a sizable work force of cheap labor was assembled from among the peasantry of the adjacent Alpine fringe and southern Italy. The diverse industries eventually included iron and steel, based on imported raw materials; automobile manufacture, including the Fiat plant at Turin; and textiles. The district is served by the port of Genoa, across the Apennines on the Mediterranean coast—a city that acquired sizable iron and steel mills and shipbuilding yards of its own. Once-proud Venice profited less than might be expected from the rise of the Po Valley industries, for the Adriatic Sea remained a backwater, leading away from the major markets and suppliers of raw materials, except for petroleum from the Middle East.

The industrial portion of Switzerland, lying to the north of the Alps on the Swiss Plateau and in the hilly Jura, developed industries adapted to a scarcity of raw materials (fig. 8.1). The Swiss relied on highly skilled labor to produce quality goods with a high value added in the manufacturing process. Hydroelectric power brought a major expansion of industry in the twentieth century. Watchmaking, concentrated in numerous small towns and cities of the Jura, is a typical Swiss industry, retaining a pre-Industrial Revolution geographic dispersal and veneration for craftsmen. St. Gallen in the east became the major textile center, producing such items as luxury silks, laces, and ribbons, while Basel in northwestern Switzerland evolved into an important chemical center at the head of barge navigation on the Rhine. Other industries specialized in the production of various kinds of machinery or food processing, including milk chocolate.

Several small areas in northern Spain also felt the effects of the Industrial Revolution, particularly the Barcelona area on the Mediterranean shore and the Bay of Biscay coast around Bilbao and San Sebastian (fig. 8.1). In the latter area, major iron ore deposits and minor coalfields supported a local steel industry, which in turn provided raw material for shipbuilders.

Despite very early industrial beginnings, Sweden had become a poor country by the late 1800s. Though endowed with iron ore and copper deposits, which had been mined since the Middle Ages, Sweden lacked coal deposits and could not share in the early Industrial Revolution. Its steelmakers, known for the high quality of their product, continued to use charcoal. Adoption of hydroelectric power finally permitted the modernization of Swedish industry around 1900, eventually creating extraordinary economic well being. Hydropower fueled electric furnaces employed in steelmaking, and while Sweden's output of steel never rivaled Germany or Britain, the quality was unsurpassed, including various steel alloys. A variety of local engineering industries rely on this steel, including manufacturers of machines, automobiles, ball bearings, electrical equipment, aircraft engines, bicycles, diesel motors, armaments, and ships.

Finland, also late to industrialize, relied upon its abundant waterpower and forests to develop a manufacturing complex in the southwest and far-flung primary industry in the woodlands. On that precarious base, the Finns, too, achieved an enviable level of economic development. Wood products remain a specialty in Finland.

By the year 1900, all of the European industrial districts combined accounted for about 90% of the world's manufacturing output, an overwhelming dominance. The power and prosperity of the Germanic industrial core reached unprecedented heights, and European colonial empires ruled much of the world. The period 1900–1960 witnessed other efforts to industrialize the European peripheries—particularly in parts of Soviet-dominated Eastern Europe. Ties to raw material sites weakened with improved transportation. Ports became favored new places for steel making because ore and coal could be shipped by sea. As a result, coastal steel mills developed at seaports such as Valencia in eastern Spain and Piombino, Genova, Taranto, and Naples in Italy.

In spite of two highly destructive world wars, Europe remained the industrial heartland of the world in the middle twentieth century, though not as dominant. Rivals had sprung up in North America and were beginning to emerge in eastern Asia. And around the corner lay a major change, as declining costs of transportation and the availability of cheap labor in other parts of the world was to usher in an era of deindustrialization. Before turning to that, however, it is important to consider some of the social, political, and environmental dimensions of industrialization.

Social and Political Dimensions of Industrialization

Industrialization cannot be understood apart from the social and political context in which it develops. As has already been suggested, governments often played a key role in facilitating industrialization, and the development of regions of heavy industry in places such as northern England and Germany's Ruhr Valley was accompanied by significant demographic shifts within those countries. To understand the nature and impacts of Europe's industrialization, it is also important to look above and below the scale of the state. At the global scale, the most critical factor is Europe's colonial extension. To a world traveler in 1400, it would not have been at all obvious that, several centuries later, Europe would be the world's preeminent economic power. But beginning in the fifteenth century, Portuguese traders began to move along the coast of Africa, establishing bases and developing trade networks. Not wanting to be left behind, the government of Spain soon got in on the act—most dramatically sending an expedition across the Atlantic in 1492 that opened up vast new areas to European influence. Aided by more effective weaponry and the devastating impacts of the diseases they brought, the Spanish and the Portuguese were able to bring much of Central and South America under their control by the end of the sixteenth century. The age of **colonialism** was at hand.

The Portuguese and Spanish established the template, and the English, French, and Dutch carried it on—eventually to be joined by the Germans, Belgians, Italians, and Russians. It is beyond the scope of this book to tell the story of European colonialism, but an endeavor that started in the Eastern Hemisphere with the establishment of bases and trading relations in South and Southeast Asia, the Middle East, and Africa eventually led to an extraordinary globe-girdling power arrangement in which a small number of modest-sized European countries controlled the better part of the land surface of the earth (fig. 1.9).

What does this have to do with industrialization? A great deal. Were it not for the accumulation of wealth that came from the very unequal political and economic relations Europe established with the rest of the world, pre-industrial manufacturing would likely not have developed nearly to the extent that it did. And once industrialization began the profits derived from colonial empires put European governments and individuals in a financial position to develop, and ensure the success and expansion of, large-scale industries.

Moreover, as European industrialization kicked into higher gear in the later nineteenth century, the relationship between Europe and the rest of the world was fundamentally transformed. Colonies moved from sites that could supply specialty goods and slave labor to resource sinks. By the early twentieth century, many of the colonies were fueling Europe's industrial growth, as colonial governments established plantations and large-scale extractive enterprises that were worked by locals who were often paid very little and had to endure terrible working conditions. Europe was the world's great economic power in the late-nineteenth/early-twentieth centuries, but it achieved that position not just by developing internally. Europe's primacy reflected a very unequal, exploitative relationship with much of the rest of the world. Even though the colonial empires have now been largely dissolved and much industry has moved to other parts of the world, the impacts of the disparities that came out of Europe's colonial era are still very much with us.

Moving to the substate scale, as we will see in Chapter 10, industrialization clearly had an impact on the growth and development of cities. It also brought about sweeping social changes. These can be most clearly grasped by considering the contrasts between life in a guild-dominated and a heavy-industry-dominated community. In the former, the percentage of the population involved in the secondary sector was relatively low. Those involved in manufacturing would spend years developing the skills to produce something of high value. They would be involved in the production process from beginning to end, and over time they would rise to a position where they had a significant say in what happened to the guild. In a community dominated by large-scale heavy industry, a much higher percentage of the population would be involved in the secondary sector, but most people working in that sector would be doing low-skill jobs with little prospect of advancement. They would be involved in only one small aspect of the manufacturing process, and they would have little prospect of ever having a say over what the business did. They would, in terms used by Karl Marx, have a different relationship to the means of production than would someone working in a guild.

The name Karl Marx is associated in many people's minds with particular twentieth-century political initiatives. Marx certainly promulgated political ideas that were later taken up (and in some cases distorted) by others, but the catalyst for his work was the social changes he saw around him during the middle of the nineteenth century. It is no surprise that Marx grew up in Germany; lived in Paris and then Belgium, where he penned (along with Frederick Engels) the *Communist Manifesto*; and then moved to England, where he wrote his greatest work, *Das Kapital*. He thus spent his life in the countries most clearly associated with the early era of industrialization. Whatever one might think of **Marxism** as a political project, Karl Marx was clearly one of the most insightful social and economic commentators of the nineteenth century. He provided penetrating insights into the profound economic and social costs of industrial capitalism.

Many nineteenth-century supporters of industrialization argued that, in critiquing industrial capitalism, Marx overlooked the poverty and social distress that was the lot of many Europeans in the pre-industrial era. They had a point, but so did Marx, for industrial capitalism led to the concentration of wealth in a few hands, and gave the lead industrialists unprecedented power over the lives of workers, who were virtually powerless in the new system. Marx also highlighted the extent to which industrialization set in motion a drive toward accumulating ever more money and goods that, if left unchecked, would lead to increasing exploitation of workers and the environment. This was borne out by developments in many industrial areas, where workers were paid little and were subjected to abominable working conditions, and where attention to public health was virtually absent.

Even to those who rejected many of Marx's ideas, it soon became clear that some kinds of checks would have to be put on industrial capitalism. By the later nineteenth century many of the early-to-industrialize areas were beginning to adopt regulations aimed at promoting public health, ensuring better conditions for workers, and putting some restraints on the ability of a small group of individuals to exert complete control over certain industries. This set the stage for political debates that are still very much in evidence: What is the appropriate balance between policies that promote entrepreneurship and those that regulate what can be done in the name of the public interest?

Environmental Dimensions of Industrialization

Not surprisingly, the Industrial Revolution and the prosperity it brought exacted a terrible environmental cost. No part of Europe has been exempt from this damage, but the highly industrialized core has suffered most, as suggested earlier in the discussion of acid precipitation in Chapter 2. Nor was the damage limited to the natural environment. The graceful, humanized landscapes of pre-industrial Europe—the fine old towns and aesthetically pleasing rural landscapes—also suffered harm. Industrial activity altered or obliterated many of the myriad places that endow Europe with its special human character, prompting geographer Douglas Porteous to coin the word **topocide**—the deliberate obliteration of a place—to describe the fate of his native Howdendyke in Yorkshire. The "Faustian bargain" which industrialized Europe made exacted its price.

Such warnings came very early. After a brief initial period of optimism about industrialization in the period before 1775, the more sensitive Europeans—poets and artists—sensed that something was amiss. They expressed their alarm in the form of paintings and poems, beginning in the last quarter of the eighteenth century. The Scottish poet Robert Burns visited an iron foundry "lest we gang to Hell, it may be nae surprise," and many artists of the period left paintings of the industrialized districts that convey a sinister, foreboding landscape. Such warnings continued over the following centuries. Charles Dickens' descriptions of London and Paris in *A Tale of Two Cities* (1859) highlight some of the squalid environmental and social conditions industrialization produced in these cities. Meanwhile, Käthe Kollwitz chronicled through her paintings and etchings the miseries of working class women and children of German cities such as Berlin during the early twentieth century. More recently the Welshman Richard Llewellyn penned the poignant novel *How Green Was My Valley* (1939), a classic lament of the economic oppression of his people and the ravaging of their countryside by industrialization.

The culprits of environmental alteration were many. Smoke and soot from the burning of coal and wood darkened the sky and the building below. Chemicals also entered the atmosphere, and carbon dioxide levels increased. The dumping of industrial wastes into rivers and oceans fouled Europe's surface waters, and seepage of industrial waste introduced noxious chemicals into the ground water. And then there were the industrial sites themselves—cleared of natural vegetation and often containing hazardous dumps and chemical-infused ponds of water.

Laws and regulations gradually began to curtail the worst environmental abuses, but these were slow in coming in many places—particularly to the east of the former Iron Curtain. The greatest concentration of environmental damage in the twentieth century occurred in the Black Triangle, the borderland between eastern Germany, Czechia, and southern Poland (fig. 8.3). Visits to ravaged industrial towns in eastern Germany until

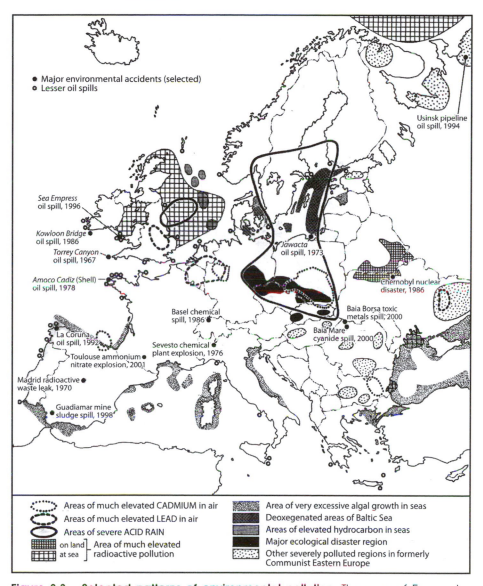

Figure 8.3. Selected patterns of environmental pollution. The core of Europe has been most disastrously affected, but the peripheries have not escaped, due to the discharge of polluted rivers, the practice of dumping toxic wastes in the sea, and oil spills in the transport lanes. *Sources:* Carré, F. 1992. Aperçu sur la Pollution de la Mer du Nord. *Hommes et Terres du Nord* 3: 142; *The Economist Atlas of the New Europe*, 1992, New York: Henry Holt, 203, 210; *Geographica Polonica*, 1962, 59: 51; Ionescu, D. 1991. Romania: The A to Z of the Most Polluted Areas. *Report on Eastern Europe* 2 (19): 20–25; Petrow, R. 1968. *In the Wake of the Torrey Canyon*. New York: David McKay, frontispiece; *Concise Statistical Yearbook of Poland, 1991*, 1992, Warszawa, PL: Central Statistical Office, 25; Clout, H. et al. 1989. *Western Europe: Geographical Perspectives*, 2nd ed., Harlow, UK: Longman, 182; Thompson 1991, 45; Vilchek G. E. et al. 1996. The Environment in the Russian Arctic. *Polar Geography* 20: 22–23.

quite recently provided a sobering experience for any sensitive person, although this has been changing dramatically in recent years. The city of Bitterfeld, near Leipzig, is practically synonymous with environmental destruction and is known for its smokestacks, chemical refineries, and horrific pollution. Since 2000, the countryside around Bitterfeld has undergone a dramatic transformation. The area called Goitzsche, known for its moonlike landscape of slag heaps and shallow coal-mining pits, was cleaned up and flooded, and is now a chain of attractive lakes used for recreation and restored animal habitat.

In spite of stories such as the ones recounted above, there are plenty of places in eastern and western Europe where one can still observe the long-term imprints of industrialization on the landscape. Russia's Kola Peninsula is plagued by nuclear wastes and the by-products of nickel smelting. Bulgaria's fishing industry has been devastated by die-offs of mackerel, sturgeons, and anchovies. Serious industrial accidents have occurred in recent decades at Seveso in northern Italy (1976), at Basel in Switzerland (1986), at Toulouse in France (2001), and at Glasgow in Scotland (2004) (fig. 8.3). The human consequences of such disasters can be profound. The chemical factory explosion at Seveso produced a dioxin cloud that led to elevated rates of leukemia, lymphoma, and liver cancer in the area.

Deindustrialization

Beginning in the mid-1960s the most important mass-production industries in Europe went into severe and irreversible decline, prompting use of terms such as **deindustrialization**, and industrial crisis. Once-prosperous industrial districts became, within no more than two decades, "derelict," "pauperized," and eligible for economic assistance. The blue-collar labor force in a single generation deteriorated into "a dispirited people who reflected a growing passivity to their plight," to use the words of geographer Shane Davies. Entire working-class communities became devastated and dependent upon unemployment relief.

The statistical evidence of deindustrialization tells the story. In the United Kingdom, birthplace of the Industrial Revolution, the labor force employed in manufacturing plummeted from 9,119,000 in 1966 to 5,172,000 by 1987. In the Midlands district, where the modern coal and steel industry was born, manufacturing employment fell by 55% during that two-decade span. In Wales, "its spirit and wealth now broken," employment in mining dropped from an all-time high of 270,000 to only 24,000 by 1982. All of Great Britain could claim only 31 coal mines, with 12,000 employees, by 1994. In the half-century after 1930, some 400,000 people emigrated from the South Wales industrial area. The Newcastle-Tyneside-Tees district of northeastern England saw its last operating shipyard and deep coal mine closed in 1994. Manchester in Lancashire and Belfast in Northern Ireland, once prosperous industrial cities, suffered particularly severe decline. Even London was not spared. Its manufacturing work force declined by 40% in the brief period between 1975 and 1982, and an additional 300,000 industrial jobs were lost in greater London during the decade ending in 1991.

Mainland industrial districts fared little better. The peak year of coal production in the Saar-Lorraine was 1957; 20 years later it was labeled a "problem region," as were the Ruhr and Sambre-Meuse-Lys regions. In western Germany, the work force employed in coal mining dwindled from 600,000 in 1955 to 95,000 by 1995. The Ligurian coast around

Genoa in Italy and the Bay of Biscay coast of northern Spain also joined the list of severely stricken industrial regions (fig. 8.4). Turin in the Po Valley suffered particularly severe manufacturing decline. In France, which had 190,000 coal miners in 1948, the number shrank to 6,000 a half-century later, and the government ended all coal mining in 2005.

The crisis began in the primary sector—in particular, coal mining. A steadily decreasing demand for coal, principally the result of a shift to alternative energy

DECLINES IN MANUFACTURING AND MINING

■ Most severe decline, 1965–1990

▨ Major decline, 1965–1990

▦ Most severe decline, 1990–1995

▧ Major decline, 1990–1995

— Borders of the new, prosperous industrial core of Europe

▦ High-tech manufacturing

▨ High quality and luxury goods manufacturing

Figure 8.4. Zones of deindustrialization and of new manufacturing growth, 1960–2000. Decline and growth remain largely separate geographically, though often in close proximity. The emerging economic core, based on high-tech, crafts, and—to a lesser extent—petroleum, favors the European west.

sources, especially petroleum, brought depression to mining. Also contributing to the decline of the mining sector was the depletion of minerals such as iron ore. Saar-Lorraine ore peaked in output in 1960, and even in Sweden, Europe's leading iron ore producer, the reserve is now small and yield falls.

Beyond the problem of declining resources in Europe, the global political and economic picture was changing in a way that worked against European industry. By the mid-1960s Europe had lost most of its colonies. At the same time, an industrial boom was taking place in eastern Asia, introducing a new source of competition for European industry. Two additional interrelated factors were of paramount importance: the declining cost of transportation and growing wage differentials between workers in Europe and the less developed world. Technological innovations and the economies of scale made possible by the expansion of shipping, airline, and railroad industries greatly reduced the cost of transporting goods across large distances. As a result, it became less important to locate industries near raw materials and consumer markets. Instead, earning a good profit meant controlling expenditures on what had become the single greatest contributor to the cost of many finished products: labor. The less developed world offered a great advantage in this regard, and it became increasingly difficult for European industry to compete.

Some industries declined earlier than others. Britain's position in the textile industry began to slip as early as the late-nineteenth and early twentieth centuries; its share of world cotton textile production dropped from 56% in 1870 to 38% in 1915. A more extreme example of decline is provided by the linen industry of Northern Ireland. Between 1950 and 1970, the labor force and number of factories in the Belfast area fell by half, a critical decline in the local economy, since a fifth of the labor force had been employed in the linen industry. Shipbuilding declined even more catastrophically. As recently as 1948, the United Kingdom produced almost half of the world tonnage launched, but by 1980 its share had fallen to only 4%. The 1960s witnessed the most rapid decline. The plight of shipbuilding is illustrated by the Clydeside district in the Scottish Lowlands. Local shipyards began their rise to world importance in the 1830s, only to find prosperity arrested a century later. Clydeside ship tonnage peaked in 1913. Foreign competition, particularly from Japan, sent the Clydeside into severe depression after the middle 1950s. In short, deindustrialization struck hardest at the traditional mass-production enterprises that had formed the core of the Industrial Revolution—textiles, steel, coal mining, shipbuilding, and chemicals—and at the districts specialized in these pursuits. Textile towns such as Troyes in France and mining centers like South Wales suffered most.

In Eastern Europe, traditional mass-production industries remained free of competition in the absence of a market economy before 1990. Many of these industries were inefficient, but that did not translate into decline as long as the Communist system of central planning survived and subsidization survived. As a result, deindustrialization came both late and very abruptly to the east, largely running its course in a half-decade and causing massive economic problems and social dislocations (fig. 8.4). Industrial collapse better describes what happened in the eastern parts of Europe.

In Russia, oil production declined to 68% of the 1990 level by 1997 and iron ore output to 59%, while coal production declined 66% in the 1990–1995 period. Russian manufactures likewise plummeted, and by 1997, chemical production stood at 46% of the 1990 output, iron and steel at 59%, and machinery and metalworking at 40%. The declines have ended, and output in some industries has risen over the last ten years. Privatization of Russian metallurgy industries was largely completed by 1996, involving 398 out of 411 enterprises.

Elsewhere in formerly Communist Eastern Europe, deindustrialization took a similar toll. In Romania, the labor force declined by 7% in just two years, from 1989 to 1991. The East German industrial city of Plauen in the Saxon Triangle lost a third of its total population between 1990 and 1994, and the East German textile work force plummeted from 320,000 in 1990 to only 20,000 by 1999. The process is ongoing. Poland, which employed 312,000 coal miners in 1993, cut its work force to 146,000 by 2002, closing well over half of its mines.

In both eastern and western Europe, deindustrialization led to high rates of unemployment, particularly in the old, decayed heavy industry districts (fig. 8.5). Persistent governmental efforts had little impact on the unemployment problem for some time,

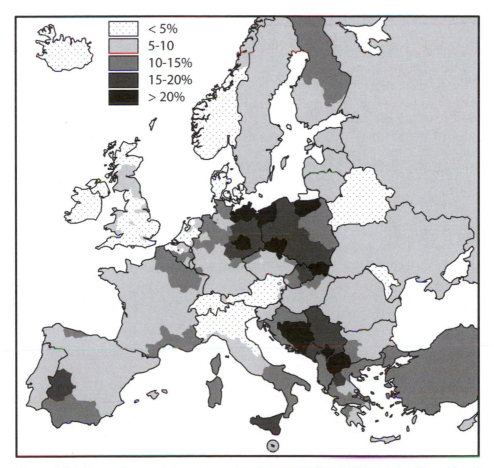

Figure 8.5.   Percentage of unemployed in Europe. Patterns at the subnational level are available for most European Union countries. Note particularly the deep pockets of unemployment in former East Germany, Poland, and the newest states in southeastern Europe. *Sources: Eurostat* and various national statistical yearbooks.

but the mid-2000s showed some improvements as European economies adjusted to new realities. We look at this issue in more depth in Chapter 11.

Industrial Rejuvenation

The impacts of deindustrialization were variable across Europe. While many major industries and districts descended into crisis, others retained stability or achieved impressive growth. In the primary sector, the collapse of coal mining and the decline of iron ore production occurred simultaneously with the development of the great North Sea oil and natural gas field—a submarine deposit shared by the United Kingdom, Norway, Denmark, Germany, and the Netherlands (fig. 8.4). The northern forests of Sweden, Finland, and Russia, a renewable primary resource, continued to yield their sizable harvests. These three northern European countries still provide about 21% of the world's sawn lumber exports and 16% of the wood pulp and paper.

Much more important than these primary industries to European rejuvenation has been the shift to the manufacture of high-quality goods requiring a skilled labor force, ongoing innovation, and/or sophisticated technology. A number of Europe's regions—particularly in the west—have successfully moved from an emphasis on mass-produced goods requiring large factories and minimally skilled labor to a focus on labor-intensive skilled operations producing items of high value, often in small workshops.

The most high-profile of these new enterprises can be grouped under the much-used term **high-tech**. Properly speaking, these include industries manufacturing high-technology products, such as electronic and microelectronic devices, data processing equipment, robotics, telecommunications apparatus, and the like. To these should be added firms that make preponderant use of high-tech products—particularly the computer—in the manufacturing process. These include pharmaceutical firms and pesticide makers. All such manufacturers invest heavily in research and development in order to foster the innovations that drive the volatile high-tech industry, though these innovations more often than not spawn new companies. Research and development activity constitutes a service industry and as such will be considered in the next chapter. While much is made of high-tech manufacturing—and several European countries have tied their industrial future to such activity—these firms employ far fewer people than the old, collapsed ones. Their rise has had only a marginal impact on problems associated with deindustrialization.

Perhaps more promising for Europe's employment future is the manufacture of high-quality expensive luxury goods, mainly for export. These factories operate as labor- and design- (rather than technology-) intensive craft industries and represent, in fact, a revival of guild-like manufacturing. Indeed, the apprenticeship system has survived from guild times, under government protection in countries such as Germany. The highly skilled workforce enjoys good wages, job security, and the satisfaction of laboring in "a positive culture of work." Creativity, skill, and craftsman pride are all essential components. Factories tend to be small and the workplace

pleasant. Typical products include ceramics, pottery, decorative glassware, fine clothing, jewelry, quality leather goods such as shoes, well-crafted wood products, and luxury automobiles. Such manufacturing survived in Europe even during the heyday of
heavy industry, especially in non-coalfield districts such as the Swiss Plateau-Jura, but
a major expansion has occurred since 1970. High quality craft industries have one
great potential weakness—their dependence upon a high level of prosperity among
consumers, many of whom reside outside Europe. Any major worldwide depression
would undermine such industries. Europe's continued prosperity and high standard
of living are always at risk.

Geographically, deindustrialization and rejuvenation occurred in distinct
European regions, with relatively little overlap (fig. 8.4). The high-tech and craft
industry districts were often close enough to the old industrial areas to have been pos-
itively affected by their former prosperity, but not so close as to have to confront the
enormous challenges of deindustrialization. Geographer Allen Scott has given these
districts the name "new industrial spaces." Southern England, southern Germany,
southern France, and northern Belgium eclipsed the northern parts of those countries
as centers of manufacturing, while the eastern part of the Po-Veneto Plain has surpassed the older Milan-Turin focus.

High-tech industry, which tends to be drawn to universities, major airports, suburbs, small towns, and medium-sized cities, has concentrated in places such as the
"M–4 Corridor," a crescent-shaped area west of London; "Silicon Glen" in the
Lothians near Edinburgh; "Scientific City," southwest of Paris; Mediterranean France;
the Dutch Randstad; northern Beligum; and the suburbs of München, Augsburg,
Nürnberg, and several other south German cities (fig. 8.4). In some cases, the older,
declining industrial centers have sought to claim a share of high-tech industry, as
northeast of Milan and at Turin in Italy, where a "Technocity" has developed, but these
efforts remain the exception rather than the rule.

The regions devoted to craft-style manufacturing include, most notably, the
"Third Italy," which as early as 1981 claimed 37% of all manufacturing employment
in that country; the provinces of Bayern and Baden-Württemberg in South Germany,
where conservative state governments fostered such development; the south of France;
southern England; central Denmark; most of south-central Sweden; and southwestern
Finland (fig. 8.4).

The so-called Third Italy, typical of these new industrial spaces, produces a great
array of goods, including luxury automobiles such as Alfa Romeo and Ferrari, silks
from Como, jewelry from Venice, tiles from Modena, and fine woolen textiles from
Biella. The district is also heavily engaged in manufacturing the precision machines
and tools required to make some of these goods, including those used in the manufacture of gold jewelry.

Europe's western industrial heartland, then, contains an odd patchwork of distressed deindustrialized districts alongside booming centers of high-tech and craft
manufacturing. Eastern Europe's condition is less fortunate, for deindustrialization
there has not been accompanied by as noteworthy a rise of new enterprises devoted
to sophisticated technology or skilled crafts. The east/west industrial contrast has
become vivid and alarming, given the social and political connotations. Decades of

central planning has made it difficult for a culture of individualistic entrepreneurialism to take root.

Still, not all is bleak in the east. Economic downturns reversed in 1995 in most countries. Many western firms opened factories in the formerly Communist countries, and some local manufacturers made the transition to a market economy. Poland's Szczecin shipyards have risen to world prominence, and the eastern German toymaking town of Sonneberg in Thüringen has regained much of its former fame and vigor, after cutting the Communist-era workforce of 18,000 down to a lean 1,200. In Russia, small private businesses, each employing fewer than 100 workers, numbered over 950,000 by 2004, giving employment to nearly eight million people. Enclaves of relative prosperity have developed in Euro-Russia, most notably in Moscow, but also in St. Petersburg and even certain provincial towns, such as Novgorod—so successful that "the Novgorod model" has entered business jargon.

There are also some environmental positives to deindustrialization. Deindustrialization, especially in eastern Europe, has greatly reduced levels of environmental pollution. Russia provides some revealing examples. Emissions of hazardous atmospheric contaminants decreased by 65% at Moscow and St. Petersburg, and 54% at Volgograd (in the south near the Caspian Sea) between 1992 and 2005. The situation in the Black Triangle has also improved, but that only says that additional damage to the regional habitat has been cut back. A network of national parks and other nature preserves offers additional hope to eastern Europe.

Core and Periphery

Both the old and new industrial orders in Europe feature a core-periphery pattern (figs. 8.1, 8.4). Under the geographical configuration that prevailed before deindustrialization, manufacturing districts lay principally in the European core, with few exceptions. In that pattern, the European periphery housed mainly primary industries that supplied raw materials for the manufacturing core. These included forest products from the north; fishing in the peripheral oceans and seas; mining, as at Kiruna and Kryvyy Rih; and the extraction of petroleum and natural gas at places such as Ploeşti in the Valachian Plain and in the hinter reaches of the East European Plain.

In Europe's new industrial order, the core has diminished in size and the periphery expanded (fig. 8.4). If the stricken manufacturing districts of Britain, northern Spain, and Eastern Europe are excluded, then the new core, represented by high-tech and craft industry concentrations as well as North Sea petroleum, displays a thinner profile than the old one. Even so, the traditional pattern of a manufacturing core and primary industrial periphery remains intact.

The industrial geography of Europe, as we have seen, is in flux. New patterns and industries emerge as old ones decline. High-tech and craft industries form only part of the changing economic geography. To obtain a more complete picture, we must now turn to another category altogether—the so-called service industries. Chapter 9 is devoted to that growing sector of the economy.

Sources and Suggested Readings

Agnew, J., M. Shin, and P. Richardson. 2005. The Saga of the "Second Industrial Divide" and the History of the "Third Italy": Evidence from Export Data. *Scottish Geographical Journal* 121 (1): 83–101.

Alfrey, J. and C. Clark. 1993. *The Landscape of Industry Patterns of Change in the Ironbridge Gorge*. London: Routledge.

Begg, B., J. Pickles, and A. Smith. 2003. Cutting It: European Integration, Trade Regimes, and the Reconfiguration of East—Central European Apparel Production. *Environment and Planning A* 35 (12): 2191–2208.

Blazek, J. and D. Uhlir. 2007. Regional Innovation Policies in the Czech Republic and the Case of Prague: An Emerging Role of a Regional Level? *European Planning Studies* 15 (7): 871–888.

Boldorf, M. 2006. *Europäische Leinenregionen im Wandel Institutionelle Weichenstellungen in Schlesien und Irland (1750–1850), Industrielle Welt Bd. 68*. Köln: Böhlau.

Bosma, N. and V. Schutjens. 2007. Patterns of Promising Entrepreneurial Activity in European Regions. *Tijdschrift voor Economische en Sociale Geografie* 98 (5): 675–786.

Bradshaw, M. 2006. Observations on the Geographical Dimensions of Russia's Resource Abundance. *Eurasian Geography & Economics* 47 (6): 724–746.

Brady, D., J. Beckfield, and M. Seeleib-Kaiser. 2005. Economic Globalization and the Welfare State in Affluent Democracies, 1975–2001. *American Sociological Review* 70 (6): 921–948.

Braun, B., and R. E. Grotz. 1993. Support for Competitiveness: National and Common Strategies for Manufacturing Industries within the European Community. *Erdkunde* 47 (2): 105–117.

Brown, D. L., B. Greskovits, and L. J. Kulcsar. 2007. Leading Sectors and Leading Regions: Economic Restructuring and Regional Inequality in Hungary since 1990. *International Journal of Urban & Regional Research* 31 (3): 522–542.

Carter, F. W. and W. Maik. 1999. *Shock-Shift in an Enlarged Europe: The Geography of Socio-Economic Change in East-Central Europe after 1989*. Aldershot: Ashgate.

Carter, F. W. and D. Turnock, eds. 2002. *Environmental Problems of East Central Europe, Routledge Studies of Societies in Transition 16*. London: Routledge.

Cumbers, A. 1995. North Sea Oil and Regional Economic Development: The Case of the North East of England. *Area* 27 (3): 208–217.

de Smidt, M. and E. Wever. 1990. *An Industrial Geography of the Netherlands: An International Perspective, Nederlandse Industrie. English*. London: Routledge.

Diamond, J. M. 2005. *Guns, Germs, and Steel: The Fates of Human Societies*. New York: Norton.

Dobruszkes, F. 2006. An Analysis of European Low-Cost Airlines and Their Networks. *Journal of Transport Geography* 14 (4): 249–264.

Douglas, K. F. 1967. Coastal Steelworks in the Common Market Countries. *Geographical Review* 57 (1): 48–72.

Dunford, M. and L. Greco. 2007. Geographies of Growth, Decline, and Restructuring: The Rise and Fall (Privatization) of the State-Owned Steel Sector and the Trajectories of Steel Localities in the Italian Mezzogiorno. *European Urban & Regional Studies* 14 (1): 27–53.

Evans, I. M. 1980. Aspects of the Steel Crisis in Europe, with Particular Reference of Belgium and Luxembourg (Manufacturing). *The Geographical Journal* 146 (3): 396–407.

Every Last Drop. July 14, 2007. *Economist* 384 (8537): 60–61.

Gatrell, A. C. and A. A. Lovett. 1986. The Geography of Hazardous-Waste Disposal in England and Wales. *AREA* 18 (4): 275–283.

Giaccaria, P. 1999. Learning and Local Competitiveness: The Case of Turin. *GeoJournal* 49 (4): 401–410.

Gregory, D. 1982. *Regional Transformation and Industrial Revolution: A Geography of the Yorkshire Woollen Industry*. Minneapolis: University of Minnesota Press.

Grotz, R. and B. Braun. 1993. Networks, Milieux, and Individual Firm Strategies: Empirical Evidence of an Innovative SME Environment. *Geografiska Annaler, Series B* 75 B (3): 149–162.

————. 1996. *Spatial Aspects of Technology-Oriented Networks: Examples from the German Mechanical Engineering Industry, Bonner Beiträge zur Geographie H. 3*. Bonn: Geograph. Inst., Lehrstuhl.

Hall, P. G. 1987. *Western Sunrise: The Genesis and Growth of Britain's Major High Tech Corridor*. London: Allen & Unwin.

Heen, K. and O. Flaaten. 2007. Spatial Employment Impacts of Fisheries Management—A Study of the Barents Sea and the Norwegian Sea Fisheries. *Fisheries Research* 85 (1–2): 74–83.

Helms, G. and A. Cumbers. 2006. Regulating the New Urban Poor: Local Labour Market Control in an Old Industrial City. *Space and Polity* 10 (1): 67–86.

Hudson, R. 2002. Changing Industrial Production Systems and Regional Development in the New Europe. *Transactions of the Institute of British Geographers* 27 (3): 262–281.

Hudson, R. and D. Sadler. 1990. State Policies and the Changing Geography of the Coal Industry in the United Kingdom in the 1980s and 1990s. *Transactions of the Institute of British Geographers, New Series* 15 (4): 435–454.

Kangas, O. E. and V.-M. Ritakallio. 2007. Relative to What?: Cross-National Picture of European Poverty Measured by Regional, National, and European Standards. *European Societies* 9 (2): 119–145.

Langton, J. 1979. *Geographical Change and Industrial Revolution: Coalmining in South West Lancashire, 1590–1799, Cambridge Geographical Studies 11*. Cambridge: Cambridge University Press.

————. 1984. The Industrial Revolution and the Regional Geography of England. *Transactions—Institute of British Geographers* 9 (2): 145–167.

Laux, J. M. 1992. *The European Automobile Industry*. New York: Twayne.

Lijewski, T. 2003. Koncentracja Osodków Aktywnosi Gospodarczej W Polsce W Sietle List 500 Firm. *Przeglad Geograficzny* 75 (3): 433–447.

Magnusson, L. 1994. *The Contest for Control: Metal Industries in Sheffield, Solingen, Remscheid, and Eskilstuna during Industrialization*. Oxford, UK: Berg.

Martin, J. E. 1966. *Greater London: An Industrial Geography*. Chicago: University of Chicago Press.

Morgan, K. 2007. The Learning Region: Institutions, Innovation, and Regional Renewal. *Regional Studies* 41: S147-S159.

Morris, J. 1987. Global Restructuring and Region: Manufacturing Industry in Wales, 1972–1982. *Tijdschrift voor Economische en Sociale Geografie* 78 (1): 16–29.

Mozhayev, P. A. 2003. Spatial Organization of Logistic Chains in Automobile Industry (the Example of Germany). *Vestnik Moskovskogo Universiteta, Seriya 5: Geografiya* (5): 38–45.

Oles, W., O. Rahmonov, M. Rzetala, S. Pytel, and I. Malik. 2004. The Ways of Industrial Wastelands Management in the Upper Silesian Region. *Ekologia-Bratislava* 23: 244–251.

Pavlínek, P. 2002. Restructuring the Central and Eastern European Automobile Industry: Legacies, Trends, and Effects of Foreign Direct Investment. *Post-Soviet Geography and Economics* 43 (1): 41–77.

Peterson, D. J. 1993. *Troubled Lands: The Legacy of Soviet Environmental Destruction, A Rand Research Study*. Boulder: Westview Press.

Plahuta, S. and G. Halder. 2006. Wirtschaftliche und Soziale Folgen der Deindustrialisierung— Das Beispiel Stuttgart. *Geographische Rundschau* 58 (6): 32–42.

Pollard, S. 1981. *Peaceful Conquest: The Industrialization of Europe, 1760–1970*. Oxford: Oxford University Press.

Porteous, J. D. 1989. *Planned to Death: The Annihilation of a Place Called Howdendyke*. Manchester: Manchester University Press.

Pounds, N. J. G. 1957. Historical Geography of the Iron and Steel Industry of France. *Annals of the Association of American Geographers* 47 (1): 3–14.

———. 1958. *The Upper Silesian Industrial Region, Indiana University Publications*. Slavic and East European Series V. 11. Bloomington.

Resmini, L. 2007. Regional Patterns of Industry Location in Transition Countries: Does Economic Integration with the European Union Matter? *Regional Studies* 41 (6): 747–764.

Rosiello, A. 2007. The Geography of Knowledge Transfer and Innovation in Biotechnology: The Cases of Scotland, Sweden, and Denmark. *European Planning Studies* 15 (6): 787–815.

Sadler, D. 1995. Old Industrial Places and Regions: The Limits to Reindustrialisation. In *Europe at the Margins: New Mosaics of Inequality*, eds. C. Hadjimichalis and D. Sadler, 133–148. Chichester: J. Wiley.

———. 2004. Cluster Evolution: The Transformation of Old Industrial Regions and the Steel Industry Supply Chain in Northeast England. *Regional Studies* 38 (1): 55–66.

Sagers, M. J. 2006a. The Regional Dimension of Russian Oil Production: Is a Sustained Recovery in Prospect? *Eurasian Geography & Economics* 47 (5): 505–545.

———. 2006b. Russia's Energy Policy: A Divergent View. *Eurasian Geography & Economics* 47 (3): 314–320.

Salet, W. G. M., and E. Gualini, eds. 2007. *Framing Strategic Urban Projects: Learning from Current Experiences in European Urban Regions*. London: Routledge.

Schulz, C. and H. P. Dörrenbächer. 2005. Grenzraum Saarland-Lothringen—Vom Montandreieck Zur Automobilregion? *Geographische Rundschau* 57 (12): 20–26.

Scott, A. J. 1988. *Flexible Production Systems and Regional Development: The Rise of New Industrial Spaces in North America and Western Europe, Research Paper / Centre for Urban and Community Studies, University of Toronto 00316–0068 No. 168*. Toronto: Centre for Urban and Community Studies, University of Toronto.

———. 2006. The Changing Global Geography of Low-Technology, Labor-Intensive Industry: Clothing, Footwear, and Furniture. *World Development* 34 (9): 1517–1536.

Smith, A., J. Pickles, R. Begg, P. Roukova, and M. Bucek. 2005. Euro-Commentary. *European Urban & Regional Studies* 12 (1): 83–91.

Steed, G. P. F. 1974. The Northern Ireland Linen Complex, 1950–1970. *Annals of the Association of American Geographers* 64 (3): 397–408.

Tuppen, J. N. 1980. *France: Studies in Industrial Geography*. Folkestone, UK: Dawson.

Warren, K. 1970. *The British Iron and Steel Sheet Industry since 1840: An Economic Geography*. London: Bell.

Wells, P. and M. Rawlinson. 1994. *The New European Automobile Industry*. New York: St. Martin's Press.

Williams, A. M. 1987. *The Western European Economy: A Geography of Post-War Development*. Totowa, N.J.: Barnes & Noble.

CHAPTER 9

The Service and Information Economy

Service industries involve neither the extraction of resources nor manufacturing, but instead include a broad range of activities that serve people's everyday needs and facilitate economic activity. These **tertiary sector** activities include health care, education, transportation, energy production, retailing, wholesaling, and tourism. Traditionally activities such as banking, consulting, information processing, legal services, and research and development were treated as part of the tertiary sector, but these have become so important that many geographers and economists now speak of a **quaternary sector** involved with the collection, processing, and manipulation of information and capital. The term **postindustrial** is sometimes used to denote the rise to dominance of these quaternary-sector industries in modern Europe, coincident with the decline of primary and secondary industries. No general agreement exists on how to categorize these diverse enterprises. Some prefer to distinguish market (or private) services from governmental (or public) services. Others suggest that the primary distinction should be between producer and consumer services. Still others continue to label all service industries as tertiary economic activities.

The most outstanding feature of Europe's tertiary and quaternary sector industries is their disproportionate growth since about 1950. Service activities have always been present, of course; the blacksmith in the traditional rural village, the road builder in a medieval city, and the engineer at an Industrial Revolution-era steel plant were all part of the tertiary sector. But as recently as the middle of the twentieth century, Europe's economy could still be described primarily as an industrial one. That is no longer the case. In recent decades in Europe, a postindustrial economy has taken root, particularly in western Europe—and tertiary and quaternary activities now dominate. Well over half of the labor force in many countries and provinces now finds employment in service industries (fig. 9.1). For example, as recently as 1961 only 30% of the workforce in Austria worked in the services sector; now, two out of three Austrian workers are involved in tertiary and quaternary sector activities. Eastern Europe, long shackled by its Cold-War industrial economy, lags behind the western part of Europe in this respect, but even there the proportion of the population employed in the service sector is growing rapidly.

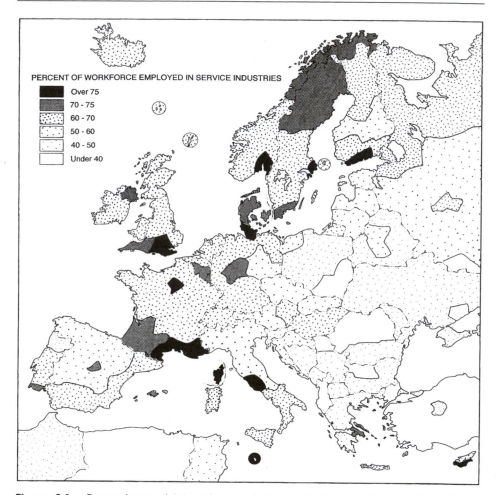

Figure 9.1. Percentage of labor force employed in the service industries. These diverse activities include government, transport, trade, finance, retailing, energy supply, tourism, education, health, and other services. An east-west contrast can be detected within Europe. *Source:* Eurostat.

What accounts for this transformation? The reasons are multiple and complex, but four interrelated catalysts are of particular importance: rising labor costs in Europe, declining transportation costs, mechanization of the production process, and expanding trade. As European industry became increasingly successful and workers gained more rights and protections as a result of collective action or government regulations, labor costs increased. At the same time, technological innovations and the expansion of transportation infrastructure led to a significant decline in the cost of shipping goods and resources over long distances. This meant that labor costs came to contribute much more to the total cost of production than did transportation. As a result, it became increasingly difficult for European industry to compete with industries established in parts of the world where cheap labor and low levels of regulation were the norm. Industries developing in other parts of the world could also take advantage of accelerating global trade to find markets for their products in distant places. Europe thus began to lose its industrial dominance, and many industrial jobs were lost.

The best way to fight back was to make the production process cheaper and more efficient, and that imperative led those European industries that did not close or move overseas to turn increasingly toward the use of sophisticated machines. The result was that many additional industrial jobs were lost. Where Europe could compete was in the development and design of the sophisticated machinery used in industry, as well as in the provision of the technologies and the financial and management services needed to sustain increasingly sophisticated tertiary and quaternary activities. Add to this the explosion in education needed to train workers for the new economy, and the growth in size of a middle class with the time and resources needed to travel and take advantage of other products of the service economy, and you begin to gain some appreciation of how and why Europe's postindustrial economy developed.

Europe's tertiary and quaternary economy is vast and complex. To understand something of its roots, and how it functions today, it is useful to look at a few key elements that are particularly important either for the role they play in sustaining economic activity, or for their overall contribution to Europe's economy. We begin by focusing on **transportation** and **communication**—for Europe has had the most complex, complete transportation and communication network of any region of comparable size in the entire world (fig. 9.2). We then turn to energy production because of its centrality to sustaining modern ways of living and doing business. We conclude by looking at several activities that are very significant contributors to the overall European economy: tourism, retailing and social services, and the set of quaternary-sector activities that sustain the postindustrial economy.

Transportation

The movement of people, information, and commodities within and between all parts of Europe is the product of a system of transport that is one of the most advanced and efficient in the world. Still, disparities exist in Europe, and there is pressure for more flexibility and reliability, higher-frequency deliveries, and ever better-articulated transportation systems. Moreover, the transport system in the core region, good as it is, cannot at present handle the demand at peak times. A look at the historical and present character of several major facets of Europe's transportation infrastructure provides insights into the ways in which this key service activity has reflected and shaped the region's changing geographical character.

HIGHWAYS

Europe's roads have provided a crucial component of the service sector at least since the time of the Romans. Desiring to rule more than the Mediterranean shores, the Romans built a truly astounding network of stone-paved roads connecting all parts of their Empire within Europe (fig. 9.3). They constructed some 320,000 kilometers of highway in the Empire as a whole, some of which, astoundingly, remain in use today.

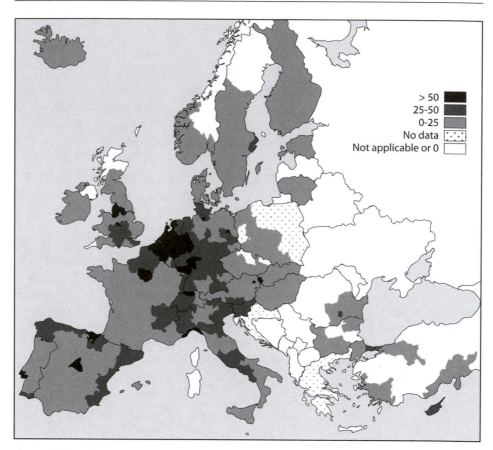

Figure 9.2. Motorable highways, kilometers per 1,000 sq km. The European road density exceeds that of any other sizable part of the world. A pronounced core-periphery pattern exists. *Source:* Eurostat.

Construction on the oldest of these Roman roads—the *Appian Way* from Rome southeast to Brindisi on the Adriatic coast—began in 312 B.C.E. Laid out by surveyors in long, straight stretches where terrain permitted, the Roman highways offered an overland mobility previously unknown to merchants, the military, and the common folk. Roman engineers bridged even major streams such as the Rhône; some of these splendid stone spans remain in use today after 2,000 years of traffic, flood, and warfare. Among them are the bridges over the Tejo River at Alcántara and the Guadiana at Mérida, both in southwestern Spain. Contrary to the popular saying, not all roads led to Rome (fig. 9.3). Indeed, the network had few major focal points.

The decline of trade during the Dark Ages curtailed the use of roads, as did political fragmentation. A rebirth of major mercantile activity in medieval times, coupled with greater internal security provided by the feudal system, renewed the demand for roads. The new routes hardly rivaled their Roman predecessors. Pavement was a rarity. Numerous streams remained unbridged, and as a consequence, river-ford sites typified many emerging towns. In time, new road patterns emerged. Regions that had undergone political unification, such as France and the United Kingdom, developed highly

Figure 9.3.   The Roman roads in Europe. The political borders are modern. *Source: Westermanns Grosser Atlas zur Weltgeschichte*, 1956. Braunschweig, D: Georg Westermann.

centralized road patterns by the eighteenth or nineteenth centuries, with the major routes radiating out from the national capital (fig. 6.5). Paris was the all-important hub of French roads, and Dublin served a similar function within Ireland. No transport focal point existed within the network of politically fragmented Germany, reflecting the lack of centralized organization. Some new routes unused in earlier times arose. St. Gotthard Pass through the Alps, ignored by the Romans, emerged as the great north-south route between Italy and the Rhine Valley in the Middle Ages, supplanting Splügen Pass to the east. The importance of the Gotthard route survives to the present.

Improvements came very slowly. A major step was taken in 1779 when Abraham Darby III built the first bridge out of cast iron over the Severn River near Coalbrookdale (a small principality in west-central England near the Welsh border). The bridge helped to spur the Industrial Revolution, and inspired people like Thomas Telford, who went on to build hundreds of bridges, including the 1826 Menai Strait Bridge—a steel suspension bridge linking the large island of Anglesey to the coast of Wales. Another major transportation innovation of the time came from John McAdam, for whom macadam roads are named. He built all-weather highways in England in the early 1800s, paved with several thin layers of tightly packed crushed rock, covered by water, and compacted by a heavy roller.

Continued improvement and elaboration of Europe's highway system occurred in the 1900s largely because of the automobile. Before long, a pronounced west-east contrast developed. Western Europe's middle class gained the financial ability to purchase cars after the middle of the twentieth century. In 1950, only 6,100,000 private automobiles existed in non-Communist Europe, about 1 for every 48 persons; but by 1970 the total had increased tenfold, and by the middle 1980s the total was 112,400,000, so that 1 western European in 3 owned a car. The proportion is now approaching 1 in 2 (fig. 9.4). Truck traffic also increased rapidly in the western part of Europe. Since

Figure 9.4.   Automobiles per person. Private car ownership remains more common in western Europe and is generally much higher in Europe than in adjacent parts of Africa and Asia. *Sources:* Eurostat and various national statistical yearbooks.

1990, trucks have carried some two-thirds of all freight, as contrasted to less than half as late as 1970.

Eastern Europe long remained a region of far lower rates of automobile ownership, much less truck usage, and sparser highway networks (figs. 9.2, 9.4). Highway infrastructure deteriorated in much of the east in the 1970s and 1980s. One of the first major tasks undertaken by the German government after reunification in 1990 involved upgrading roads in its new eastern provinces. Automobile ownership is increasing rapidly today in eastern Europe, even in the poorest countries such as Albania, where the number of passenger cars rose from 3,000 to 103,000 between 1985 and 2005. The gap between west and east is closing.

Private automobiles now account for 83% of all passenger-kilometers in western Europe, and around half in the east. Trucks and vans dominate goods transport, except in eastern Europe. The rise of private automobile and truck transport caused a major boom in highway construction that continues to the present in most parts of Europe. An already dense network has become even denser. Controlled-access expressways have proliferated since 1970, building upon the prototype of Germany's *autobahn* system, the origins of which date to the Nazi era (fig. 9.5). As the highway network has

Figure 9.5.   Controlled-access divided highways. Germany built the prototype of such expressways in the 1930s, and they remain a trait of the European core.

Figure 9.6.   Recently constructed highway bridge over the lower Seine River in Normandy, France. Europe has a superb road network but one nevertheless congested by traffic. (Photo by T.G.J.-B., 1999.)

expanded, many new bridges have been erected, some of which rank as grand works of art (fig. 9.6). One of the most ambitious recent projects was a bridge linking Denmark and Sweden, just north of Copenhagen. Plans are now in the works for a bridge that will span the Straits of Messina (linking Sicily to the Italian peninsula), as well as for a 19-kilometer bridge between the German island of Fehmarn and the Danish island of Lolland (linking Germany with Scandinavia) across the Baltic Sea.

While east-west contrasts remain in highway transportation, the more compelling and vivid contrast is that between European core and periphery (figs. 9.2, 9.6). The densest network exists in the center, while peripheries have a sparser pattern. Some settlements in Norway, for example, remain unconnected to the country's highway system, though an ambitious program of road, tunnel, and bridge construction has linked even some sparsely settled offshore islands to the road network.

Efforts to integrate Europe's highway system have progressed for decades, with the aim of more effectively meshing together the various national networks of roads. The "European highway" designation is one result. In addition to having a national number, these routes also have a standard E designation. For example, the E8 highway runs from Gravenhage eastward through Hannover, Berlin, Poznan, Warsaw, and Minsk to Moscow. The E1 extends from Sicily in the far south to Rome, Genoa, Lyon, Paris, Le Havre, and, after a ferry connection, to London. New routes of this type include the *Via Baltica,* an upgraded highway from Tallinn to Riga, Vilnius, and into Poland. Efforts to create an integrated European highway system have not translated into full harmonization of automobile travel in Europe. England, Scotland, Wales, and Ireland continue to have a right-hand drive system (i.e., they drive on the left side of the road), whereas drivers in continental Europe conform to the international norm of the steering wheel on the left-hand side. Incidentally, differences in what is viewed as the "correct" side for travel extend beyond roads. Trains travel on the left-hand track on British and Irish railways. Curiously, most Belgian and French railways also use the left track because they were originally built by British engineers, even though cars in both of those places conform to the right-hand model.

In spite of the ambitious programs of highway and expressway construction, the road network of the European core has become overwhelmed by the volume of automobile and truck traffic. Bottlenecks have formed at natural obstacles such as the Alps and sea channels, and traffic jams of enormous size develop on some expressways. Germans regularly endure the *Autobahnstau*—"expressway dam," when freeway traffic comes to a halt even in the countryside. Many international borders also produce jams (fig. 9.7). Within cities such as Paris, London, and Milan, traffic congestion is an acute problem as well. In London, where a decade of population growth had brought inner-city traffic to a nearly perpetual standstill, a system of tolls ("congestion charges") has been introduced to limit traffic inside London's inner ring road. This system has been proposed in a number of other global cities facing constant gridlock, including New York.

As John Whitelegg noted two decades ago, high levels of motorization constitute a major source of "disturbance, nuisance, health hazards, land-take, and ecological disruption," not to mention an appalling death rate from accidents and frequent gridlock traffic jams on the freeways. Germany, the epicenter of these problems, has seen picturesque towns such as Idar-Oberstein mutilated by highway construction and watched forests die from automobile exhaust, while suffering nearly 330,000 traffic accidents annually resulting in death or injury. As a result, public opinion has begun to turn against additional road building in Germany. Switzerland heavily taxes transit trucks to reduce traffic, noise, and pollution.

Efforts to relieve some of the bottlenecks have been partially successful. Perhaps most ambitious have been the bridge/tunnel between Denmark and Sweden and the English Channel tunnel, through which cars and trucks move by rail. In addition, the Schengen Agreement, in which many of the long-standing European Union member countries removed all internal border passport control, alleviated numerous chokepoints. In the final analysis, however, the road congestion problem cannot be solved short of a radical shift way from automobiles. Europe has too many people, too many vehicles, too many barriers, and not enough space.

RAILROADS

Europeans invented the railroad, just as they did the all-weather highway. Thus it is not surprising that Europe possesses almost one-third of the world's rail tracks by length. Railroad network density is greatest in a band stretching from England across northern France, the Low Countries and Germany, and into Czechia and western

Figure 9.7.   Road traffic bottlenecks and chokepoints. Europe has a splendid network of highways, but its large population, high automobile ownership rate, indented coastline, and numerous international borders, coupled with the position of the Alps in the central core, create many chokepoints.

Poland. (fig. 9.8). Outlying islands such as Iceland, the Shetlands, Malta, and Cyprus have no railroad lines, nor do the northernmost provinces of Norway. European railroads are state-owned or semi-privatized rather than wholly private, with the result that relatively little duplication of routes has developed.

The European railroad system derives from the English Industrial Revolution. In 1767 a British ironworks cast the first rails, initially for use by horse-drawn trams. A crude steam locomotive appeared by 1804 and, ten years later, a locomotive first pulled a train. By 1825 the British opened regularly-operated railroad service connecting the industrial towns of Darlington and Stockton on the River Tees in northeastern England. The British invention, prompted by increased demands for bulk transport, spread rapidly to mainland Europe, reaching France by 1832, Belgium and Germany by 1835, Austria-Hungary by

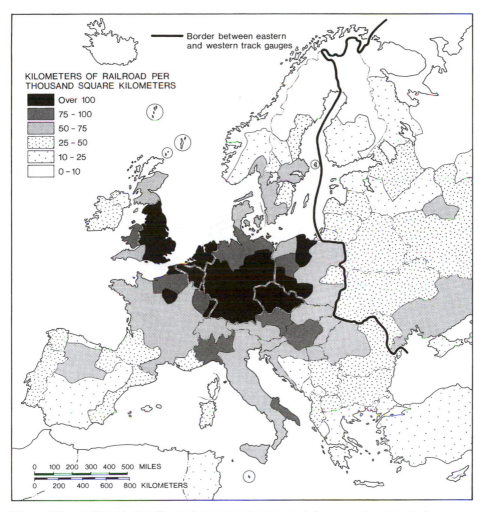

Figure 9.8.   Railroad density and gauge. A core-periphery contrast is obvious, and the gauge difference adds an east-west component to the pattern. The western gauge is typically 1.64 m and the eastern 1.74 m.

1838, Italy and the Netherlands by 1839, and Switzerland by 1844. By mid-century, a railroad network had developed in England, and significant beginnings had been made in the Paris Basin, Belgium, and northern Germany (fig. 9.9). The great era of rail construction ended by 1900 in Europe, by which time much of the present network existed. Albania, the final country to join the railroad age, built its first line in 1947.

Deindustrialization and the rise of motorized highway transport caused a notable shrinkage of the railroad network in the twentieth century, particularly in western Europe. As early as the 1920s, over 700 kilometers of line had been abandoned in Great Britain. In western Germany, the number of passenger rail cars on the *Bundesbahn* (Federal Railroad) declined from 22,600 in 1958 to 18,700 as early as 1967, and the volume of riders decreased in almost every western country. The downward trend

Figure 9.9.   Diffusion of the railroad in nineteenth-century Europe. A striking core-periphery pattern appears. Political borders shown are modern.

ended in the early 1990s, and since 1995 the number of passengers traveling by rail has inched up. Nonetheless, the growing number of passengers traveling by train has not kept pace with increases in automobile ridership.

Freight movement by rail has historically been less important in Europe than passenger movement. Rail freight also experienced a decline between 1970 and 1990. The trend has been reversed over the past decade, but growth in rail freight is modest and, like passenger service, it has not kept pace with increases in freight movement by road. This reflects in part the move toward smaller and more frequent deliveries that accompanied the shift away from heavy industries to those manufacturing high-quality and luxury goods. Another problem the railroads faced was that, until very recently, no real European-wide network ever existed. Instead, a series of patched-together national systems with different gauge widths was the norm. Postindustrial Europe made transport demands that the railroads were poorly designed to meet.

Nonetheless, Europeans have by no means given up on either freight or passenger rail transport. Indeed, rail transport is far more important in Europe than it is in the United States. For every 1,000 passengers using a car in Europe, 80 use a train. In the United States the ratio is 1,000 to 3. Moreover, throughout much of Europe rail transport is well organized and efficient—a reflection of government oversight and subsidies. Finally, the European railroad network is becoming faster and is increasingly well-integrated across national boundaries. The first step came in the late 1950s, when the international *Trans-Europ Express* was introduced. The service attracted business travelers by offering luxurious rolling stock and quicker service. Then, in the early 1980s, France led the way in ultra-high-speed passenger rail service (TGV), followed a decade later by Germany with its ICE.

Expansion of high-speed passenger rail transport now has top priority in the EU, and enormous sums are being spent. A master plan for a Europe-wide network is being implemented (fig. 9.10). When completed, this high-speed system will extend to all

Figure 9.10.   The European master plan for twenty-first-century high-speed railroads. This plan will be difficult to implement, especially in parts of the East. Part of the system, particularly in the west, is already operational. *Source:* European Commission.

Figure 9.11. The Channel Tunnel, providing a railroad link between England and France. Completed in the 1990s, it links Britain directly to the high-speed rail system of the mainland. The Chunnel, or Eurotunnel, as it is also called, transports both passengers and automobiles.

corners of Europe, including the east, where railroads have retained their traditional importance in spite of deteriorated track quality. High-speed trains operating in Europe today travel at 160 to 350 kilometers per hour. They compete successfully, time- and cost-wise, with many airline connections. (However, as we will see, the rise of low-cost air carriers is changing the calculus in some places.)

The most compelling evidence of Europe's future commitment to rail transport is provided by the completion of the 50-kilometer English Channel *Eurotunnel*, or "Chunnel," which links England and France by railroad (fig. 9.11). Trains move through the tunnel at speeds of up to 160 kilometers per hour carrying freight, passengers, and ferried automobiles. The Eurotunnel project has yet to be the financial success that its founders hoped it would be, but ridership has increased and the outlook for the future looks reasonably bright. Once a major hindrance to land transport, the English Channel can now be crossed in less than 30 minutes.

WATERWAYS

Complementing the road and rail systems is an intricate network of waterways. It consists of Europe's rivers and peripheral seas, connected by a series of canals (see fig. 2.7). The interconnected oceans and seas flanking Europe on three sides provide a splendid opportunity for transportation. The outline of Europe shows deep indentations on all shorelines, with the result that no place lies very far from the sea; small wonder that Europeans have long taken advantage of the pattern of peripheral seas to move their commodities from place to place.

The Mediterranean, the first sea used extensively for transportation, proved admirably suited to early navigators who needed few advanced marine skills, because ships could sail about its waters without ever losing sight of land. High, rocky coasts, with promontories made even more visible by the erection of temples and shrines atop them, guided the sailors of ancient Greece, as did the many mountainous islands (fig. 9.12). By

Figure 9.12. Templed promontories of the ancient Aegean. The seagoing Greeks placed great importance upon promontories, both as hazards to sailing and as landmarks. Temples both heightened the visibility of the promontories and allowed placation of the relevant gods. *Source:* Semple 1927.

"coasting" parallel to the shore or keeping island landfalls in sight, the sailors overcame much of the danger of sea transport. At a remarkably early date, Mediterranean seamen ventured out beyond Gibraltar, as far as Cornwall in Great Britain, attracted by tin mines. Still, at the time depicted in the Homeric epics, about 1200 B.C.E., the Greeks apparently remained ignorant of even the western part of the Mediterranean. Ulysses' relatively short voyage to western lands such as Malta and Tunisia placed him in unknown waters, where fear and imagination led him to people the shores with one-eyed cannibalistic giants and sorceresses who changed men to swine. In later centuries, the Greeks searched out every bay and cove around the Mediterranean and used the sea as the highway of their far-flung commercial empire. The Romans succeeded the Phoenicians and Greeks. They in turn gave way to other great Mediterranean seafaring peoples, including the Byzantine Greeks and Venetians.

The use of the North and Baltic seas for trade came later. By the eighth century, a trade in furs, slaves, and amber developed in the Baltic, while merchants in the North Sea handled cloth, wine, and wool. The Middle Ages brought the **Hanseatic League**, or *Hansa*, a trading union of many towns, in countries around the shores of the North and Baltic seas. With the Age of Discovery, the Atlantic assumed its present position as the major trade route of Europe.

Complementing the peripheral seas are numerous navigable rivers, improved through dredging, removing rapids, constructing locks, and digging connecting canals. Only after the commercial focus of Europe shifted north of the Alps did river traffic become important. The North European Plain is drained by a series of parallel navigable rivers trending southeast-to-northwest, most of which rise in the hills and mountains south of the plain. Some achieved major use by the 1100s and 1200s, and feudal lords who resided along the banks of such streams as the Rhine collected tolls from ships passing beneath their strongholds. In modern times, many rivers have been internationalized, and the countries through which they flow cannot charge unnecessary tolls or restrict traffic.

The navigable rivers of Europe became bound together early by canals. The building of canals predated railroad construction, beginning in earnest in the late 1700s and reaching a peak in the first half of the nineteenth century. Most canals connected the different rivers on the North European Plain. The English led the way in canal building as well as railroads, and by 1790 they had established a good network. Some 8,000 kilometers of canals existed in the United Kingdom by the middle 1800s, and the Industrial Revolution experienced a "canal phase." Inland waterways became the prime carriers of bulky products with a low per-unit value, particularly raw or semi-processed materials. Canals and rivers provided the most important linkages for early industrial districts.

By the end of the great era of European canal building, barges could cross the entire Great European Plain, from France to Russia (fig. 2.7). The densest concentration of canals anywhere in the world lay in the region from the Seine and English Scarplands eastward to the Oder River. That link remains open today, part of which is Germany's *Mittelland Canal.* Other major water linkages included the *Kiel Canal,* shortening the distance between the Baltic and North seas, and the *Canal du Midi* through the Gap of Carcassonne. Russia long ago linked the headwaters of the Volga, Don, and Neva rivers with canals to allow movement through the East European Plain.

After the great age of canals ended, many became derelict, bypassed by railroads and highways. Once-famous waterways such as the Göta Canal of Sweden became largely recreational routes used by vacationers. Canals experienced a decline even more profound than that afflicting the railroads. By 1948, some 6,500 km of the British waterway system had been abandoned. Usage continues to decrease; inland waterways carried 12.5% of Europe's freight tonnage in 1970 but only 3.3% by 2006, though the actual tonnage decline was slight. Waterways are now primarily for bulk transport, as well as for tourism.

Even so, several European countries have continued to upgrade their waterways for transport use, most notably Germany and France. Canalization of the Mosel/Moselle River with 14 locks between Thionville in Lorraine and Koblenz in Germany, where it joins the Rhine, greatly enhanced the navigability of the river in the 1960s—ironically just before deindustrialization struck the Saar-Lorraine district. Romania opened the *Danube-Black Sea Canal* in 1984, shortening the route by avoiding the river delta, and in 1992 Germany completed the extraordinary *Main-Danube Canal*, linking the Rhine River and North Sea with the Black Sea by way of Nürnberg. The canal uses a series of locks to traverse the 175-meter-high continental divide, and can accommodate huge "Eurobarges" carrying as much freight as 90 truck trailers or 60 rail freight cars.

The elaborate network of seas, rivers, and canals focuses on Europe's numerous port facilities, most of which lie at the transshipment points between inland waterways and the open ocean. A string of major ports lines the shores of the North and Baltic seas, at the mouths or on the lower courses of the rivers of the Great European Plain. These include, from west to east, Bordeaux on the Garonne, Nantes on the Loire, Le Havre and Rouen on the Seine, London on the Thames, Antwerp on the Schelde, Rotterdam-Europoort on the Rhine, Bremerhaven on the Weser, Hamburg on the Elbe, Szczecin on the Oder, Gdansk on the Vistula, Riga on the Daugava, and St. Petersburg on the Neva (fig. 2.7). In contrast, most major ports of southern Europe, including Barcelona, Genoa, and Naples, are generally not riverine, but instead lie some distance removed from the silted river deltas. An exception is Marseille, where a major port, Fos, operates west of the city at the mouth of the Rhône, at the southern access to the core of Europe. Traffic volume at Marseille/Fos increased enormously since World War II, and it now ranks as one of Europe's larger ports. Europoort, serving Rotterdam and the rest of the Randstad Holland, as well as the European industrial heartland, ranks as the greatest port of Europe, reflecting the huge volume of traffic carried by the Rhine and Maas rivers. Rotterdam began to grow rapidly in the last three decades of the nineteenth century, coincident with the rise of the Ruhr and other industrial areas along the Rhine. By 1938, the Dutch port ranked as the largest in Europe in terms of tonnage handled, and in 1962 it became the leading tonnage port in the world, surpassing New York City. Europe's seaports are all containerized, handling freight in standard-sized rectangular containers that are easily stacked in ships or moved by truck and railroad flatcar (fig. 9.13). Hamburg's port, meanwhile, has benefited greatly from the opening of Central European trade since the fall of communism, and it is now the second busiest in Europe.

Figure 9.13.   Containerized port of Bremerhaven, at the mouth of the Weser River in Germany. Ships are quickly loaded and unloaded, and the standardized containers can be put on trucks or railroad cars. (Photo by T. G. J.-B., 1999.)

PIPELINES

After 1950, as Europe shifted steadily away from coal as its primary energy source, adopting instead petroleum and natural gas, a system of pipelines was built. Most lines connect the European core area, where consumption is centered, to peripheral and external sources. One major supplier consists of oil and gas fields in the hinter reaches of Russia's East European Plain and beyond, in western Siberia and Central Asia. Oil and gas pipelines operated by Russia's state-owned *Gazprom* bring these fossil fuels westward to Europe (fig. 9.14). Much of the oil has long flowed through a pipeline that crosses southern Russia and Belarus to Lviv in Ukraine, home of a major pipeline depot, and on into the heart of Europe. This antiquated line can handle only about 1.25 million barrels of petroleum per day. In 2005, construction of a new pipeline linking Russia and Germany was initiated. This will help alleviate the gas supply problem in western and central Europe, but the decision to adopt a route that bypasses Ukraine and Poland has raised energy security concerns in those countries. There is more general unease that Europe is becoming overdependent on Russian natural gas—particularly in light of Russia's new strength, and concerns that it is moving in a more authoritarian direction. Plans for several major new pipelines in and around the Black and Caspian Seas and into southeastern Europe do little to alleviate these concerns, since the source of most of the pipelines is in Russian territory.

Figure 9.14.   Gas pipelines. The main sources lie in the east, in Siberia and Central Asia, while the principal consumers are in the European core region. *Source:* Based on a map in *The Economist,* January 26, 2008.

North Sea oil flows to Great Britain, Denmark, Germany, and the Netherlands in a series of pipelines, some of which cross the floor of the sea. The Middle East remains Europe's largest supplier of petroleum. To accommodate this oil, pipelines lead northward from the Mediterranean, beginning at Trieste and Genoa in Italy, Marseille in France, and Málaga in Spain. Two of these lines cross the Alps to the German city of Ingolstadt, a major refining center. The pipeline from Marseille passes north through the Rhône-Saône Corridor, Belfort Gate, and Upper Rhine Plain, reaching Karlsruhe in southwestern Germany and the Lorraine area of France. Since virtually all pipelines have been built since 1950, their routes reflect international planning. Cooperation within the EU led to the selection of southern Germany as an oil-refining center, fed by the pipelines originating in France and Italy.

AIR TRANSPORT

Europe has a dense network of air routes and a large number of airlines that started as national carriers, including Lufthansa (Germany), Alitalia (Italy), Air France, Swissair, KLM (Netherlands), British Airways, Aer Lingus (Republic of Ireland), and SAS (Sweden, Denmark, and Norway). Many intercity air connections within the European core carry over one million passengers annually. The numbers have grown rapidly over the past decade, due to an explosion in budget carriers that now make it possible to buy a roundtrip ticket from southeast England to southern France for the cost of a nice meal back in England.

The largest volume of passenger traffic in Europe moves through London's Heathrow Airport, followed by Charles de Gaulle at Paris, Frankfurt International Airport, Schiphol at Amsterdam, Madrid's Barajas International Airport, and London's Gatwick Airport. As for cargo, Paris's Charles de Gaulle is in the lead, followed by Frankfurt, Amsterdam, and London Heathrow. Congestion at some of these airports, notably London Heathrow, has prompted airport enlargements and the construction of new airports. Competition has also arisen. Munich now rivals Frankfurt with its splendid facility, situated in the virtual center of Europe.

When travel restrictions between east and west loosened after 1990, airlines proved better able than any other mode of passenger transport to exploit the demand for increased movement within Europe. It is a decades-long process to upgrade railroad and highway infrastructure sufficiently to allow ease of movement, but airline connections are already in place. Even eastern cities formerly difficult to reach by air, such as Riga, now enjoy much enhanced airline linkages.

Communications

Much of Europe has excellent internal communication connections, especially telecommunication, including computer-to-computer data exchange, e-mail, telefax, and cellular phone service. The growth of the European telecommunication system has been particularly rapid in the 1990s and early 2000s. By 2007, over 50 million Germans were using the Internet, as were more than 30 million citizens of the United Kingdom, France, and Italy. Per-capita Internet use is highest in northern Europe, but Portugal stands out as a country of particularly great Internet penetration in the European south (fig. 9.15). The figures are much lower for parts of eastern Europe and Turkey.

Europe leads the world in the percentage of the population using cell phones, with an extraordinary 94 cellular mobile subscribers per 100 inhabitants in 2006. Moreover, Europe plays host to leading cellular phone providers—most notably Nokia, based in Finland.

Energy Production

Europeans consume vast amounts of energy to sustain their high standard of living. A sizable service industry thus exists to supply the needed power. Traditionally, indigenously produced coal provided the greater part of Europe's primary energy, but after about 1950, when consumption levels in Western Europe began rising beyond all expectations, coal gradually lost its dominance. Petroleum and natural gas soon surpassed coal in most of western and southern Europe, though most oil had to be imported, placing Europeans in a vulnerable position. The sharp oil price increase instigated by the Organization of Petroleum Exporting Countries in 1973 sent shock waves through Western Europe, and the Russian turnoff of the subsidized oil flow to its sphere of domination in eastern Europe in the early 1990s had a similarly traumatic impact.

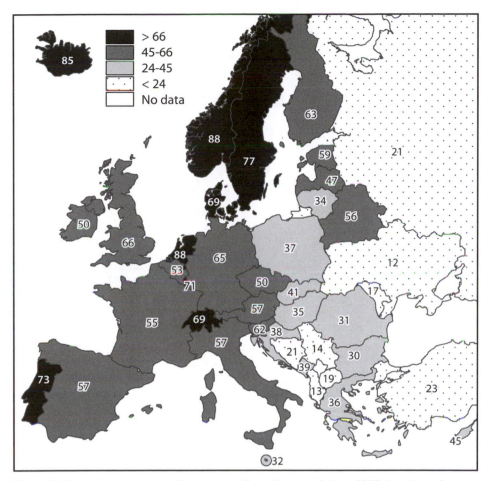

Figure 9.15.   Internet connections proportional to population, 2007. Northern Europe is the most "wired" region, and eastern Europe the least. Italy and France lag far behind the remainder of the European core. *Source:* Based on data from http://www.Internetworldstats.com/stats4.htm

One European reaction to the rapidly growing need for energy and the problem of foreign dependency has been increased development of indigenous sources such as hydroelectric, wind, and geothermal power (fig. 9.16). Denmark pioneered the effort to harness the westerly winds for electric power generation, and tens of thousands of graceful, three-bladed wind turbines now line the North Sea, Atlantic coast, and river estuaries, from Denmark to France and Spain. Germany now generates the greatest amount of *aeolic* power in the world, followed by Spain, the United States, and Denmark. But Italy, the Netherlands, and the United Kingdom are also among the top ten countries in the world in wind energy production. Denmark leads the world in terms of per capita wind energy production, and the Danish government has launched an ambitious plan for the construction of five huge offshore wind turbine parks that will boost wind energy production 200% by 2040. Iceland gets over 25%

Figure 9.16.   The geography of electrical energy. *Sources:* United Nations, *Energy Statistics Yearbook;* World Bank statistics; *European Marketing Data and Statistics.*

of its electricity from geothermal power, tapping the island's superheated volcanic subsurface.

The far more controversial nuclear power industry also grew in response to rising consumption. The United Kingdom put the first nuclear power plant on line in 1956, followed by France two years later, and western Germany in 1961. The five countries in the world with the greatest reliance on nuclear plants to meet their power needs are all European countries: Lithuania, France, Slovakia, Belgium, and Sweden (in that order) (fig. 9.16). The largest number of nuclear power reactors in Europe is in France (59), Russia (30), and the United Kingdom (27).

During the 1980s, concerns over safety, the disposal of nuclear wastes, and terrorism led many European countries to curtail production. A particular shock arrived in 1986, when the worst nuclear power accident in world history occurred at the Chernobyl plant in northern Ukraine (then part of the Soviet Union). This meltdown, apparently caused by a low-intensity earthquake, spewed radioactive pollution over much of Europe, causing noteworthy contamination as far afield as northern Scandinavia. Closer to the site of the disaster, 5 million hectares of farmland were contaminated, and neighboring Belarus had to abandon 20% of its arable land (fig. 9.4). Over 1,600,000 Belarussians today live in radioactive contamination zones, 80% of them in Homel province, which experienced a 6% decline in population between 1989 and 1999. Children living near the plant experienced an elevated incidence of thyroid tumors, and perhaps 10,000 persons have died as a direct or indirect result of the catastrophe.

In the wake of Chernobyl, most countries stopped building new plants; Italy phased out its modest industry, and voters in Sweden demanded that their country follow suit, though that has not happened. However, some newly independent eastern countries, including Lithuania and Slovakia, increased their nuclear dependence when cheap Russian oil ceased to flow. There is considerable concern that some of the older eastern European power plants remain dangerous, due to obsolete design, inadequate maintenance, or poor management.

Nuclear power is getting a second look in the 2000s in the wake of growing concern about the role of fossil fuels in global climate change. Even in Germany, where the parliament voted in 2002 to shut down all nuclear plants by 2020, debate has been rekindled by those asking if nuclear energy isn't a lesser evil than global warming. In 2008, Italy became the first western European country to conclude that it was—committing to building nuclear power plants by 2013. Proponents of nuclear power are pushing governments to follow Italy's lead, citing doubts about the ability of alternative energy sources to meet increasing energy demand, and the enhanced safety features of new-generation nuclear power plants. But opponents of nuclear energy point out that the problem of waste disposal continues to be unsolved, and that no plant can ever be completely safe. It is not yet clear how different parts of Europe will respond to the debate, but it appears that growing concern over rising temperatures and sea levels is ushering in a new era of expansion in the nuclear industry.

The complex spatial pattern of energy production in Europe (fig. 9.16) reflects the lack of consensus concerning energy—how to provide an adequate supply safely, dependably, and at an affordable cost, while at the same time avoiding significant ecological damage. Europeans must find a solution to this pressing problem if their prosperity and high living standards are to survive. Environmental costs remain high, however, and inefficiencies are not hard to find. For example, pigs from the Netherlands go by truck to Italy for slaughter so that the prestigious label "Parma ham" can be affixed to the meat, yielding a higher price, while Bavarian potatoes journey to Italy for washing, only to be reshipped to Germany to sell, wasting fossil fuel and clogging Alpine highways in order to benefit from less expensive Italian labor.

Tourism

Tourism—the short-term movement of people to destinations away from their place of permanent residence for reasons unconnected to livelihood—forms an integral part of the European lifestyle and of the European economy. In the western half of Europe, tourism experienced very rapid growth after 1950, and especially in the two decades following 1965, during which the number of tourists doubled. Tourism constitutes an important growth sector in the economy, and provides one of the reasons why employment in the service sector has grown so large. Prior to World War II, tourism remained an elitist activity of the upper class, but today most Europeans participate. The large majority of tourists are Europeans. Today tourism is directly responsible for 5% of Europe's GDP, and indirectly responsible for as much as 10% of GDP.

Tourism displays a vivid geography in its sources, destinations, and flows. Most tourists come from the wealthy countries of northern and western Europe, and their vacation destinations most often lie to the south. Over half of all European tourists seek out beaches for their holidays. Spain possesses the greatest concentration of southern seaside resorts, grouped in such coastal districts as the Costa del Sol and Costa del Azahar, as well as the Balearic Isles (fig. 9.17). Between 1959 and 1964, the number of tourists coming to Spain increased from 4 to 14 million, and the country's foreign currency earning grew tenfold, marking the beginning of the Iberian beach resort era. Today, some 55 million international visitors come to Spain each year, and a fifth of all cash receipts derive from tourism, making it the country's largest industry. As is often the case with tourism, the economic impact in Spain remains highly localized in a coastal corridor and a few inland cities. Even today, the tourism infrastructure is less well developed in most interior areas, away from the beaches, in spite of the cultural richness of the country.

Many beach resorts also developed in Mediterranean France, northern Italy, the Dalmatian coast of Croatia, the Black Sea shore of Bulgaria, and Ukrainian Crimea. The tourist industry's main shortcoming is extreme vulnerability to economic downturns and political unrest. Tourist flows to beach resorts tend to be channeled. Two-thirds of the vacationers in Malta, where the tourist boom began in the 1960s, come from the United Kingdom, in part because the islands were once a British colony. Germans prefer the Italian beaches, and also heavily patronize the Dalmatian coast and southern Spain.

The second most common tourist flow is from lowland to highland. Mountain and hill areas attract abundant visitors in both winter and summer, and the Alps, benefiting from a central location, dominate the highland tourist industry (fig. 9.17). Together, Switzerland and Austria annually receive almost twice as many visitors— 27,200,000—as their combined resident population (fig. 9.18).

At least a quarter of all EU tourists seek out rural areas for their vacations. Many farms in favored districts offer guest accommodations. A third of all farmers in Finland's Åland Islands house vacationers, as do about a fourth of those in the Austrian Alps. In some Norwegian municipalities, the proportion runs as high as 40%.

Cultural tourism also ranks high in Europe, directed to places offering museums, well-preserved medieval or Renaissance quarters, theatrical and musical festivals, notable archaeological sites, and the like. Fifteen million tourists visit Venice each year. Stonehenge in England became so overrun by visitors that protective measures became necessary, as also occurred at the Acropolis in Athens. The very names of certain cities—Paris, Vienna, Florence—connote culture and refinement, attracting many tourists. More bucolic in message and appeal, the numerous open-air folk museums of

Figure 9.17.   Major tourist destinations in Europe. The most important tourist flow is from north to south, favoring the Mediterranean beaches and Alpine mountain resorts. *Sources:* Mayer, F. ed. 1975. *Diercke Weltatlas*, Braunschweig, D: Georg Westermann, 55, 98–99; Hoffman, G. ed. 1989. *Europe in the 1990s: A Geographical Analysis*, New York: John Wiley 184–185; White 1987.

Europe remind visitors of a romanticized, lost rural past. Such outdoor museums, centered upon collections of traditional farmsteads relocated from the countryside, appeared first in Scandinavia, the prototype being Skansen in Stockholm. The concept has spread through most of trans-Alpine Europe, from Kizhi Island in Russian Karelia to the Ulster Folk Museum in Northern Ireland and the Schweizerisches Freilichtmuseum in central Switzerland. Following the Skansen example, many of these open-air displays combine the appeals of folk museum and amusement park.

European tourists are less likely than their American counterparts to spend their vacations traveling to one place after another. A "tour" differs from a "holiday," and most Europeans prefer the latter. Their normal pattern is to get as quickly as possible

Figure 9.18. Tourism, two statistical measures. Dependence upon tourism varies widely within Europe, with both north-south and east-west contrasts. *Sources:* United Nations World Tourism Organization; various national statistical yearbooks.

from home to the desired destination—no small achievement, given the frequent summer traffic jams on European roads—and then spend the entire holiday there, perhaps making day excursions to other, nearby attractions. Self-contained holiday resorts offering diverse amusements have recently gained in popularity, catering to the European mode of tourist travel.

Linking the penchant for single-destination tourism to the craving of the urban European for the rural countryside led also to the widespread practice of owning vacation homes. Most of these are modest cottages of recent construction, but some are old farmhouses abandoned as the agrarian population left the land and migrated to urban areas. This is especially common in the Dordogne River valley of France, a favorite area for British vacationers. In some Spanish provinces, over 30% of all residences are vacation homes—many owned by Germans. The rural environs of Helsinki in southern Finland average more than five vacation cottages per square kilometer. In eastern Europe, where tourism remains a less important activity due to lower living standards, the *dacha,* or country cottage, has long been common. In Bulgaria, some 32% of all city dwellers own a dacha in the countryside.

Another distinctly European type of tourism involves "taking the waters" at one or another of a huge assortment of health resorts, a practice most common in Germany and France. The generous health-care systems of such countries make it possible for citizens to receive treatment, at government expense, for real or imagined ailments and afflictions. The road signs posted at the limits of many towns in Germany tell the traveler that the name of the place is *Heilbad* or *Kurort* Such-and-Such, treating one or more problem of the lungs, kidneys, joints, stomach, or some other part of the anatomy. Amusements receive abundant attention as part of the cure, and the stay at such a place can be most enjoyable. Visitors spend a pleasant holiday, sometimes drawing full wages from work all the while. Needless to say, spas have prospered and proliferated in this subsidized system of health-related tourism, although in recent years the generous reimbursements from health insurance are no longer as certain as they once were (see Chapter 11).

The removal of most political barriers to travel in eastern Europe has opened up that huge area to mass tourism from the affluent west. Virtually every formerly Communist country benefits from this west-to-east tourist flow, and some places and regions, such as Prague, Budapest, Dresden, the Harz Mountains and Thüringer Forest of eastern Germany, St. Petersburg, Moscow, Riga, and Tallinn are especially popular.

When mass tourism arrives in full force, residents find it a mixed blessing. Economic benefits come with tourism, but so do assorted problems. The experience of the Alps is instructive. As late as 1955, most of that mountain range remained a land of traditional, anachronistic, and in places impoverished dairy farmers living in picturesque log houses. The elitist tourism of the previous century had touched few of these residents and changed little in their way of life. Many young people fled the mountains, seeking a better living in the lowland cities. Then, in a single generation between 1955 and 1975, mass tourism came to the Alps, prompting a pervasive shift from dairy farming to dependence upon winter and summer visitors. Certain isolated, poverty-stricken places became prosperous, highly desirable tourist destinations within the span of two decades. Money injected into the rural Alps by tourism provided a cure for the depressed economy, prompting the construction of an excellent road network and halting the emigration of the young. As a result, most residents of the Alps benefit from tourism and regard it as a good thing.

Even so, they paid a high price. The local mountain culture was disrupted. A folk society based upon mutual cooperation, egalitarianism, and respect for tradition gave way to a popular culture in which neighbors competed for tourist income, and the old ways were discarded. An ancient adaptive system of land use in ecological balance with the fragile Alpine environment yielded to a new one that required massive, and necessarily destructive, habitat modification. Ski runs, cut through protective belts of communal forests on slopes above the valley floors, scarred the mountainsides, caused erosion, and removed natural protection against avalanches. Also, tourism greatly increased the number of people tramping about the Alpine countryside, further damaging the local flora and fauna. Highway construction brought additional massive damage. In short, the people of the Alps lost their ancient traditional culture, and the land suffered extensive ecological modification as a result of mass tourism. A proven, sustainable system of land use gave way to an unsustainable and economically vulnerable one.

The legendary Greek isle of Crete provides another cautionary tale. Home of the ancient Minoan civilization, Crete was long sought out mainly by culturally oriented tourists, who visited its numerous archaeological sites. As recently as 1971, only 15,000 tourists visited the island annually. True, Crete was impoverished and suffering from emigration to the mainland, but it was home to a traditional Mediterranean way of life that possessed both charm and dignity. Then, in the 1980s, came mass tourism—fun-in-the-sun, beach-based, and wildly successful. The number of tourists rose to 2 million by 1995, and much of the island's beautiful north coast was converted into an unbroken row of hotels—a "vacationer ghetto." Almost no planning or restrictions were imposed. Many inhabitants find work in the hotel industry or other tourist-related businesses (car rental agencies, restaurants, etc.). Most of Spain's best beaches and the Algarve region of southern Portugal have similarly been overdeveloped.

Tourism of any sort has the tendency to destroy the basis of its existence. Mass tourism will certainly do that. Is there an alternative? Intelligently written land-use zoning and building codes can retard the worst excesses of mass tourism. The French Riviera provides an encouraging example, though at the cost of creating an "elitist landscape" that is largely inaccessible to the average tourist. **Ecotourism** offers yet another alternative. Its goal is sustainability, causing little damage to nature or local cultures. Necessarily, ecotourism involves small numbers of tourists willing to "rough it" in less than resort-like conditions. But many tourists do not want that sort of vacation, and in any case Europe has few natural habitats or native cultures left.

Retailing and Governmental/Social Services

The remainder, and far greater, part of the service sector consists of retailing and the provision of governmental and social services. Retailing is, of course, ubiquitous. Its distribution largely mirrors the population patterns discussed in Chapter 3, although the size of the retail sector is particularly large in the wealthiest parts of Europe and in tourist areas. Governmental and social services include various public agencies, health care and welfare systems, educational facilities, and other enterprises serving collective and individual needs. The majority of Europeans are employed in the retailing, governmental, and social services sectors. Most hold jobs paying modest wages—often lower than those recently lost in the primary and manufacturing industries. For some Europeans, the postindustrial age has brought diminished living standards. We will look in greater detail at such social issues in Chapter 11.

The Quaternary Sector

Another sector of activity consists of higher-order services catering principally to the needs of business, education, and research. These services include banking, stock and bond exchanges, accounting, legal services, research and development, various types of consulting, and the processing and provision of knowledge and information. Such activities, as well as many corporate headquarters, cluster strikingly in the inner core

Figure 9.19. **Major centers of producer-service industry.** Banking, insurance, research and development, information processing, stock and bond exchanges, and other producer services are highly concentrated in an inner core region of Europe.

of western Europe, revealing the dominant economic position of that part of Europe—especially Germany, France, and the United Kingdom (fig. 9.19).

London and Paris early became the financial centers of not just Europe, but the world. In the twentieth century, and especially in the 1990s, London eclipsed its rival. Centered in "The City"—the old central part of London—the financial service industry employs hundreds of thousands of workers today. London has hundreds of banks, many of the world's largest insurance companies, a famous stock exchange, and handles a third of the world's currency trading. Deindustrialization hardly touched London's prosperity, due to the city's role as the world's financial leader. Dubbed the "Thames tiger," London's rate of employment in the financial sector has expanded steadily during the early 2000s. If Greater London, a city of 7.5 million, were an independent country, it would rank among the top ten largest economies in Europe. Frankfurt, Zürich, and Paris also rank as major financial centers, but far behind London. The United Kingdom's rejection of the EU's common currency, the euro, has not had a notable impact on the city's role as a major international financial center.

The segment of the quaternary sector devoted to the generation, storing, and processing of diverse types of information forms a mainspring in this age of rapid technological change. It includes an institutionalized research and development component, and subsidiary consultancy firms. This information sector tends to be clustered in the same European inner core that houses financial services (fig. 9.19). Locationally, the information services remain linked to the major centers of high-tech manufacturing, in particular the western suburbs of London, the southern and southwestern satellite cities of Paris, the Randstad Holland megalopolis, and southwestern Germany (figs. 9.5, 9.19).

The striking concentration of quaternary activities represents a powerful statement of core-periphery contrasts in Europe. Even though such services, in a time of instant communications, need not be concentrated geographically, the fact is that the core of Europe has, in some respects, grown smaller and more powerful in the postindustrial age. Eastern Europe, in particular, faces significant obstacles to achieving prosperity given the dominant position of the inner core region. Most of the decisions and innovations that shape and reshape the economy and future of Europe derive from the inner core, from a small, elite group engaged in the quaternary sector.

Europe, then, has evolved into a postindustrial status, in which most people find employment in a diverse array of service industries. This development leads Europeans into uncharted waters, just as the original Industrial Revolution did a quarter-millennium ago. Uncertainties, even pessimism, about the postindustrial future abound among some Europeans, including those living in the wealthiest lands, but change has long been an inevitable constant. In no place is that more clear than in the cities where Europe's secondary, tertiary, and quaternary economy is principally concentrated. It is to these that we turn in the next chapter.

Sources and Suggested Readings

Amin, A., and N. J. Thrift, eds. 1994. *Globalization, Institutions, and Regional Development in Europe*. Oxford; New York: Oxford University Press.

Arentsen, M. J. 2006. Contested Technology: Nuclear Power in the Netherlands. *Energy and Environment* 17 (3): 373–382.

Ashworth, G. J., and P. J. Larkham. 1994. *Building a New Heritage: Tourism, Culture, and Identity in the New Europe*. London: Routledge.

Bailly, A. S. 1995. Producer Services Research in Europe. *Professional Geographer* 47 (1): 70–74.

Bathelt, H. 2005. The German Variety of Capitalism: Forces and Dynamics of Evolutionary Change. *Economic Geography* 81 (1): 1–9.

Briassoulis, H. 2003. Crete: Endowed by Nature, Privileged by Geography, Threatened by Tourism? *Journal of Sustainable Tourism* 11 (2–3): 97–115.

Brulhart, M., and P. Koenig. 2006. New Economic Geography Meets Comecon—Regional Wages and Industry Location in Central Europe. *Economics of Transition* 14 (2): 245–267.

Bryson, B., and G. Ludwig. 1992. Main-Danube Canal: Linking Europe's Waterways. *National Geographic* 182 (2): 3–31.

Bryson, J. R. 2007. The 'Second' Global Shift: The Offshoring or Global Sourcing of Corporate Services and the Rise of Distanciated Emotional Labour. *Geografiska Annaler Series B: Human Geography* 89 (Supplement 1): 31–43.

Button, K. J., P. Nijkamp, and H. Priemus. 1998. *Transport Networks in Europe: Concepts, Analysis, and Policies.* Cheltneham, UK: Edward Elgar.

Capuzzo, P. 2003. Between Politics and Technology Transport as a Factor of Mass Suburbanization in Europe, 1890–1939. In *Suburbanizing the Masses: Public Transport and Urban Development in Historical Perspective*, eds. C. Divall and W. Bond, 23–48. Aldershot, UK: Ashgate.

Casado-Diaz, M. A. 2006. Retiring to Spain: An Analysis of Differences among North European Nationals. *Journal of Ethnic and Migration Studies* 32 (8): 1321–1339.

Clark, G. L. 2004. Globalization and Competitive Strategy in Europe's Vulnerable Regions: Firm, Industry and Country Effects in Labour-Intensive Industries. *Regional Studies* 38 (9): 1085–1100.

Dicken, P., and M. Quevit, eds. 1994. *Transnational Corporations and European Regional Restructuring.* Vol. 181, *Nederlandse Geografische Studies.*

Dobruszkes, F. 2006. An Analysis of European Low-Cost Airlines and Their Networks. *Journal of Transport Geography* 14 (4): 249–264.

Garcia, C., and J. Servera. 2003. Impacts of Tourism Development on Water Demand and Beach Degradation on the Island of Mallorca (Spain). *Geografiska Annaler, Series A: Physical Geography* 85 (3–4): 287–300.

Gibb, R., ed. 1994. *The Channel Tunnel: A Geographical Perspective.* Chichester, England: Wiley.

Glückler, J. 2007. Geography of Reputation: The City as the Locus of Business Opportunity. *Regional Studies* 41 (7): 949–961.

Goetz, A. R., and B. Graham. 2004. Air Transport Globalization, Liberalization and Sustainability: Post-2001 Policy Dynamics in the United States and Europe. *Journal of Transport Geography* 12 (4): 265–276.

Gonen, A. 1981. Tourism and Coastal Settlement Processes in the Mediterranean Region. *Ekistics* 48 (290): 378–381.

Green, A. E., and J. R. Howells. 1988. Information Services and Spatial Development in the UK Economy. *Tijdschrift voor Economische en Sociale Geografie* 79 (4): 266–277.

Hall, C. M., and A. A. Lew, eds. 1998. *Sustainable Tourism: A Geographical Perspective.* Harlow, UK: Longman.

Hall, D. R. 1993. Impacts of Economic and Political Transition on the Transport Geography of Central and Eastern Europe. *Journal of Transport Geography* 1 (1): 20–35.

Hall, P. G., and K. Pain, eds. 2006. *The Polycentric Metropolis: Learning from Mega-City Regions in Europe.* London: Earthscan.

Hermelin, B. 2007. The Urbanization and Suburbanization of the Service Economy: Producer Services and Specialization in Stockholm. *Geografiska Annaler Series B: Human Geography* 89 (Supplement 1): 59–74.

Holloway, L., R. Cox, L. Venn, M. Kneafsey, E. Dowler, and H. Tuomainen. 2006. Managing Sustainable Farmed Landscape through 'Alternative' Food Networks: A Case Study from Italy. *Geographical Journal* 172: 219–229.

Howkins, T. J. 2005. Changing Hegemonies and New External Pressures: South East European Railway Networks in Transition. *Journal of Transport Geography* 13 (2): 187–197.

Krätke, S. 2002. Die Globale Vernetzung von Medienzentren. Zur Diversität von Geographien der Globalisierung. *Geographische Zeitschrift* 90 (2): 103–123.

————. 2007. Metropolisation of the European Economic Territory as a Consequence of Increasing Specialisation of Urban Agglomerations in the Knowledge Economy. *European Planning Studies* 15 (1): 1–27.

Leo, M. D. 2007. Chernobyl Revisited. *Discover.* 68–75.

Lopez-Bazo, E. 2005. Geographical Distribution of Unemployment in Spain. *Regional Studies* 39 (3): 305–318.

Marples, D. R. 2004. Chernobyl: A Reassessment. *Eurasian Geography & Economics* 45 (8): 588–607.

Nijkamp, P., ed. 1994. *Missing Transport Networks in Europe*. Aldershot: Avebury.

Peattie, R. 1954. The Ruts and Routes of Europe: A Study in Historical Geography. *Journal of Geography* 53: 336–341.

Roper, S. 2007. Cross-Border and Local Co-Operation on the Island of Ireland: An Economic Perspective. *Political Geography* 26 (5): 554–574.

Rosiello, A. 2007. The Geography of Knowledge Transfer and Innovation in Biotechnology: The Cases of Scotland, Sweden and Denmark. *European Planning Studies* 15 (6): 787–815.

Schimmelfennig, F., and U. Sedelmeier, eds. 2005. *The Europeanization of Central and Eastern Europe, Cornell Studies in Political Economy*. Ithaca, NY: Cornell University Press.

Selstad, T. 1990. The Rise of the Quaternary Sector. The Regional Dimension of Knowledge-Based Services in Norway, 1970–1985. *Norsk Geografisk Tidsskrift* 44 (1): 21–37.

Ter Brugge, R. 1984. Nuclear Energy in the Netherlands. *Tijdschrift voor Economische en Sociale Geografie* 75 (4): 300–304.

Turnock, D. 1986. The Danube-Black Sea Canal and Its Impact on Southern Romania. *GeoJournal* 12: 65–79.

van der Heijden, H. A. 2006. Multi-Level Environmentalism and the European Union: The Case of Trans-European Transport Networks. *International Journal of Urban and Regional Research* 30 (1): 23–37.

Ward, K. 2003. UK Temporary Staffing: Industry Structure and Evolutionary Dynamics. *Environment and Planning* 35 (5): 889–907.

CHAPTER 10

The European City

Cities are relatively large, permanent settlements containing a dense cluster of socially heterogeneous people engaged in specialized, primarily nonagricultural, types of work. Cities are distinguished from traditional rural villages by their size, the comparatively high level of **occupational specialization** of their residents, and their relatively elaborate systems of governance, which amass and spend capital for public projects. Much that we regard as "European" has its roots in the city. Virtually all of the Europe's most influential innovations, changes, and great ideas discussed in Chapter 1 came out of urban settings.

Cities also play host to the vast majority of the European population. But this was not always so. As recently as the turn of the twentieth century, the majority of Europeans lived in rural areas. But the twentieth century saw a tremendous migration from the countryside to urban areas, and now more than 80% of Europe's population lives in cities and towns. The proportion in Belgium exceeds 97% (fig. 10.1).

To appreciate the nature and significance of the European city, it is useful to look at the development of urbanization over time. We thus look at where and why cities developed, the sites they occupied, and their **morphology** (material form and organization) from ancient to modern times. We then focus on key attributes of the contemporary European city as well as some of the major differences among cities in different parts of Europe. We conclude with a brief assessment of the overall urban pattern found in Europe today.

The Rise of the European City

The city represents an ancient, vital European institution, but its origins lie elsewhere. In fact, the diffusion of urbanism followed the same northwest path from the Near East that brought the Indo-European languages, Christianity, agriculture, and the political state into Europe (fig. 10.2). Many of these innovations were interrelated in that agriculture greatly increased food production per capita, freeing a portion of the population to engage in urban activities, such as trade, crafts, the military, and political

Figure 10.1. Urban population as a percent of total population and distribution of large metropolitan areas. Countries differ somewhat in their definition of *urban* and *metropolitan area,* but the figures are roughly comparable. For purposes of this map, urban is defined as settlements of 10,000 or more population. The core of Europe is more highly urbanized, in general, than the peripheries.

administration. These occupations all became centered in cities and in fact provided the very reason for urban existence. Trade represented the most important single function. Hence, the term **mercantile city** best describes European urban centers prior to the eighteenth and nineteenth centuries.

Cities have also served as centers of administration. Rulers found cities convenient bases from which to rule. Many early cities arose as religious sites, centered on temples that were often built in prominent places, for example, on hilltops. The priestly class also formed an influential part of the urban population from the time that cities started to develop. Scholars, artists, and philosophers joined the merchants, artisans, rulers,

Legend: Pre-Roman Diffusion of Urbanism

Figure 10.2. Diffusion of the city. The source and paths of diffusion show striking similarities to the diffusion routes of the Indo-European languages, agriculture, the political state, and Christianity. Just as was probably true in the spread of agriculture and languages, Iberia received its first urban impulse from Afro-Asiatic peoples by way of North Africa. *Source:* Pounds 1969, with modifications.

soldiers, and clerics as urbanites, making the city a center of learning and creativity. Human heterogeneity and crowding energized the urban population, leading to new ideas and inventions.

The Greeks were the first Europeans to adopt urbanism from the Near East and Anatolia. Small cities began to develop about 2000 B.C.E., and, within seven centuries, small city-states, each ruling a modest-sized tributary rural territory, dotted the Peloponnesus and Aegean shores. These formed the basis of the so-called Greek Heroic Age (that is, the age of Homer), which ended about 1100 B.C.E. Most of these early cities were small in size and rather unimpressive in appearance. Unlike farm villages, they often boasted a temple, palace, theater, and marketplace. Many of them were eventually surrounded by walls.

Having grown up over time without planning, street patterns were irregular, although the larger streets would tend to wind toward the marketplace, which also functioned as the center of public affairs. After a period of decline following the Heroic Age, the Greeks began their greatest era of city-founding around 850 B.C.E., culminating in the Hellenic Golden Age. The great **city-states** of Ancient Greece reached their apex. Rarely did cities exceed 5,000 in population, though Athens may have had as many as 300,000 residents in the peak of its classical glory and Corinth perhaps had 90,000. Only the larger cities acquired importance beyond their local areas. Even at the height of classical urban development, as little as 25% of the Greek population lived in cities.

Ancient Greece's impact on European urbanism was limited to Greece proper. Greek colonists carried urbanism as far afield as the Black Sea coasts, southern Italy, and the south of France. Syracuse on Sicily and Marseille in Languedoc represent their work. Unlike the cities in the homeland, Greek colonial cities were the product of planning. The Greeks would choose a site of strategic or economic importance and then lay out a grid of streets that would shape the development of the city. Their interest in mathematics and geometry led them to adopt a north-south-oriented **rectilinear street pattern**, an approach to urban design that is still with us today. There was no single dominant intersection in the Greek colonial city. Instead, important buildings were simply aligned along streets in the central part of the town. The external perimeter of the town was often irregular, reflecting how far it was feasible to extend the grid.

By about 500 B.C.E., some 600 cities existed in peninsular Greece and the Aegean Islands. The Phoenicians, a Mediterranean people of the Near East, also founded some cities as trading colonies in Europe, especially in southern Iberia. By that time, peoples who were beyond the Greek realm, but influenced by Greek ideas, had begun establishing cities as well. Beginning about 800 B.C.E., the Celts established a number of small cities in the Alpine peripheries, most notably at Hallstatt in Austria, and the Etruscans of Italy became active city builders in the same period. Romans, destined to become the greatest of all European city founders, were influenced by both Greeks and Etruscans. They eventually replaced the concept of the city-state and their troublesome small wars with empire and the *pax Romana*. At the dawn of Roman greatness, the imperial core districts of Latium (modern Lazio) and Etruria (modern Tuscany) contained some 42 cities. By midpoint in the Roman Empire's life span under Augustus, 430 new cities existed in Italy alone (fig. 10.3). In its classical grandeur, Rome may have boasted a population of close to a million people, packed into an area of barely 23 square kilometers.

The Roman city was similar in form to the Greek colonial city—planned and with a rectilinear street pattern—although the Romans tended to establish major intersections at the heart of the city where the most important buildings would be located. Central plazas were also common. The Romans speeded the diffusion of urban life through Europe by founding new cities in France, Germany, Britain, and interior Iberia as well as along the Danube River. Some new towns grew around military barracks or camps, an

Figure 10.3.   Cities of the Roman Empire by the third century CE. Note the clusterings in central Italy, southern Spain, and Greece. *Source:* After Pounds 1969.

origin suggested by the British town suffixes of *-caster* and *-chester*, as in Lancaster or Winchester, derived from the Latin word *castra* (army camp). The Romans also took over and expanded fortified villages. Three areas stood out as centers of urban development under Roman rule: central Italy, Greece, and Andalucía in Spain (fig. 10.3). Most of the Roman cities remained small by modern standards. In France, the towns ranged from about 600 to 35,000 in population, whereas in the British periphery of the Roman Empire, the size varied from 500 or fewer up to the 17,000 inhabitants of London.

The heritage of Roman urbanization is considerable. Many sites have been continuously occupied since Roman times, for example, the city of Trier in Germany. Other sites were reoccupied after a period of abandonment. Even names are often corruptions of the original Latin form, for example, London (Londinium). One of the most interesting names, Zaragoza, began as the Roman Caesarea Augusta and was corrupted by the Arabic Moorish conquerors to Zarakusta and again by the Christian "reconquerors" of Spain to its present form.

The Medieval City

After the fall of the Roman Empire, Europe's urban population shrank, and some towns became totally abandoned, particularly north of the Alps. Europe entered its last great age of city-founding in the Middle Ages, taking advantage of increased security provided by the mature feudal system and increasingly agricultural productivity as the climate warmed between the ninth and fourteenth centuries. Germanic peoples established most of the new cities during this era. Europe's urban focus shifted to new regions, particularly the Po–Veneto Plain and the Germanic Low Country/Rhinelands in northwestern continental Europe (fig. 10.4). A combination of factors explains the concentration of cities in these two regions. First, they were both areas of relative political stability. Second, they were agriculturally rich areas, for example, the Po Valley and the rich agricultural lowlands and deltas of the North European Plain. Finally, they were geographically strategic sites for the development of significant trade networks. Northern Italy was in a position to capture a share of trade movements across the Alps and could take advantage of the Po River and the northern Adriatic Sea to build a far-flung

Figure 10.4.   Distribution of important cities, about 1500 C.E. Northern Italy and northwest continental Europe had become the new urban centers in Europe. Thousands of smaller towns do not appear on the map. *Source:* Pounds, N. J. G. 1989. *Hearth and Home,* Bloomington, IN: Indiana University Press, 260.

trade network. The Low Country/Rhinelands area could take advantage of the great rivers draining northwestern continental Europe and their strategic location adjacent to the meeting point of the English Channel and the North Sea. This helps to explain why some of the largest cities at the time were Bruges, Ghent, Antwerp, and, across the English Channel, London.

Most of the towns in the Germanic Low Country/Rhinelands region grew from fortified preurban cores, sites dominated by the stronghold of a feudal lord. The ninth and tenth centuries had been a major period of castle construction by feudal landowners as they sought to secure the surrounding countryside. The catalysts in changing most preurban cores to towns were itinerant traders, who initially made use of secure marketplaces adjacent to strongholds along transport routes. In time, the desire for safe winter quarters led the traders to establish permanent residence at the preurban cores, creating merchant colonies. Artisans were attracted by the presence of merchants, and the town population grew steadily. In an early stage of development, a town often consisted of several distinct nuclei: the feudal fortress; one or more marketplaces; scattered, fortified houses of merchants; a church; and some farmhouses. The German city of Braunschweig, for example, originated in 1269 through the union of five distinct nuclei, each of which had its own name. In an earlier era, Rome had arisen in a very similar manner as the union of adjacent hilltop villages.

CITY SITES

Geographers study diverse spatial and ecological aspects of urbanization. Perhaps none is more fundamental than an analysis of the specific physical location, or **site**, of a city. Decisions that determined the sites of most medieval European cities reflected the need for defense and access to trade routes. An easily defended site was particularly important to feudal lords who built strongholds during the insecure period after the Roman Empire fell. Romans themselves rarely chose protected sites for their army camps and other settlements because their military force enjoyed superiority to that of neighboring tribes. Roman camps typically possessed offensive advantage along roads and navigable streams rather than on high points. Still, episodes of piracy in the classical and preclassical Mediterranean may well have influenced the defensive siting of Athens and Rome, both of which lie a short distance inland from the coast.

Many types of defensive sites exist. The **river-meander site**, with the city located inside a loop where the stream turns back upon itself, leaves only a narrow neck of land unprotected by the waters. Besançon on the Doubs River in far eastern France provides an example of a river-meander site. Incised meanders proved particularly popular because the river loop became permanent by cutting down to form a steep-sided valley. The city of Bern, capital of Switzerland, on the Aare River, offers a splendid example of an incised river-meander site, as does Toledo in Spain (fig. 10.5).

Similar to the river-meander site but even more advantageous, the river-island site combined a natural moat with an easier river crossing, the latter an advantage for the merchant trade. Paris began on an island in the middle of a major river (the Île de la Cité in the Seine River), as did Limerick in Ireland and others. Stockholm, the capital

Figure 10.5.   Toledo, in the central Meseta of Spain, an example of a river-meander urban site. The original settlement, now the core of the city, lay inside the loop of the incised meander of the Tajo River. Such a location provided natural defense on three sides. (Photo by T.G.J.-B., 1986.)

of Sweden, occupies a lake-island site, originating on a dozen or so small islands in the area where Lake Mälaren joins the Baltic Sea. Perhaps even more appealing, the offshore-island site combined defense with a port facility. The classic example, Venice, rests on wooden pilings driven into an offshore sandbar, which separated a coastal lagoon from the open Adriatic Sea. Larch wood imported from Russia serves as Venice's foundations. Defensive concerns were also an ingredient in the choice of sheltered harbor sites, where narrow sea entrances could be easily defended from attack by sea. Oslo, at the head of a fjord in Norway, and the Portuguese capital of Lisbon both occupy sheltered harbors.

High points offered obvious defensive advantages. Many towns lie at the foot of a fortified high point (fig. 10.6). Such cities often derived their names from the stronghold, as is indicated by many place names ending or beginning in *-burg, -bourg, -borg, castelo-, -grad,* and *-linna,* all of which mean *fortress* or *castle* in various European languages. Scottish Edinburgh (Edwin's fort), dominated by the impressive Castle Rock, provides a good example, as do Salzburg in Austria and Castelo Branco in Portugal. Other cities sited adjacent to fortified high points include Prague, Vaduz in Liechtenstein, Sion in Switzerland, and Budapest. Closely akin are those towns and cities that, in their formative stage, lay entirely on high ground, often adjacent to the stronghold. Examples include Belgrade (white fortress) on a high bluff overlooking the confluence of the Danube and Sava Rivers; Segovia and Zamora in Spain; Laôn in France; Shaftesbury,

Figure 10.6.   The city of Sion/Sitten, in the Swiss Canton of Valais/Wallis, an example of the high-point urban site. Sion developed at the foot of not one but two fortified high points, secular and ecclesiastical. The beautifully preserved fortresses still dominate the skyline of the city. Merchants who were responsible for creating the original urban nucleus chose to locate adjacent to the fortresses, for security. (Photo by T.G.J.-B., 1978.)

a Saxon hill town in England; and Castelo de Vide in Portugal. Often such hill towns in Romance-language lands bear the place name prefix *Mont-* or *Monte-*, as in Monte Corno, Italy.

Merchants, largely responsible for the development of cities from preurban cores, generally selected stronghold sites that lay on trade routes. Numerous types of sites possessed advantages for the merchants. In the early medieval period, before bridges became common, river ford sites, where the stream was shallow and its bed was firm, offered good sites. Some cities bear names that indicate the former importance of fords, including the German and English suffixes of *-furt* and *-ford*. Frankfurt (Franks' ford) in Germany lies at an easy crossing of the Main River, where the ancient trade route from the Upper Rhine Plain passes northward toward the North European Plain. Upstream on the Main River from Frankfurt, we find the towns of Ochsenfurt (ford for oxen), Schweinfurt (swine-ford), and Hassfurt (Hessians' ford). The English cities of Oxford on the Thames, Hertford on the Lea, and Bedford on the Ouse again suggest the former importance of river shallows in urban siting.

A similar function was served by sites where narrowed streams and firm banks and beds facilitated the building of bridges. Town names, including *pont, bridge, brück,* and the like, signal the centrality of the bridge to the urban area. Good bridge sites help explain the location of many cities back in Roman times. Historic London Bridge, of which several have existed through history, originally stood at a point on the Thames River just upstream from the marsh-flanked estuary, at a site where the banks were firm and the stream was narrow. It served as an important river crossing on the Roman route from the Strait of Dover to the interior of England. Examples of bridge-centered cities from the medieval period include Cambridge (bridge on the Cam River) in England, Pontoise (bridge on the Oise River) near Paris, Bersenbrück (broken bridge) in northwestern Germany, Innsbruck (bridge on the Inn River) in Austria, and Puente-la-Reina (queen's bridge) in Spain.

Many city sites north of the Alps are riverine because navigable streams have long served as trade routes. Confluence sites, where two rivers meet, are common. The German city of Koblenz, at the juncture of the Rhine and the Mosel Rivers, actually derived its name from the Latin word for *confluence*, while Passau in the German province of Bavaria may be the only city where three rivers—the Danube, Inn, and Ilz—meet at precisely the same point. The rise of Paris was facilitated by the convergence of the Marne, Oise, and Seine Rivers in the general vicinity of the city, and Lyon profited from its position at the confluence of Rhône and Saône Rivers. Head-of-navigation sites serve as transshipment points, such as Basel on the upper reaches of the navigable sector of the Rhine River in Switzerland. In countries such as Finland, where an intricate network of lakes and rivers provided the major trade routes, fortifications built at strategic narrows sometimes provided urban nuclei, as at Savonlinna (castle in Savo province) and Hämeenlinna (castle in Häme province).

Crossroad sites occur throughout Europe. One of the more famous is Vienna, the Austrian capital, located where an east-west route connecting the Hungarian Plain with southern Germany along the Danube Valley met the ancient north-south route, which skirted the eastern foot of the Alps and passed through the Moravian Gate to Poland and the Baltic Sea. Hanover in Germany stands at the juncture of an old route that runs along the southern edge of the North German Plain and the road that follows the course of the Leine River through the Hercynian hills south of the city. Leipzig was made famous by its trade fair, which occurred there because the city was situated at the intersection of two main trans-European trading roads during the Middle Ages.

Seaport sites often are found at or near the juncture of navigable rivers or estuaries and the coast, for example, London, Hamburg, Bordeaux, and Gdansk. In southern Europe, however, the seasonality of precipitation and short length of many streams rendered rivers less useful for transportation. Great ports usually developed at the juncture of highways and the coast rather than at the marshy, shallow river mouths. Cádiz lies some 30 km south of the mouth of the Guadalquivir River, and Marseille is well to the east of the Rhône delta marshes in southern France. Other Mediterranean rivers such as the Po and Tevere also have no major ports at their mouths, in part because of silting.

Although mercantile activity was by far the most significant of the economic functions served by the medieval city, other economic factors were occasionally determinant in siting, in particular mining and the operation of health resorts. Extraction of iron ore, copper, salt, silver, and other minerals or metals often gave rise to mining towns. In Germany and Austria, place names, including *salz* or *hall* (salt), *eisen* (iron), *gold*, and *kupfer* (copper), as in Salzburg in Austria as well as Eisenach and Kupferberg in Germany, indicate the present or former importance of mining. The German city of Halle still has a saline spring in its very center, where the settlement began in Celtic times. Spa sites include towns that developed around mineral or hot springs, long sought by Europeans for relief from any number of ailments. Spa towns often date to Roman times. These places typically bear names indicative of their function, including elements such as *bains, bad(en),* or *bagni,* all of which mean *bath.* Examples include Wiesbaden in Germany, Bagnoli (bath) near Naples in Italy, and Luxeuil-les-Bains in eastern France. The English city of Bath, known to the Romans as Aquae Sulis, has an ancient resort tradition. In the Slavic lands, the name elements *-vody* (waters), as in Mineralny Vody (mineral waters), a city near the Caucasus Mountains, and *-vary* (hot springs), as in Karlovy Vary, Czechia, describe resort towns.

CITY ATTRIBUTES

The three essential attributes of the medieval northwestern European city were the charter, town wall, and marketplace. The charter, a governmental decree from an emperor or lesser ruler granting political autonomy to the town, freed its populace from the manorial restrictions of the rural areas. The city became self-governing and responsible for its own defense. Charters were typically requested by colonies of well-to-do merchants, who found that manorial restrictions hindered the mobility and exercise of personal initiative so vital in trading activities. Many cities date their founding from the granting of a charter, though most existed prior to that time. City-states similar to those of classical Greece, legitimized by charter, appeared throughout most of central and western Europe. So important were the charters that the citizens of the cities of medieval Flanders would build great towers to house them and to symbolize their freedoms. These towers dominated the skyline, sometimes even overshadowing the main church (fig. 10.7).

Self-government demanded self-defense, and the castles and fortified houses found in feudal kingdoms gave way to city walls (fig. 10.8). All important parts of the city lay inside the wall, including the mercantile and manufacturing establishments, fortress, church, and homes of the majority of the population. Urban expansion often required the construction of new, more inclusive walls, and some larger cities eventually needed three or four rebuildings. In the period before gunpowder came into widespread use, city walls were usually sufficient to repel invaders.

The marketplace, often supplemented by a trading hall (*bourse*), served as the focus of economic activity in the town, for the mercantile function remained dominant throughout the medieval period. Larger places held annual trade fairs, some of which began in the days of itinerant traders before permanent settlement had transformed the preurban cores into towns. Some of the more famous of these fairs survive to the present day, as at Leipzig, Frankfurt-am-Main, Milan, Lyon, and Lübeck (fig. 10.9).

Many of the cities in the northern Italian realm developed out of towns that could trace their roots to Roman times. There were exceptions. Most notably, Venice

Figure 10.7.   The skyline of Bruges, Belgium. The structures that attract attention are not just the church spires but the tower that housed the charter representing the freedoms of the city. (Photo by A.B.M., 1986.)

Figure 10.8.   Avila, on the Castilian Meseta of interior Spain. The city retains its splendid ring of medieval walls. (Photo by T.G.J.-B., 1986.)

Figure 10.9.   The central market square in Lübeck, Germany. An important site for traders when Lübeck was a leading city in the Hanseatic League, the square continues to be used today for weekly markets and annual trade fairs. (Photo by A.B.M., 1973.)

developed as a major city between the ninth and twelfth centuries on a series of inauspicious islands in a lagoon off Italy's northwestern coast. From that position, however, merchants were able to build it into a major center that, for a time, dominated the exchange of goods between western/central Europe and the Byzantine and Islamic realms to the south and east. But Venice was joined by a variety of other northern Italian towns that prospered through a combination of trade, agricultural production, and the manufacture of specialty goods.

Whether north or south of the Alps, most of the towns of the Middle Ages were modest in size. Few exceeded 100,000 in population. The famous textile center of Ghent had only 56,000 inhabitants in the mid-fourteenth century. Paris, the largest European city, and Naples were the only cities with more than 100,000 inhabitants by 1400. Moreover, the vast majority of people continued to live in rural areas. When viewed at a global scale, however, the level of urbanization in Europe by 1400 was greater than any part of the world other than parts of South and East Asia.

MEDIEVAL URBAN MORPHOLOGY

Europe's medieval urban places were characterized by a distinctive morphology, or cityscape. In most cities north of the Alps and Pyrenees, the street pattern was

Figure 10.10. **Street plans of medieval towns in Germany.** In Heilbronn the castle-fortress, the Deutschherrenhof, was the successor to an ancient Frankish fortress. The church, town hall, and marketplace shared the center of the city with the fortress. Heilbronn was heavily damaged in World War II. Nördlingen, where the old outer wall is still intact, has the maze of streets typical of medieval towns. An earlier wall that was outgrown is clearly traced by the circular street. *Sources:* Gutkind, E. A. 1964–69. *International History of City Development.* New York: Free Press; Dickinson 1945.

irregular, a function of a lack of planning (fig. 10.10). The city's most important church, marketplace, and civic buildings were often found near the center of the town, but streets met at odd angles, and blocks (to the extent one can use the term) took on the shape of parallelograms or triangles. Many of these cities had walls, which gave rise to an abrupt urban-rural transition. As cities expanded and those walls had to be built farther out, the traces of the former walls were left in the street pattern. Note the inner circle of streets in the urban plan for Nördlingen (fig. 10.10).

In marked contrast to the irregular street pattern of most northern European cities, the cities of the south that could trace their roots to the Romans, Etruscans, or Greek colonists were characterized by a grid pattern. One can still see traces of the ancient pattern today in cities such as Pavia and Naples in Italy, Cologne (Köln) in Germany, Zaragoza in Spain, and Chester in England (fig. 10.11), although later irregularities in the street pattern often make it difficult to detect the original grid. In the late Middle Ages, the gridiron plan experienced a revival and served as the model for new towns founded by the Germans in east-central Europe and by the French kings in southern France. The latter were often fortified towns designed to

Figure 10.11.   Survival of the Roman grid pattern in Pavia, Italy. To walk in the central section of modern Pavia (Roman Ticinum) is to tread in the footsteps of the ancient Romans. The degree of survival of the Roman checkerboard pattern is quite remarkable, for most of the original streets are still in use after 20 centuries. The two main intersecting streets of Roman times have maintained their dominance. Note how much less regular the streets are outside the old Roman core. Pavia is on the Ticino River south of Milan. *Source:* After Gutkind, E.A. 1964–69, *International History of City Development,* New York: Free Press.

help extend the control of the monarchy farther south during the thirteenth and fourteenth centuries. Sometimes they started with preexisting settlements, as was the case with the famous walled city of Carcassonne. The older city has an irregular street pattern, but the part constructed in the fourteenth century has a grid street pattern.

Renaissance–Baroque Urban Development (1500–1800)

After about 1500, the founding of new cities declined markedly, except in the far north. City-states gave way to larger, more powerful kingdoms. Urbanization continued to affect a small part of the European population. In 1600, only 4 million of the 85 million Europeans lived in towns with populations of 15,000 or more, about 5% of the total. The Low Countries and northern Italy, the most highly urbanized areas, could claim only about 12 or 13% of their populations as urban, whereas only 2% of the Germans, French, and English lived in large towns at that time.

Nonetheless, a number of noteworthy developments in the urban structure of Europe occurred from about 1500 to 1800. Most notably, this period saw the rise of national capital cities to urban primacy, particularly in western Europe. Fueled by the growing concentration of wealth associated with the increasingly successful European state-building project (see Chapter 6) and by the wealth flowing into parts of Europe from the early period of colonization, some cities exploded in size. In 1400, London had only 50,000 inhabitants, and Bristol, its major rival English port, had 30,000. Three centuries later, London had grown to 700,000, while Bristol remained at 30,000. Cities such as London, Amsterdam, Paris, and Madrid underwent dramatic modifications as they grew, as seen in major public projects that served to enhance their grandeur. But, in many cases, it was a grandeur not just borne of internal successes but of an exploitive colonial relationship with other parts of the world.

A related feature of the Renaissance and Baroque periods was the development of urban planning. Inspired by classical ideas and the field of geometry, Renaissance town builders laid out districts with, for example, radial street patterns focused on a royal palace. Cases such as Palmanova, Italy, provide an extreme case, with a street pattern radiating out in a full circle from a point at the center of the town (fig. 10.12). Not all parts of Europe had the resources or space to devote to such projects, however, and in some places, towns declined during this period. The disruption of trade ties in northern Italy, for example, led to some outmigration from towns and cities.

The Industrial City

European cities changed rapidly after about 1800 as a result of the Industrial Revolution. Manufacturing became the dominant function of many urban centers, putting an end to the age of mercantile cities (see Chapter 8). The hallmark of the industrial phase was a great increase in city size, prompted by the gravitation of the majority of the European population to urban, industrial areas. England and Wales urbanized more than half their population by the 1850s. A half-century later, more than three-quarters of the English and Welsh lived in cities, and Germany had become the second country to have over half of its population living in urban areas. Many other countries, especially in northwestern Europe, reached this level by 1930, and the trend continues to spread toward the peripheries (fig. 10.1).

Figure 10.12. Central part of Palmanova, Italy, in the far eastern Po–Veneto Plain. Founded in 1593 during the Renaissance era, Palmanova displays a highly planned street pattern, as did most of the cities established after the end of the Middle Ages.

The Industrial Revolution produced new cities in places such as northern England and Germany's Ruhr Valley. It also gave rise to the first European cities to have more than a million inhabitants. London passed the million mark in the first decade of the nineteenth century and exceeded 2 million by 1850. Paris claimed more than a million by 1846. By the turn of the twentieth century, Berlin, Vienna, St. Petersburg, and Moscow had reached this level. As people and industry arrived in already established cities, they found a **preindustrial core** that was often relatively densely packed and fairly prosperous. Around that core was a **preindustrial periphery** where more recent, poorer immigrants had concentrated. As industrialization unfolded, this was the area where the railroad stations could be built. The tight clustering of venerated, old structures made it impossible for railroad lines to penetrate the preindustrial core. Large cities such as Paris and London have a circle of rail terminals, and the stations typically bear the name of the major city that lies on their rail route. In Paris, one finds the Gare de Lyon (station of Lyon) at the terminus of the rail line leading out to that city, the Gare St. Lazare, the Gare d'Orléans, and so on. In some instances, one suburban railroad station serves as the main one, where trains for all destinations may be taken, but the traveler must sometimes choose correctly among five or more stations to find the right train.

In time, the slum hovels of the preindustrial periphery gave way to more substantial buildings as the city grew, and some prosperous neighborhoods developed. In function, this ring came to be dominated by residences, railroad stations, and retail activity. In capital cities, a nationalist-infused desire to develop visually impressive symbol of greatness, and a concern to break up or control worker ghettos led to plans to build grand, straight ceremonial avenues or boulevards in the preindustrial periphery, sometimes even penetrating into the preindustrial core. Thousands of Parisians, for example, lost their homes through royal decree to make way for the Champs Elysées (fig. 10.13). These impressive avenues provide a marked contrast to the remainder of the street pattern.

As the preindustrial periphery was made over, the poorer people, the new migrants, and many of the factories were pushed out to another ring around the European city, that is, the **industrial suburb**. This area was characterized by a dingy halo of factories, huge apartment blocks or row houses for the workers, and railroad

Figure 10.13.   The Champs Elysées in Paris, a classic example of a nineteenth-century urban development project designed to highlight the glories of France and facilitate movement within the French capital. (Photo by A.B.M., 2001.)

yards. Yet this became the largest part of the typical European city, dwarfing the older preindustrial core and periphery. It housed the burgeoning population that made Europe dominantly urbanized, as commoners finally became urbanites.

Characteristics of the Mid-Twentieth-Century European City

By the middle of the twentieth century, the effects of industrialization had been felt in most European cities, and some were on the cusp of entering a postindustrial era. Most European cities have experienced significant change since then, but a template had been set around 1950 to 1960 that still is very much in evidence and that continues to influence what these cities look like and how they function. That template reflected many of the different influences on city development described above. As we review its main characteristics, it may be useful to think about how the identified characteristics differ from the typical North American city, as such an exercise can provide insights into the role urban morphology and social geography play in the life of cities.

The most notable characteristics of the mid-twentieth century European city were:

1. *A set of more or less concentric rings with the preindustrial core at the center, surrounded by the preindustrial periphery, surrounded by the industrial suburbs.* The preindustrial core was the mercantile city of past times, including all districts that formerly lay within the ramparts and walls. Remnants of these walls often survived, marking the outer limits of the core. The famous Porta Nigra (black gate) in the German city of Trier is a Roman survival, while the Holstentor (Holstein gate) at Lübeck survives as a remnant of medieval walls. In some instances, the entire circuit of city walls continued to enclose the old core, and that is still the case today. Lugo in Spanish Galiza retains its Roman walls, and Ávila in the Castilian heartland of Spain boasts a medieval ring of walls and gates that ranks among Europe's finest (fig. 10.8). More often, the walls no longer exist, their place taken by a ring street and a string of parks. Riga in Latvia and Frankfurt-am-Main fit this description, as do many other places.

2. *A low degree of **functional zonation**, that is, the separation of different functions into different spaces.* Each of the rings had a mix of residences, retail establishments, and manufacturing activities. The medieval custom of combining residence and place of work continued on, and most cities never had zoning ordinances such as those common to North American cities. Many bakers, butchers, and restaurant owners lived above their shops, and it was not unusual to encounter small-scale manufacturing and a variety of services activities taking place on the same block with apartments and retail establishments.

3. *A high degree of compactness.* In comparison to North American urban centers, mid-twentieth-century European cities of comparable population covered much less geographical area (figure 10.14). A foreign visitor could easily gain the impression that European cities were smaller in terms of population than they actually were. In 1960, for example, single-family detached homes accounted for only

Figure 10.14. Munich, Germany, and Milwaukee, Wisconsin, metropolitan areas drawn to the same scale. The two urban areas have similar populations, but notice how much more compact the built-up area of Munich is. *Source:* After Holzner, L. 1986. In *Research Profile,* Milwaukee, WI: University of Wisconsin–Milwaukee Graduate School, 9 (2): 18.

16% of all urban residences in West Germany. Throughout Europe, many urbanites preferred to live close to the center of town, where the old city core served as a place to gather after work, to stroll, and to dine. Many city dwellers resided at least within walking or cycling range of their place of employment, though commuting was becoming increasingly common.

4. *An irregular street pattern in the preindustrial core and periphery.* This was a product of the unplanned development that occurred before the Industrial Revolution, and it was only broken up in parts of some cities by the decision to channel industrial wealth into the kinds of grand urban planning initiatives described above. But irregularity was the norm. In parts of southern Europe, particularly Iberia, Arabic influence in street pattern produced a particularly twisted maze with numerous dead ends, as in the old quarters of Toledo, Lisbon, and Seville. As cities industrialized and grew, planners often succeeded in creating more regular street patterns farther from the core, but, even there, a strict regularity was hard to a achieve because of the need to connect the new street pattern with the old, winding pattern of the core. Most of the streets in the core were narrow and ill-suited for the age of the automobile, and, in many instances, attempts to modify the crazy quilt pattern of streets and render it more suitable for motorized traffic flow were resisted. Wartime destruction leveled as much as 80% of the buildings in some German cities, providing an opportunity to revise street patterns in the central portions. Urban planners wanted to lay out broader and straighter streets, but

few West German cities actually acquired thoroughfares in the process of rebuilding. There were exceptions to this, of course. The Dutch and British reconstruction of Rotterdam and Coventry produced cities better adapted to the needs of the automobile. But most cities kept their irregular street patterns, leading to traffic problems that have become ever more critical because of the narrowness of thoroughfares and the scarcity of parking space.

5. *A religious building or palace at the symbolic center of the city.* Unlike American urban areas such as Chicago, where an intersection at the center of the commercial district has long served as the focal point of the city, the equivalent in most European cities was a building of religious or governmental significance at the heart of the old preindustrial core, often in conjunction with a square or marketplace. Impressive cathedrals are particularly common focal points, bearing witness to the extraordinary importance and vitality of Christianity in the Middle Ages. Even as early as the era of classical Greece, municipal pride in public buildings and religious edifices was one of the traits that distinguished townsfolk from residents of farm villages, and citizens bore the large expense involved in cathedral construction with little complaint. Many of these churches—such as Notre Dame de Paris on the Île de la Cité; San Marco in Venice; St. Stephen's in Vienna; the magnificent cathedral at Chartres southwest of Paris; and Santa María in Burgos, Spain—rank among the great architectural treasures of the world. If the city served as the residence of a royal family, the focal point might have been a palace or fortress. Examples include Edinburgh Castle in Scotland and the Palazzo Ducale in Venice, the latter located right next to the cathedral.

6. *A skyline with the tallest buildings on the periphery.* Standing in contrast to the North American city, which is dominated by high-rise buildings at the center of the city, most of the commercial skyscrapers and tall apartment blocks in the typical European city were constructed outside the urban core, often in the industrial suburbs (fig. 10.15). This is still true today. The central skyline of most cities will have a few tall structures such as church spires, a venerable hilltop fortress, or a special landmark such as the Eiffel Tower. But the urban core is dominated by historic buildings of considerable age, erected before the elevator and modern structural technology permitted thin-walled buildings to reach great heights. Edifices of more than five or six stories are uncommon. Even when catastrophes destroyed the old urban cores, Europeans generally rebuild them as before, keeping the taller buildings on the periphery. Photographs of pre- and post-World War II Munich reveal striking similarities, even though 80% of the city was destroyed by bombing. Perhaps the most remarkable re-creation took place in the former German Baltic port city of Danzig (present-day Gdansk) in Poland since 1945. The German population of the severely damaged city was expelled, but the Poles then proceeded to spend huge sums of money to produce a duplicate of the old German Hanseatic city. Their attention to detail in reconstruction was simply astounding. The end product was a museum town from another age. Yet with time, effort, and money, Poland solidified a valid claim to a city that Germans and Russians had destroyed.

Figure 10.15.   Paris, looking westward from the Eiffel Tower. An American would mistake this for a view toward the center of the city, whereas in reality the modern high-rise buildings stand in Paris's outer ring. (Photo by T.G.J.-B., 1978.)

7. *A concentration of significant wealth in the core.* Many North Americans think of the inner city as a zone of poverty and crime. But the cores of most European cities were very different. Traditionally, the most expensive and prestigious residences had been near the city center, creating a concentration of wealth at the heart of the city that often endured. There were pockets of poverty nearby and areas where only those of a certain ethnic background or those practicing a particular craft would live (see Chapter 11), but the heart of the preindustrial core was generally a prosperous area with a variety of small retail stores, cafés, restaurants, multifamily residences, and workshop-like factories of craftsmen workers. Guild houses of the medieval crafts still stood in some preindustrial urban cores, as did the old trading hall for merchants. Institutional functions also remained common in the central city, including governmental agencies and museums. By contrast, more recent immigrants and members of the poorer working class had moved to the peripheries where land was cheaper and low-skills jobs were found.

The Late/Postindustrial European City

Sweeping changes have occurred in the European city over the past five to six decades. The catalysts for change are:

- The decline of secondary industry
- The rise of tertiary and quaternary activities

- The expansion of public transportation networks
- Growing automobile ownership
- The arrival of new immigrants
- The growing size and prosperity of the middle class

These circumstances, in turn, helped to bring about suburbanization, counterurbanization, and gentrification, that is, three developments that have had a significant impact on the character of the typical European city over the last 60 years.

Since about 1950, some wealthier Europeans began to move out beyond the industrial suburbs to a newly developing outer ring of **postindustrial suburbs**. The outer ring consists of a loose assemblage of low-density residences dominated by detached single-family houses, modern factories devoted to high-tech industry, and firms specializing in data gathering and processing. Some planned satellite towns also appear here, as do the garden plots and dachas (cottages used sometimes as summer homes, particularly in Russia) of the inner-city population. In spite of the low density of building, the outer ring sometimes contains American-inspired, high-rise commercial structures made of glass and steel. Access to the city center by mass transit is normally available. Typically, the outer ring developed in segments and usually remains incomplete. In London, where the outer ring lies beyond a zoned, largely open green belt, a high-class residential fringe began taking shape in the western periphery by the 1950s, and it has since spread clockwise around to the northeast.

In other words, **suburbanization** is occurring in Europe. Though it began later than it did in North America, due in part to a lag in accepting the private automobile to commute to work, suburban development is bringing urban problems very similar to those in the United States, especially sprawl on the peripheries of cities and decay in the center. The suburban shopping mall, another symptom of urban Americanization, made its appearance in Europe's outer rings in the 1980s. France, the United Kingdom, Italy, and Germany now have hundreds of malls. From Lisbon to Budapest and beyond, shopping malls with hundreds of stores have opened over the past fifteen years, and they are transforming the retail landscape. Some countries have passed legislation in an effort to control the proliferation of malls, but the retail patterns of most sizable cities have been Americanized to a fairly significant extent.

In the period after about 1965, **counterurbanization**, the movement of population from the largest cities to areas that lie beyond the commuting range of those cities, also began to influence Europe. For a time, counterurbanization caused some of Europe's larger cities to stagnate or decline, while villages and smaller urban places grew. This, in turn, helped to create larger second- and third-order cities in Europe. The movement away from cities is typically driven by the more affluent segment of the population, and it often occurs in stages, beginning with the acquisition of a second home for vacation purposes. An author, data processor, or designer comes to realize that his or her job can be performed just as well in locations remote from the urban office. The products of their work can be shipped, mailed, or electronically transmitted to the city.

The sudden, rapid decline of such traditional manufacturing industries as textiles and steel also caused many overspecialized cities to lose less well-off segments of the population. Among the hardest hit by manufacturing decline were Glasgow, Manchester, Belfast, Turin, and many cities in the formerly Communist East. Equally important, waves of foreign immigrant guest workers began arriving in parts of many cities, causing some longer-term residents to flee.

The United Kingdom, the first country to urbanize massively, also became the first to feel the effects of counterurbanization in the 1960s. West Germany experienced an almost simultaneous onset of the phenomenon, followed by the Low Countries, France, and Denmark. In France, the period from 1975 to 1982 saw the rural population grow more rapidly than the urban population for the first time in well over a century. France's Atlantic coastal, Mediterranean, and Alpine provinces gained population most rapidly.

Counterurbanization slowed in most countries in the 1980s, leading some urban geographers to label it as a temporary shift. France experienced a resurgence of growth in the largest metropolitan areas by 1990, and only the decaying heavily industrial cities exhibit long-term population losses. Germany, too, saw a slowing down of counterurbanization in the late 1980s, following 15 years during which the trend intensified. Today, counterurbanization is occurring most profoundly in eastern Europe. The cities of the southern Urals region in Russia are among the most severely impacted.

The slowing or reversal of counterurbanization throughout much of Europe can be attributed in part to the **gentrification** of areas within major cities. Gentrification refers to the rehabilitation of deteriorated or abandoned areas and the concomitant replacement of low income by more affluent populations. Gentrification can occur either through the private property market, that is, individuals or firms buying up and converting areas, or it can be a product of urban redevelopment policies. Both are common in Europe, and they have made the cities more attractive places to live for the middle and upper classes. But the less well-off often face displacement and the prospect of moving to even less desirable areas.

Generous social welfare policies have blunted the social impacts of gentrification in some parts of Europe (see Chapter 11), but gentrification can still pose significant challenges for the poor. Perhaps the group most adversely affected consists of urban squatters, that is, homeless people who illegally take up residence in derelict, empty buildings. Called *kraakers* in the Netherlands and *squats* in Britain, this preponderantly young group began moving into abandoned central city buildings in the 1960s. Amsterdam, London, Hamburg, West Berlin, and Copenhagen became the major scenes of urban squatting. The movement peaked in the 1980s, and it has since largely succumbed to police pressure and gentrification.

On a more positive note, the gentrification of abandoned areas in old industrial cities can be a boost to the city at large. The redevelopment of former industrial areas in cities such as Duisburg in Germany's Ruhr Valley is bringing new people into the city and even attracting some tourists (fig. 10.16). Gentrification is also improving the fiscal viability of some cities that were struggling from the loss of tax revenue as people moved out to the suburbs and beyond.

These general processes have worked together with the economic, social, and technological developments mentioned at the beginning of this section to change the character of the typical European city to some degree over the past 60 years. But the change

Figure 10.16.   Urban redevelopment in Duisburg, Germany. Middle-class residents, and even some tourists, are being drawn into old industrial districts. (Photo by A.B.M., 2001.)

has only been partial because many of the characteristics of the industrial city described above could not easily be altered. The best way to see what has remained the same and what has changed is to look at the modern city in terms of its various zones.

THE PREINDUSTRIAL CORE

Changes to the preindustrial core have been comparatively minor. As in the industrial period, this part of the city is generally prosperous and suffers relatively low levels of blight, decay, and crime. In most instances, the preindustrial core is still dominated by compact settlement, low levels of functional zonation, older buildings, and winding streets. Automobile traffic moves with great difficulty, for thoroughfare avenues are rare. Though some European central cities remain choked by automobile traffic, a number have taken major steps to restrict motorist access. Parking space has been drastically reduced, bicycle routes have been provided, and mass transit has been upgraded. Zürich eliminated 10,000 central city parking spaces, and governmental restrictions on automobile traffic in cities such as Amsterdam, Freiburg in Germany, and (most recently) London have led to significant declines in the use of cars in the inner city. In places such as Amsterdam and Heidelberg, bicycles seem to outnumber automobiles. A particularly noteworthy response to the challenges presented by the street pattern has been to designate certain streets or even entire districts as pedestrian zones. Pedestrians in these areas no longer feel intimidated by traffic or repelled by the visual blight of machine space.

Certain well-preserved urban central areas have become virtual outdoor museums, bypassed by the usual range of economic activity. Some central city dwellers complain that they cannot be expected to live in an unchanging, romanticized setting of past times. The crumbling architectural heritage of the past is expensive to maintain and difficult to adjust to the modern age. Venice's core area, largely a historic district, provides an extreme example. Plagued by flooding, decay, and pollution, Venice's central area population has declined from 137,000 in 1961 to only 62,000 today.

In an effort to preserve the historic character of central cities while adapting them to the needs of the twenty-first century, **façadism**, that is, the complete gutting and remodeling of the interior of a building while preserving its façade, has become increasingly popular. Outwardly, buildings look much as they did 500 years ago; inwardly, they are a product of the Contemporary Era.

THE PREINDUSTRIAL PERIPHERY

The preindustrial periphery is a zone where redevelopment and gentrification has been particularly concentrated. As a result, in the typical city, there are fewer pockets of poverty in this zone than in previous times. Much of the urban landscape remains historic in character, but it is more likely to be punctuated by modern structure and developments than is the landscape of the preindustrial core. Former industrial sites are particularly common candidates for redevelopment. Since this part of the city is often redeveloped in chunks, functional zonation is somewhat higher than in the preindustrial core, but it is still low in comparison with the typical North American city. In some cases, major upscale shopping districts have developed in this part of the city, taking advantage of the proximity of many well-to-do consumers and easy-to-use public transportation facilities.

A controlled access perimeter highway now often marks the outer limits of the preindustrial periphery. Inside that highway, regulations often keep buildings at relatively low heights. Street patterns remain fairly irregular, but there are more thoroughfares and arteries than in the preindustrial core. In many cases, the most important of these follow the routes of former roads leading out of the medieval city. Paris's Avenue d'Italie, running through the southern part of the city's preindustrial periphery, is the old road one would have taken out of the old city to go to Italy. Street names can be tricky in Europe, though, as they change frequently, even in places where the street does not take a notable turn. Munich provides an extreme example. Over a length of only six blocks, one reasonably straight street bears the names Maxburgstrasse, Löwengrube, Schäfflstrasse, Schrammerstrasse, and Hofgraben.

THE INDUSTRIAL SUBURBS

Since these areas were not developed prior to the Industrial Era, most buildings are relatively modern, and many are tall. Modern and tall does not necessarily mean nice, however. Many were erected hurriedly and cheaply to house an influx of low-wage

Figure 10.17.   La Défense, a hub of Paris's quaternary economy, lies just beyond the preindustrial periphery. (Photo by A.B.M., 2001.)

workers. Others were developed to meet the industrial needs of the late nineteenth and early twentieth centuries, only to fall into wrack and ruin as the economic tides turned. The industrial suburbs are not uniformly areas of poverty. Some parts developed as middle-class areas with good, quality housing and nice public amenities. Whether the housing is in good shape or not, much of it takes the form of high-rise apartment complexes. This is true in countries as diverse as Iceland, Spain, Czechia, and Latvia.

Population density is generally high in the industrial suburbs, but parks and shopping centers are relatively common, and streets are relatively wide. In some places, large tracts of land in particularly poor parts of the industrial suburbs were entirely redeveloped in the post–World War II era. Basically, everything was cleared, and a district of a very different character was planned and built from scratch. In some cases, the goal was to create a middle-class residential area. In others, it was to make room for a postindustrial center for business and commerce. Perhaps the most famous example is La Defense, just outside of Paris proper (fig. 10.17). To the extent that Paris has a downtown reminiscent of something like midtown Manhattan, this is where it is found.

THE POSTINDUSTRIAL SUBURBS

On the periphery of most European cities lie the newest suburbs, home to the residences of wealthier people and selected tertiary and quaternary economic activities. We have already reviewed the principal characteristics of these suburbs, including less compact with a mix of nice apartment blocs, stand-alone houses, and tertiary and quaternary sector businesses. Where single-family houses are found, lots tend to be considerably smaller than in the suburbs of Canada or the United States, and front yards are often absent. For the apartment dwellers in this zone as well as in the nicer industrial suburbs, garden allotments serve in effect as backyards. Large tracts of *kleingärten* (small garden complexes) can be found on the periphery of many German cities; indeed, this phenomenon has spread to cities throughout Europe. These allotments were intended as places where urban dwellers could escape their apartments and the unhealthy inner-city environment to the relative solitude of a small hut or garden. These became increasingly widespread during the nineteenth century when railroads were being built on a large scale. Hence, these complexes often adjoin train tracks.

Generally, population densities are much lower in the postindustrial suburbs, and street patterns are more regular, a function of modern planning. Nonetheless, it is much rarer in Europe than in North America to find houses standing off completely by themselves. Instead, they tend to be built adjacent to one another, creating a relatively sharp break between urban and rural. The break may be less abrupt than in the days when city walls were common, but the inertia of a long-standing settlement pattern with a sharp break between urban and rural may help explain why the edges of European cities are so much more distinct that their North American counterparts.

Regional Variations

Preceding sections of this chapter perhaps led you to believe that a European type of city exists; indeed, some features occur widely. For example, most cities have a preindustrial core, most are compact, and most have an important religious structure, civic building, or old market square at the center. Still, we have been operating at a very high level of generalization. Each European city possesses its own distinct character and personality, and many aspects of European urbanism vary regionally. To provide a little more sense of some of the differences, it is useful to look at a few of the distinctive characteristics of urban areas in different parts of Europe (fig. 10.18). Even this exercise requires us to generalize at a fairly high level, but it provides interesting insights into the variable influences on urban development found in different parts of Europe.

The **British city**, more than others in Europe, resembles the urban centers of the United States, but major differences between the two can also be identified. A high rate of owner-occupied housing, detached or semidetached single-family residences, as well as flight to the suburbs of the outer ring characterize both British and American cities. Inner urban decay and blight, coupled with poverty, diminishing services, and crime, afflict most of the major British conurbations. Britons devote less attention to the preservation of inner-city historic structures than most Europeans do. Concerns over urban decline and crisis have long been heard in Great Britain. As a result, counterurbanization and suburbanization have worked more vigorously in Great Britain than the rest of Europe. This dispersal also feeds upon the British perception that the real England lies in the countryside and that the city is an anomalous aberration. Suburban

Figure 10.18. Distribution of European city types. Considerable overlapping of types occurs but is not shown, as for example where socialist influences partially reshaped many Central European cities in the Communist era. *Sources:* Leontidou 1990, 4; Hamilton 1978; Ford 1985; Gritsai 1997 a and b; Argenbright 1999; Pacione 1997; Sabelberg 1986.

expansion causes the British city to be less compact than normal for Europe and produces a steep population density gradient from core to periphery. Americans find all these British conditions familiar, but continental Europeans are more likely to regard them as odd and generally undesirable.

At the same time, the British city has experienced far more inner area gentrification than its American counterpart has, and the government is quite active in the effort to stem decay. In Belfast, for example, the proportion of unfit housing declined from 25% to 8% between 1978 and 1992, largely as a result of public expenditures on urban regeneration. The figure now lies below 5%. The walled inner city of Londonderry (or

Derry, as Irish separatists prefer) has undergone refurbishment, the once-blighted East End district of Glasgow became transformed in the 1980s, and many similar projects are presently under way. In urban regeneration, the British city occupies an intermediate position between those of the United States and western Europe.

The **Central European city** conforms most closely to what we have been describing as the typical European city (fig. 10.18). In origin, the Central European city reflects mainly the period of urban genesis led by Germanic peoples during the feudal Middle Ages. The early attainment of city-state status, which allowed a quasi-democratic form of government to take root in the Germanic cities while the countryside remained under feudal despotism, fostered a sense of urban superiority and a strong antirural bias. One is either a *burgher* (a city-dweller) or a *bauer* (farmer). City governments, visually represented by the town hall, retain considerable importance. Some cities even preserve a vestige of their former independent city-state rule; for example, Hamburg and Bremen enjoy provincial status within Germany, and Luxembourg remains, in effect, a free city-state. Central European citizens attach great importance to the preindustrial core, the root of urban self-government and democracy. As a result, central city decay has never approached the British levels (fig. 10.19). The preindustrial core, wreathed by parks and remnant walls, remains a prestigious place to live, and historic preservation and renewal

Figure 10.19.   The preindustrial core of the small Hessian city of Weilburg, on the Lahn River in Germany. A typical Central European city, Weilburg perches on an incised meander of the river. The urban core retains its royal palace, cathedral, and town hall. Many people still reside in the central city, though new suburbs appear in the distance. Little evidence of urban decay can be found in such places. (Photo by T.G.J.-B., 1991.)

projects, including abundant façadism, typify the Central European city. The central public square retains great importance. In World War II, many German preindustrial cores were destroyed by bombing, but these old districts, so prized by the citizenry, were lovingly rebuilt, a process still underway today in cities such as Dresden (fig. 10.20).

Counterurbanism and suburbanization, blunted by the appeal and snobbery of the city and the antirural bias, proved weaker than in Britain. In housing density, the

Figure 10.20.   War damage to housing in Hamburg, Germany. Destruction was most profound in the old preindustrial core, but the visitor today will not find much evidence of the damage. Most Europeans prize very highly their medieval urban cores. *Sources:* City of Hamburg. 1951. *Hamburg in Zahlen,* Statistisches Landesamt, 29: 6; *Erdkunde.*

Central European city falls between the extremes of the British urban area with its relatively high number of single-family residences and the cities of southern and eastern Europe, where apartment housing prevails. Urban planning and land use zoning enjoy popular support and have greatly contributed to the renewal, aesthetic appeal, and livability of cities. The pedestrian zone movement began here and still enjoys its greatest acceptance in central Europe.

In some areas, the problems associated with British cities have taken root in central Europe, but they are aggressively combated. Economically depressed industrial cities in Germany's Ruhr area and the coalfields of the Belgian–French border region offer examples of blight and decay, as do many cities in the east that long remained under Communist rule.

Some Central European cities experienced a half-century or more of Communist rule, which imposed rigid socialist control over what had been a capitalistic urban structure. Warsaw, Budapest, Leipzig, Prague, and Riga provide examples. These cities all bore the earlier imprint of Central European urban culture, reflecting a long tradition. Socialist ideals and planning never completely transformed them, though change did come. In Warsaw, for example, an early Communist-directed residential mixing of social groups after 1945 steadily gave way during the following 40 years to a reemergence of class-based neighborhoods. Budapest became an odd amalgamation of Central European and Communist urbanism (fig. 10.21). Most of these cities have

Figure 10.21.   A stylized scheme of modern Budapest. A Central European type of city in heritage, Budapest reflects that tradition in its preindustrial core and inner ring. A socialist city from the late 1940s until 1990, Budapest accordingly has peripheral apartment blocks located adjacent to industrial complexes. The high-prestige green belt represents an anomaly for a communist city and reflects significant new influences on urban development in Hungary, beginning as early as 1970. *Source:* Enyedi/Szirmai 1992, 99.

even more rapidly regained their central European character and identity since the fall of Communism in the early 1990s.

In the **Mediterranean city**, a greater spontaneity of growth and development occurred with minimal attention to urban planning or zoning (fig. 10.18). The Germanic rural-urban dichotomy is less common in Mediterranean civilization, and the transition from the city to the countryside is more gradual. Since classical times, many farmers and rural laborers have resided in Mediterranean cities. Less social segregation occurs, and the juxtaposition of good and bad districts is common. A diversity of social classes is found in most parts of the Mediterranean city in mixed neighborhoods, though squatter slums and low-income apartment high-rises dominate the outer peripheries.

Small workshops of self-employed artisans are scattered through the city, and mixed land use reflects the lack of zoning, or, more exactly, widespread disregard for zoning regulations. Owners more typically live above their place of business than in the British or Central European cities, and most other people live close to their place of work. Inhabitants tend to view the city rather than the home as the principal venue for life, and, as a result, more people are to be seen in the streets, plazas, and shops. A central business district in the British/Germanic sense does not exist, and small shops appear even in the finer residential neighborhoods. To the Germanic eye, the Mediterranean city seems disorderly, but the people of the south instead see their cities as places of light, heat, and spontaneity, a welcome contrast to the cold, disciplined cities beyond the Alps.

Mediterranean cities represent the most compact type in Europe, with very high residential densities and virtually no development of an outer ring. High-status residential areas instead lie in the preindustrial periphery, adjacent to the preindustrial core and linked to it by a fine boulevard (fig. 10.22). While the old, walled part of the town retains great prestige and swarms with life, it is often largely given over to institutional functions, especially schools, museums, churches, and convents. A failure to restrict automobile access to the center creates a nightmare of traffic congestion, noise, and air pollution in the preindustrial core, and the pedestrian zone concept remains in its infancy here. The periphery of the Mediterranean city is the most stigmatized section, in contrast to the British model. Industries are concentrated there, as are poor people. Many of them live in spartan, high-rise apartment blocks.

The **Eastern European city** bears the residual imprint of socialism and Communism (fig. 10.18). In fact, this urban type was formerly called the **socialist city**. Eastern Europe was very weakly urbanized prior to the Communist era. In the Soviet Union in 1926, for example, only 18% of the population lived in cities, but, by 1989, the proportion there reached 66%. In such countries, socialist doctrine shaped urban development in diverse ways, and the legacy will persist long into the future. Under Communism, the government controlled urban development, including the demand for and supply of housing. Land, in effect, had no monetary value.

In its idealized form, the socialist city would have:

- Abolished socioeconomic residential segregation
- Guaranteed availability of public services such as child care

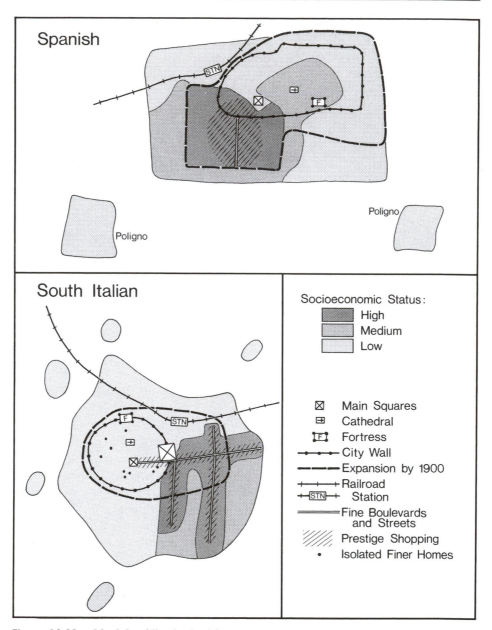

Figure 10.22.   Models of the typical Spanish and southern Italian city provide examples of the Mediterranean city type, but they are sufficiently distinctive to be considered regional subtypes. The outlying clusters, called *polignos* in Spain, are recent laborer apartment blocks or squatter settlements. In the southern Italian type, the core has a maze of dead-end streets and remains largely residential, while in the Spanish type, most of the core is now institutional and has connecting streets. *Sources:* Ford 1985, 268; Sabelberg 1986; Fusch 1994; Pacione 1987.

- Provided abundant public green space
- Offered equal, if rudimentary, access to all consumer goods
- Created self-sufficient, small neighborhoods where residents lived, worked, and shopped

In many respects, eastern European cities still reflect these socialist goals, particularly in Russia, Ukraine, Belarus, and the Balkans. The Eastern European city resembles a collection of separate towns tied together. Population densities remain remarkably high in comparison to cities in most of the remainder of Europe, and the normal gradient toward lesser densities on the urban periphery is retarded and, in some cities, even reversed, with an outer rim of higher concentration of people (fig. 10.23). All of Moscow has a population density comparable to that of central London.

Less marked functional zonation occurs within the city than in the West, including a much more even spread of industries throughout the urban area, a phenomenon associated with the former absence of cash values for land. Social, economic, and ethnic segregation by districts or sectors is diminished. Workers in a particular industry might be segregated in response to a desire to minimize the journey to work. Public mass transportation prevails, and the automobile remains a less important means of moving about the city than in countries to the west. Even those workers who inhabit the characteristic

Figure 10.23. The northern periphery of Moscow. Huge complexes of high-rise apartments produce dense concentrations of population even on the outer margins of the city, a typical phenomenon in the Eastern European city type. Even so, much green space is preserved, catering to the Russian love of the forest. (Photo by T.G.J.-B., 1997.)

belt of prefabricated high-rise apartments, grouped in neighborhoods of 2,000 to 5,000 people, enjoy easy access to the city center. In comparison to the West, a higher proportion of the urban workforce finds employment in manufacturing, construction, and transportation, with lower percentages in trade, administration, and services.

Other socialist ideals will long leave a visible legacy in the European East. During the Communist era, authorities sought to convey the power of the state and the insignificance of the individual person. Governmental buildings of overwhelming size, reflecting monumentality in architecture, provide one example. Oversized public squares, in which mass political rallies could be held, appear gargantuan, cold, and empty at other times. And the cult of personality associated with some Communist dictatorships, most notoriously in Romania and Albania, allowed megalomaniacal leaders to massively reshape cities, often destroying much of the beauty from earlier eras. The pre-Communist city disappeared from central Bucharest, and the imprint of a personality cult will long linger there.

At the same time, infrastructure is decaying alarmingly in many eastern European cities. Shoddily constructed and inadequately maintained buildings abound. The eastern European cities inherited these from the socialist era, and the cost of correcting them creates enormous fiscal challenges. Still, pervasive change has come since the fall of Communism. Moscow, the Russian capital, provides an example, if somewhat atypical. A July 1991 decree provided for privatization of apartments in Russian cities. In Moscow, some 25% of all housing had been privatized by 1993, as had nearly 5,000 businesses, mainly those engaged in consumer services. The socialist city had few shops, but, in Moscow today, retail outlets abound, from upscale boutiques to makeshift sidewalk markets. One finds more automobiles. Moscow now has legendary traffic jams. One also finds more light, including neon signs. One finds more litter, color, outdoor advertising, and crime. By contrast, many Communist monuments have toppled, and the socialist slogans that formerly festooned public places have all vanished. Numerous factories closed, and the proportion of the urban workforce employed in manufacturing plummeted. Service sector jobs multiplied rapidly, involving everything from clerks and fast-food workers to realtors, banks, lawyers, and stockbrokers. The proportion of Moscow's labor force engaged in service activities passed 50% as early as 1993 and is substantially higher today.

A less widespread city type, the **Nordic city**, occurs in Scandinavia and Finland. More recent in origin, these cities generally date from the seventeenth and eighteenth centuries, the era of the Swedish Empire when new cities were laid out by planners. A grid pattern of streets characterizes the core of the Nordic city, though often that pattern breaks down in the suburbs (fig. 10.24). A waterside site was unfailingly chosen for the Nordic city, whether marine, riverine, or lakeside. Of the various European urban types, the Nordic city is the least compact, with broad avenues; abundant freestanding, single-family residences (fig. 10.25); and spacious open areas. In fact, some Nordic cities consist of several different clusters separated by green space or even farmland, heightening the dispersed urban character. Trees grow more abundantly along the urban streets, revealing the strong northern love of forests. The Nordic city is modest in size, usually having less than 100,000 inhabitants, and the local industries typically consist of small firms manufacturing high-quality, even luxury products. In spite of

Figure 10.24.   Oulu, a Nordic city of Finland. Clearly preserved in its central section is the gridiron plan and public squares laid out by its Swedish founders. The city dates from 1605 and was originally protected by the island fortress on Linnansaari.

their size, Nordic cities offer an impressive array of amenities, from museums, sport complexes, and hospitals, to symphony orchestras and bicycle paths.

The Modern Urban Pattern

Site, morphology, and internal cultural/economic patterning, while essential geographical attributes of cities, do not complete the spatial analysis of urbanism. The distribution of cities must also be considered. In spite of the fact that Europe forms the most highly

Figure 10.25. **Single-family detached private housing** in the small Swedish mill town and service center of Torsby, in Värmland province. Surrounded by a well-kept, fenced lawn and garden, this home is typical of smaller urban centers in northern Europe. (Photo by T.G.J.-B., 1985.)

urbanized culture area in the world, **megalopolis** development is not common there. A megalopolis forms when adjacent cities grow until they coalesce, forming a poly-nucleated urban complex. The region from Boston to Washington, DC, in the United States is a megalopolis. In most parts of Europe, land use planning and green belt preservation worked against the development of megalopolises. Among the few examples are Randstad in the Netherlands (fig. 10.26) with a collective population of 7.5 million; the Rhine–Ruhr in western Germany, containing about 11 million inhabitants; Lancs-Yorks in the old industrial heart of England; Donbas in eastern Ukraine; and the somewhat more spread-out Flemish Triangle of northern Belgium (fig. 10.27). These megalopolises retain more open space than might be expected, thanks to rigorous zoning policies. Randstad Holland, for example, remains doughnut-shaped, due to a largely successful plan to keep the center (the Green Heart) open (fig. 10.26).

The area encompassing Randstad Holland, the Rhine–Ruhr, and the Flemish Diamond contains the greatest concentration of cities in Europe. Moving up in scale, some geographers make reference to a great arc of urban areas stretching from Lancs-Yorks to Rome, sometimes called the *big banana* because of its shape (fig. 10.27). Since the urbanized banana is interrupted by the Alps, it should not be seen as a zone of continuous urbanization, but much of it is an area of unusually high levels of urbanization and urban-related economic activities. There are, of course, many important cities outside of the banana, but they tended to be somewhat more widely separated from one another and less intimately interconnected with a wider hyper-urbanized zone.

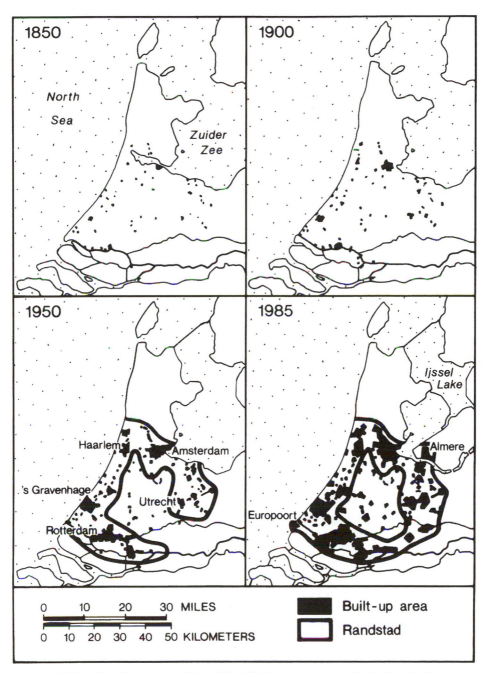

Figure 10.26.   Development of Randstad Holland, megalopolis in the Netherlands. Land-use planning and zoning are being employed to keep the central area, or "doughnut hole," open, but suburban development is encroaching. Note the use of some reclaimed Zuider Zee polderland for expansion of the Randstad. *Sources: Randstad Holland,* 1980, Utrecht and 's Gravenhage, NL: Centre for the Geography of the Netherlands, 14; van Wessep et al. 1993.

Figure 10.27. European megalopolises and the "Big Banana" dominate Europe's core. *Sources:* After Wessep et al. 1993; Dieleman and Faludi 1998.

Our focus in this chapter has been on the locational, morphological, and economic attributes of European cities. Since the vast majority of Europeans live in urban areas, they play a major role in Europe's social and ethnic geography as well. We turn to these matters in the next chapter.

Sources and Suggested Readings

Agnew, J., J. Mercer, and D.E. Sopher. 2007. *The City in Cultural Context.* London: Routledge.

Agnew, J.A. 1994. *Rome, World Cities Series.* Chichester: John Wiley & Sons.

Argenbright, R. 1999. Remaking Moscow: New Places, New Selves. *Geographical Review* 89 (1): 1–22.

Balsas, C. 2001. Commerce and the European City Center: Modernization, Regeneration and Management. *European Planning Studies* 9 (5): 677–682.

Bater, J.H. 2006. Central St. Petersburg: Continuity and Change in Privilege and Place. *Eurasian Geography & Economics* 47 (1): 4–27.

Beaujeu-Garnier, J. 1986. Urbanization in France since World War II. Research Paper, University of Chicago, Department of Geography: 47–62, 217–218.

Belina, B., and G. Helms. 2003. Zero Tolerance for the Industrial Past and Other Threats: Policing and Urban Entrepreneurialism in Britain and Germany. *Urban Studies* 40 (9): 1845–1867.

Benevolo, L. 1993. *The European City, The Making of Europe*. Oxford, UK: Blackwell.

Bollens, S.A. 2007. *Cities, Nationalism, and Democratization, Questioning Cities*. London: Routledge.

Bontje, M. 2005. Edge Cities, European-Style: Examples from Paris and the Randstad. *Cities* 22 (4): 317–330.

Burtenshaw, D., M. Bateman, and G. J. Ashworth. 1991. *The European City: A Western Perspective*. New York: Halsted Press.

Byfuglien, J. 1995. Urbanisation and Centralisation in Norway. *Norsk Geografisk Tidsskrift* 49 (1–2): 35–44.

Cardoso, A.S. 1983. *The Illegal Housing Sector in Portugal Bairros Clandestinos, Geographical Papers 0305–5914 No. 78*. Reading, UK: University of Reading.

Carter, F.W. 1972. *Dubrovnik (Ragusa): A Classic City-State*. London: Seminar Press.

Cherry, G.E. 1994. *Birmingham: A Study in Geography, History, and Planning, Belhaven World Cities Series*. Chichester, UK: Wiley.

Christaller, W. 1966. *Central Places in Southern Germany*. Translated by C. W. Baskin. Englewood Cliffs, NJ: Prentice-Hall.

Clark, D. 1989. *Urban Decline*. London: Routledge.

Clark, P., ed. 2006. *The European City and Green Space: London, Stockholm, Helsinki and St. Petersburg, 1850–2000, Historical Urban Studies*. Aldershot: Ashgate.

Clout, H.D., ed. 1994. *Europe's Cities in the Late Twentieth Century, Nederlandse Geografische Studies 176*. Utrecht: Royal Dutch Geographical Society.

Cornish, V. 1923. *The Great Capitals: An Historical Geography*. London: Methuen.

Costa, F.J., and A.G. Noble. 1990. The Growth of Metro Systems in Madrid, Rome and Athens. *Cities* 7 (3): 224–229.

Cummins, S., and S. Macintyre. 2002. A Systematic Study of an Urban Foodscape: The Price and Availability of Food in Greater Glasgow. *Urban Studies* 39 (11): 2115–2130.

Dale, B., and P. Sjoholt. 2007. The Changing Structure of the Central Place System in Trondelag, Norway, over the Past 40 Years—Viewed in the Light of Old and Recent Theories and Trends. *Geografiska Annaler Series B: Human Geography* 89 (Supplement 1): 13–30.

Danta, D. 1993. Ceausescu's Bucharest. *Geographical Review* 83 (2): 170–183.

David, T. 1963. London's Green Belt: The Evolution of an Idea. *The Geographical Journal* 129 (1): 14–24.

Dawley, S. 2007. Fluctuating Rounds of Inward Investment in Peripheral Regions: Semiconductors in the North East of England. *Economic Geography* 83 (1): 51–73.

Dekker, K., and R. Van Kempen. 2004. Large Housing Estates in Europe: Current Situation and Developments. *Tijdschrift voor Economische en Sociale Geografie* 95 (5): 570–577.

Dennis, R. 1984. *English Industrial Cities of the Nineteenth Century: A Social Geography, Cambridge Studies in Historical Geography 4*. Cambridge: Cambridge University Press.

Dieleman, F.M., and A. Faludi. 1998. Randstad, Rhine-Ruhr and Flemish Diamond as One Polynucleated Macro-Region? *Tijdschrift voor Economische en Sociale Geografie* 89 (3): 320–327.

Dingsdale, A. 1999. Budapest's Built Environment in Transition. *GeoJournal* 49 (1): 63–78.

Doherty, P., and M.A. Poole. 1997. Ethnic Residential Segregation in Belfast, Northern Ireland, 1971–1991. *Geographical Review* 87 (4): 520–536.

Drever, A. I. 2004. Separate Spaces, Separate Outcomes? Neighbourhood Impacts on Minorities in Germany. *Urban Studies* 41 (8): 1423–1439.

Dunford, M., and G. Kafkalas, eds. 1992. *Cities and Regions in the New Europe: The Global-Local Interplay and Spatial Development Strategies.* New York: Belhaven Press.

Enyedi, G., and V. Szirmai. 1992. *Budapest: A Central European Capital, World Cities Series.* London: Belhaven Press.

Ewen, S., and M. Hebbert. 2007. European Cities in a Networked World during the Long 20th Century. *Environment & Planning C: Government & Policy* 25 (3): 327–340.

Ford, L.R. 1985. Urban Morphology and Preservation in Spain. *Geographical Review* 75 (3): 265–299.

Fusch, R. 1994. The Piazza in Italian Urban Morphology. *Geographical Review* 84 (4): 424–438.

Gaspar, J., and A.M. Williams. 1994. *Lisbon.* London: Belhaven.

Glebe, G., and J.V. O'Loughlin, eds. 1987. *Foreign Minorities in Continental European Cities, Erdkundliches Wissen 0425–1741 Heft 84.* Stuttgart: F. Steiner-Verlag.

Gomez, M.V. 1998. Reflective Images: The Case of Urban Regeneration in Glasgow and Bilbao. *International Journal of Urban and Regional Research* 22 (1): 106–121.

Graham, S., and S. Marvin. 2001. *Splintering Urbanism: Networked Infrastructures, Technological Mobilities and the Urban Condition.* New York: Routledge.

Gritsai, O. 2004. Global Business Services in Moscow: Patterns of Involvement. *Urban Studies* 41 (10): 2001–2024.

Gritsai, O., and H. Van der Wusten. 2000. Moscow and St. Petersburg, a Sequence of Capitals, a Tale of Two Cities. *GeoJournal* 51 (1–2): 33–45.

Hagen, J., and R. Ostergren. 2006. Spectacle, Architecture and Place at the Nuremberg Party Rallies: Projecting a Nazi Vision of Past, Present and Future. *Cultural Geographies* 13 (2): 157–181.

Hall, P.G. 1998. *Cities in Civilization.* New York: Pantheon Books.

Hall, P.G., and K. Pain, eds. 2006. *The Polycentric Metropolis: Learning from Mega-City Regions in Europe.* London: Earthscan.

Hall, T., and P. Hubbard, eds. 1998. *The Entrepreneurial City: Geographies of Politics, Regime, and Representation.* New York: Wiley.

Harvey, D. 2003. *Paris, Capital of Modernity.* New York: Routledge.

Hermelin, B. 2007. The Urbanization and Suburbanization of the Service Economy: Producer Services and Specialization in Stockholm. *Geografiska Annaler Series B: Human Geography* 89 (Supplement 1): 59–74.

Hoggart, K., ed. 2005. *The City's Hinterland Dynamism and Divergence in Europe's Peri-Urban Territories, Perspectives on Rural Policy and Planning.* Aldershot: Ashgate.

Hoggart, K., and D. Green, eds. 1991. *London: A New Metropolitan Geography.* London: Edward Arnold.

Hoyle, B.S., and D. Pinder, eds. 1992. *European Port Cities in Transition.* London: Belhaven Press.

Illeris, S. 1990. Counter-Urbanization Revisited: The New Map of Population Distribution in Central and North-Western Europe. *Norsk Geografisk Tidsskrift* 44 (1): 39–52.

Ioffe, G., and T.G. Nefedova. 2000. *The Environs of Russian Cities, Mellen Studies in Geography,* vol. 3. Lewiston, NY: Edwin Mellen Press.

Isenberg, A.C., ed. 2006. *The Nature of Cities, Studies in Comparative History 1539–4905.* Rochester, NY: University of Rochester Press.

Johnston, R., J. Forrest, and M. Poulsen. 2002. Are There Ethnic Enclaves/Ghettos in English Cities? *Urban Studies* 39 (4): 591–618.

Jones, E. 1960. *A Social Geography of Belfast*. London: Oxford University Press.

Kearns, G., and C.W.J. Withers, eds. 2007. *Urbanising Britain: Essays on Class and Community in the Nineteenth Century, Cambridge Studies in Historical Geography 17*. Cambridge: Cambridge University Press.

Kemper, F.J. 2003. Binnenwanderungen in Deutschland: Rückkehr Alter Muster? *Geographische Rundschau* 55 (6): 10–15.

Kiss, E. 2004. Spatial Impacts of Post-Socialist Industrialtransformation in the Major Hungarian Cities. *European Urban & Regional Studies* 11 (1): 81–87.

Kloosterman, R.C., and B. Lambregts. 2007. Between Accumulation and Concentration of Capital: Toward a Framework for Comparing Long-Term Trajectories of Urban Systems. *Urban Geography* 28 (1): 54–73.

Knox, P., and S. Pinch. 2006. *Urban Social Geography: An Introduction*, 5th ed. Harlow, UK: Pearson.

Korec, P. 2003. Population Development, Urbanization and Regional Disparities of Slovakia. *Acta Universitatis Carolinae, Geographica* 38 (1): 167–180.

Kotus, J. 2006. Changes in the Spatial Structure of a Large Polish City—the Case of Poznan. *Cities* 23 (5): 364–381.

Krätke, S. 2004a. City of Talents? Berlin's Regional Economy, Socio-Spatial Fabric and "Worst Practice" Urban Governance. *International Journal of Urban & Regional Research* 28 (3): 511–529.

———. 2004b. City of Talents? Berlin's Regional Economy, Socio-Spatial Fabric and "Worst Practice" Urban Governance. *International Journal of Urban & Regional Research* 28 (3): 511–529.

Kühn, M. 2003. Greenbelt and Green Heart: Separating and Integrating Landscapes in European City Regions. *Landscape and Urban Planning* 64 (1–2): 19–27.

Kunzmann, K.R., and M. Wegener. 1991. The Pattern of Urbanization in Western Europe. *Ekistics—The Problems and Science of Human Settlements* 58: 282–291, 350–351.

Ladd, B. 1997. *The Ghosts of Berlin: Confronting German History in the Urban Landscape*. Chicago: University of Chicago Press.

Le Galès, P. 2002. *European Cities: Social Conflicts and Governance*. Oxford: Oxford University Press.

Leetmaa, K., and T. Tammaru. 2007. Suburbanization in Countries in Transition: Destinations of Suburbanizers in the Tallinn Metropolitan Area. *Geografiska Annaler Series B-Human Geography* 89B (2): 127–146.

Lentz, S., and P. Lindner. 2003. Privatisierung des Öffentlichen Raumes—Soziale Segregation und Geschlossene Wohnviertel Moskaus. *Geographische Rundschau* 55 (12): 50–57.

Leontidou, L. 2006. *The Mediterranean City in Transition: Social Change and Urban Development*. Cambridge Human Geography. Cambridge: Cambridge University Press.

Lichtenberger, E. 1993. *Vienna: Bridge between Cultures*. World Cities Series. London: Belhaven Press.

MacLaran, A. 1993. *Dublin: The Shaping of a Capital*. World Cities Series. London: Belhaven Press.

Maloutas, T. 1993. Social Segregation in Athens. *Antipode* 25 (3): 223–239.

Maloutas, T., and N. Karadimitriou. 2001. Vertical Social Differentiation in Athens: Alternative or Complement to Community Segregation? *International Journal of Urban and Regional Research* 25 (4): 699–716.

Marcuse, P., and R. v. Kempen, eds. 2002. *Of States and Cities: The Partitioning of Urban Space*. Oxford Geographical and Environmental Studies. Oxford: Oxford University Press.

Meijers, E. 2007. Clones or Complements? The Division of Labour between the Main Cities of the Randstad, the Flemish Diamond and the Rhein–Ruhr Area. *Regional Studies* 41 (7): 889–900.

Michael, P. 1987. Socio-Spatial Development of the South Italian City: The Case of Naples. *Transactions of the Institute of British Geographers, New Series* 12 (4): 433–450.

Murphy, A. B. 2002. Brussels: Division in Unity or Unity in Division? *Political Geography* 21 (5): 695–700.

Nefedova, T., and A. Treivish. 2003. Differential Urbanisation in Russia. *Tijdschrift voor Economische en Sociale Geografie* 94 (1): 75–88.

Pacione, M. 1995. *Glasgow: The Socio-Spatial Development of the City.* World Cities Series. Chichester: J. Wiley.

———. 1998a. The Social Geography of Rome. *Tijdschrift voor Economische en Sociale Geografie* 89 (4): 559–570.

———. 1998b. The Social Geography of Rome. *Tijdschrift voor Economische en Sociale Geografie* 89 (4): 359–370.

———. 2004. New Settlements for the United Kingdom in the Twenty-First Century. *Geography* 89 (2): 152–164.

———. 2007. Sustainable Urban Development in the UK: Rhetoric or Reality? *Geography* 92 (3): 248–265.

Papadaskalopoulos, A. 2005. The Spatial Impact of EU Pan-European Transport Axes: City Clusters Formation in the Balkan Area and Developmental Perspectives. *Transport Policy* 12 (6): 488–499.

Parr, J.B. 2007. Spatial Definitions of the City: Four Perspectives. *Urban Studies* 44 (2): 381–392.

Petsimeris, P. 2002. Population Deconcentration in Italy, Spain and Greece: A First Comparison. *Ekistics* 69: 163–172, 412–414.

Plaza, B. 2006. The Return on Investment of the Guggenheim Museum Bilbao. *International Journal of Urban and Regional Research* 30 (2): 452–467.

Pounds, N.J.G. 1969. The Urbanization of the Classical World. *Annals of the Association of American Geographers* 59 (1): 135–157.

Price, E.T. 1964. Viterbo: Landscape of an Italian City. *Annals of the Association of American Geographers* 54 (2): 242–275.

Regulska, J., and A. Kowalewski. 1993. *Warsaw, World Cities Series.* London: Belhaven Press.

Rizov, M. 2006. Rural Development Perspectives in Enlarging Europe: The Implications of Cap Reforms and Agricultural Transition in Accession Countries. *European Planning Studies* 14 (2): 219–238.

Robert, E.D. 1945. The Morphology of the Medieval German Town. *Geographical Review* 35 (1): 74–97.

Rowland, R.H. 1998. Metropolitan Population Change in Russia and the Former Soviet Union, 1897–1997. *Post-Soviet Geography and Economics* 39 (5): 271–296.

Rudolph, R., and I. Brade. 2005. Moscow: Processes of Restructuring in the Post-Soviet Metropolitan Periphery. *Cities* 22 (2): 135–150.

Rutherford, J. 2005. Networks in Cities, Cities in Networks: Territory and Globalisation Intertwined in Telecommunications Infrastructure Development in Europe. *Urban Studies* 42 (13): 2389–2406.

Steinführer, A., and A. Haase. 2007. Demographic Change as a Future Challenge for Cities in East Central Europe. *Geografiska Annaler Series B: Human Geography* 89 (2): 183–195.

Thomas, D. 1963. London's Green Belt: The Evolution of an Idea. *The Geographical Journal* 129 (1): 14–24.

Till, K. E. 2005. *The New Berlin: Memory, Politics, Place.* Minneapolis: University of Minnesota Press.

Turok, I., and V. Mykhnenko. 2007. The Trajectories of European Cities, 1960–2005. *Cities* 24 (3): 165–182.

Van Criekingen, M., M. Bachmann, C. Guisset, and M. Lennert. 2007. Towards Polycentric Cities. An Investigation into the Restructuring of Intra-Metropolitan Spatial Configurations in Europe. *Belgeo* (1): 31–50.

Vance, J.E. 1971. Land Assignment in the Precapitalist, Capitalist, and Postcapitalist City. *Economic Geography* 47 (2): 101–120.

———. 1990. *The Continuing City: Urban Morphology in Western Civilization.* Baltimore: Johns Hopkins University Press.

CHAPTER 11

Europe's Changing Social and Ethnic Geography

As in all places, wealth is unevenly distributed to Europe, but geographical disparities in well-being are less dramatic than in almost any other part of the world. This was not always the case, of course; throughout much of European history, prosperity was concentrated in the hands of a few aristocrats. But the last one hundred fifty years has seen the rise of a large middle class, and a dramatic reduction in the percentage of the population living in abject poverty. Hence the large areas of destitution one can find in the megacities of South Asia or South America, or even on the Appalachian Plateau of the United States, are largely absent from Europe. Geographically, there are differences in levels of **human development**, but the visitor is often struck by the degree of socioeconomic evenness amongst places. Shanty towns on the outskirts of large cities such as Rome and Bucharest exist, but evidence of poverty at this scale is relatively rare. Crime rates spike in sections of some urban areas, but violent crime in European cities is the exception. And Europeans enjoy some of the highest life expectancies found anywhere in the world.

Why is this? The answer lies in part in matters we have examined in previous chapters: the head start Europe got in the Industrial Revolution; the growth of its manufacturing, agriculture, and services sectors; and a system of colonialism that allowed Europe to extract wealth from afar. But understanding the region's social geography also requires consideration of a particular social model that has taken root there in the past century and a half. There are variations in the way the social model is understood and implemented, but in general terms, European societies are characterized by a comparatively active governmental role in the provision of education, health care, housing, child care, and other basic needs. The term **welfare state** reflects this state of affairs and shows that state governments are the principal providers of social goods.

A second feature of the European social model—in many senses a corollary of the first—is that Europeans pay relatively high taxes and are generally accepting of those taxes. It follows that a larger percentage of the gross domestic product is consumed by the state in Europe than in places such as the United States or Japan. This arrangement has been challenged to some degree in recent years. New market economies in eastern Europe, such as Slovakia and Poland, have attempted to fuel industrial growth by introducing rates of taxation much lower than western European countries. Meanwhile, there have been successful moves to lower taxes in countries such as Germany, the Netherlands, and the United Kingdom in an effort to stimulate growth. Nonetheless, corporate, income, and consumption ("value added") tax rates in Europe are among the highest in the world.

Europe's strong tradition of labor unionization is a third element of the European social model. In many parts of Europe, citizens are relatively sympathetic toward workers seeking protections and benefits through their employers and the state. Employees tend to have generous fringe benefits, and these benefits are often guaranteed by law. The most commonly cited example is vacation time, which in many places in continental Europe accrues at the rate of five weeks or more per year for everyone from the factory worker to the white-collar manager. In addition, European countries have some of the longest maternity/paternity leave periods anywhere in the world. In Sweden, 18 months' paid leave is legislatively guaranteed—with the government picking up half the cost and the employer the other half. Bulgaria has even more generous maternity leave policies. In the case of Sweden, at least 3 months out of 18 must be taken by the other parent (usually the father) to ensure both parents play a role in rearing the child.

Yet another example of the benefits accruing to labor can be found in the unemployment realm. Many countries have laws making it difficult to fire workers—particularly those working in the large civil service sector—and most countries offer comparatively generous unemployment benefits. When one reads in the newspaper about frequent labor strife and work stoppages in places such as France, it becomes clear that labor movements play an important role in French society—and that the relative prosperity of France makes it possible for its workers to expect much in return for their labor.

Underpinning Europe's social model is a broad social commitment to equality and *communitarianism*. The phrase inscribed on the façade of almost every public building in France sums up the concept: *"Liberté, Egalité, Fraternité"* (Freedom, Equality, Brotherhood). There are certainly many instances in which reality does not live up to this ideal, but there is nonetheless broad support for the idea that the responsibilities of the state lie in all three areas. The term "equality" is understood to mean not just that citizens should be equal before the law and enjoy equal opportunities, but that the state should facilitate social and economic equality. This helps to explain the commitment to the welfare state. It also provides insight into the support many Europeans express for equal rights—which is not to say that there is no gap between rhetoric and reality.

The concept of *fraternité* can best be understood against the backdrop of what geographer Nicholas Entrikin describes as an imaginary continuum of social values, with individualism lying at one end of the continuum and civic communitarianism at the other. European values and ideals, as reflected in politics, media, and other social activities, have historically tended toward the communitarian side of the spectrum. While making generalizations about the views of large, diverse groups of people is inherently problematic, the communitarian impulse is evident when one contrasts Europe at large with places such as the United States and Australia. By most measures, the latter societies tend to emphasize the role of the individual, whereas the European focus is more on the collective.

For all the strength of the communitarian tradition, over the past two decades more and more Europeans have started wondering whether the emphasis is shifting more towards the individualistic norms that dominate in the United States and Australia. The pressure to move in this direction reflects the challenge of maintaining the European social model in changing economic and social times. The social model has served to spread wealth relatively widely, but it has also made it difficult for European economies to respond quickly and flexibly to larger economic shifts. Some also argue that it has failed to reward individual initiative, and has even promoted a culture of complacency.

In recent years, much of the discussion of the social model has focused particularly on its consequences for the competitiveness of European business. The active involvement of the state in assessing high taxes, as well as mandating generous worker benefits and workplace standards, amounts to a highly effective safety net for employees and their families. Someone laid off from an Italian auto factory need not worry that her immediate needs will not be met, thanks to this social safety net. But such a model makes the car produced in Italy more expensive than one produced in a place with lower social standards. In an era of relatively free trade, this can cause the Italian automobile business to down-size, to leave, or to close down.

The challenges facing the European social model are further complicated by the aging of Europe's population (see Chapter 3). Simply put, the working population is increasingly shrinking as a percentage of the total population. Such a dynamic raises a whole host of issues, since everything from pension schemes to health care programs are premised on the idea that the population is fairly evenly distributed across different age groups, with the population pyramid weighted towards the youngest age groups. In nearly every European country, the population pyramid is inverted, with elderly retirees making up a larger segment of the population than school-aged children (fig. 11.1).

Immigration offers a partial solution to this problem, but it carries with it other challenges to the traditional social model. Rapidly increasing rates of immigration over the last few decades have brought large numbers of new residents into western European countries—some of whom are placing additional strains on welfare resources. Then there are the prejudices and resentments against immigrants that can undermine support for a social model that first developed during the late nineteenth and early twentieth centuries, when the nation-state ideal was at its strongest and when most people saw the commitments of states in terms of the ethnic nations that they theoretically represent (see the discussion of the nation-state idea in Chapter 6).

To make sense of Europe's changing social and ethnic mix, we turn first to basic patterns of social well-being, health, employment, education, gender roles, and ethnic differences that lie behind the general picture sketched above. We then look in more detail at how changes in economy, demography, and migration are altering the European social scene.

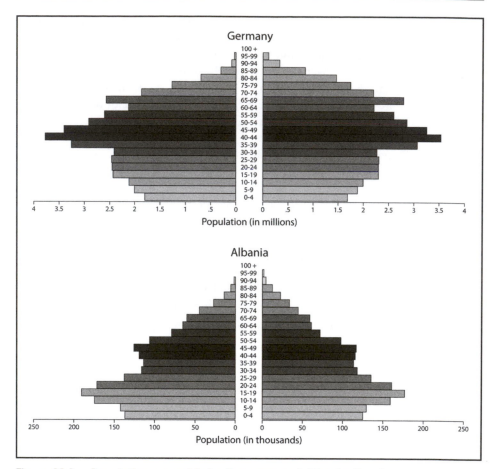

Figure 11.1.   Population pyramids for Germany and Albania. The German pyramid is more typical for Europe. The bulge representing the greatest number of people of a particular age appears in the 40s. The pyramid for Albania, by contrast, shows a bulge in the 15–19 age range. This is more typical of areas surrounding Europe, but not of Europe itself. *Source:* U.S. Census Bureau.

Patterns of Social Well-Being

The European social model traditionally emphasized "cradle-to-grave" care by the state, including parental leave and subsidies to parents with children, universal health care, unemployment insurance and welfare, and old-age pensions. The model's roots lie in nineteenth-century Germany, when Otto von Bismarck was the chancellor. He is credited with implementing the first health insurance scheme for the poor (1883), work accident insurance (1884), and social security for the elderly (1889). This social safety net was introduced partly out of genuine concern for the plight of disadvantaged populations confronting rapid industrialization and urbanization. But most historians agree that Bismarck's initiatives were also pragmatic political responses to an increasingly unruly working class clamoring for social reforms.

By the early twentieth century, other forms of social insurance, such as unemployment insurance, were introduced in Germany. Of course, prior to Bismarck's reforms there was a tradition of charity in Germany and throughout Europe. A poor person who became sick might receive treatment at a charity hospital run by the church, an unemployed worker might have access to handouts through the church or some other charity organization, and an old person might be able to remain housed and fed thanks to family members or municipal homes set up for indigents. What was revolutionary about Bismarck's reforms is that they put a secular, national government in charge of the social safety net. They also made benefits available to most of the population. Like other contemporaneous policies that established the "nation-state" as the focus of identification for people—the establishment of national parliaments, armies, and even post offices—the welfare state was instrumental in shifting people's orientation from their local community, their regional king, or even their church, towards the state. From these beginnings, the social model spread throughout Europe, not immediately or everywhere, but eventually most Europeans came to enjoy social protections that resemble those that began in Germany in the late 1800s.

Nonetheless, within Europe there are notable regional differences in the degree to which states are involved in the provision of social services. Since social welfare programs are so diverse, it is difficult to gain a precise picture of these differences; but the general pattern becomes clear when one maps data on the percentage of gross domestic product devoted to social welfare programs in states belonging to the Organization for Economic Cooperation and Development (OECD) (fig. 11.2). The continental European countries that lie to the north of the Alps and Pyrenees and to the east of the former Iron Curtain tend to have the most generous social welfare benefits. By contrast, the welfare state is less well developed in countries lying at the northeastern, southeastern, and eastern peripheries of Europe.

An indication of more general patterns of socioeconomic well-being can be gained from mapping differences in GDP per capita. The European Spatial Planning Observation Network, an EU program, developed an interesting cartographic representation of differences in GDP per capita in "Europe and its neighborhood" in 2002 (fig. 11.3). The figure shows both the generally favored position of western over eastern Europe, and the places where the sharpest differences can be found across international borders. The Mediterranean stands out as a socioeconomic dividing line, but so does the border between Finland and Russia and, to a lesser extent, the border between former Western and Eastern Europe. Less dramatically, the border between the countries that joined the EU in 2004 and other parts of eastern Europe stands out.

Of course these state-scale patterns tell us nothing about differences within states. Figure 11.4 shows the differences in per capita GDP within EU member states when this variable is mapped at the scale of first-order substate regions. The figure shows relatively little internal regional variation within the Nordic countries, but much greater

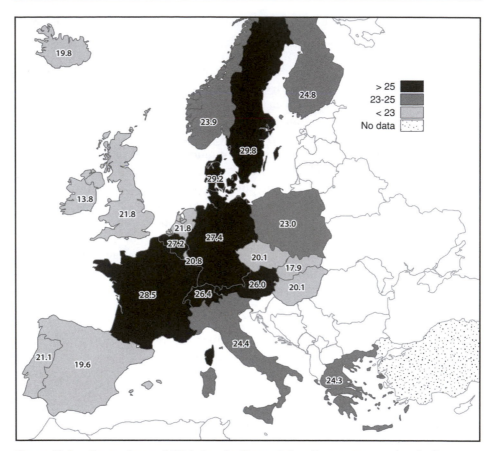

Figure 11.2.   Percentage of GDP devoted to social welfare programs (excluding education) in states belonging to the Organization for Economic Cooperation and Development. The welfare state is most in evidence in the western part of continental Europe, but most European states spend more on social welfare than do states in most other parts of the world. *Source:* OECD 2001.

variation in most other western European countries—particularly Italy and Spain. The continuing challenges faced by eastern Germany are also evident from this figure. Regional differentiation tends to be lower throughout much of eastern Europe, but the overall base is lower. It is interesting to note, however, that the regions around a few of the capital cities stand out as areas of particular prosperity—notably Prague (Czechia), Bratislava (Slovakia), and Warsaw (Poland).

Moving to an even smaller scale (or a larger scale if one is thinking in map terms), the differences in socioeconomic well-being within city regions described in Chapter 10 are prominent features of Europe's social geography. Within the better sections of the preindustrial city, segregation often occurred along occupational lines. Surviving street names provide clues. In Munich, we find the *Ledererstrasse* ("Street of the Leather-Workers"), *Färbergraben* ("Street of the Cloth-Dyers"), *Sattlerstrasse* ("Street of the Saddlers"), and others. Such names referred to the artisans' places of work and

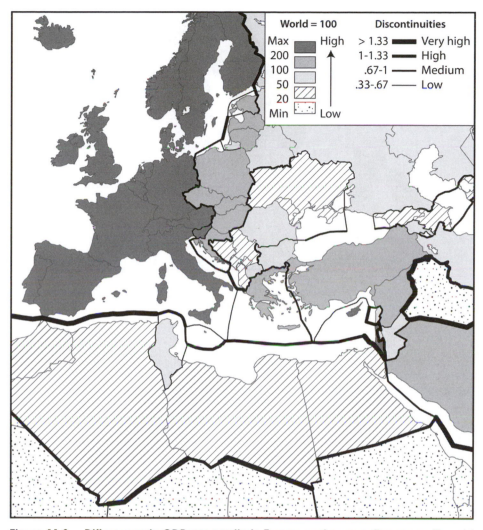

Figure 11.3.   Differences in GDP per capita in Europe and surrounding areas. The old Iron Curtain is still very much in evidence, as are the gaps across the Mediterranean Sea. *Source:* Based on a map in European Spatial Planning Observation Network, *ESPON Synthesis Report III,* October 2006: 35.

usually also their residences. In medieval Lübeck, merchants lived to the west of a main north-south street, while artisans resided to the east. Ordinary laborers lived outside the town walls.

Residential neighborhoods in European cities today remain rooted in class. The clustering of foreign laborers in certain districts speaks of their socioeconomic status as much as their ethnic background. A map of socioeconomic differences in the Paris metropolitan region shows the extent of the contrasts in a single city (fig. 11.5). The central and western sections of Paris proper are zones of significant prosperity— as are areas immediately to the west where new urban development has taken hold.

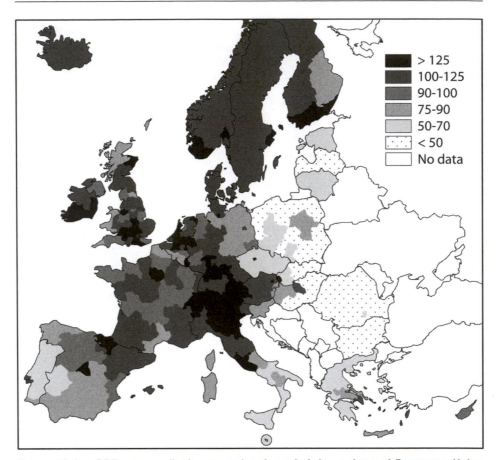

Figure 11.4. GDP per capita in second-order substate regions of European Union and European Free Trade Association member states, 2004, relative to the EU average (percentage). The map highlights the significant regional differences within countries such as Italy and Germany, as well as the comparative prosperity of capital-city regions in countries such as France, the United Kingdom, and Spain. Note also that the poorest areas are heavily concentrated in the former Eastern Europe. *Source:* Eurostat.

A notable decline is evident in the northeastern section of Paris proper, and the inner ring of suburbs to the north, west, and south stand out as zones of considerable distress.

After World War II, a more American-like pattern began to emerge in Europe's metropolitan areas, with prestigious neighborhoods developing in the outer ring. In present-day Liverpool, England, for example, persons engaged in the professions, business owners, and administrators live in residential areas farthest from the city center, whereas unskilled and semiskilled laborers reside in and near the preindustrial core. In Paris, the impact of this trend is evident in the greater prosperity of the suburbs lying far from the urban core (fig. 11.5).

Figure 11.5. Unemployment levels in the Paris metropolitan area (percentage). Unlike many American cities, the poorest parts of Paris and other western European cities are found in the first ring of suburbs. *Source:* IPUMS database.

Health

Europe has one of the healthiest populations in the world, as measured by average lifespan, rates of infant mortality, access to health care, and infection rates of life-threatening communicable diseases. Of the top twenty countries in the world in life expectancy as ranked by the World Health Organization, thirteen are in Europe (including the microstates of Andorra, Liechtenstein, and San Marino). The average infant mortality rate in the EU is 4.8 deaths per 1,000 live births, compared with 6.4 for the United States, 12.4 for Saudi Arabia, and 22.1 for China (Angola has the highest rate of infant mortality in the world at 184.4 deaths per 1,000 live births.) Part of the explanation lies in the fact that access to health care is among the best in the world. Europeans are accustomed to either government-provided or government-mandated health coverage. While this could be considered an expensive "luxury," it is interesting to note that per capita spending on health care in European countries is about half of what it is in the United States.

The nature of health coverage differs from place to place in Europe. The United Kingdom has a single-payer system of health coverage, with all hospitals publicly owned. Most medical personnel in the U.K. are employees of the government. England's National Health Service, begun in the late 1940s, is now one of the five largest employers in the world; only the Chinese military, Indian railways, and Wal-Mart employ more people. Countries in southern Europe such as Greece, Italy, and Spain, as well as the Nordic countries, also have health systems that are primarily financed through taxation at the national level, though in some cases regional or, in the case of Finland, local administrations are involved.

In France and Germany, as well as many of the former communist states of central and eastern Europe, the norm is a combination of public and private health insurance (the "social health insurance" model), typically involving complicated formulas of employer, individual, and income tax contributions. Unlike in Britain, French and German doctors are typically not government employees. Instead they are self-employed, and participate voluntarily in government-organized systems. In these countries, patients have the freedom to "shop around" for their doctor or hospital. Regardless of the precise form, European countries typically have virtually universal health coverage for their citizens. The prospect that a person between jobs could be uninsured for a time—commonplace in the United States and much of the less-developed world—is unknown to most Europeans.

Although Europeans enjoy some of the highest life expectancies in the world, there are health problems worth noting. As in all industrialized societies, heart disease and cancer are leading causes of death. Alcohol and tobacco dependency are also chronic public health concerns, particularly in central and eastern Europe, especially many of the countries within the former Soviet Union (fig. 11.6). Some 60% of Russian men, for example, report smoking regularly, and this is reflected in much higher mortality rates from smoking-related illnesses such as lung cancer and emphysema. The cultural norm in much of Europe emphasizes alcohol consumption as a regular part of the daily routine. Of the top ten countries in terms of beer consumption in the world, only Australia (ranked number four) is not in Europe; in top-ranked Czechia, the average citizen consumes some 160 liters (approx. 42 gallons) of the sudsy liquid per year. Likewise, the top 13 wine-consuming countries are European, and the average French person consumes 56 liters (approx. 15 gallons) of wine annually.

There is evidence that modest alcohol consumption can have health benefits, but alcoholism is a significant problem in parts of Europe, as are alcohol-related incidents in the workplace and on roadways. In the United Kingdom, a culture of binge drinking and associated antisocial behavior among young people has become a national topic of concern. A 2006 government report indicated that 40–50% of British 15-year-olds report drinking alcohol in a given week. The rates of alcohol and drug abuse among British people were consistently among the highest in Europe. By the early 2000s, the street scene in many English town centers on a Friday or Saturday night had become so disorderly that former Prime Minister Tony Blair declared binge drinking a "British disease" that could only be combated through the intervention of parents, government, and business.

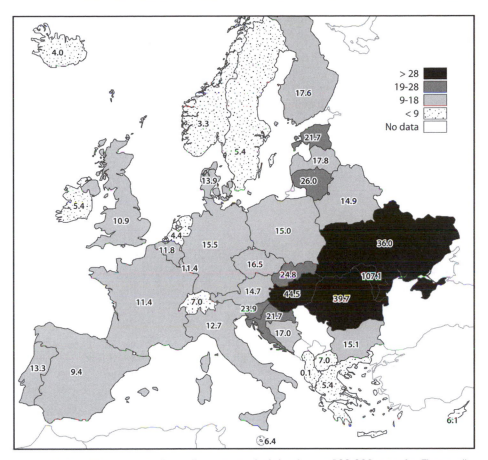

Figure 11.6.   SDR, chronic liver disease, and cirrhosis per 100,000 people. These diseases are primarily associated with the excessive consumption of alcohol. Note the particularly high incidence levels in eastern Europe. *Source:* World Health Organization, Regional Office for Europe.

Other drug use is also relatively widespread in Europe. In the Netherlands, a country known for liberal laws on the consumption of marijuana and hallucinogenic mushrooms, a drug tourism industry has emerged, drawing people from throughout the continent, and as far away as North America, to Amsterdam's and Rotterdam's famed coffeehouses, where cannabis can be legally dispensed. Recently, a movement has been launched to curb both the tourist aspect of the trade and drug use among young people. In 2007, for example, the mayor of Rotterdam announced that he would close all marijuana dispensing coffeehouses within 250 meters of a school, which meant half of the existing shops. It seems there are limits to Holland's culture of tolerance, though it is not clear if the recent trend will be short lived.

Two other public health concerns bear mentioning. Although global statistics on suicide are notoriously unreliable (given taboos associated with the subject in many cultures), according to the World Health Organization, sixteen of the top twenty suicide rates in the world are found in European countries. The highest four suicide rates in the world were reported in former Soviet republics (Lithuania, Belarus, Russia, and Kazakhstan), with men having much higher rates than women. Obesity is also a growing problem in much of Europe. Decreased physical activity and increasing caloric intake, particularly of fatty and sugary foods, combine to make obesity one of the "greatest public health challenges of the 21st century" in Europe, according to the World Health Organization. Even places with traditionally slender people, such as Norway and France, are seeing a clear upward trend in the number of obese people. Nonetheless, this problem is much less pronounced in Europe than it is throughout much of the United States.

Employment

Despite the generally high level of prosperity found throughout most of Europe, many European countries have been plagued by persistently high levels of unemployment. Currently the worst problems are found in western Europe (fig. 8.5), where unemployment is tied to the transition away from the industrial economy, as well as a relatively inflexible labor market in which job transition can be difficult and generous unemployment benefits can undermine the incentive to return to work. Significant parts of eastern Europe also experienced high levels of unemployment in the 1990s, as wrenching economic adjustments were made in the shift from communism to capitalism. Many of the eastern European countries now have some of the lowest rates of unemployment in Europe, but significant pockets of unemployment remain. Some regions of western Poland, for example, have some of the highest rates of unemployment in Europe; the same is true for eastern Slovakia, away from the urban economic engine of Bratislava near the Austrian border.

Countries in northwestern Europe, such as the Netherlands and the United Kingdom, as well as the Nordic countries, have had consistently low unemployment rates during the last decade or so. Finland, for example, which was facing rather dramatic economic challenges during the early 1990s, had an unemployment rate of just over 15% in 1995. Thanks in part to booming telecommunications and high technology sectors, the unemployment rate was nearly halved in a decade, and in late 2007 stood at just under 7%. Denmark has one of the lowest unemployment rates in the world at just under 3%.

Denmark's southern neighbor, Germany, has struggled with relatively high unemployment rates (between 8 and 11%) since the mid-1990s. Many attribute this to the post-unification economic boom petering out in that country. In eastern Germany specifically, unemployment rates of 20% are not uncommon in some districts, while in southern parts of Germany, around boomtowns Munich and Stuttgart, unemployment rates have rarely risen above 5% during the past decade.

In southern Europe, it is not uncommon to have higher overall unemployment rates, though the economic boom in Spain during the past decade has resulted in the rate being more than halved in just over a decade (from over 18% in 1995 to just over 8% in 2007). Urban growth centers such as Madrid, Barcelona, and Bilbao have the lowest unemployment rates, whereas comparatively high rates of unemployment are found in many rural areas of southern and western Spain. Italy exhibits a classic north-south division. In the north, where almost all Italian industry is located around such cities as Turin and Milan, unemployment is not a noteworthy problem. By contrast, in the Italian south, or *Mezzogiorno*, high unemployment has been the norm for over a century.

All of this reflects and reinforces the gaps between rich and poor noted above. Again, the social model ensures that contrasts in income are not as noticeable as if, for example, the free market were allowed to function unimpeded, but important contrasts remain. Just a few hours by train north of central London, one of the richest places in the EU—and indeed the world—lies Liverpool's derelict river frontage in the center city. Similarly, Düsseldorf and Gelsenkirchen, in Germany's Ruhr Valley, are separated by less than 50 kilometers. Düsseldorf is a wealthy center of finance and industry, but Gelsenkirchen has never recovered from the mining and steel industry bust of the 1970s.

Education

Another distinctly European demographic trait is a high level of formal education. By any measure, Europe possesses among the best-schooled peoples in the world. Access to basic education for the great majority of Europeans came about in the nineteenth and early twentieth centuries, beginning in northwestern Europe and spreading southward and eastward. German peasants learned to read and write in the first half of the 1800s, while most Russians, Italians, and other Mediterranean and Slavic farm folk remained illiterate. Only after the Communist takeover did education become available to the average Russian. In most of Europe, education spread to the masses because of ambitious government-supported education plans. European central governments generally oversee the operation of schools, which do not charge tuition.

The literacy rate offers a crude, but still revealing, measure of basic education. The overwhelming majority of Europeans above the age of 15 can read and write, and in most countries, from Ireland to Russia, the proportion stands at 99% or even higher. Only in Bosnia, Malta, and Portugal does the literacy level fall below 95%. The Mediterranean forms an educational fault line along Europe's southern boundary, beyond which literacy rates are far lower, as in Morocco, at 63%, Algeria at 70%, and Libya at 82%.

More revealing than basic literacy is the level of reading proficiency. A survey done in the late 1990s found that the proportion of adults reading at the lowest of 5 levels stood at only 7% in Sweden, 11% in the Netherlands, 14% in Switzerland, and 15% in Germany. Interestingly, 40% of adults in France ranked in this lowest reading category, comparable to Poland's 43%.

Other measures of education also prove revealing, as for example book readership. Northern Europe leads in the number of book titles published each year. Germany ranks first, followed by the United Kingdom, France, Spain, and the

Netherlands. On a per capita basis, Iceland, Denmark, Finland, and Switzerland lead. The Icelandic, Danish, and Finnic achievements are made even more remarkable by the fact that little or no foreign demand exists for books in the languages of those nations. Lowest levels of book production per capita occur in Ukraine, Romania, Belarus, and Albania, but even these countries compare favorably to many other parts of the world.

Universities in Europe are open to qualified students. Traditionally these were free, but a growing number of countries are now charging students at least a nominal fee (much less than their counterparts in the U.S.). There is growing concern that these fees will rise significantly as universities cope with rapid enrollment growth and stagnant or declining state funding. There is also concern that relatively few continental European universities are ranked among the world's best any more. Given that the graduates of European high schools are, by many measures, the best educated in the world, this is surprising. Reform movements are underway in several countries, but embedded hierarchies within institutions and pressures on state budgets make significant change difficult.

The Role of Women

The status of women in Europe has improved dramatically since the early twentieth century. In the decades after World War II, most governments implemented legislation mandating the equal treatment of women in the workplace and in public life. Gradually the pay disparities between men and women decreased, women began assuming positions of greater authority in the private sector, and a growing number of women started entering public life.

Despite these advances, women have not achieved parity with their male counterparts. Most parliaments throughout Europe are still dominated by men, and there are few women heading major corporations. Even equal pay for equal work is elusive. Most assessments show women earning between 4 and 22 percent less than their male counterparts who hold comparable jobs. Interestingly, gender pay gaps are less pronounced in Portugal and Italy (9%) than in the United Kingdom, the Netherlands, and Finland (between 20 and 22%) (fig. 11.7).

Behind these figures lie some interesting complexities. If one looks at the absolute employment gap (i.e., the difference between the number of men and women in the workforce), the Nordic countries stand out as places where the gap is small (fig. 11.8). This may well reflect a low level of discrimination and a high level of support for working women in that part of Europe. Also, behind the gender pay gap lie notable differences between the public and private-sector pay gaps. Both Portugal's and Italy's relatively small pay gap is the result of public-sector salaries that put women on an equal—or in the case of Portugal, more than equal—footing with men. The pay gap in the private sector is much less variable across Europe—hovering between 15 and 25 percent in almost all EU countries.

There is also evidence that women still face a "glass ceiling" in the private sector. Corporate leadership positions in most European countries are far more likely to be

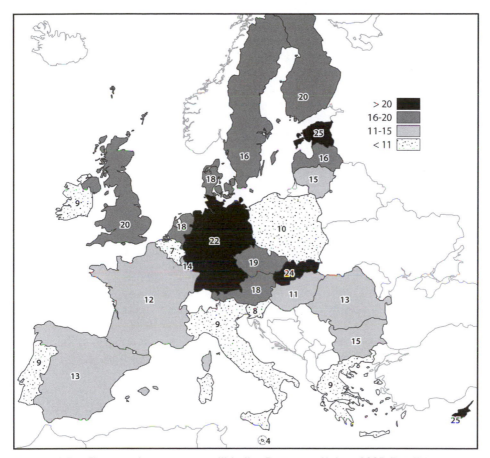

Figure 11.7.   The gender pay gap within the European Union, 2005. The EU average at this time was 15%. *Source:* Eurostat.

occupied by men than in the United States. A telling study in Germany in 2003 found that of the top forty public companies ranked by total sales, none had a woman on its board of management executives; this included such companies as DaimlerChrysler, Volkswagen, Siemens, and Deutsche Bank.

In national-level politics, the ranks of women in positions of authority are increasing: witness the election of Angela Merkel as the first female chancellor of Germany in 2005. Nonetheless, as of 2008, women occupied on average less than 25% of the seats in the lower houses of parliament in EU countries, and the representation of women was even smaller in the upper houses of parliament. Regional variations can be found that are somewhat similar to those found in the absolute employment gap, but not in the pay gap (compare fig. 11.7, 11.8, and 11.9). The data on parliamentary representation suggests that women are most visible in public life in the Nordic countries and in northern continental Europe. They are less well represented in eastern Europe and in the British Isles.

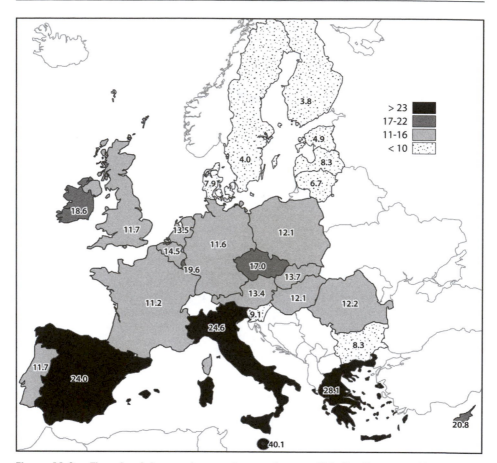

Figure 11.8.   The absolute gender employment gap within the European Union, 2005 (percentage). This is the difference between the number of men and the number of women in the workforce. *Source:* Eurostat.

Continuing disparities between women and men show the limitations of focusing solely on legislation requiring equal treatment of women and men. Many European countries, and the EU itself, are increasingly recognizing the importance of considering the conditions that can lead to unequal outcomes, and the challenges of overcoming those conditions. Affirmative action programs have been introduced in many places, and are supported under EU law. Moreover, networks of experts and advocates in women's rights have sprung up, and governments have taken a more aggressive role in everything from child care to highlighting the accomplishments of women in education. Increasingly, the call is heard for "gender mainstreaming"—the incorporation of gender issues throughout the full range of governmental policies and institutional arrangements. Gender mainstreaming has emerged as a significant EU policy commitment, although there is a lively debate over its direction and effectiveness.

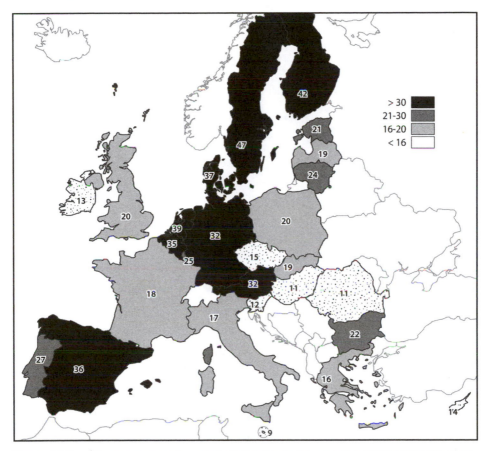

Figure 11.9. Women occupying seats in the lower houses of parliament in EU countries, 2008 (percentage). The highest numbers are generally found in northern Europe, but Spain and Portugal have a substantial number of female parliamentarians as well. *Source:* European Commission.

Ethnic Patterns

In chapter 6, we discussed the division of Europe into historical nations, which both helped to produce, and were shaped by, the political pattern. But a system of states based on the nation-state idea has never been fully implemented, because states have not been entirely successfully in forging a single nation out of disparate peoples. Even leaving aside the complexities introduced by recent streams of migrants, Europe does not consist solely of Spanish, French, Belgian, and Dutch peoples; it also encompasses Galicians, Basques, Catalans, Walloons, Flemings, Frisians, and many more. These latter groups represent a source of unevenness in Europe's social space that is different from the geographical variability associated with socioeconomic conditions, health, or the role of women.

Most of Europe's historically rooted ethno-cultural groups occupy discrete regions and live in uneasy tension with the dominant political-territorial order (fig. 11.10). It

Figure 11.10.   Areas of separatism or significant ethno-cultural difference within states. The map shows only areas that are the object of separatist sentiment or where significant ethno-cultural minorities can be found. More than a dozen new recognized independent states have appeared as a result of separatist movements since 1980, and several others, such as Turkish North Cyprus and Abkhazia, have achieved de facto independence.

is difficult to generalize about the socio-economic situation of these groups. Some are located in areas of significant economic prosperity (Basques and Catalans in Spain, Flemings in Belgium), whereas others are found in more economically marginal regions (Galicians in Spain, Bretons in France, Walloons in Belgium). What they share in common is some desire to maintain distinctiveness from the "nation-state" in which they live.

In pursuit of that desire, many members of Europe's long-standing ethno-regional minority communities seek some degree of autonomy from the state in which they are situated, and in some instances the call is for complete independence. The degree of radicalization is directly related to the extent to which state authorities seek to impose a single ethno-national norm throughout the territory. When states are actively engaged in such efforts (e.g., Franco's Spain), radicalization usually follows. On the other hand, when states take a more conciliatory and inclusive attitude toward ethno-cultural minorities (such as Finland toward its Swedish-speaking minority, or the Netherlands toward the Frisians), there is less incentive to demand extreme autonomy or independence.

Of course, Europe's ethnic diversity is not just a function of these longer-standing ethno-cultural differences. Many European countries have been destinations for migrants coming from other parts of the world. Unlike the United States, large-scale immigration is a relatively recent phenomenon in Europe. Even Britain's vast colonial empire did not produce a large wave of immigration until, ironically, direct colonial rule came to an end during the middle of the twentieth century. Spain's deep involvement in Latin America, dating to the sixteenth century, likewise did not result in large-scale migration to the Iberian Peninsula.

As we saw in Chapter 3, however, over the past sixty years the wealthiest countries in Europe, almost without exception, have been destinations for large numbers of new immigrants from south Asia, southeast Asia, the Middle East, and Africa. Most of the immigrants have ended up in western Europe, with Switzerland, France, Germany, Belgium, Denmark, and Sweden taking on a particularly large number in relation to population size (fig. 11.11). Only eastern Europe has largely missed out on large-scale immigration, but sizable numbers of eastern Europeans have become migrants themselves. Refugees from the war-torn former Yugoslavia have ended up in Germany and the United Kingdom, while many Romanians (particularly ethnic *Roma*, or gypsies) have made their way to Italy. Increasingly, workers from poorer parts of eastern Europe are moving to the west.

These migration streams have complicated Europe's social geography, but in a very different way from historical ethno-regionalism. Many of the new migrants have come to Europe to fill particular economic niches—particularly as low-wage, menial laborers. They are thus often at the lower end of the socioeconomic ladder. Moreover, they and their families have settled overwhelmingly in and around cities—making many western European urban areas decidedly heterogeneous.

It is important to remember that European cities have been culturally and ethnically diverse since the time of ancient Greece, when the first European urbanites segregated themselves along tribal lines. Religion long acted as one of the most powerful forces segregating people within the towns of Europe. In Roman cities, evidence strongly suggests that Christians occupied certain neighborhoods early in the diffusion of their faith. The term **ghetto**, to designate a Jewish neighborhood, derives from medieval Venice, and most European towns of the Middle Ages had separate Jewish districts, reminders of which are still seen in names such as the German *Judengasse* ("Street of the Jews") or Sevilla's *Judaría* ("Jewish Quarter"). Even today, residential segregation along religious lines can be seen in Belfast and Londonderry, Northern Ireland, where one finds Catholic and Protestant neighborhoods (fig. 5.13). The level of denominational segregation in Belfast rose sharply in the 1970s, and more gently in subsequent decades, ghettoizing the city's Catholics, who make up a third of the population.

Linguistic differences also traditionally separated people within European cities—most commonly in multi-lingual areas. Brno, in the Czech province of Moravia, had a medieval residential pattern in which Germans lived in the northern part of the city

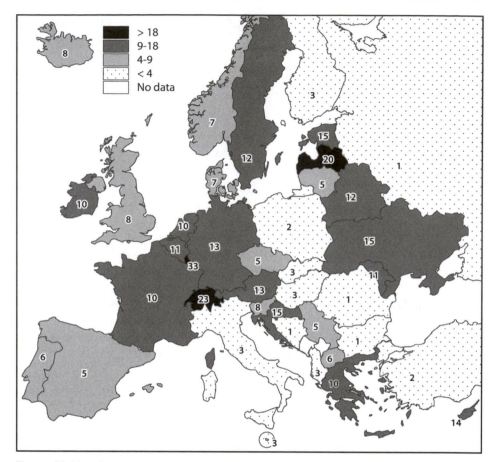

Figure 11.11.   Percentage of the population that is foreign-born in European countries. The relatively high numbers in eastern Europe are a result of migration from Russia to neighboring countries to the west, whereas substantial foreign-born populations in western European countries reflect migration from north Africa and southwest Asia. *Source:* OECD and selected national statistical sources.

and Czechs in the south. Towns such as Armagh and Downpatrick in Northern Ireland developed distinct quarters in the seventeenth century, as is indicated by the survival of English Street, Irish Street, and Scotch Street. In medieval Caernarfon, Wales, the portion of the town enclosed by walls housed the English, while Welsh clustered in the **faubourg** just outside the walls.

Whatever the historical patterns, the recent wave of foreign immigration to western European cities has greatly increased cultural diversity and led to the development of a growing number of ethnic and racial neighborhoods (fig. 11.12). In London, for example, the district of Wembley, where the famous soccer stadium is located, is over 50% immigrants; you are just as likely to see *paan* shops, a Bollywood video shop, African hair salons, or a Muslim-run *halal* butcher shop there as you are a traditional British pub. Frankfurt-am-Main had a population that was more than 27% foreign-born

Figure 11.12. Evidence of Middle Eastern immigrants in Brussels. The Arabic language is very much in evidence in sections of the city. (Photo by A.B.M., 1986.)

by 2000, as did Vienna. Many of these immigrants found homes in the decaying residences of the preindustrial core and inner ring—often occupying apartments abandoned by natives who had moved to the periphery.

Some ethnic neighborhoods and ghettoes developed from this influx. In Paris, for example, foreigners cluster in the northeastern quadrant, including parts of both the inner and middle rings. Many Muslims live in segregated neighborhoods in Paris and other cities of mainland Europe. Nonetheless, ethnic residential segregation is generally lower in European cities than in American cities. In Europe, foreign ethnic segregation often occurs at the level of individual apartment houses rather than at larger scales; tiny, multiple concentrations of individual foreign ethnic groups are relatively common.

The presence of large numbers of new culturally and ethnically different residents has, perhaps unsurprisingly, created social tensions. Some Europeans express concerns about the social and landscape changes brought by immigrants—and prejudice against immigrants is distressingly common. Riots in several Parisian suburbs during 2005, and again in 2007, reflected disenchantment amongst North-African immigrants who felt they were denied economic opportunities for advancement in France (fig. 11.13). Terrorist attacks on transportation targets in Madrid (2004) and London (2005) by Islamist extremists, meanwhile, have given rise to overtly anti-immigrant sentiments such as those aired by the **xenophobic** British National Party (BNP), which distributed recruitment fliers after the London bombings, arguing that the U.K. had become an "overcrowded multi-cultural slum." Faith-based hate crimes rose by five-fold in the two weeks after the bombings of public transit in the British capital city.

Figure 11.13. The geography of the 2005 riots in the Paris metropolitan area. The pattern provides a clear reflection of the spatial distribution of immigrants in the city. *Source:* Based on a map in *The Economist*, November 10, 2005.

In Germany, an ongoing debate is simmering about that country's large immigrant population, including 2.4 million immigrants from Turkey (of those, slightly over 400,000 have obtained German citizenship). The debate centers on the lack of integration of most Turks into German culture, as exemplified by the failure of a substantial number of Turks to learn the German language. Yet many Turks believe that their isolation within German society is due to an unwelcoming environment by Germans who once desperately needed their labor, but who have made little attempt to accommodate their cultural practices and differences. The mere term "guest workers" (*Gastarbeiter*) used to describe Turkish immigrants—in other words, you may stay as a temporary guest—offers some credence to this widespread belief among Turks.

France is home to the largest concentration of Muslims in Europe (some five million). France's Muslims come primarily from Morocco and Algeria; many end up in the Paris conurbation in subsidized housing complexes on the periphery of the city. Although predominantly Roman Catholic, France, like the United States, has a strong tradition of secularism, which dates from the French Revolution in the late eighteenth century. Government-funded schools (nearly all schools in France) may not teach any particular religion, and religious displays, such as Christian crosses, are banned in classrooms.

When a presidential commission recommended in 2003 that personal attire associated with a particular religion be banned, there was an outcry among Muslims who felt targeted by the measure. Many Muslim girls wore headscarves to cover their hair, ears, and neck, in line with Islamic dictates on proper attire for women. The report also recommended banning Jewish yarmulkes and Sikh turbans, but Muslims in particular felt singled out by the new law. The "headscarf law" set off a firestorm of protest, but immigrant communities felt largely powerless in the face of a large majority of the French public (as well as school teachers) who supported the ban. This policy has fueled feelings of discontent among immigrants of the Muslim faith in France, who must balance their precarious socio-economic status in French society with cultural traditions rooted in their faith.

Although France perhaps is the most extreme example of secularist traditions in Europe, tensions between the dominant culture and immigrant populations play out across all of European space. Switzerland, once thought to be comfortable in its insularity, is now a major site of immigration. A 21% foreign-born population gives it one of the highest non-native populations in Europe. Obtaining Swiss citizenship is quite difficult, for Europeans and non-Europeans alike. Of the foreign residents in Switzerland, more than half are from EU countries (particularly Italy, Portugal, and Germany), though a sizeable number came as refugees and economic migrants from the former Yugoslavia. 'Foreigner criminality' (*Ausländerkriminalität*) is an oft-discussed political topic in Switzerland. As in several other countries, nationalist parties have profited at the polls by exploiting this issue. In 2007, for example, the right-wing Swiss People's Party (SVP) won the most votes ever recorded by a party in a Swiss general election (29%), boosted in part by its stance on criminality by foreigners. In a poster ad campaign, the party showed four sheep, three white and one black, with one of the white sheep kicking the black sheep off the Swiss flag. In spite of domestic and international attention to such explicitly racist politics, the party scored well among voters with its promise to clean up what it called "rampant crime" by expelling foreign criminals from the country. Some even called for banning the construction of minarets (towers built adjacent to Islamic mosques); polls in 2007 showed more than half the population favored such a ban.

There is often a gap between rhetoric and reality in these circumstances. Violent crime in Switzerland has increased nominally since 2000, but crime rates remain well below those of many other industrialized countries, and immigrants and native Swiss alike have profited from a consistently booming economy. The typical street scene in Berne or Zürich, and even in much smaller towns, is of high levels of prosperity, and often of foreign-born workers fulfilling important service sector jobs. Like in other places with strong economies and large immigrant populations, such as the United Kingdom, Germany, and Sweden, Switzerland shows that the issue of immigration is not merely an economic one in Europe; rather, it goes to the heart of people's conceptualization of their cultural identity. As much as European governments, including the

Swiss government, like to paint their countries as beacons of tolerance and openness, it would be naïve to think that the opening of their borders to higher levels of immigration during the last four or five decades has been welcomed with open arms by most native-born peoples.

The Traditional Social Model in Transition

With European businesses, communities, and states struggling to maintain their competitiveness in an era of global trade, communication, and movement, the traditional European social model has come under increasing pressure. Moreover, the ability of states to provide for everyone is being challenged by the aging of the population and by migration. It should come as little surprise, then, that a growing number of Europeans are questioning whether they can maintain their relatively high standard of living and preserve the social model. To understand the dimensions of the problem, it is useful to look at the key challenges to the social model.

THE CHALLENGE FROM GLOBALIZATION

Production and consumption patterns in the twenty-first century are increasingly global. A visit to any corner of Europe reveals evidence of globalization. In most places, the small-scale manufacture of basic goods for the local market has given way to highly specialized production systems geared towards global markets. Consider, for example, the geographical changes that have occurred over time in the production and use of goods such as dishes. During pre-industrial times, the dishes used by a typical European were likely produced within a few miles of his or her home. The town potter, with the help of perhaps a handful of assistants, would have made enough plates and cups to meet the demand of the local community; the practice of shopping around, or of traveling to another place to buy pottery from a distant potter, was a privilege reserved for only the wealthiest in society.

Industrialization—from the late eighteenth century onward—greatly increased the scale of production-consumption patterns. An individual's choice of dishes might have increased to a host of brands carried by the local pottery shop, even though most of those brands still would have come from factories within the same region or country. Some pottery manufacturers during this era even had royal consent to produce in the name of the king or queen, offering evidence of their "national-ness." Although the cost of production might have been cheaper in some distant locale, the cost of transportation, as well as stiff duties assessed on imported goods, worked against goods being imported from afar. It was during this era that the social model in Europe as we know it today began to emerge.

The vast increase in the scales of production during the last century, combined with a dramatic decrease in the cost of transporting goods (through containerization, for example), as well as the lowering of barriers on imports, dramatically altered the scale of the production-consumption relationship. Were you to head today to a major department store in any European city, or surf an online shopping site, you would be confronted by a wide array of dishes with various brand names from around the world. Some might be European, from such well known brands as Waterford (England), Bernardaud (France), or Rosenthal (Germany)—successor enterprises to age-old manufacturers—but these would be substantially more expensive than most people can afford for normal, evening dinnerware. For all its appeal aesthetically and environmentally, pottery produced locally by craftspeople is typically uncompetitive in terms of price with the goods arriving from afar by the container-load at ports such as Rotterdam and Hamburg.

Even as globalization has altered the ways goods are produced, marketed, and sold—moving the scale from local to global—new pressures have been placed on social goods as well. The European social model developed with the assumption of a national political context, national industries, and minimal in- and out-migration. That model is not easily maintained when businesses can move halfway around the globe in search of more favorable conditions (fewer regulations, less taxation, etc.), and when competitors can offer lower wages and fewer protections. To maintain competitiveness, government and business leaders have increasingly looked at reducing the size of the public sector and exploring ways of making the labor market more flexible by, for example, making it easier to let employees go. Yet many Europeans are understandably uneasy with the proposition that their accustomed standard of living—from long vacations to job security to generous pensions—is being called into question.

The debate over such issues was very much in evidence during the 2007 French election campaign, during which the conservative candidate, Nicolas Sarkozy, openly criticized France's famous 35-hour work week, saying it showed an inadequate work ethic in France. He argued that France was behind the times in terms of its inflexible labor market, and he made it clear that he thought French workers should spend more time at their jobs. He went on to win the presidential election by a wide margin against his socialist opponent.

Other European countries have been having this debate as well. In Scandinavia—particularly Denmark and Sweden—serious economic crises during the early 1990s (high unemployment and massive government debt) led to labor and welfare reforms. These countries are now held up throughout Europe as models of globally fit, socially responsible market economies. As for Germany, during the 1990s and early 2000s, the country's fitness as a business location became somewhat of a national obsession; again, the debates centered largely on the inflexibility of the labor market and a social model that arguably encouraged able workers to stay at home and collect generous unemployment benefits rather than work a menial job for less pay. Since 2000, a series of reforms—corporate and income tax cuts, reduced unemployment benefits, and a liberalization of the rigid system of craft guilds—have been introduced under the mantra of "reform or lose out" in the global economy.

The case of "workfare" replacing "welfare" in Germany is worthy of attention. The huge costs associated with the unification of West and East Germany in 1990, combined with other political and economic factors, led the German government to adopt a variety of reforms designed to encourage able-bodied social assistance recipients not to become dependent on state aid. Curiously, the country that gave the world the first comprehensive social safety net looked to the New World for inspiration for its reforms. Since about 2000, reforms to unemployment and social security benefits that resemble the so-called "Wisconsin Model" have come into effect. In the American state of Wisconsin during the 1980s, a series of reforms were introduced that were designed to decrease dependence on social assistance by making receipt of aid dependent on holding a job (even a volunteer job in the community). This was called "workfare," which of course was a play on the word "welfare." Similar policies were later implemented under President Bill Clinton at a nation-wide scale in the United States in the 1990s. The idea was that individuals who received state aid would eventually become dependent upon it. The reforms, which were designed to encourage work and make the welfare state less expensive, caused a firestorm of protest throughout Germany, with protesters declaring the reforms "anti-social." Nonetheless, they have remained in place, and may well signal the beginnings of a new phase for the European social model that is less expansive than its predecessor.

THE DEMOGRAPHIC CHALLENGE

When Bismarck introduced old age pensions during the 1880s in Germany, the retirement age was set at 70 years old—an age that only 30% of males reached at the time. The retirement age was subsequently lowered to 65, where it remained for many decades. Then during the 1970s, when children born after World War II were entering the labor market in large numbers, there was a surplus of available labor. During this time, the idea of "early retirement" was introduced to make room for the new pool of labor. Someone who had worked for thirty years could retire at age 60 and collect a pension until death. The system was financially viable because of the relatively small number of retirees to workers. The ratio of current workers to retired persons throughout most of Europe was between five and eight to one.

But times have changed. The aging of the European population has reduced the ratio of the working population to those collecting pensions to as low as 4 to 1; and the trend is in the direction of even lower worker-to-retiree ratios. Future population growth trends are notoriously difficult to predict, but the potential dimensions of the demographic problem come into focus when one looks at some basic numbers being generated by the European Commission. Currently, no EU country has a total fertility rate (TFR) above 2.1 children per woman (the rate needed for replacement of the existing population)—and most European countries are well below that number (fig. 11.14). A 2005 European Commission report predicts that the EU's population will continue to grow until 2025, thanks largely to immigration, but thereafter it will begin to decline. Between 2005 and 2030, the working age population is predicted to decline by 21 million in the EU, a significant figure when one considers that the entire population of the EU is about 460 million. In eastern Europe, population declines are predicted to be particularly dramatic. By 2030, Bulgaria and Romania may well lose 21% and 11% of their populations, respectively. Turkey, which is not a member of the EU, is the only country along the eastern frontier of the EU where the population is likely to increase during that time period.

Figure 11.14.   Total fertility rates in the countries of Europe. In marked contrast to their southern and southwestern neighbors, European countries have fertility rates that are below replacement levels. *Source:* CIA World Factbook.

The share of the world's population living in Europe is also decreasing rapidly. Whereas Europe comprised 12% of the global population in 1970, that number is expected to shrink by half by 2030, while the share in Africa and parts of Asia will grow. Ireland, which in 1960 had the highest TFR in Europe (3.7 children per woman), now still has the highest in Europe after being nearly halved to 1.9 children per woman. By contrast, the highest TFR in the world is in Mali, where the average woman will bear 7.38 children during her lifetime. In the United States, the rate is 2.1, or just at the replacement level (these figures, of course, do not take into account immigration).

The causes of these demographic changes are complex. Certainly, in a place such as Ireland, there is strong correlation among economic growth, gender equalization in the labor market, and decreasing birth rates over the past few decades. The same trends are observable in Spain, also a predominantly Roman Catholic country experiencing slowed natural population increase on the one hand, and a rapidly growing economy on the other. Curiously, in several former communist countries, population decline coincided with the collapse of communism. In a country such as Poland, before 1989 access to nicer, larger housing was controlled by the government and linked to factors such as family size. This certainly may have encouraged couples to have children earlier in life.

In western Europe, rising levels of prosperity also correspond to decreasing birth rates. It is important to remember the difference between correlation and causation, however. As educational systems and labor markets have opened to women, there has been a large increase in the number of couples in which both partners work outside the house. Despite a social model that provides generous leave benefits for new parents, career trajectories often complicate extended breaks for child rearing.

In addition to having fewer children, couples are typically waiting longer to have their first child—often until their mid-30s or later, when careers are better established and the risk of setbacks are fewer. Societal expectations are also changing. A path that was once taken as natural and expected—schooling, marriage, babies, in that order— is no longer the absolute norm. Longer stints in pursuit of higher education, cohabitation without marriage, extended stays abroad, and high mobility are quite typical, particularly among 20-somethings of higher socio-economic status. Societal and familial pressures towards child rearing have given way, or at least been delayed, in favor of an emphasis on self-exploration, self-expression, and career development. Again, this differs somewhat based on class, but the elements of the social model that make European societies some of the most equitable in the world, such as universal access to free, quality education, make such opportunities available to large segments of the population.

Many governments are now faced with trying to come to terms with the impacts of these demographic tendencies. How will economies continue to grow as workers retire and fewer and fewer people are present to replace them? Is it possible to implement policies that stop or reverse these trends? Are the potential impacts of demographic change really so bad? Are these trends the inevitable consequence of particular development paths in Europe? Should additional immigration be encouraged to offset declining birth rates?

There is, of course, much debate over questions such as these, but one thing is clear: the social systems of the post-World War II decades cannot be sustained unless changes are made. Immigration has provided a reprieve for a time in parts of Europe, but not in others, and immigration carries with it other social costs (see below). Hence much of the attention is focused on adjusting social benefits and looking for ways to encourage larger families.

On the social benefits side, the trend in recent years has been in the direction of decreases in guaranteed benefits, lengthened periods of service to collect full pensions, and increases in the mandatory retirement age—from 65 to 67, and even higher. As for the issue of population growth itself, many European countries have adopted **pronatalist policies** (i.e., policies designed to increase fertility rates, or at least slow the decline in the birth rate). Population policies are not without controversy, as some people believe this is not an area that is appropriate for state intervention. But with low population growth presenting states with increasingly significant challenges, governments see few options other than to encourage more births. Four brief case studies illustrate what is happening.

Spain had a moderately high TFR until relatively recently—particularly during the forty-year reign of dictator Francisco Franco, who died in 1975. Under Franco, contraception and abortion were illegal (Spain still has some of the strictest abortion laws in Europe), and women's roles were largely confined to the home. Following democratic reforms, economic growth took off, and employment possibilities for women opened up. This led to a precipitous decline in Spain's TFR. It was not until the 1990s that the state began to assume a more active role in encouraging more births, but Spain's fairly decentralized system of governance made it difficult to implement a coordinated set of population policies. Nonetheless, Spain has adopted some pronatalist policies, such as improved maternity leave. In keeping with more traditional views on family in Roman-Catholic Spain, however, the overall emphasis has been more on creating more favorable overall conditions for families with children. The steps have been modest, but include increasing the availability and lowering the cost of preschool education, and increasing the availability of affordable housing (a large percentage of 20- to 29-year-olds in Spain live with their parents, in part because of the high expense of housing.) These measures are showing some positive results. Under any circumstances, the demographic issue is less acute in Spain because of the large number of immigrants coming to the country (fig. 11.11).

Sweden has had a more proactive family policy than Spain. In keeping with its liberal reputation, there are fewer taboos on children being born to unwed parents in Sweden, and abortion and contraceptives are readily available. During the 1980s, Sweden showed fairly dramatic gains in fertility rates. These corresponded to the introduction of proactive family policies such as generous family leave; universal, inexpensive child care; and even "speed premiums"—a bonus for parents having babies in quick succession. Gains in fertility in Sweden during the 1980s also corresponded to strong economic growth, while economic stagnation during the 1990s led again to a downward trend in birthrates. This prompted some demographers to speculate that pronatalist government policies are only one part of the birthrate equation in Sweden. Just as important is the fact that women are highly integrated into the workforce there, and are more likely to contribute significantly to overall family earnings. During periods of economic growth, mothers with stable work were more likely to have children, whereas during periods of stagnation, uncertainty and job insecurity may have lowered birth rates.

Population policies in Germany lie somewhere between those of Spain and Sweden. Unlike Sweden, the idea of a traditional nuclear family is still very much a part of German government policy. There is, for example, a German ministry of "Family, Seniors, Women, and Youth" at the federal level, and the German constitution recognizes marriage as a cornerstone of society. The symbolism of the governing coalition's decision to choose Ursula von der Leyen, a married, working woman with seven children, to be the Minister of Family in 2005, was widely commented in the German media. Yet there are still taboos associated with government involvement in population policy, because of the history of the Third Reich and Hitler's explicitly pronatalist (and racist) family policy. Since the 1970s, the German government has compensated families for each child, under the assumption that the state has a role to play in assisting families in the costs of child-rearing. Until recently, each household received the same basic amount per child, but this was changed as of 2007 to reflect the fact that women who were employed in the workforce were still having fewer children, later in life, than those not in the workforce. Now, rather than a standard rate given to each family with a child, a system of "parents money" replaces a percentage of the income of a stay-at-home parent for a specified period of time. This change was designed to encourage working professionals to have children. It is too early to know whether it will produce a sustained increase in fertility rates, but there was evidence of a spike in births after the date when the generous new benefits went into effect. There have been some criticisms of this program as elitist, however, since its goal is to subsidize well-educated, employed (and therefore better off) individuals having children, while at the same time eliminating the simple "educational" grants to all children regardless of family income.

Poland provides a case study of the demographic challenges to the European social model in the formerly communist east. Poland's birth and death rates are estimated to be identical in the late 2000s. Hence, the net rate of migration determines whether the population grows or not. Since more are emigrating than immigrating, Poland has been losing population. The country's total fertility rate of 1.26 children per woman is significantly below replacement levels. With its large agricultural sector and strong Roman Catholic traditions, Poland long had high fertility rates—the highest in Eastern Europe outside the Soviet Union in the period after World War II. Aggressive pronatalist policies during the communist era kept Poland's fertility rate high for a time, but the TFR fell to the replacement level of 2.1 in 1989—the year when free-market reforms were first introduced in the country. During the 1990s, fertility rates fell even further, as government benefits to parents were restricted or privatized, and material conditions worsened for segments of the population. Unlike Spain and Germany, Poland's low rate of natural increase is not offset by immigration. This poses significant challenges for Poland and most other eastern European countries, which are in a similar situation. It will be a struggle at best to maintain reasonably far-reaching social welfare programs in the face of these highly unfavorable demographic trends.

THE IMMIGRATION CHALLENGE

The welfare state has traditionally been organized primarily at the national scale, and the very notions of mutual assistance and social solidarity have carried with them strong nationalist tendencies (of Italians helping Italians, or French helping French). In the wake of the recent wave of immigrants, many countries are wrestling with how far the social model should extend. With the EU now comprised of 27 countries, these questions are likewise played out in Brussels and Strasbourg. Is, for example, a Roma from Bulgaria (an EU member state since 2007) who emigrates to Italy entitled to the rights and privileges of the Italian welfare state? Previously, the answer to that question was unequivocally 'no,' but EU membership theoretically puts European citizens on equal footing.

Far more pressing a concern, of course, is the question of immigration from non-European countries. The arrival of large numbers of new, relatively poor immigrants raises the prospect of increased strains on the European social model. The offset comes in the form of an expanding working-age population—and by extension a growing tax base. But in situations where immigrant unemployment is high and where immigrant workers bring with them large families who are not necessarily contributing to the tax base, extending the social support network to immigrants can be a significant challenge. That many of these immigrants came at the invitation of European governments in an effort to address labor shortages presents, in the minds of many, a moral obligation to include immigrants within the social model. But in an era of demographic decline and growing unease among native-born populations about the changing ethnic makeup of European societies, this is no easy task.

Not surprisingly, then, immigration remains a lively topic of discussion throughout Europe, and that discussion itself can serve to undermine some of the core values that have sustained the social model. It seems that populist sentiments are fairly easily mobilized when complex issues involving race, belief systems, taxation, and the provision of services are reduced during election campaigns to questions such as: Are you willing to finance the arrival of yet more immigrants from some of the poorest spots on earth? Can "our" culture afford more new arrivals? Why should immigrants have jobs when so many (Germans, Dutch, French, etc.) are unemployed? This is not to suggest that European societies are necessarily more racist than others, and there are certainly vast differences in attitudes toward immigrants in Europe along geographic, class, and educational lines. Moreover, even in areas with limited social programs for immigrants, non-native Europeans benefit from certain aspects of the European social model, including social housing, heavily subsidized transit, and free schooling. Clearly, though, immigration has not just been a source of economic dynamism and cultural richness; it has also produced substantial material and psychological strains on the underpinnings of the European social model. How Europe confronts those strains is one of the region's fundamental challenges in the years ahead.

As the foregoing discussion suggests, in recent years Europe's social trajectory has been affected not just by developments at the local and state levels, but by the expanding role of the EU. As the EU has broadened its reach, both geographically and administratively, it has also become a growing focus of controversy. Understanding what is happening with the EU is vital to an appreciation of the geographical changes unfolding in Europe in the twenty-first century. We thus turn our attention to the possibilities and prospects of European integration in the final chapter of this book.

Sources and Suggested Readings

Allen, J. T. 2006. The French-Muslim Connection: Is France Doing a Better Job of Integration Than Its Critics? In *Pew Global Attitudes Survey*. Washington, DC: Pew Research Center. Available from http://pewglobal.org/reports/display.php?ReportID=253.

Amin, A., and S. Graham. 1997. The Ordinary City. *Transactions of the Institute of British Geographers* 22 (4): 411–429.

Bontje, M., and J. Latten. 2005. Stable Size, Changing Composition: Recent Migration Dynamics of the Dutch Large Cities. *Tijdschrift voor Economische en Sociale Geografie* 96 (4): 444–451.

Bouma-Doff, W. V. D. L. 2007. Confined Contact: Residential Segregation and Ethnic Bridges in the Netherlands. *Urban Studies* 44 (5/6): 997–1017.

Buzar, S., P. Ogden, R. Hall, A. Haase, S. Kabisch, and A. Steinfuhrer. 2007. Splintering Urban Populations: Emergent Landscapes of Reurbanisation in Four European Cities. *Urban Studies* 44 (4): 651–677.

Dekker, K., and R. van Kempen. 2004. Large Housing Estates in Europe: Current Situation and Developments. *Tijdschrift voor Economische en Sociale Geografie* 95 (5): 570–577.

Dingsdale, A. 2002. *Mapping Modernities: Geographies of Central and Eastern Europe, 1920–2000.* London; New York: Routledge.

Dodgshon, R. A. 1987. *The European Past: Social Evolution and Spatial Order.* Houndmills, UK: Macmillan Education.

Doherty, P., and M. A. Poole. 1997. Ethnic Residential Segregation in Belfast, Northern Ireland, 1971–1991. *Geographical Review* 87 (4): 520–537.

Entrikin, J. N. 2003. Political Community, Identity, and Cosmopolitan Place. In *Europe without Borders*, eds. M. Berezin and M. Schain, 51–63. Baltimore: Johns Hopkins Press.

European Commission. 2005. Confronting Demographic Change: A New Solidarity between the Generations, 27. Available from http://ec.europa.eu/employment_social/news/2005/mar/comm2005–94_en.pdf.

Foucher, M. 1995. *The New Faces of Europe.* Strasbourg: Council of Europe Press.

Graham, S., and S. Marvin. 2001. *Splintering Urbanism: Networked Infrastructures, Technological Mobilities and the Urban Condition.* New York: Routledge.

Grant, J., S. Hoorens, S. Sivadasan, M. v. h. Loo, J. DaVanzo, L. Hale, S. Gibson, and W. Butz. 2004. Low Fertility and Population Ageing: Causes, Consequences, and Policy Options, 152. Leiden and Brussels: RAND Europe and the European Commission. Available from http://www.rand.org/pubs/monographs/2004/RAND_MG206.pdf.

Häkli, J., and D. H. Kaplan. 2002. Learning from Europe? Borderlands in Social and Geographical Context. In *Boundaries and Place: European Borderlands in Geographical Context*, eds. D. H. Kaplan and J. Häkli, 1–17. Lanham, MD: Rowman & Littlefield.

Hamnett, C. 2003. *Unequal City: London in the Global Arena.* New York: Routledge.

Jonas, A. E. G. 2006. The Globalized City: Economic Restructuring and Social Polarization in European Cities. *International Journal of Urban and Regional Research* 30 (1): 233–234.

Koopmans, R. 2005. *Contested Citizenship: Immigration and Cultural Diversity in Europe, Social Movements, Protest, and Contention.* Minneapolis: University of Minnesota Press.

Lubbers, M., and P. Scheepers. 2007. Explanations of Political Euro-Scepticism at the Individual, Regional and National Levels. *European Societies* 9 (4): 643–669.

Malheiros, J. 2002. Ethni-Cities: Residential Patterns in the Northern European and Mediterranean Metropolises—Implications for Policy Design. *International Journal of Population Geography* 8 (2): 107–134.

Monzini, P. 2007. Sea-Border Crossings: The Organization of Irregular Migration to Italy. *Mediterranean Politics* 12 (2): 163–184.

Musterd, S. 2005. Social and Ethnic Segregation in Europe: Levels, Causes, and Effects. *Journal of Urban Affairs* 27 (3): 331–348.

O'Loughlin, J., and J. Friedrichs, eds. 1996. *Social Polarization in Post-Industrial Metropolises.* Berlin; New York: Walter de Gruyter.

Organisation for Economic Co-operation and Development. 2003. *Berlin: Towards an Integrated Strategy for Social Cohesion and Economic Development.* Paris: Organisation for Economic Co-operation and Development.

Pacione, M. 2005. The Changing Geography of Ethnic Minority Settlement in Glasgow, 1951–2001. *Scottish Geographical Journal* 121 (2): 141–161.

Price, M., and L. Benton-Short. 2007. Immigrants and World Cities: From the Hyper-Diverse to the Bypassed. *GeoJournal* 68 (2): 103–117.

Saltman, R. B., R. Busse, and J. Figueras. 2004. Social Health Insurance Systems in Western Europe. In *European Observatory on Health Systems and Policies Series*, eds. J. Figueras, M. McKee, E. Mossialos and R. B. Saltman, 298. Maidenhead: Open University Press and the World Health Organization. Available from http://www.euro.who.int/document/E84968.pdf.

Samers, M. 2004. An Emerging Geopolitics of 'Illegal' Immigration in the European Union. *European Journal of Migration & Law* 6 (1): 27–45.

Sardon, J. P., and G. D. Robertson. 2002. Recent Demographic Trends in the Developed Countries. *Population (English Edition)* 57 (1): 111–156.

Thrift, N. 2005. But Malice Aforethought: Cities and the Natural History of Hatred. *Transactions—Institute of British Geographers* 30 (2): 133–150.

Trenz, H.-J. 2007. Reconciling Diversity and Unity. *Ethnicities* 7 (2): 157–185.

United Kingdom. Home Office. Advisory Council on the Misuse of Drugs. 2006. Pathways to Problems: Hazardous Use of Tobacco, Alcohol and Other Drugs by Young People in the UK and Its Implications for Policy, 100. London. Available from http://drugs.homeoffice.gov.uk/publication-search/acmd/pathways-to-problems/Pathwaystoproblems.pdf?view=Binary.

Vallely, P. 2007. Switzerland: Europe's Heart of Darkness. *The Independent*, September 7.

Van Marissing, E., G. Bolt, and R. Van Kempen. 2006. Urban Governance and Social Cohesion: Effects of Urban Restructuring Policies in Two Dutch Cities. *Cities* 23 (4): 279–290.

Western, J. 2007. Neighbors or Strangers? Binational and Transnational Identities in Strasbourg. *Annals of the Association of American Geographers* 97 (1): 158–181.

Wilkes, R., N. Guppy, and L. Farris. 2007. Right-Wing Parties and Anti-Foreigner Sentiment in Europe. *American Sociological Review* 72: 831–840.

CHAPTER 12

Whither European Integration?

Of the geographic changes that have unfolded in Europe over the past several decades, the most dramatic may well be in the political arena. Most Europeans are no longer simply French, Germans, or Hungarians; they are also citizens of the European Union. But what does that mean—both practically and perceptually? What are the implications of European Union citizenship for longer-standing national allegiances—both now and in the future? More broadly, what is the future of the European experiment with integration? The answers to these questions are far from clear, but there is much to be learned from looking at the on-going process of European integration through a geographic lens. This means focusing not simply on institutions and political arrangements, but on the spatial arrangements and territorial ideas that bear on the integration process.

Geographic circumstances have influenced European integration from the beginning. The EEC might never have gotten off the ground in the late 1950s if the two core powers behind the initiative—France and Germany—had not had products they wanted to trade with one another. France was a ready market for the output of Germany's rebuilt heavy industries, and Germany was an obvious outlet for French agricultural production and specialty manufacturing. The French-German trading relationship provided a geographic foundation around which early European cooperation could be built. Of relevance as well was the new willingness in the Europe of the 1950s to challenge the traditional role of the European "nation-state" in light of the disastrous conflicts of the first half of the twentieth century and the growing dominance of the United States and the Soviet Union on the global stage.

As we saw in Chapter 6, in general terms European integration has made great strides over the last fifty years. More countries have come into the fold, the economies of those countries have become increasingly interdependent, the reach of EU governmental and regulatory institutions has expanded, and more and more Europeans have come to think of the EU as part of their lives—and even their identities. With the partial exception of a period of stagnation during the 1970s, from the 1950s through the early 2000s the general trajectory was in the direction of both widening (adding more territory) and deepening (expanding the EU's authority)—with neither occurring at the expense of the other.

Over the past several years, however, the European integration experiment has been in some turmoil. The May 2004 enlargement of the EU (fig. 6.19) set off a vigorous debate in Europe over the advisability of further enlargement. Then, in 2005 the voters in both France and the Netherlands rejected a proposed Constitution for the EU that was designed both to coordinate the various treaties under which the EU had been operating and to give the EU more administrative power and autonomy over matters such as foreign policy. The EU has continued to move forward—adding Romania and Bulgaria in 2007, continuing negotiations over entry with Croatia, Macedonia, and Turkey, and hammering out treaties that deal with many of the key operational issues that were in the draft Constitution. But new questions are being raised about what the EU is and where it should be going, and there is evidence that the level of support for the EU has been slipping in key parts of Europe.

Public opinion is constantly changing and is tricky to gauge, but "Eurobarometer" surveys run by the EU are helpful because they are fairly comprehensive and are administered frequently. They regularly include questions about support for European integration. A Spring 2007 survey asking Europeans whether they thought membership was a good thing for their countries yielded strong positive responses in the Netherlands, Ireland, Luxembourg, Spain, and Belgium, but on average only 57% of the population in EU countries regarded membership as a good thing, and in seven countries the figure fell below 50% (fig. 12.1). The lowest support came from Austria (36%), but the United Kingdom, Hungary, and Latvia were all below 40%. When the question becomes whether people trust the EU, the picture is even more discouraging for proponents of European integration. On average only 48% of the population indicated trust in the EU in 2006, and the figures were as low as 25% in the United Kingdom, 39% in Germany, and 40% in Sweden (fig. 12.2).

Clearly, then, the EU faces some obstacles as it seeks to move forward. Many are feeling somewhat disaffected from the European integration experiment, and there is widespread concern over the future. None of this means that the EU is about to be derailed, however. The strongest support for the EU tends to come from members of the better educated, more economically successful segments of the society who exert considerable influence over political and social affairs. Moreover, the EU tends to be viewed more favorably by younger people than by those who are aged 55 or over. Even more importantly, the impacts of European integration are so pervasive that it would be extremely difficult to abandon the project now.

The question, then, is not so much whether the EU will continue to exist, but what form it will take. At the heart of the discussion are two fundamentally different perspectives on the future of European integration. One perspective views the EU as a big state in the making. Proponents of this perspective concede that much power remains vested in individual states and that the EU has some formidable internal divides to overcome, but they note that it took the United States nearly a century to forge a fairly unified state out of a disparate set of colonies. Europe, they argue, is simply engaged in the same drawn-out process.

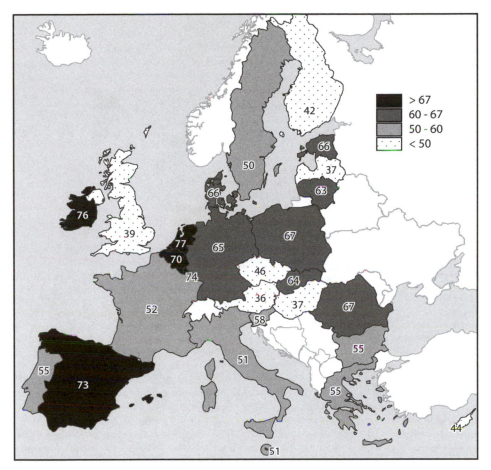

Figure 12.1. **Attitudes toward European integration in 2007 (percentage).** The numbers reflect agreement with the statement, "Membership in the EU is a good thing." *Source:* Eurobarometer.

In opposition to this perspective are those who view the idea of creating a big European state as infeasible, as a mistake, or both. They acknowledge that Europe has taken major strides both in widening and in deepening, but they argue that the great uncertainties unleashed by the recent expansion of the EU, the defeat of the proposed Constitution for the EU, and the divisive debate over new members reflect fundamental differences in Europe than cannot and should not be resolved through the concentration of ever greater powers in the central institutions of the EU. Instead, they see the future of the EU largely as an economic club where substantial powers continue to reside in the individual national capitals and where non-economic powers were limited to those areas only directly necessary to facilitate economic arrangements.

To make sense of the circumstances that give rise to these different positions, if not to resolve them, it is useful to look at some of the most important impetuses for integration and disintegration in contemporary Europe. We start on the integration side,

Figure 12.2. Trust in the European Union among EU member states and applicant countries, 2006 (percentage). Trust tends to be lowest in northern Europe (excluding Ireland) and a swath of countries through the European center. General levels of trust are comparatively high among the newest EU members *Source:* Eurobarometer.

but as we review the key catalysts of integration it is useful to keep in mind that some of them can be sources of disintegration as well.

Impetuses for Integration

GLOBALIZATION

As we have seen throughout this book, Europe has been shaped by forces beyond its borders for centuries, if not millennia. But the extent and pace of globalization has greatly accelerated over the past fifty years—most obviously in the economic arena. In the face of rapidly expanding networks of investment and economic exchange, many

European economists, business people, and everyday citizens believe that the region will be at a decisive disadvantage if its economies are divided among more than 45 relatively small-scale territorial units. They view the EU as a fundamental source of economic competitiveness—promoting intra-European trade, allowing major economic ventures to develop across state lines (a good example is the European consortium, Airbus), and enhancing Europe's clout in international economic and financial circles.

Bolstering this view is the great expansion of intra-European trade that has occurred as the European integration project has moved forward. No one knows exactly how much of the increase in trade can be attributed to integration, but the rise of the EEC/EC/EU has clearly played a key role in bolstering Europe-wide economic exchange. The adoption of a common currency by most long-standing EU members reflects and reinforces the growing integration of Europe's economic space (fig. 6.20). Integration has also given Europe more external economic clout by allowing European countries to speak as a bloc in global summits on economic and policy issues.

Given these circumstances, it is not surprising that some of the greatest support for European integration is found in Europe's major business and financial centers. This was well illustrated when the citizens of the Nordic countries voted on whether to join the EU in the mid-1990s. The Norwegians ultimately rejected EU membership, whereas the Swedes and Finns voted to join. Interestingly, though, the people living in the major urban nodes of all three countries supported EU membership (fig. 12.3), whereas those in rural areas were more hesitant to join. This pattern is common throughout much of Europe.

THE CHANGING GEOPOLITICAL ORDER

As was discussed in Chapter 6, the superpower-dominated Cold War order that took shape after World War II was an initial driver of European integration in the 1950s. Much has changed since then, but the idea that larger units are more likely to have influence at the global scale has endured. Thus there are still many Europeans who feel that the region is unlikely to be able to shape global developments, or even to chart its own path, if there is no significant coordination among its peoples and states.

Of course the Cold War is no longer with us, and there is much debate over where the global geopolitical order is, or should be, heading. But growing discussions about the breakdown of the world into competing regions based on religion and history has promoted integrationist impulses in some circles. Perhaps more importantly, the rise of an increasingly assertive, less collaborative United States during the early years of the twenty-first century fostered considerable support for integration in Europe because of a perceived need to provide a counterweight to the United States in the global arena. This argument was made with particular force in the aftermath of the U.S. invasion of Iraq in 2003 when a considerable majority of Europeans (although not all European governments) strongly opposed the U.S. initiative. The argument has become more muted in recent years as the U.S. has assumed a more consultative posture and as

Figure 12.3. The Nordic vote on European Union membership, 1995. Mapping the vote at the scale of the first-order substate regions highlights the continuities across the three northern European countries; even though the membership vote failed in Norway and succeeded in Sweden and Finland, the yes vote in all three countries was concentrated in the urban-economic core. *Source:* Based on a map in Murphy 1996, 286.

Europe has had to confront its own divisions over foreign policy matters. But the concern over the need for a counterweight to the United States in world affairs still serves as a strong impetus for European integration.

Looking back over the past fifty years, it is interesting to note how the United States has shifted from being a strong advocate of European integration in the 1950s to a position of ambivalence in the early 2000s. Yet the relationship with the United States is as strong a catalyst for integration as ever. What once was produced by persuasion, foreign aid, and a desire to emulate is now produced by concerns over domination and a struggle for influence in the international arena.

RELATIONSHIPS WITH SURROUNDING REGIONS

A corollary of the impetus for integration provided by global geopolitical developments is the advantage integration provides in the effort to confront issues and problems in and around Europe's margins. A particularly significant moment in this regard came when the Iron Curtain fell and the then-EC was confronted with a radically changed political and economic environment immediately to its east. Having long opposed the Soviet presence and championed the cause of democracy and economic liberalization in the eastern part of Europe, many in the EC felt a moral obligation to reach out to their newly liberated neighbors to the east. There were also practical concerns: If the EC did not step in and help what used to be called Eastern Europe get on its feet, the countries in the west could be faced with a set of unstable and potentially dangerous societies on their doorstep.

All of this produced a move to bring much of former Eastern Europe into the European integration project. The EC/EU provided the umbrella under which west and east could reengage, and the regulatory requirements that had to be met by the eastern countries in order to join the EC/EU were seen by many as critical to the process of reform. Thus, even though the recent expansion of the EU has introduced a new set of problems, it was also seen as a triumph for the idea of European integration. And European integration continues to be viewed as a force that is producing positive results in parts of southeastern Europe (including Turkey) that are not yet part of the EU. This is because the prospect of membership has fostered what many see as constructive reforms in would-be member states and may even have helped to quell violence in places such as Bosnia.

Somewhat farther afield, the EU as a bloc engages in negotiations with political entities in the Middle East and Africa over matters ranging from security to trade. Differences among EU countries sometimes turn these negotiations into sources of fragmentation rather than integration, but the ability of the EU to speak for Europe at large is often seen as a source of strength. For example, there is mounting concern that China's single-minded pursuit of economic exchange in Africa is undermining Europe's efforts to promote human rights or democratization in a region that has traditionally fallen principally within Europe's sphere of influence. Many Europeans feel that they are in a poor position to challenge China's approach if Europe cannot speak with one voice.

HEIGHTENED INTERACTION

European integration has clearly facilitated interactions and arrangements that make it difficult to think of Europe simply as a collection of states. Most obviously, European integration has served to make it almost inconceivable that another conflict will erupt in Europe like the ones set off in 1914 and 1939. The magnitude of this achievement should not be underestimated, nor should its importance as a catalyst for integration go unappreciated. A comparable achievement today would be to create the foundations for lasting peace and cooperation between Israelis and Palestinians. The magnitude of what has been achieved in Europe is widely recognized and it keeps many committed to the idea of European integration, even when disagreements arise over the ways in which integration is being pursued.

Furthering this sense is the increasing ease and frequency of movement of Europeans from one country to another. Students regularly travel to other countries to pursue their studies under an EU program known as Erasmus. Throughout most of Europe one no longer engages in the long waits to cross international borders that are characteristic of many parts of the world. This is because most longstanding EU members are signatories to the Schengen Agreement, which eliminates most border formalities between them (fig. 12.4). The "Schengen area" in Europe has been steadily expanding, and it is likely to continue to do so—furthering the momentum of the European integration project.

The economic interactions that have developed across Europe mean that people's well-being in one European state is intimately linked with what goes on in another. People regularly buy products aimed at the EU market as a whole. The packaging on those products reminds consumers that they are part of something larger than the state in which they live. They drive cars with license plates incorporating the EU flag. They carry passports with an EU designation, and they are often surrounded by organizations and businesses with a Europe-wide focus. All of this contributes to the sense that the EU represents a more-or-less irreversible process.

ECONOMIC ADVANCES

Considerable support for the integration project in some parts of Europe has come from gains in prosperity that have come from joining the EEC/EC/EU. States such as Ireland, Spain, and Greece have benefited heavily from the EU's "structural funds" (fig. 12.5)—and these are states where support for European integration is particularly strong. Similarly, the previously mentioned tendency for those in Europe's key urban-economic centers to support European integration reflects a widespread sense that integration has worked in favor of its major cities. Also, the development assistance that is dispersed by the EU has fostered support for the integration process—both in parts of the EU that have been beneficiaries, and in neighboring countries and regions where EU investment and aid has brought greater prosperity.

Growing prosperity in the newest member states in the European east is also helping to foster support for integration throughout much of that region. The economies of the newest member states lag behind their counterparts to the west (a source of

Figure 12.4.   Schengen Agreement countries, 2008. Many countries in eastern Europe only recently joined. More than 400 million Europeans can now travel across borders without formalities.

fragmentation, as we will see later), but since joining the EU, growth rates in the east have generally been strong, foreign direct investment from the western part of Europe has grown, and trade with longer-standing EU members has increased. Moreover, integration has opened a job market in western Europe for those from the east that has helped to reduce unemployment and bring money into some poor parts of the region. It is thus not surprising that the majority of citizens in countries such as Estonia, Poland, Slovakia, and Slovenia hold favorable views of European integration.

The adoption of the euro by many long-standing EU members (fig. 6.20) has also deepened the penetration of the European integration project into people's daily lives. Not everyone has been in favor of the euro, of course, and some argue that the common currency has increased the cost of living. Moreover, joining the **eurozone** requires meeting certain economic benchmarks, and membership means losing the ability to make the sorts of monetary adjustments that individual countries use to respond to

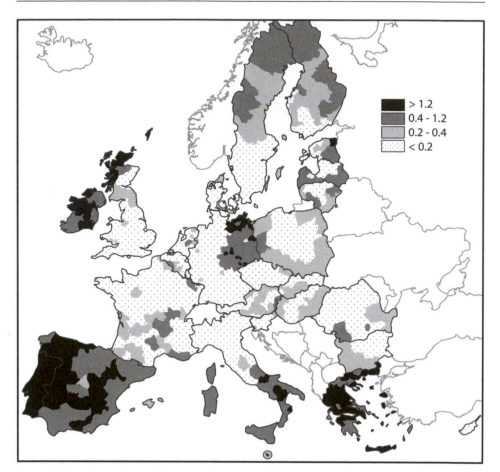

Figure 12.5.   Areas benefiting from European Union regional development funds (assistance funds as a percentage of regional GDP). Regions in newer EU member states are beginning to benefit, but the map shows the longstanding importance of regional assistance funding to Ireland, Portugal, Spain, and Greece. *Source:* Based on a map in European Spatial Planning Observation Network. *ESPON Synthesis Report III.* October 2006, 73.

specific national circumstances. This, in turn, has raised concerns in some circles about the loss of national autonomy and authority. Nevertheless, the euro has promoted yet more interaction of people and capital across national boundaries. It has also been accompanied by the establishment of a European Central Bank and a set of related economic arrangements that bring the member-state economies and fiscal practices into ever-closer alignment. It has made it increasingly difficult even to think about distinctly national economies in contemporary Europe.

THE "IRRATIONALITY" OF THE PATTERN OF STATES

Looking back over the many maps we have examined in this book, it is often easy to see how patterns on one map reflect those on another. Maps of terrain and precipitation help us understand agricultural patterns; population distribution maps reflect the influence of agricultural and environmental patterns; and so on. When it comes to the political pattern, however, it is almost as if all the other maps were thrown away and a new map was created from scratch. This is because political territories are more likely to come out of the vicissitudes of conquest and power balances than any underlying environmental or social arrangement. This also means that political boundaries rarely delimit discrete physical or human territories. Instead, the pattern of states bears little relationship to other human or physical patterns.

Even though the logic for the pattern of states rarely lies in underlying geographic conditions, states can work to change those geographic conditions and try to make them correspond more closely with their boundaries (e.g., by enforcing language policies that create language regions). Nonetheless, many "irrationalities" inevitably remain. States necessarily represent awkward territorial frameworks for dealing with environmental issues, economic development challenges, infrastructure planning, and much more because the spatial dimensions of these problems do not coincide with the territorial reach of the state. Against this backdrop, integration offers the potentially appealing prospect of being able to develop approaches to issues and problems that are more in keeping with the underlying geography of the problems themselves than is possible in a more territorially fragmented world region.

Many Europeans recognize that whether the issue is the construction of a high-speed transit network, the disposal of nuclear waste, the regulation of fisheries in surrounding waters, or the development of poor border areas, the European state system represents an obstacle to coordinated planning that can only be overcome through some kind of suprastate institutional initiative. They are thus drawn to the possibilities inherent in EU initiatives that take a non-state-based approach to issues and problems (see, e.g., fig. 12.6). On a more individual level, the ability to take advantage of people, resources, and even job opportunities outside one's country of birth represents an appealing prospect to many Europeans—particularly those living in towns and villages in border regions that would be cut off from their natural **hinterlands** if borders were to function the way they did during the first half of the twentieth century.

ETHNO-REGIONALISM

Despite the ability of most European states to create large-scale national communities within their borders, many ethno-regional minorities remain within and between European states—and many are looking for some degree of autonomy, or even independence (fig. 11.11). In one sense this might be thought of as an example of fragmentation, as ethno-regionalist movements have promoted a substantial **devolution** of authority in several European states over the past several decades—most notably in Belgium, Spain, and the United Kingdom. In all three of these cases, ethno-regionalist groups have managed to wrest considerable power from central authorities—and devolutionary pressures continue. Some Basques and Catalans in Spain, Corsicans in France, and Flemings in Belgium see independence as the ultimate goal.

Figure 12.6.   Future development scenarios within the European Union. The starting place is not the state but underlying patterns of socio-economic well-being. *Source:* Based on a map in European Spatial Planning Observation Network. *ESPON Synthesis Report III.* October 2006, 54.

Despite the disintegrative potential of these movements, they also serve as catalysts to integration because ethno-regionalists groups are often too small or vulnerable to go it alone, and the EU offers an appealing, alternative political-territorial framework to that of the traditional state. It is for this reason that some partisans of ethnic autonomist and separatist movements have been proponents of European integration. They see it as a development that ultimately weakens the power of the central governments of countries such as Spain, France, and the United Kingdom and as an alternative locus of power that is not rooted in the nation-state idea (Chapter 6). Many Catalans can identify more easily with Europe than with Spain.

As we will see in the next section, European integration has not been embraced by all proponents of ethno-regionalism. But the EU offers possibilities for ethno-regionalists that make European integration appealing to many. Regions can have direct access to Brussels, integration facilitates the cooperation of regions across state boundaries, and regionalists can even bring state governments to account in front of the judicial organs of the EU. These possibilities make ethno-regionalism a force favoring integration in a number of corners of Europe—as well as at the very core of the EU, where a substantial number of Flemings, and some Walloons, view Europe as an attractive alternative to Belgium.

Impetuses for Fragmentation

GLOBALIZATION

One of the principal critiques leveled against economic globalization is that it makes it increasingly difficult for local communities, or even states, to control their own economic futures. European integration is implicated in this critique, in that it has facilitated the process of expanding the scale of economic decision making and activity. Important fiscal and monetary decisions in Europe are now made above the level of the state. The elimination of trade barriers has made it hard for some small-scale farmers and business people to turn a profit. The ease of transacting business across national borders has facilitated the rise of large-scale, multi-national corporations that can take advantage of economies of scale that are not available to smaller businesses and industries.

All of these things help make Europe more competitive at the global scale and foster support for European integration among many of Europe's economic and political elite. But they can also foster resentment—particularly where local, traditional, smaller-scale interests are losing out to larger, more impersonal, externally controlled entities. The point is that globalization is a double-edged sword. Yes, it offers economic opportunities for some, but it can also erode the traditional protections offered by individual states and undermine people's quality of life. For the many Europeans who are concerned about the latter side of this equation, European integration is a mixed blessing at best.

The mid-1990s vote on EU membership in northern European countries (noted above) shows that skepticism about European integration is particularly intense in the rural sector (fig. 12.3). Many of the voters outside of the major cities were concerned that joining the EU would undermine the small-scale farming and business activities that are the mainstays of life in significant parts of the rural European north. Many of the areas with high numbers of "no" votes were eligible for EU regional development aid, but that was not enough to offset local voters' concerns over the erosion of their traditional modes of livelihood.

The phenomenon noted in the Nordic case can be found elsewhere in Europe as well—and not just in rural areas. Many Europeans are concerned about the erosion of the European welfare state (Chapter 11) and about the depersonalization of everyday life in the face of globalization. With the EU looking like the face of globalization to some, this inevitably has implications for the extent and depth of support for the European integration project.

THE CHANGING GEOPOLITICAL ORDER

Even though the geopolitical shifts of the past several decades have served as a catalyst for integration, they have also put Europeans in the position of needing to take positions on issues that are viewed in dissimilar ways in different parts of Europe. As such, they have exposed some of the region's more significant internal divisions and highlighted the challenges of creating a more integrated political space in Europe.

The EEC and EC had little authority over questions of international relations, but the EU has played an ever-more-significant and visible foreign-policy role. Foreign policy decisions often require confronting sensitive, highly charged matters that have traditionally been the prerogative of state governments. On matters ranging from the U.S. intervention into Iraq, to the Iranian nuclear program, to climate change, differences within the EU have not been easy to resolve. The difficulty of reaching agreement intensified when the new eastern-European member states joined in 2004 and succeeding years. These countries were faced with radically different political and economic circumstances during the decades after World War II. As a result, many of their citizens and leaders view foreign policy questions through a different lens than their counterparts in the west do.

The uncertainty of the geopolitical environment of the early twenty-first century heightens the potential for fragmentation that lies in Europe's encounter with the rest of the world. Is the world breaking down into competing blocs based on religious "civilizations?" To what extent is the rise of China an opportunity or a challenge? What role should NATO play in conflicts outside of Europe? Intense differences exist over questions such as these within states. When the EU becomes involved, the complexities grow. It is not surprising, then, that critics of the integration project highlight the inability of the EU to function as a strong international actor as an example of the limitations of integration. They further suggest that strengthening the EU's foreign policy competence would lead either to incoherence or to an unacceptable imposition of the views of some parts of Europe on other parts of the region.

NATIONALISM

Proponents of the integration process frequently herald the growing tendency for Europeans to identify with Europe. This tendency is well illustrated in public opinion surveys that ask people to indicate whether they consider themselves to be a particular nationality, European, or some combination of the two. The last such poll—taken in 2004 among the 15 members of the EU prior to May 1 of that year—shows that over 50% of the population in several important EU countries identified with the notion

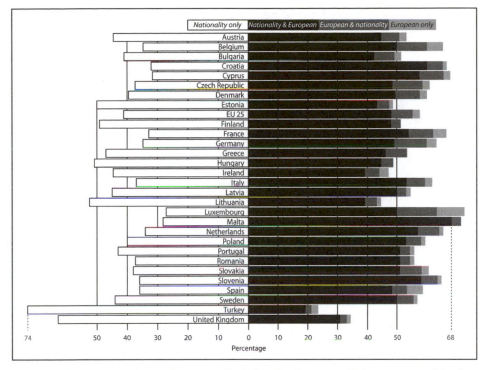

Figure 12.7.   Degree of identification with states, the European Union, or a combination of the two in longstanding EU member states. Even though a substantial number of Europeans identify to some degree with Europe, questionnaires of this sort highlight the continuing importance of nationalism in Europe. *Source:* Eurobarometer 2004.

of being "European" as well as being a member of a particular nationality—and the figure exceeded 35% in all countries except the United Kingdom (fig. 12.7).

For all the significance of these findings, there is another way to read these surveys. Respondents can choose among European only, European followed by nationality, nationality followed by European, and nationality only. The percentage of people who put Europe ahead of their own nationality (by answering either European only or European followed by nationality) is fairly small. Only in Luxembourg did the percentage exceed 20%, and in more than half the then-member states it was below 10%. Moreover, more than half the population in seven of the countries expressed no identification with Europe.

What this suggests is that nationalism is far from dead in Europe. Indeed, it remains a potent force that affects how most Europeans view integration. The bottom-line question for many Danes and Britons is whether integration is working in the interests of Denmark and the United Kingdom. There is much to suggest that the greater reservations toward the EU that were expressed by French and Swedes in the aftermath of the 2004 enlargement reflected a concern that their countries were losing clout within a larger EU. The enthusiasm of Poles and Hungarians for joining the western club has been tempered by a desire to ensure that their own distinctive national cultures do not get lost in the mix. And as has already been noted, the loss of the ability to set monetary policies has produced resentments in some countries within the eurozone and has kept other countries—notably the United Kingdom and Denmark—out of the zone.

The greatest problem that comes from comparing the Europe of the last fifty years with the early United States is that, for all the differences that existed among the original 13 U.S. colonies and the States that joined them in the decades following 1776, the peoples living in those States did not have a sense of identity or territorial attachment that was in any way comparable to the nationalist affinities that have been part of the modern European scene. Europe is clearly no longer in the Age of Nationalism that gave rise to World War I, but for the majority of Europeans, the "nation-state" still comes first. Nationalism thus remains the single greatest source of fragmentation in Europe—making it difficult for the EU to move beyond a system where individual states can veto important decisions or take actions that may be in the collective interest, but that disadvantage a few key states.

BUREAUCRATIZATION

The EU is a large, complicated institution with multiple branches—each accompanied by its own system of administration. A fair degree of bureaucratization is thus an inevitable part of European integration. But the EU's reputation for bureaucratization is enhanced by at least two aspects of the way it functions. First, at the heart of the project of creating a common European economic space is the development and enforcement of regulations. As such, many people see the EU primarily as a rule-generating bureaucracy. Second, much of the power in the EU is vested in a Council of Ministers from the various states, none of whom have been elected, and in a Commission of representatives appointed by state governments. Substantial power is thus wielded by individuals who were not directly elected, giving rise to concerns that the organization is encumbered by a "democratic deficit" (see Chapter 6). This too fuels a sense that the EU can be a bureaucratic maze.

Not surprisingly, concerns over bureaucratization are a source of fragmentation in Europe. Those opposing further integration frequently argue that Europeans should not delegate control over their fates to a distant, unresponsive bureaucracy in Brussels. This is an argument with growing traction in an enlarged EU. With ever more peoples and territories gathered under the EU umbrella, it becomes increasingly difficult for individuals and communities to see the EU as an organization over which they have meaningful control.

And then there are the concerns over administrative costs, which are substantial and which many regard as doing little to enhance well-being or the quality of life of most Europeans. Consider, for example, the cost of language services within the EU. Even before the 2004 enlargement, language services accounted for a significant percentage of the EU's administrative budget (see Chapter 4). With the addition of twelve new countries and multiple new languages, those costs have grown considerably. Another area of controversy is the cost of maintaining Strasbourg as the official seat of the European Parliament, even though much of the day-to-day parliamentary business is conducted in Brussels. Every month vast sums are expended shipping people, documents, and equipment back and forth between the two cities. This irks many, but there is little incentive for France to let the European Parliament go to Brussels.

DIFFERENCES OVER WIDENING AND DEEPENING

From the perspective of those living in Western Europe prior to 1989, the only possible candidates for admission into the EEC/EC were those countries lying to the west of the Iron Curtain. The disintegration of the post-World War II order, however, opened up the question of what exactly constituted Europe, or at least what areas might or should be eligible for inclusion in the European integration project. There was little debate over the first tier of countries abutting former Western Europe's eastern boundary, but the situation beyond that was much murkier. The very process of opening up the question of what might constitute Europe (at least for integration purposes) fostered uncertainty and debate that has not yet been resolved. The EC/EU could no longer define itself in opposition to a Soviet-dominated east; it now needed a different *raison d'être*.

Confronting the diversity of views on this matter is a major and on-going challenge for the EU. Some want to see the EU as little more than a loosely linked economic space; they tend to favor as much widening as makes sense in terms of Europe's economic relationships, but they are not interested in further deepening. Many in this camp see widening as a guarantee against further deepening, as widening makes it more difficult to develop centralized approaches to issues and problems that are supported throughout the EU. At the other end of the spectrum are those who want to see Europe emerge as an ever better integrated economic, social, and even political space. Many of them are concerned that widening will undermine the ability of the EU to move in this direction—making them cautious about admitting new members. In between these two positions are a diversity of alternative perspectives, some of which do not treat widening and deepening as oppositional, some of which highlight the advantages of admitting specific countries for particular strategic or economic reasons, and some of which want to see some parts of the EU move faster toward integration than others.

Reconciling these different views is not an easy task; indeed they are at the heart of the current impasse over where the EU is headed. Differences in perspective are manifest most clearly in the debate over Turkey's potential membership in the EU. Turkey has long been a candidate to join the EU. Some see this as a positive step for Turkey and the EU—rewarding Turkey for reforms in recent years, bringing an important new economy into the mix, and undermining the notion that Europe stands in opposition to a purported Islamic regional bloc. Others oppose Turkish membership out of concern that Turkey is too different culturally and economically and that Turkish membership would make further deepening almost impossible. Proponents of this view argue that if Turkey joins the EU, there is no logical basis for denying membership to Ukraine, and perhaps Russia down the line—leading to an EU that stretches from the Atlantic to the Pacific. Former French President Valery Giscard d'Estaing echoed this line of thinking when he headed the group charged with drafting a new Constitution for Europe. He suggested that if Turkey were admitted to the EU, Morocco would reasonably expect to follow, and perhaps Lebanon and Israel—leading to the end of the EU as we know it.

It is not yet clear how these debates will be resolved. Opinion polls indicate that Turkish membership does not have broad support among the citizens of current EU member states, but public opinion can be fluid. What lies behind the Turkish debate, though, are the more fundamental differences in how European integration is conceived, which were sketched out at the beginning of this chapter. A considerable majority of Britons are interested in little more than an economic union, whereas most Dutch, Irish, and Belgians are looking for something very different.

HEIGHTENED INTERACTION

At the heart of the widening versus deepening debate are questions about the impacts of growing interactions between places with different socioeconomic and cultural characteristics. As we saw earlier, interaction has been an important catalyst for integration in Europe, but when peoples with substantially different standards and ways of living are joined together in a formal process of integration, interaction can serve as a source of fragmentation as well. The disintegrative tendencies of interaction typically revolve around the difficulties of forging formal linkages among countries in very different economic circumstances and the tensions associated with the movement across international boundaries of peoples from divergent economic and cultural backgrounds.

Difficulties and tensions of this sort have been in evidence each time the EEC/EC/EU has been joined by new states that were clearly less well off and that had been isolated from longer-standing member states (for example, Greece, Spain, and Portugal). But the addition of ten new eastern European countries in the mid-2000s raised the stakes considerably. The recent enlargements were different from their predecessors both in the number of states and peoples involved and in the economic diversities they brought into the fold. As figure 12.8 shows, the newest EU members in the east are far behind their western counterparts in terms of gross national product per capita; even with relatively high growth rates, it will take decades for many of them to reach parity with most western European countries.

The difficulty of confronting these differences has raised significant doubts in the minds of many about the future of the European integration project. Exacerbating the problem is the growing movement of people between lesser and better-off parts of the EU. Even before the recent enlargements, concerns were being raised in the United Kingdom and France about the potential for a flood of Polish plumbers (the symbolic example) to come in and swamp local labor markets. Of course, many recognized that migrant laborers could fill important vacant niches in the labor markets of the receiving countries, but there was significant concern that

Figure 12.8.   Gross National Product per capita in EU member states (in U.S. dollars).
The impact of Europe's post-World War II division remains very much in evidence.
Source: CIA. The World Factbook.

jobs would be taken from locals and that salaries and social protections would be diminished. In the early years after the mid-2000s enlargements, the movement of peoples from east to west was modest, but mobility has been accelerating, as have concerns over the impacts of growing mobility on local economies and workers. Those concerns, in turn, translate into negative attitudes toward European integration more generally.

The disintegrative potential of mobility can be the greatest when cultural differences are at play. As was noted in Chapter 11, the movement of Roma peoples into Italy has led to violence and has fostered considerable concern about European integration among segments of the Italian population. To a lesser extent, the growing visibility of Polish, Slovakian, and Bulgarian communities (to use three random examples) in parts of western European has ignited social tensions that are undermining support for integration among some segments of the population.

ETHNO-REGIONALISM

Earlier we noted the interest of some ethno-regionalists in supporting European integration as an alternative to the state. Yet ethno-regionalism must be thought of as a force promoting fragmentation, not just integration. There are two reasons for this: ethno-regionalist movements have not been uniformly supportive of integration, and ethno-regionalism carries with it the potential for an increasingly disaggregated Europe that can make integration ever more difficult to achieve.

Turning to the first of these points, integration presents a dilemma for ethno-regionalist leaders seeking to promote greater autonomy. Europe may represent an alternative to the state, but there is little interest in substituting one source of external rule (the state) for another, even more distant, source of authority (the EU). With that in mind, some ethno-nationalists are hesitant to support European integration. Those taking this position are not necessarily opposed to a loosely constructed EU, but they do not want to see the EU evolve into a state-like entity.

The ultimate goal of the more assertive ethno-nationalist movements is to create new spaces on the European political map with considerable capacity to control their own affairs. To the extent that such goals are achieved—if there were to be a Flanders and a Wallonia instead of just a Belgium sitting at the EU table, for example—the European integration challenge could become yet more complicated because there would be a growing number of units to accommodate. This is not a major issue at the moment, as there are relatively few ethno-regionalist movements that are likely to give rise to independent or quasi-independent territories in the near future, but devolution cannot be ignored as a potential source of fragmentation in the decades to come.

Where from Here?

In 2006 the international affairs editor of the *Financial Times*, Quentin Peel, made reference to an "underlying concern that the EU has become too big, too distant and, for a growing number, too threatening to their livelihoods." This quote captures much of the concern that is circulating in Europe today about the status of the European integration experiment. Predictions are inevitably hazardous, but European integration appears to be facing a rocky period in the short-to-medium term. This is because, for all the progress that has been made in the name of integration, recent developments have raised questions about whether "widening" can be accomplished without threatening "deepening," even as they have challenged the idea that state nationalism will increasingly recede in the face of an ever more integrated union.

Most obviously, the recent enlargements of the EU have introduced important new differences and complexities. Adding twelve new members during the mid-2000s necessitated significant adjustments in the way the EU functions. Important steps are being taken to address the new realities, but a host of fiscal and power-sharing issues will continue to occupy the EU for some time to come, including politically difficult matters, such as the degree to which some areas in the EU are willing to subsidize the economic development of other areas. And those adjustments have to be worked out at a time of growing distrust of the EU.

All of this suggests that, at least for a time, the EU is likely to take a cautious approach to admitting new member states. It also suggests that it will be difficult to assemble the consensus needed to expand significantly the authority of the EU. There is already much discussion of what some call enlargement fatigue among the populace of the EU's long-standing member states. Despite evidence to the contrary, many western Europeans are even questioning whether the enlarged EU continues to be economically beneficial. A 2006 Eurobarometer survey showed that only 43% of Europeans agreed with the statement "in economic terms, the enlargement of the European Union increases prosperity for all Europeans." Agreement with the statement exceeded 50% in only five EU-15 countries: Greece (52%), Belgium (51%), Sweden (51%), Spain (51%), and Ireland (61%). By contrast, only 30% of Germans and only 34% of the French agreed with this statement.

Among countries that have expressed interest in joining the EU, only Croatia, Turkey, and Macedonia were officially candidate countries by early 2008. Croatia and Macedonia could join without any major adjustments in institutional arrangements, and their admission would likely not be seen as a major enlargement. Turkey is another matter. As we have seen, many Europeans are quite concerned about adding Turkey to the EU. Managing the debate over the issue is likely to be one of the more volatile challenges facing the European integration project in the years ahead.

As for deepening, the depth and extent of the negative attitudes toward the EU in countries such as the United Kingdom, Austria, Sweden, and Finland make it very difficult for the EU to assume greater powers. Until the early 2000s, most significant EU decisions had to be agreed to unanimously by all member states. A system of qualified majorities came into play in 2001 with the signing of the Treaty of Nice, but it is still difficult to push through major reforms when they are opposed by one or more of the larger states. Unless opinion swings more favorably toward the EU, then, it will be difficult to extend the EU's administrative and judicial competence into new areas.

The EU had to work out new procedures in the wake of the 2004 enlargement and the 2005 defeat of the Constitution. By late 2007 a treaty was signed in Lisbon (known as the Treaty of Lisbon or the Reform Treaty) embodying many of the principles that were contained in the Constitution, but eliminating references that make the EU sound like a state (including the word Constitution) and providing opt-outs for the United Kingdom, Poland, and Ireland on matters deemed to be invasive of national sovereignty by the leaders of those countries. The treaty was designed to create an EU president and foreign minister, adjust the qualified-majority voting system, set the distribution of parliamentary seats, and reduce the number of EU Commissioners. By framing it as a treaty rather than a Constitution, ratification could occur in national parliaments rather than by referendum—thereby increasing the likelihood of passage. Nonetheless, Ireland held a public vote on the treaty in 2008, and it was defeated. The precise legal character of the EU thus remains in flux.

Whatever the precise configuration of the EU in the years ahead, the challenge of confronting disaffection will likely remain significant. Moreover, it seems increasingly clear that efforts aimed largely at making the EU bigger and more powerful will not address that challenge, and may even be counterproductive. With that in mind, the time may be at hand when the EU needs to move away from large-scale, state-like projects, such as monetary union, and toward the sorts of initiatives that can give people a stronger sense that the EU is not just a replacement for the state—but instead offers possibilities beyond the state.

In considering what those possibilities might be, it is important to recognize that even though many Europeans define their interests and their larger identity in European terms, they are not necessarily doing so at the expense of their traditional cultural identities and concerns. By extension, many do not want to see a large, economically oriented bureaucracy assume responsibilities in areas that threaten traditions of local autonomy. This suggests that the much-talked about, but little-followed, EU principle of "subsidiarity"—the idea that decisions should be made at the lowest level and

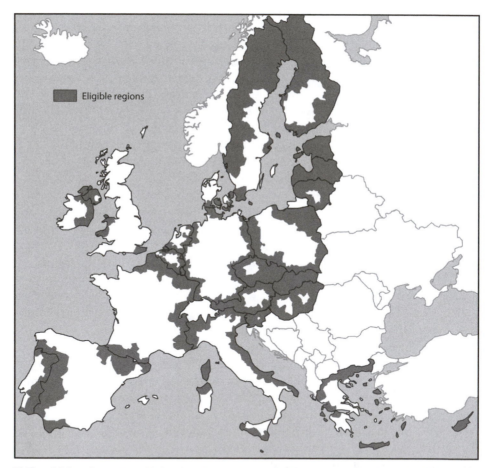

Figure 12.9.   European Union border regions eligible to participate in the EU's Interreg III program. The program fosters transboundary and transnational cooperation. Some kind of active transboundary cooperation is now taking place across many borders in the EU, as well as between border regions in EU and non-EU states. *Source:* European Union, http://ec.europa.eu/regional_policy/index_en.htm.

Figure 12.10.   Regions participating in the Four Motors Agreement. The agreement links economically dynamic regions in four core European states. Agreements such as this have the potential to alter the economic geography of Europe and to destabilize the idea that most of what matters in Europe can be captured by the traditional map of states. *Source:* Murphy 1996.

smallest scale appropriate to the issue at hand—needs renewed consideration. It also suggests that the EU, if it is to be successful, should not be a framework promoting homogeneity, but should be a forum that facilitates flexible cooperation across Europe at a variety of different levels. This means focusing not just on interstate relations, but on regions as well.

The idea that integration could give rise to a "Europe of the Regions" has always been part of the movement for European unity. The regions encompassed by this expression are usually understood to be simply administrative subdivisions of states, but more imaginative regional constructions can be part of the picture as well. One of the most interesting spillover effects of European integration is the development of increasingly important links among and between regions in different countries. Some of these are developing directly across international boundaries (fig. 12.9), whereas others involve geographically dispersed regions (e.g., fig. 12.10). In a potentially significant departure from the state-based perspective that has dominated most decision making in the EU, efforts are now being made to facilitate these regional linkages. Beginning in the early 1990s the EC established a funded program to support cross-border cooperation schemes (INTERREG). Local representatives from border areas may apply for funds to encourage administrative and economic cooperation across the border. The program has expanded over the years, and the EU has adopted new programs aimed at encouraging collaborations among more geographically distant regions. Developments such as these demonstrate the role the EU can play in overcoming problems arising from the fragmentation of Europe into many relatively small states.

As we saw in Chapter 6, the modern state system is premised on the idea that the surface of the earth should be divided up into discrete national territories, each with its own sovereign government. That idea is currently being challenged, yet it continues to shape the way Europeans and others see the world. Nowhere is this more apparent than in the traditional way of viewing European integration, which measures progress in terms of whether the EU is able to wrestle more and more power away from the state. But the current challenges facing the EU highlight the problem with that approach. Although the EU is not about to go away, its future is uncertain if it can only be seen as a big state where there used to be many small ones. Instead, the EU's most promising prospects arguably lie in arrangements that help Europeans overcome the rigidities of the traditional European state system without sacrificing respect for local interests and concerns. If it succeeds in this endeavor, the part of the world that gave birth to the modern state might well be the place that ultimately transcends it.

Sources and Suggested Readings

Agnew, J. A. 2001. How Many Europes? The European Union, Eastward Enlargement Uneven Development. *European Urban and Regional Studies* 8 (1): 35–38.

Bauman, Z. 2004. *Europe: An Unfinished Adventure.* Malden, MA: Polity Press.

Brunt, B. M. 1995. Regions and Western Europe. *Journal of Geography* 94: 306–316.

Cameron, F., ed. 2004. *The Future of Europe: Integration and Enlargement.* New York: Routledge.

Clout, H. 1986. *Regional Variations in the European Community.* Cambridge: Cambridge University Press.

Cole, J. and F. Cole. 1997. *The Geography of the European Union, 2nd ed.* New York: Routledge.

Dahlman, C. 2004. Turkey's Accession to the European Union: A Geopolitical and Cultural Assessment, *Eurasia Geography and Economics* 45 (8): 553–574.

Delamaide, D. 1994. *The New Superregions of Europe.* New York: Plume/Penguin.

Heffernan, M. 1998. *The Meaning of Europe: Geography and Geopolitics.* New York: Arnold.

Hudson, R. and A. M. Williams. 1999. *Divided Europe: Society and Territory.* London: Sage.

Judt, T. 1996. *A Grand Illusion?: An Essay on Europe.* New York: Hill and Wang.

Kepka, J. and A. B. Murphy. 2002. Euroregions in Comparative Perspective: Differential Implications for Europe's Borderlands. In J. Hakli and D. Kaplan, eds. *Boundaries and Place.* Boulder: Rowman & Littlefield, 50–69.

Kramer, S. P. 2006. The End of French Europe? *Foreign Affairs* 85 (4): 126–138.

Kramsch, O. T. and B. Hooper, eds. 2004. *Cross-Border Governance in the European Union, Transnationalism.* Routledge Research in Transnationalism. New York: Routledge.

Mau, S. 2006. Die Politik der Grenze: Grenzziehung und Politische Systembildung in der Europäischen Union. *Berliner Journal für Soziologie* 16 (1): 115–132.

Morris, J. 1997. *Fifty Years of Europe.* New York: Villard.

Murphy, A. B. 2006. The May 2004 Enlargement of the European Union: View from Two Years Out. *Eurasian Geography and Economics* 47 (6): 635–646.

Murphy, A. B. 2006. The Changing Face of U.S.—Europe Relations: Geopolitical Causes and Possible Consequences. *GeoJournal* 66 (4): 285–293.

Murphy, A. B. and A. Hunderi-Ely. 1996. The Geography of the 1994 Nordic Vote on European Union Membership. *Professional Geographer* 48 (3): 284–297.

Murphy, A. B. and C. M. Johnson. 2004. German Geopolitics in Transition. *Eurasian Geography and Economics* 45 (1): 1–17.

Newhouse, J. 1997. Europe's Rising Regionalism. *Foreign Affairs* 76 (1): 67–84.

Pedersen, Roy N. 1992. *One Europe/100 Nations.* Clevedon, UK: Channel View Books.

Pfaff, W. 2005. What's Left of the Union? *The New York Review of Books* 52 (12): 26–29.

Timmins, G. and D. Jovi´c. 2006. Introduction: The Next Wave of Enlargement: The European Union and Southeast Europe after 2004. *Journal of Southern Europe and the Balkans* 8 (1): 1–5.

Schott, M. 2007. Geopolitical Imaginations about the European Union in Recent Political Discussions. *Tijdschrift voor Economische en Sociale Geografie* 98 (2): 284–295.

Sellar, C. and J. Pickles. 2002. Where Will Europe End?: Ukraine and the Limits of European Integration. *Euraisan Geography and Economics* 43 (2): 123–142.

Sidaway, J. D. 2006. On the Nature of the Beast: Re-Charting Political Geographies of the European Union. *Geografiska Annaler, Series B* 88 (1): 1–14.

Stephanou, C. A., ed. 2006. *Adjusting to EU Enlargement.* Cheltenham Glos, UK: Edward Elgar Publishing.

Stuart, E. and B. Luiza. 2006. The New Geopolitics of Division and the Problem of a Kantian Europe. *Review of International Studies* 32 (4): 623.

Zielonka, J. 2006. *Europe as Empire: The Nature of the Enlarged European Union.* Oxford: Oxford University Press.

Glossary

Acid precipitation—Rain or snow that has a higher level of acidity because of a chemical reaction between water in the atmosphere and industrial pollutants.

Afforestation—The replanting of forests.

Afro-Asiatic—The language family that dominates much of the Middle East and North Africa. Includes Arabic, Hebrew, and Maltese.

Age of Discovery—The period from the fifteenth to the seventeenth centuries during which European mariners, notably the Spanish, Portuguese, British, Dutch, and French, traveled the world in search of resources, lands, and peoples to claim for their respective crowns.

Agribusiness—Large-scale, commercialized, market-oriented agriculture.

Alpine Period—Period of significant tectonic activity between c. 100 and 60 million years ago that resulted in the creation of east-west mountain ranges in Europe, such as the Alps and the Pyrenees.

Altaic—A language family thought to have originated around the Altai Mountains of Central Asia. Includes Turkish, Tatar, Azeri, and Gagauz.

Animism—Religious practices that imbue objects such as rocks, heavenly bodies, mountains, forests, and rivers with souls.

Anti-empire nationalism—The effort by a national group living within an empire to create a sovereign nation-state of their own.

Arable land—Land suitable for agriculture.

Armenian Orthodox Apostolic Church—Officially a branch of Eastern Orthodoxy, it has an independent status because it never acknowledged the supremacy of the Patriarch at Constantinople.

Ashkenazim—Jews who settled primarily in western and southern Germany and the Kingdom of Poland. They often spoke Yiddish, a German-derived language written in Hebrew.

Azores anticyclone—A high-pressure system generally situated in the North Atlantic. Its seasonal movement off the northwest African and southwest European coasts contributes to the Mediterranean climate found throughout much of southern Europe.

401

Baltic—A subfamily of the Indo-European languages originating west of the Pripyat Marshes. Over time it lost ground to Germanic and Slavic speakers and is now represented by Latvian and Lithuanian.

Bora—A periodic wind that blows from north to south into the Adriatic, Greece, and Turkey, particularly in the winter. It brings cold snaps to parts of southeastern Europe.

British city—The type of city found in the British Isles that generally has a higher degree of semidetached, single-family residences and greater functional zonation than the typical continental European city.

Capitalism—An economic system based on private ownership in which land and goods are exchanged at prices determined by free-market competition.

Caucasic—A language family to the southeast of the Indo-European family in the Caucauses. Includes Georgian.

Celtic—A subfamily of Indo-European that was once dominant throughout Europe, but now is mostly confined to the northwestern periphery. Includes Welsh, Breton, Cornish, and Gaelic.

Central European city—The most common type of city found in Europe, characterized by compactness, a low degree of functional zonation, a core that is both historic and relatively prosperous, and surrounding suburbs, some of which are industrial and relatively poor.

Checkerboard village—A village with a relatively rigid rectilinear street pattern, a legacy of the Roman imperial land survey.

City-states—Cities that function as independent political entities. The ancient city-states of Greece are classic examples.

Collective agriculture—The system implemented in Communist states in which fragmented private landholdings were replaced by large communal farms.

Colonialism—Rule by an autonomous power over a subordinate, usually distant people. Because of the scope and scale of European colonialism that began in the sixteenth century, the term is often used to refer specifically to the European colonial project of the last 500 years.

Communication—The transmission of information and ideas among and between peoples and places.

Composite language—A language whose form was taken from more than one language.

Continent—Conventionally a sizeable landmass standing more or less separate from other landmasses. In the case of Europe and Asia the term is stretched to denote major world regions that were once considered to be separate realms.

Corriolis effect—The process by which the rotation of the earth deflects the movement of ocean and atmospheric currents clockwise in the northern hemisphere and counter-clockwise in the southern hemisphere.

Cottage industry—Secondary economic activities produced at home using simple technology. Generally confined to farm villages as a sideline to agriculture.

Counterurbanization—The movement of people from the largest cities to smaller towns and cities that lie beyond the commuting range of their former places of residence.

Cuesta—A ridge of tilted sedimentary rock with a gentle slope on one side and a moderately steep drop-off on the other.

Cultural landscape—The visible trace of human presence on the land, consisting of an assemblage of tangible physical and human features found in an area.

Culture area—A region that is thought of as the homeland of a people who hold numerous beliefs, behaviors, and overall ways of life in common, including ideology, technology, social institutions, and material possessions.

Dechristianization—A term used to describe the move toward secularization that has occurred recently in parts of Europe.

Deindustrialization—The decline or abandonment of industrial activity in a region.

Demographic transition—The shift from high birth rates and high death rates to low birth rates and low death rates in the wake of industrialization and urbanization. Because death rates historically fell before birth rates, the demographic transition is associated with a period of rapid population increase followed by low, or even negative population growth.

Desire paths—Paths through natural areas that are chosen for convenience, which then gradually solidify into streets.

Devolution—The transfer of governmental competencies from the state to sub-state regions.

Dialect net—A linguistic zone of multiple dialects in which the speakers of each dialect can understand the neighboring ones but not those farther away in regions with which they have no regular contact.

Dialects—Variants of standardized languages.

Diaspora—The dispersal of a cultural or ethnic group from a homeland. Originally referred to the dispersal of the Jewish people from Ancient Palestine.

Dikes—Human-constructed banks along the edges of water bodies that are designed to protect against flooding.

Eastern European city—An eastern European variant of the Central European city characterized by large public spaces, massive public housing projects, and a particularly low degree of functional zonation.

Eastern Orthodoxy—A form of Christianity prevailing in eastern Europe that arose from the church in Byzantine Constantinople.

Ecotourism—Tourism designed to promote sustainability by minimizing long-term damage to nature or local customs.

Esker—Narrow gravel-lined channel that is produced by a stream lying under an ice sheet.

Ethnic cleansing—The attempt by one ethnic group to eliminate another ethnic group from a place or region.

Eurasia—Term combining Europe and Asia into a single continent instead of two.

Eurocentrism—A perspective that looks at developments around the world through the lens of European circumstances and beliefs. Eurocentrism typically is premised on the idea of European superiority.

Eurorussia—The portion of Russia to the west of the Ural Mountains often regarded as belonging to Europe.

Eurozone—The states that have adopted the European Union's common currency: the euro.

Façadism—The complete gutting and remodeling of the interior of a building while preserving its façade.

Faubourg—An early form of suburb, particularly in France.

Federal state—A state in which internal states or provinces retain considerable power or even autonomy.

Feudal system—A loosely-organized, not strictly hierarchical political-economic system binding nobles, local landowners, and peasants together through a set of reciprocal obligations. The feudal system was found throughout much of Europe in the Middle Ages.

Föhn—In southern Germany, a warm, dry wind from the south that results when a cyclonic storm moving north of the Alps in the winter draws drier, warmer winds over the mountains from the Mediterranean lands.

Fontanili—An east-west line of springs in the Po-Veneto Plain where the groundwater table reaches the surface.

Functional zonation—The segregation of different functions (retailing, manufacturing, residential) in different areas within a city.

Gentrification—The rehabilitation of deteriorated or abandoned areas and the concomitant replacement of low-income people by those who are more affluent.

Geolinguistics—The study of language changes over space and through time.

Geomorphology—The scientific study of landforms, including the processes that shape them.

Germanic—A major subfamily of the Indo-European languages that arose in Jutland and spread throughout northern and west-central Europe. Includes German, English, Danish, Swedish, Norwegian, Icelandic, and Dutch.

Ghetto—Originally a Jewish neighborhood, in particular the Jewish quarter in medieval Venice. The term now refers to a poor area dominated by minority groups who have little choice but to stay there.

Green village—A compact village in which the houses are grouped around a central green or commons that serves as a market place, a festival ground, and a protected enclosure for livestock.

Guest workers—Immigrants invited by national governments to come into a country for a time in response to labor shortages. Many guest workers end up staying more or less permanently.

Guild—A professional organization of free artisans skilled in a particular craft; skills were passed down generation to generation through an apprenticeship system.

Gulf Stream—A warm ocean current originating in the Gulf of Mexico that influences the climate of the eastern United States and Canada as well as western Europe.

Hanseatic League (Hansa)—A trading union of towns around the shores of the North and Baltic seas in the Late Medieval and Early Modern periods.

Hardscrabble belts—Regions separating and surrounding the favored lands of the three-field farming and Mediterranean agriculture, afflicted with broken terrain, excessive cloudiness, and/or sterile soils.

Heat island—A zone of higher temperatures in cities resulting from the reflective properties of urbanized landscapes.

Hellenic—A subfamily of the Indo-European languages to which modern Greek belongs.

Hercynian Period—Period of significant tectonic activity between c. 280 and 240 million years ago resulting in the uplift of areas along Europe's northwestern fringe and into the main west-European landmass (including the Ardennes, Vosges, and Blackforest).

High-tech industry—Industries producing high-technology products such as electronic and microelectronic devices, data processing equipment, and robotics, as well as firms that make use of high-tech products in the manufacturing process.

Hinterland—The zone surrounding an urban area that regularly provides goods and people needed to sustain the urban area.

Holocene—The current interglacial period, which began some 10,000 years ago.

Homo sapiens—Modern humans.

Human development—A measure of human well-being that includes not just economic circumstances, but also health, social and psychological well-being, education, and human security.

Hydrogeography—The study of the distribution and spatial character of streams and bodies of water on the surface of the earth.

Ice Age—A geologic period characterized by multiple cold episodes, called glacials, interrupted by periodic warmer times known as interglacials. The earth has been in an ice age since at least the beginning of the Pleistocene, some 1.65 million years ago.

Indo-European—One of the major language families of the world, and the dominant language family in Europe. In Eurasia, Indo-European languages are spoken from Europe to India.

Industrial Revolution—The invention of diverse machines and the harnessing of inanimate power that began in Great Britain in the 1700s, leading to countless crucially influential inventions such as the steam engine, railroad, internal combustion engine, automobile, expressway, radio, orbital satellites, manned space flight, and the digital computer.

Industrial suburb—An area immediately outside a city proper—characterized by factories, huge workers' apartment blocks or row houses, and transportation facilities.

Infant mortality rate—The number of children per thousand who do not survive to the age of one year.

Islam—A religion arising out of the Arabian Peninsula and based on the teachings of the prophet Mohammad, as set forth in the Koran.

Isogloss—A line on a map signifying a linguistic boundary of some sort.

Isostatic rebound—The gradual uplift that occurs when a segment of the earth's surface that has been depressed by the weight of an ice sheet loses the heavy layer of ice that depressed it. As the area rebounds, adjacent areas are sometimes pulled downward.

Karst topography—A landscape dominated by permeable limestone, which has numerous large sinks or troughs caused by water filtering down through the limestone.

Land consolidation—Redrawing property lines to reduce or eliminate the fragmentation of holdings.

Land reform—A process intended to distribute land more equally. Often large landholdings are broken up to allow more people to own their own land.

Language families—A grouping of languages that share broad similarities in structure and vocabulary.

Latifundia—System in which nobility has control over large estates, which are divided into small units and farmed by indentured peasants.

Lingua franca—A common language that is used as a means of communication among speakers of diverse tongues.

Littoral—The coast or shore of a water body.

Loess—Wind-deposited, fine-textured sediment that was originally produced by glaciers and ice sheets grinding up rock.

Market gardening—Also known as truck farming. Small-scale agriculture, typically orchards, vineyards, and vegetable plots.

Marxism—A body of political, economic, social, and cultural theories based on the writings of Karl Marx and Friedrich Engels. Marxism particularly seeks to explain the economic and social consequences of industrial capitalism.

Medieval Warm Period—Sometimes called the Medieval Optimum, a period between the ninth and twelfth centuries that brought warmer average temperatures to much of Europe.

Mediterranean agriculture—The distinctive agrarian system traditionally practiced in Cyprus, Greece, the eastern Adriatic coast, peninsular Italy, the Languedoc Plain, and southern Iberia.

Mediterranean city—A southern European variant of the Central European city characterized by greater spontaneity of growth and development and less segregation by socio-economic class.

Megalopolis—An immense conurbation resulting from the growing-together of several large cities.

Mercantile city—An urban center in which trade is the most important economic activity.

Mercantilism—An economic system based on commercial production and trade.

Milankovitch Cycle—A cycle of global warming and cooling cause by changes in (1) the shape of the earth's orbit, (2) the tilt of the earth on its axis, and (3) the earth's position in its orbit at equinox. The Milankovitch cycle has produced repeated glacial advances and retreats during the Pleistocene.

Mistral—A regular wind that blows from north to south down the Rhône-Saône corridor into the Mediterranean, particularly in the winter and spring. The mistral brings cold air into the coastal fringe of France and beyond.

Modernity—A set of ideas and practices set in motion by the sixteenth-century European Enlightenment that was rooted in the idea that reason and scientific rationality would lead to progress.

Monotheism—The religious practice of worshipping a single deity.

Moraine—Debris scraped up and deposited at the foot of glaciers.

Morphology—The external form, structure, and organization of a thing or place.

Motes—Small hills in Ireland erected as fortifications by invading Normans in the Middle Ages.

Nation—A group of people with a shared sense of culture and history and a desire to control their own affairs.

Nationalism—The glorification of a particular nation and the historic homeland it claims as its own.

Nation-state—Originally a sovereign political territory associated with a group of people with a shared sense of culture and history. In many circles the term has come to be used as a synonym for an independent state.

Neanderthal—A hominid living in Europe between c. 200,000 and 30,000 years ago that became extinct in the wake of the arrival of *Homo sapiens*.

Neolithic Revolution—The domestication of plants and animals.

Nomadic herders—People who move with their animals, often in a regular cyclic pattern, to take advantage of multiple natural grazing areas.

Nordic city—The type of city found in Scandinavia and Finland that is relatively recent in origin and that bears more evidence of planning and functional zonation than most other European cities.

North Atlantic Drift—An extension of the Gulf Stream, bringing warm ocean currents to northwestern Europe.

Occupational specialization—Also known as division of labor. A circumstance in which workers perform particular tasks within a production chain, thereby increasing productivity.

Orographic Effect—Process by which humid air masses moving from west to east rise over hill and mountain barriers, cooling and decreasing their ability to hold moisture in an evaporated state. This produces precipitation on west-facing slopes.

Othering—Defining one group or area in negative opposition to other groups or areas.

Polders—Areas of land that have been reclaimed from the sea by dikes and water-pumping systems.

Polytheism—The religious practice of worshipping multiple deities.

Postindustrial—The rise to dominance of quaternary-sector industries coincident with the decline of primary and secondary industries.

Postindustrial suburbs—The outer ring of suburbs that developed since the 1950s, consisting of a loose assemblage of low-density residences dominated by detached single-family houses, modern factories devoted to high-tech industry, firms specializing in data gathering and processes, and high-rise commercial towers.

Potential Support Ratio—A measure of the number of persons aged 15–64 years per one older person aged 65 years or older.

Preindustrial core—The densely packed center of a city that was already built up before the Industrial Revolution.

Preindustrial periphery—The part of a city surrounding the preindustrial core into which urbanization was spreading before the Industrial Revolution.

Primary economic activities—Those involved in extracting resources from the earth and seas, such as agriculture, mining, fishing, and lumbering.

Primate city—A city that contains by far the largest population and greatest concentration of economic and cultural functions within a state.

Primogeniture—A system of inheritance found principally in Germanic Europe under which the holdings of one generation pass intact to the oldest male child of the next generation.

Pronatalist policies—Policies designed to increase fertility rates, or at least slow the fall in the birth rate.

Protestantism—A fragmented agglomeration of many denominations such as Lutheranism, Presbyterianism, and Anglicanism that split off from the Roman Catholic Church. Generally concentrated in northern Europe.

Quaternary sector—Economic activities associated with the collection, processing, and manipulation of information and capital, such as education, consulting, and research and development services.

Reconquista—Literally, "reconquest." The term refers to the ultimately successful effort of Christian kingdoms to push the Islamic Moors out of the Iberian Peninsula. The reconquista began with the Battle of Covadonga in 722 and ended with the defeat of the last Moorish stronghold in Granada in 1492.

Rectilinear street pattern—A grid pattern of parallel and perpendicular streets.

Return migration—The return of migrants or their descendants to the historical homeland whence they or their ethnic ancestors originally came.

River-meander site—A piece of land created when a stream turns back upon itself, leaving only a narrow neck of land surrounded almost completely by water. River-meander sites could be easily defended, making them good choices for settlements in unstable regions.

Roman Catholicism—A form of Christianity centered on the Pope in the Vatican City, dominant in southern and parts of eastern Europe.

Romance—A subfamily of the Indo-European languages derived from Latin, dominating the western and southern edges of Europe that were once part of the Roman Empire. Includes Italian, Spanish, French, Portuguese, and Romanian.

Sclerophyllous—Protective external tissues of plants found in dry areas that serve to retard evaporation.

Secondary economic activities—The processing of resources into finished goods, also known as manufacturing.

Sephardim—Iberian Jews who were expelled from Spain and Portugal following the reconquest and resettled throughout North Africa and northern Europe, particularly Britain and the Netherlands.

Sharecropping—A system in which a landowner allows a peasant to use a piece of land in exchange for a share of what is produced on the land.

Shifting cultivation—Also known as slash-and-burn agriculture, the practice of cultivating crops for a few years in one place, and then abandoning that place for another after soil fertility declines.

Siltation—The build-up of sediment in a stream or lake.

Site—The physical setting and specific location of a place or phenomenon.

Slavic—A major subfamily of the Indo-European languages spoken throughout much of eastern Europe. Includes Russian, Polish, Czech, Slovakian, Ukrainian, Belarusian, Serbo-Croatian, Slovenian, Bulgarian, and Macedonian.

Socialist city—See Eastern European city.

Sovereignty—The idea that independent countries should be free from external interference.

Specialization—A system in which diverse traditional subsistence agriculture is replaced by cash crops that are sold to obtain a profit.

Standardized language—The form of writing and speech promoted by elites to foster communications across a broad area.

Street village—A village aligned along a single road.

Suburbanization—The movement of people from city cores to the outskirts of an urban areas.

Terpen—Mounds of earth upon which structures were built to avoid flooding in the Low Countries.

Tertiary sector—The service industries; those that involve neither the extraction of resources nor manufacturing but instead include a range of activities that serve people's everyday needs and facilitate economic activity. Includes health care, transportation, energy production, retailing, wholesaling, and tourism.

Thracian (Thraco-Illyrian)—A subfamily of the Indo-European languages originating from the Stara Planina and Rhodopi Range, but today represented only by Albanian.

Three-field farming—Agricultural system in which land was divided into three segments, one planted with a summer grain, one with a winter grain, and one left fallow. The segment devoted to each of these activities was rotated every year.

Topocide—The deliberate obliteration of a place. Coined by Douglas Porteous in reaction to changes to the physical environment during the Industrial Revolution.

Total Fertility Rate—The number of children born to women of child-bearing age.

Transhumance—Nomadic system in which herds move to high pastures in the mountains in the summer and down to the lowlands during the winter.

Transportation—The movement of people and goods between locations using something constructed by humans.

Uniate Church—A hybrid of Eastern (Orthodox) and Western (Catholic) Christianity centered in western Ukraine and surrounding areas.

Unification nationalism—The effort to bring together, within a single state, peoples who are thought to share a common culture and history.

Unitary states—States with executive and legislative power concentrated in a central government.

Uralic—A language family that was pushed to the periphery by Indo-European languages. Includes Finnish, Estonian, Sámi, and Hungarian.

Welfare state—Social model under which the state provides services such as health care, education, unemployment insurance and pensions to its population as a "safety net."

Xenophobia—Fear of the foreign or of foreigners.

Zero population growth—A demographic situation in which the mortality rate is equal to the birth rate, producing a stable, or even declining, population.

Index

About the Authors

Alexander B. Murphy is professor of geography at the University of Oregon, where he holds the James F. and Shirley K. Rippey Chair in Liberal Arts and Sciences. He specializes in political, cultural, and environmental geography, with a regional emphasis on Europe. Murphy is vice president of the American Geographical Society and a past president of the Association of American Geographers. He co-edited *Progress in Human Geography* for eleven years, and currently serves as an editor of *Eurasian Geography and Economics*. Murphy is the author or co-author of more than seventy-five articles and several books. He has won teaching awards both from his university and from the National Council for Geographic Education. In the late 1990s Murphy led the effort to add geography to the College Board's Advanced Placement Program. He holds a bachelor's degree in archeology from Yale University, a law degree from Columbia University, and a Ph.D. in geography from the University of Chicago.

Terry G. Jordan-Bychkov (1938–2003) was the long-standing Walter Prescott Webb Professor of History and Ideas in the Department of Geography at the University of Texas, Austin. Prior to that he spent many years as chairman of the geography department at the University of North Texas in Denton. At the time of his death, he had completed field research in sixty-five countries, exploring topics as diverse as the origins of livestock ranching, folk architecture, burial customs, forest colonization, agricultural practices, and village life. As one of the most published and cited cultural geographers of his generation, he published a number of lauded books. He was the recipient of numerous professional and teaching awards and served as president of the Association of American Geographers. He earned his Ph.D. in geography at the University of Wisconsin at Madison.

Bella Bychkova Jordan is a lecturer in the Department of Geography and at the Center for Russian, East European, and Eurasian Studies at the University of Texas, Austin. A native of Djarkhan, Siberia, she specializes in the ethnic geography of the region. Her books include *The European Culture Area: A Systematic Geography*, fourth edition (with Terry G. Jordan-Bychkov) and *Siberian Village: Land and Life in the Sakha Republic* (with Terry G. Jordan-Bychkov). She holds a Ph.D. in geography from the University of Texas, Austin.